THE HISTORY OF
THE SECOND DIVISION

About
The Naval & Military Press

The Naval & Military Press offer specialist books
for the serious student of conflict. The range of titles
stocked covers the whole spectrum of military history
with titles on uniforms, battles, official histories,
specialist works containing Medal Rolls and Casualties Lists,
and numismatic titles for medal collectors and researchers.

Their Book Lists, which are issued approximately
every six weeks, are legendary. The variety of titles
which are listed covers every facet of military history.
Each title is accompanied by a concise critical review
which enables the prospective purchaser to make
an informed judgement.

The innovative approach they have to military
bookselling and their commitment to publishing
have made them Britain's leading
independent military bookseller.

The Naval & Military Press Ltd
Unit 10, Ridgewood Industrial Park, Uckfield,
East Sussex, TN22 5QE, England

Tel: 01825 749494
Fax: 01825 765701
Email: order.dept@naval-military-press.co.uk

Websites:
www.naval-military-press.co.uk
www.great-war-casualties.com
www.great-war-trench.maps.com
www.world-war-2-casualties.com

GENERAL SIR C. C. MONRO, G.C.B., G.C.S.I., G.C.M.G., A.D.C.,
COMMANDED THE 2ND DIVISION IN FRANCE AND FLANDERS
FROM AUGUST 1914 UNTIL 26TH DECEMBER 1914.

THE HISTORY
OF THE
SECOND
DIVISION

Vol. I. 1914 – 1916

By
EVERARD WYRALL

WITH A FOREWORD BY
FIELD-MARSHALL EARL HAIG OF BEMERSYDE

PUBLISHED BY
THE NAVAL & MILITARY PRESS

FOREWORD.

THERE must always be a peculiar interest attaching to the war histories of the Divisions that composed the original Expeditionary Force and, from August 1914 to November 1918, saw the full course and development of the struggle on the Western Front. Those Divisions were not merely the advance guard to the far mightier forces that followed them to France, they were also their example, and set the standards to which the younger Divisions of our Army afterwards lived up so worthily. Of these older Divisions, the Second Division formed, prior to the outbreak of the war, part of my own Aldershot Command, and afterwards fought under me in France in the First Army Corps. I am the more glad to write this Foreword to their Divisional History, for I am thereby given the opportunity to express something of my appreciation of the loyal and gallant service all ranks of the Division gave me in those early days, and of the pride I then felt—and still feel—to have commanded such fine troops.

Until January 1915, in fact, the story of the Second Division is practically the history of my own command, and I can speak with the assurance of close personal knowledge regarding the very high standard of military efficiency set and maintained by all ranks, in spite of the greatest difficulties. The Army as a whole owed a big debt to the Divisions of the old Army that served as a pattern and inspiration to the splendid material furnished in the course of the war by all parts of the Empire.

The pages of this book tell how well the Second Division, though its personnel constantly changed owing to the filling up of gaps with freshly recruited troops, yet preserved throughout the long years of war the high level of its early days in France. Among so great a number of gallant actions, so many tales of duty well and truly done, it is difficult, and perhaps invidious, to single out incidents for especial praise. Else I would have referred to the holding of the line at Bourlon Wood on November 30, 1917, when the Second Division, in the centre of the German Northern attack on that day, with the stout-hearted London Divisions on either side of them, prevented a local reverse on another part of the line from developing consequences far more serious.

This incident can at least stand as an example of the work and worth of the Second Division, and it is with the memory of such deeds before my mind that I thank all past and present members of the Division for what they did in the days of the Great War.

HAIG OF BEMERSYDE, F.-M.

LONDON, *July* 5, 1921.

CONTENTS.

II. TRENCH WARFARE, 1914–1916.

WINTER OPERATIONS.

NOVEMBER 1914 TO MARCH 1915.

SUMMER OPERATIONS, 1915.

MARCH TO OCTOBER.

III. THE ALLIED OFFENSIVE, 1916.

LIST OF MAPS.

INTRODUCTORY.

THE SECOND DIVISION FROM ITS EARLIEST DAYS.

THE history of the 2nd Division dates from June 18, 1809—five years before Waterloo—when the British army in the Peninsula was organized into divisions, a formation which has been followed ever since. Prior to the Peninsular War, the recognized fighting unit was the brigade ; and the armies engaged in the Austrian War of Succession, the Seven Years' War, and the campaigns in America fought in brigades—*i.e.*, stiff rows of troops difficult to manœuvre.

The generals of the French Revolutionary armies were the first to recognize the value of the division, for the levies for the republican army were at first badly drilled and greatly undisciplined, unused to maintaining alignment and brigade formation. They therefore formed their armies into columns in place of lines, and hurled them against selected points of their opponents' defences, rather than employ them in a general line. So successful were these tactics that they broke up the system of war inculcated by Frederick the Great. By 1794, however, the Republican army had learned to manœuvre, and although it retained the principle of avoiding dispersion of forces, and concentrated against crucial points, its tactics were considerably modified. The separation of the French armies into divisions became a regular organization.

The first campaign in Portugal in May 1809 was fought by the British army under Sir Arthur Wellesley in brigade formation. The infantry (18,000 men) was distributed over eight brigades of two or three battalions each, each battalion numbering from 1,400 to 2,500 troops.

In the following month, on June 18, the British army was first organized into divisions, and consisted of :

Cavalry Division (Payne) : three brigades of two regiments and attached troops.
1st Division (Sherbrooke) : four brigades of two regiments.

2nd Division (Hill) : two brigades, one of two regiments and one of three regiments.

3rd Division (Mackenzie) : two brigades of three regiments.

4th Division (Campbell) : two brigades of two regiments.

Detached companies of rifles (5/60th) were attached to brigades.[1]

But in 1810 and 1811 the army was again added to, until at Waterloo the formation was a cavalry division, seven infantry divisions, a light division, and a Portuguese division.

The capture of Talavera seems to have been the first action in the Peninsular Wars in which the 2nd Division (as such) took part. Thenceforward the 2nd Division was engaged throughout the subsequent campaigns against the Spaniards and French in the operations in Andalusia in 1810, at Barrosa and Albuhera in 1811, Ciudad Rodrigo and Salamanca in 1812, the campaign of Vittoria in 1813, and the battles of the Pyrenees of the same year which ended in the operations in the south of France ; and finally at Waterloo in June 1814, where the 2nd Division formed part of the IInd Corps, under Lieut.-General Lord Hill.

In the Crimean War the 2nd Division, under General de Lacy Evans, fought at the Alma, at Inkerman, and before Sevastopol.

The Divisional formation was again used in the South African War of 1899–1902, the 2nd Division being under the command of Lieut.-General Sir C. F. Clery. Throughout the above campaign the Division gained many honours.

On August 5, 1914, when war was declared between Great Britain and Germany, the 2nd Division[2] formed part of the Aldershot Command. With the exception of the 4th (Guards) Brigade (Brigadier-General R. Scott-Kerr, M.V.O., D.S.O.), of which three battalions—2nd Grenadiers, 3rd Coldstream, and 1st Irish Guards —were quartered in London and the 2nd Coldstream at Windsor, the troops forming the Division were located in, or in the vicinity of, Aldershot. The 5th Infantry Brigade (Brigadier-General R. C. B. Haking, C.B.), formed by 2nd Worcester Regiment, 2nd Oxford and Bucks Light Infantry, 2nd Highland Light Infantry, and 2nd Connaught Rangers, and the 6th Infantry Brigade (Brigadier-General R. H. Davies, C.B.), formed by 1st King's (Liverpool) Regiment, 2nd South Stafford Regiment,

---

[1] This formation was nearly that at the Battle of Mons in 1914, the British Expeditionary Force consisting of a cavalry division and four infantry divisions, plus one cavalry (5th) and one infantry (19th) brigade.

[2] See Appendix for Order of Battle.

1st Royal Berks Regiment, and 1st King's Royal Rifle Corps, were at Headquarters. Of the Divisional troops, the XXXIVth Brigade R.F.A., 5th and 11th Field Companies and 2nd Signal Company Royal Engineers, and the Divisional train, Cyclist Company, and Field Ambulances were also at Aldershot; the XXXVIth Brigade R.F.A. at Ewshott, the XLIst Brigade R.F.A. at Bordon, and the Divisional Cavalry, B Squadron 15th Hussars, at Longmoor. The XLIVth (Howitzer) Brigade R.F.A. and 35th (Heavy) Battery Royal Garrison Artillery were in the Eastern and the Southern Commands.

Late on the afternoon of 4th August Lieut.-General Sir Douglas Haig,[1] the General Officer Commanding at Aldershot, received orders to mobilize the troops under his command. On the following morning the declaration of war was officially announced. 4TH AUG 1914.

Mobilization proceeded rapidly. The majority of the troops had just completed their summer manœuvres, and were in very fit condition. The reservists required to bring units from peace to war establishment began to arrive from the very first day of mobilization. The new arrivals were put through courses of drill and musketry. At midnight 7th–8th August, the 6th Brigade (with a few minor exceptions) reported mobilization complete. By midnight 8th–9th August, the 5th Brigade had also received its full complement. The 4th (Guards) Brigade, Royal Artillery, Royal Engineers, Divisional train, and the remainder of the Divisional troops also reported complete to full establishment and ready to sail.

Major-General C. C. Monro,[2] C.B., had been selected to command the 2nd Division, which with the 1st Division (Major-General S. H. Lomax) formed the Ist Army Corps under Sir Douglas Haig. The IInd Army Corps, consisting of 3rd Division (Major-General H. I. W. Hamilton) and 5th Division (Major-General Sir C. Fergusson), was commanded by Sir James Grierson, and on his death shortly after arriving in France, by Sir Horace Smith-Dorrien.

The Royal Artillery and the Royal Engineers of the 2nd Division were under the commands of Brigadier-General E. M. Perceval, D.S.O., R.A., and Lieut.-Colonel R. H. H. Boys, D.S.O., R.E., respectively.

On the 12th August the three infantry brigades embarked at Southampton for France. On the 13th, the 4th (Guards) Brigade and half of the 6th Infantry Brigade (1st King's and 2nd South 12TH AUG.

[1] Afterwards Field-Marshal Earl Haig.
[2] General Sir C. C. Monro, G.C.B.

Staffords) disembarked at Havre, the 5th Infantry Brigade at Boulogne, and the remaining half of the 6th Infantry Brigade (1st Royal Berks and 1st King's Royal Rifle Corps) at Rouen.

At various dates from 16th to 19th August, the Divisional troops left England and disembarked at Boulogne, Havre, and Rouen.

Divisional Headquarters left Aldershot shortly after 6 a.m. on 15th August, and reaching Havre on 16th, disembarked and went into billets. On 18th, Divisional Headquarters again entrained and arrived at Wassigny very early in the morning of 19th August.

The point of assembly for the 2nd Division was Wassigny and area, with Divisional Headquarters in the town. The area included Grougis (4th Guards Brigade), Verly-le-Petit (5th Infantry Brigade), and Hanappes (6th Infantry Brigade).

During the 19th and 20th, Divisional troops and other details were arriving, and at 5.20 p.m. on the latter date the first " 2nd Division Operation Order " (No. 1) was issued : the Division would move on the morrow towards its allotted place in the line of battle.

21ST AUG. On the 21st August billets were occupied at Noyelles, Maroilles, Landrecies, and Lagruise, and on the following day the Division rested on the line La Longueville (4th Guards Brigade), Hargnies (6th Infantry Brigade), and Pont-sur-Sambre (5th Infantry Brigade).

I.

THE GERMAN INVASION, 1914.

THE RETREAT FROM MONS.

THE BATTLE OF MONS.
THE RETREAT.
The Affair of Landrecies.
The Retreat resumed.
The Rearguard Actions of Villers-Cotterets.

THE BATTLE OF MONS.

ON the evening of 21st August, the Ist and IInd Corps, the Cavalry Division, and 5th Cavalry Brigade had reached their objectives. The IIIrd Corps was still in the process of formation, but the 19th Infantry Brigade, formed from troops on the lines of communication, arrived in time to play an important part in the subsequent retreat from Mons. Concentration complete, Sir John moved his troops forward to their allotted positions in the Allied line.

"The concentration was practically complete on 21st," said Sir John French,[1] the commander-in-chief, in his first dispatch, " and I was able to make dispositions to move the force during Saturday the 22nd to positions I considered most favourable from which to commence operations which the French commander-in-chief, General Joffre, requested me to undertake in pursuance of his plans in prosecution of the campaign."

Nothing of interest seems to have happened during the advance, though on the 21st August, as the troops marched northwards to their billets, news that the enemy's cavalry had been seen north and east of Mons was passed along the line ; and on the 22nd, a British cavalry brigade engaged the enemy's patrols near Bray.

But before detailing at length dispositions which even at that early date played so great a part in the final results of the War, a brief appreciation of the relative positions of the French and the German armies is necessary.

In his dispatch Sir John referred to General Joffre's plans for " the prosecution of the campaign," but these plans were very different from the original scheme designed by the French General Staff in case of invasion.

From the time of the Franco-Prussian War, France had spent many millions of pounds on fortifying her eastern frontier from Belfort to Longwy, or, in other words, from Switzerland to Luxembourg. The powerful forts at Belfort, Epinal, Nancy, Toul, St.

[1] Afterwards Viscount French of Ypres.

Mihiel, Verdun, and Longwy—all, with the exception of Epinal and Toul, having strongly fortified areas between them—were, backed by the French armies, considered practically impregnable.   And although in the early stages of the Great War [1] it was proved that the strongest fortress cannot be held against modern howitzer fire, had Germany elected to observe the international laws governing neutral states in time of war, she would have found extreme difficulty in obtaining a footing in France if she had attacked the French by flinging her armies at the line of forts which guarded the frontier and the line of the Meuse.

The movement of the bulk of the German invading forces through Belgium had not been considered probable, and Mezières, Maubeuge, Lille, and Dunkirk were lightly held along the northern frontier.   This is evident from the disposition of the French armies when war was declared.   For General Joffre, in pursuance of the French plan of attack, had massed the bulk of his armies between Belfort and the line of the Meuse northwards to a point at which the river cuts the Belgian frontier at Givet.   Between Belfort and Lunéville lay the Alsace group and the First French Army under General Dubail ; then in succession northward the Second (de Castelnau), Third (Ruffy), and Fifth (de Lanzerac).   De Castelnau watched the Lorraine frontier with his right at Lunéville, his centre in front of Nancy, and his left on the frontier opposite Metz ; Ruffy continued the line in front of St. Mihiel and Verdun to Montmédy ; and de Lanzerac's right lay just north of Malmédy and his left at Rocroi, guarding all exits from the Ardennes.   Behind the Third Army was massed the Fourth Army under Langle de Cary, acting as a reserve.

Against these dispositions the German General Staff had moved up the Alsace group between Colmar and Strassburg, facing the First French Army ; the Seventh Army, under von Heeringen, lay opposite the Second French Army ; the Sixth Army, under Prince Rupprecht, behind Metz ; the Fifth Army, under the German Crown Prince, north of Metz between Thionville and Trèves, on the Luxembourg frontier; the Fourth Army, under Duke Albrecht, lay along the north-eastern frontier of Luxembourg ; the Third Army under von Hausen, the Second under von Bülow, and the First under von Kluck, carried the line north along the Belgian frontier to the borders of Holland.

A map will reveal at once the intentions of the German General Staff.

[1] At Liége and Namur.

General Joffre had already begun an offensive in Alsace and Lorraine when reports reached him that the First and Second German Armies, under von Kluck and von Bülow, had violated the Belgian frontier and were already advancing on Liége. A few days later the fall of Liége and the rapid advance of von Kluck and von Bülow towards the northern frontier of France was reported. Immediately Joffre moved the Fifth Army under de Lanzerac into Belgium on the line of the Sambre between Charleroi and Namur, and southwards along the Meuse from Namur to Dinant. His Fourth Army was then pushed forward to fill the gap between de Lanzerac and Ruffy. He was also compelled to abandon his offensive in Alsace and Lorraine and detach the XVIIIth and IXth Corps from the Second Army, which, by occupying Saarburg, had already succeeded in cutting the enemy's communications between Strassburg and Metz ; and General d'Amade was ordered to Arras in command of French Territorial Divisions spread out between Douai, Arras, St. Omer, Lille, and Valenciennes.

Such was the position on Saturday morning, 22nd August, 22ND AUG. when Sir John French moved his force to the line Condé–Mons–Binche, with the Cavalry Division (General Allenby) behind his centre ready to act on either flank, and the 5th Cavalry Brigade (Brigadier-General Sir Philip Chetwode) on his right at Binche.

Even at this date the strength of the German forces advancing through Belgium was not understood, for the plan agreed upon between General Joffre and Sir John French was that the British Expeditionary Force and the Fifth French Army, the latter pivoting on Namur, should advance in an enveloping movement against the enemy, and, rolling up his right flank, force him back upon the eastern frontier of Belgium.

From subsequent events it was obvious that a similar plan of action had been determined upon by the German General Staff. That it did not succeed—though it came perilously near doing so—was almost entirely due to the stubborn resistance and indomitable pluck of the British soldier.

Unaware, therefore, of the real strength of the oncoming enemy with whom he was soon to join action, and having been given to understand that " one or at most two of the enemy's Army Corps [1] with perhaps one Cavalry Division " were in front of him,

---

[1] The First German Army (General von Kluck) at Mons consisted of : IXth, IIIrd, IVth, and IInd Corps, from right to left, in the order given. The IInd Corps was west of Condé ; the IInd Cavalry Corps about half-way between Tournai and Douai ; the IVth Reserve Corps was still behind the line.

Sir John gave orders on 22nd for the following positions to be occupied :

IInd Corps (5th and 3rd Divisions) : from Condé to Mons inclusive.

Ist Corps (2nd and 1st Divisions) : from Mons—exclusive—to Binche.

British General Headquarters were at Le Cateau with Advanced Headquarters at Bavai.

From Condé to Mons the line ran perfectly straight along the southern banks of the canal, but from Mons to Obourg the semi-circular course of the waterway formed a dangerous salient, and in a flank attack would be untenable. Sir John had foreseen this, for he says : " In view of the possibility of my being driven from the Mons position I had previously ordered a position in the rear to be reconnoitred. This position rested on the fortress of Mau-beuge on the right, and extended west to Jenlain, south-east of Valenciennes, on the left."

The 2nd Division, as already explained, was at this date in billets at La Longueville, Hargnies, and Pont-sur-Sambre, and in the evening received the following order : " The 2nd Division will move to-morrow from its billets to a fresh area on the left of the 1st Division. . . . Divisional Mounted Troops (B Squadron 15th Hussars, under Captain Hon. W. Nugent) will clear La Longue-ville by 4.30 a.m. and will reconnoitre the area Givry–Noirchain–Sars-la-Bruyère–Quevy-le-Petit–Havay, thus covering the advance of the Division in its assigned position."

Orders were first of all received for the Division to move at 7 p.m. on 22nd. These orders were cancelled about 5.30 p.m., and the Division ordered to be in readiness to move at 3 a.m. At 9.30 p.m. an A.D.C. left Pont-sur-Sambre to take these orders round to the various brigades. On returning at 11.45 p.m. he was informed that fresh orders had just come from the corps : the Division was to move as soon as possible and to be at Mons at 6.30 a.m. The A.D.C. was sent to fetch in the brigadiers by car, and arrived with Brigadier-Generals Davies and Scott-Kerr at 1.45 a.m., General Haking being already in the town. They given their instructions, and Brigadier-General Scott-Kerr returned to his headquarters in La Longueville, arriving there at 2.40 a.m.

23RD AUG.
MAP.

At 3 a.m. on the 23rd the Hussars set out with instructions to reconnoitre the area as ordered, and then to hold a portion of the road from Mons to Bray.

The Divisional Cyclists had already been placed under the

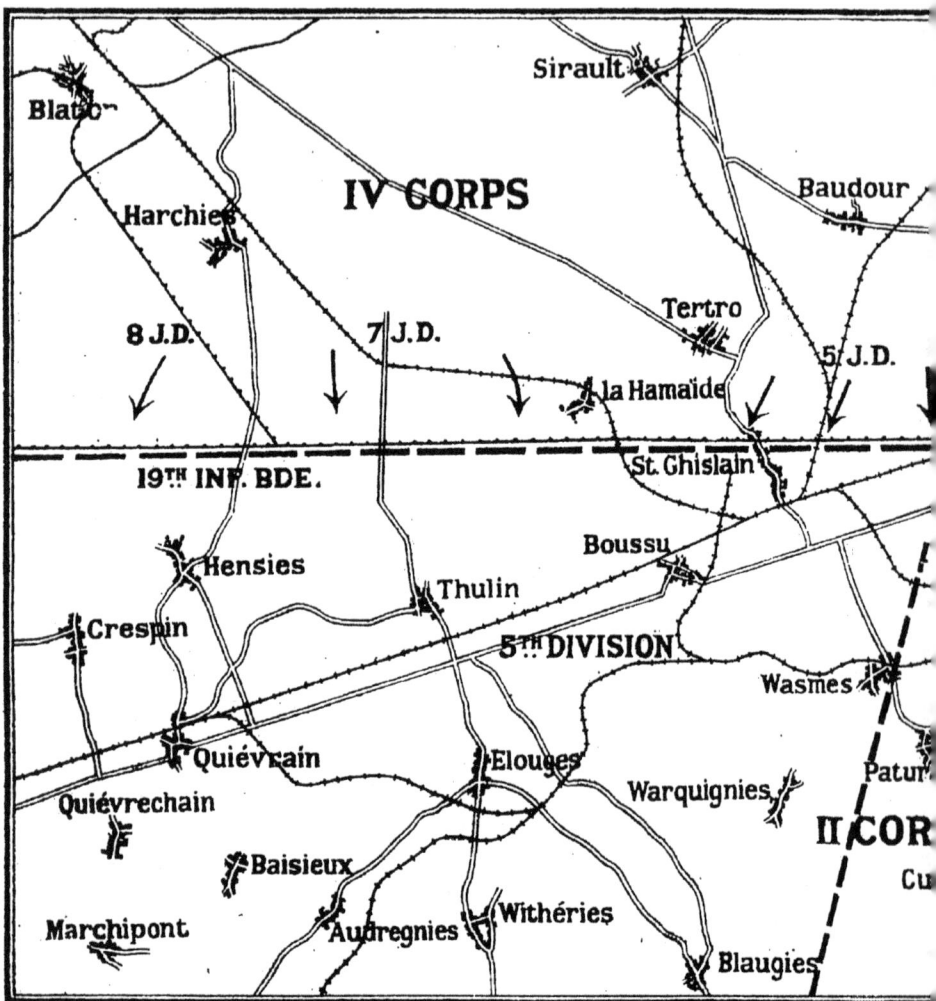

Blaton

Harchies

Sirault

Baudour

IV CORPS

8 J.D.

7 J.D.

Tertro

5 J.D.

la Hamaïde

St. Ghislain

19TH INF. BDE.

Hensies

Boussu

Thulin

Crespin

5TH DIVISION

Wasmes

Quiévrain

Quiévrechain

Elouges

Warquignies

Patur

II COR

Baisieux

Cu

Marchipont

Audregnies

Withéries

Blaugies

THE BATTLE OF

Position of 2nd Division (Ist Corps) and
British Army ; and

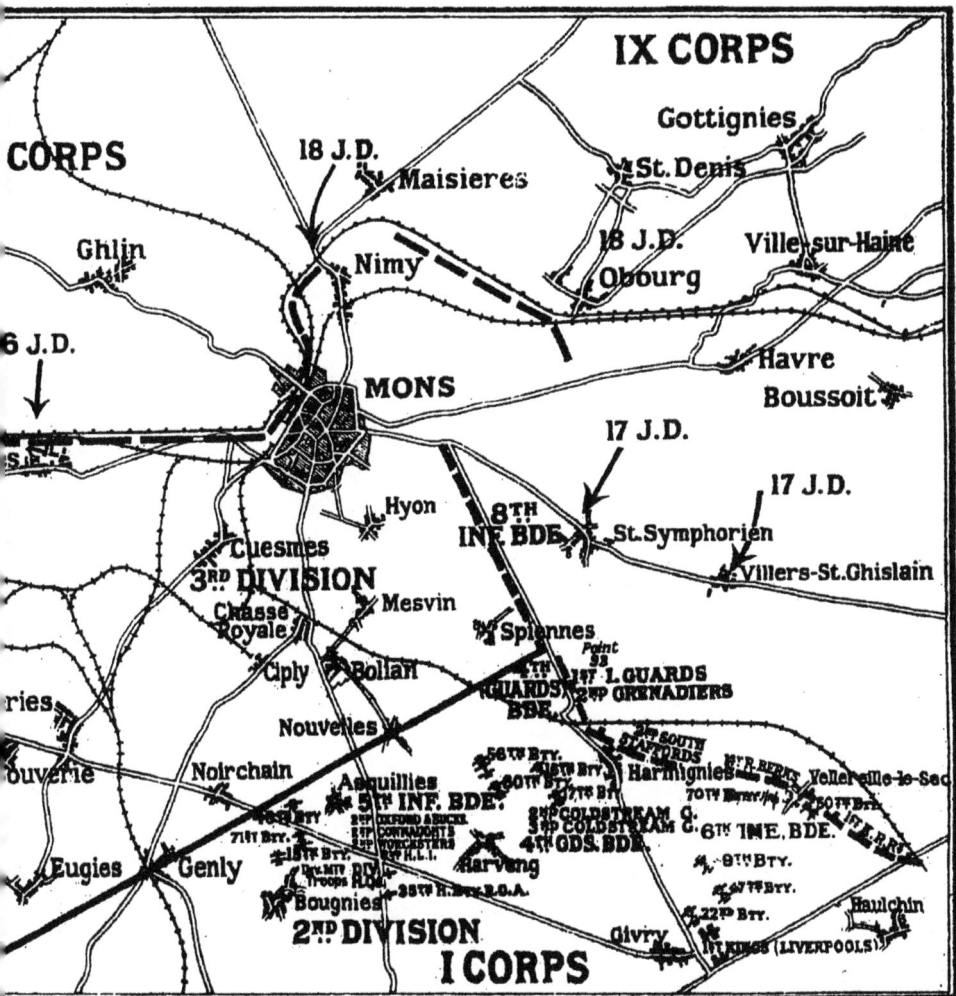

IX CORPS

CORPS

Gottignies

18 J.D.

St. Denis

Maisieres

Ghlin

18 J.D.

Ville-sur-Haine

Nimy

Obourg

6 J.D.

Havre

S.R.E.

Boussoit

MONS

17 J.D.

Hyon

8TH INF. BDE.

17 J.D.

Cuesmes

St. Symphorien

3RD DIVISION

Villers-St. Ghislain

Chasse Royale

Mesvin

Ciply

Spiennes

Bollan

Point 93

4TH L. GUARDS

ries

2ND GRENADIERS

GUARDS BDE.

Nouvelles

SOUTH STAFFORDS

Noirchain

56TH BTY.

N.R. BERY.

Velleville-le-Sec

ouverie

38TH BTY.

Harmignies

Asquillies

80TH BTY.

5TH INF. BDE.

77TH BTY.

70TH BTY.

70TH BTY.

71ST BTY.

2ND OXFORD & BUCKS.

2ND CONNAUGHTS

2ND WORCESTERS

9TH COLDSTREAM G.

3RD COLDSTREAM G.

6TH INF. BDE.

Eugies

Genly

15TH BTY.

1ST H.L.I.

4TH GDS. BDE.

8TH BTY.

Div. MTD. Troops R.C.A.

35TH H. BTY. R.C.A.

Harveng

46TH BTY.

Bougnies

Givry

22ND BTY.

Haulchin

2ND DIVISION

1ST KINGS (LIVERPOOLS)

I CORPS

5, 23rd August 1914.

mate Positions of other Divisions of the
irst German Army.

(Facing p. 22.)

command of the Officer Commanding Divisional Mounted Troops, and these set off with the Hussars.

At 3.30 a.m. the Division marched in the order as given : the 4th (Guards) Brigade (Brigadier-General Scott-Kerr) leading, followed by the XLIst Brigade R.F.A. (less one battery), 5th Field Company Royal Engineers, and B Section 4th Field Ambulance, taking the route Riez de l'Erelle–Blaregnies, its destination being Quevy-le-Petit to the Mons–Bettignies road exclusive ; the 6th Infantry Brigade (Brigadier-General R. H. Davies), 11th Field Company Royal Engineers, XXXIVth Brigade R.F.A., and A Section 4th Field Ambulance *via* Riez de l'Erelle vicinity of Gognies, its destination being Havay to Mons–Bettignies road ; Headquarters 2nd Division, 5th Infantry Brigade (Brigadier-General R. C. B. Haking), XXXVIth Brigade R.F.A., XLIVth (Howitzer) Brigade R.F.A., 35th (Heavy) Battery R.G.A., Divisional Ammunition Column, and C Section 4th Field Ambulance *via* La Longueville–Riez de l'Erelle, destination the vicinity of Gognies on the Binche–Bavai road.

The head of the main body of the 2nd Division (which included Divisional Headquarters) reached the crossroads immediately east of Frameries at 8.15 a.m.   On arrival there General Monro heard the 3rd Division was to his front, and he immediately rode forward to 3rd Divisional Headquarters, and a readjustment of the front was mutually agreed upon—General Monro moving his troops into billets about Quevy-le-Petit and Genly, the 6th Infantry Brigade holding the line Estinne station to Vellereille-le-Sec. The 1st Division later took over Estinne station.

In the meantime the Divisional Mounted Troops, having very early in the morning reconnoitred the country ahead and covered the advance of the Division, penetrated as far as the village of Villers St. Ghislain and sent out patrols to Obourg, Havre, and Boussoult.   Small parties of the enemy were encountered, evidently advanced guards, and the patrols had to retire under shell-fire to Squadron Headquarters in the village.   Here they were attacked in force.   Eventually, having delayed the enemy considerably, they withdrew, but not without casualties, the Hussars losing Lieut. J. M. Tyler and 1 man killed, Captain S. S. Rylands wounded, and 4 men missing.[1]   Of the Cyclists, Captain Hall and Lieut. Blacker were wounded, the latter dying later of his wounds.

[1] At Harmignies on 23rd August 1914, and subsequently for bravery on 3rd September at Dammartin, Corporal C. E. Garforth, 15th Hussars, was recommended for the V.C., awarded him in the *London Gazette* of 16th November 1914.

Already the IInd Corps had joined battle with the enemy, who had opened fire with his artillery and later launched a strong infantry attack especially against the Mons–Obourg salient, obviously the weak spot in the British line.

At 1.45 p.m. the General Officer Commanding 6th Infantry Brigade reported to Divisional Headquarters that the Royal Scots (8th Infantry Brigade, 3rd Division) were being attacked, and had appealed for help to the 2nd South Staffords. The troops were then ordered from their billets.

The 2nd Grenadier Guards and 1st Irish Guards moved up to Point 93—high ground north of Harmignies station ; 2nd and 3rd Coldstream Guards to Harveng ; and entrenched a position covering the village from the north-east.

The 5th Infantry Brigade entrenched in front of Divisional Headquarters, situated between seven and eight kilometres from Mons at the crossroads on the Mons–Maubeuge road.

The Divisional Artillery was disposed as follows :—XXXIVth Brigade R.F.A. : 50th and 70th Batteries near Vellereille-le-Sec, and the 22nd Battery in observation east of Givry.

XLIst Brigade R.F.A. : 17th and 16th Batteries north-east of Harveng, and 9th Battery detached with the 6th Infantry Brigade.

XLIVth (Howitzer) Brigade R.F.A. : 56th and 60th Batteries near Harveng, and 47th Battery near Givry.

XXXVIth Brigade R.F.A. and the 35th (Heavy) Battery R.G.A. in the rear of Divisional Headquarters at the crossroads, one mile W.S.W. of Harveng.

About 6 p.m. the Grenadiers and Irish Guards at Point 93 came under a heavy shell and rifle fire, and the latter had five casualties, though generally the enemy's shrapnel burst high and did little damage. It is interesting to note that here on a chalk hill near Harmignies, for the first time in the history of the Irish Guards since they were formed, the regiment came under fire of an enemy's guns. Later during the night the Grenadiers and Irish Guards were withdrawn from Point 93.

The two Coldstream battalions were then ordered to dig themselves in, in front of the village of Harveng, facing Harmignies. With their comrades of the Division they had been for eighteen hours under arms, and, having spent most of the time beneath a scorching sun, could hardly keep awake. But the trenches were completed just before midnight. Although exposed to shell-fire of varying intensity the Coldstream suffered no casualties.

The 5th Infantry Brigade came into position at the crossroads about the same time, 6 o'clock, and, with the two Artillery Brigades, proceeded to entrench themselves. At 10 p.m. an urgent message was received from Ist Corps Headquarters ordering three battalions to march and counter-attack Frameries, where the enemy was reported to have captured the village and penetrated the British line between the 5th and 3rd Divisions. The 2nd Oxford and Bucks Light Infantry, 2nd Worcesters, and 2nd Highland Light Infantry of the 5th Infantry Brigade set out immediately. The three battalions reached Frameries without firing a shot. The Worcesters entrenched themselves north of the village ; but the night passed without incident, nothing occurring until dawn. It was evidently a false alarm, for not a single German was found in Frameries. The Oxford and Bucks and the Highland Light Infantry went on to Pâturages, arriving at 3 a.m., where they acted as reserves ; but here also nothing happened, and the two battalions lay down in the market-place for an hour's rest.

The 6th Infantry Brigade, on the line Harmignies–Vellereille-le-Sec–Estinne station, was for some hours subjected to a heavy shell-fire. The infantry were entrenched in the following order : 2nd South Staffords, Harmignies ; 1st Berks, Vellereille-le-Sec ; 1st King's Royal Rifles, Estinne ; Brigade Headquarters and 1st King's (Liverpool) Regiment in Givry. The Berks had 4 casualties, Second-Lieut. T. V. B. Dennis and 3 men being wounded.

Of the artillery, the XXXVIth, XLIst, and XXXIVth Brigades were heavily engaged, the 9th Battery of the XLIst Brigade and the 50th and 70th Batteries of the XXXIVth Brigade being continuously shelled. The 9th was attached to the 6th Infantry Brigade defending Harmignies–Estinne station, and was a special target for the German gunners, who fired from concealed positions which could not be located. The battery lost 2 officers killed, and 10 men killed and wounded.

The 70th Battery of the XXXIVth Brigade, also defending the Harmignies Ridge, suffered even more severely, losing 2 officers wounded (Lieuts. Robertson and Durand), 3 N.C.O's and men killed, and 27 wounded. Two hostile howitzer batteries were turned on to the 50th and 70th Batteries, with the result that three of the guns of the latter were damaged by direct hits on the outer spring case of the buffer. One was repaired in the battery, but the other two had to be sent to the base. The " Heavies " (35th Battery R.G.A.) did not go into action but entrenched west of Harmignies. The men were dismounted, and lined the side of the road as an alarm had been given that an attack was imminent. This is the first record in the Great War of artillery acting as dismounted troops.

It was said that at Mons on 23rd August the troops had no time to entrench themselves; but the records of the Royal Engineers mention barbed-wire entanglements, trenches with traverses, and emplacements with head-coverings for machine guns. These probably were not used, for with the advance of the enemy and the sudden and unexpected orders to retire, the trenches were not only abandoned but many tools also.

When darkness fell on the 23rd the 2nd Division had done little or no fighting. Casualties certainly were sustained, but excepting artillery duels, the Division cannot be said to have joined action with the enemy. The casualties were caused mainly by the artillery fire (field guns and howitzers) of the enemy, who searched the ground thoroughly over which his infantry was to advance.

North-west and west of the Division the 3rd and 5th Divisions had during the day fought hard, and had delayed the enemy in his attempt to cross the Condé Canal and capture Mons; and time was a very important factor. The German General Staff had designed to strike a swift blow at France and overwhelm her before she was ready to take the field in full strength, and all that stood between the enemy and his plans on this flank was the British Expeditionary Force.

At nightfall the troops, such as were not engaged in desultory fighting, which went on along practically the whole front, bivouacked full of confidence in the morrow. They were in ignorance of the surprise awaiting them. For at 5 p.m. that afternoon Sir John French had received a most unexpected telegram from General Joffre informing him that Namur had fallen on the previous day, the Fifth French Army had evacuated Charleroi and were retiring (they were even then a day's march from the British forces), and that Sir John had on his front " at least three German corps, viz., a Reserve Corps, the IVth Corps, and the IXth Corps ... and that the IInd Corps was engaged in a turning movement from the direction of Tournai." [1]

In addition to these four corps, German cavalry divisions were operating on his left flank, while his right was exposed to attacks from the Second German Army [2] under von Bülow, who, having

[1] The IXth, IIIrd, and IVth Corps, with the IInd at and west of Condé.
[2] VIIth Corps.

won the passage of the Sambre, was in rapid pursuit of the Fifth French Army then retiring in a south-westerly direction towards Avesnes.

There was nothing for Sir John to do but retire in conformity with the French army.[1]

THE RETREAT.

The retreat began in the very early hours of the 24th August. During the night there had been desultory fighting along the whole front. At dawn the 2nd Division made a powerful demonstration from the Harmignies area towards Binche as if to retake the town, which had been evacuated by the 1st Division. On the afternoon of the previous day Sir Douglas Haig had retired the right flank of the Ist Corps in a southerly direction towards Peissant, from which position the 1st Division supported the 2nd Division. The demonstration was designed to cover the retirement of the 3rd Division (IInd Corps) to the line Dour–Quarouble–Frameries, General Hamilton's troops having suffered heavy casualties on the previous day.

The enemy opened fire at 3 a.m., but made no attempt to advance. At 4.45 a.m. the retirement began. Simultaneously every available gun of the 2nd Division artillery opened fire upon the enemy, the 1st Division also lending artillery support. Under cover of the guns and a rearguard formed of the 5th Cavalry Brigade and the XLIst and XXXVIth Field Artillery Brigades under the command of General Horne, the infantry were gradually withdrawn. The retirement was covered by the 4th (Guards) Brigade.

Of the 5th Infantry Brigade, the three battalions (2nd Highland Light Infantry, 2nd Oxford and Bucks, and 2nd Worcesters), which had been hurriedly dispatched on the previous night to Frameries and Pâturages to fill the gap between the 5th and 3rd Divisions, still remained in the latter villages, and in consequence saw more fighting on the first day of the retreat than any other unit of the 2nd Division.

The enemy opened with a heavy bombardment of Frameries which lasted for five hours—from 3 a.m. to 8 a.m.—and the 2nd Worcesters, who stuck to their trenches, had 26 casualties, 5 wounded and 21 missing. The Highland Light Infantry and the Oxford and Bucks in Pâturages were also heavily shelled, the former bat-

24TH AUG.

---

[1] The losses of the 2nd Division at Mons were : Officers killed, 1 ; wounded, 8 ; other ranks : killed, 9 ; wounded, 71 ; missing, 18.—" Q " Diary, 2nd Division.

talion losing 14 N.C.O's and men, and the latter 7 men wounded. At 9.30 a.m. the order to retire was given, and the three battalions fell back *via* Sars–La Bruyère–Bois de Montreuil. As the 3rd Division gradually drew away from the enemy, the 2nd Division also fell back towards the line Bavai–La Longueville.

The Irish Guards and 2nd Grenadiers entrenched a position north of Quevy-le-Petit from the third kilometre stone on the Genly–Quevy-le-Petit road to the tenth kilometre stone on the Mons–Bettignies road. Through this position the whole of the 2nd Division, with the exception of the three battalions (which later rejoined the 5th Infantry Brigade) from Frameries and Pâturages, passed on their way southwards practically unmolested by von Kluck's IXth Corps, though the British Expeditionary Force was never in greater danger of being enveloped on both flanks had the enemy's troops persisted. There is little doubt that when he allowed the withdrawal of Sir John French's force to the Valenciennes–Bavai–Maubeuge line without a more vigorous pursuit, von Kluck threw away his first chance of complete success. For the British troops, though fighting valiantly, were at this stage verging on exhaustion. The diaries of the 2nd Division on the 24th August contain references in no uncertain tones when speaking of the condition of the troops. Early in the morning—2.30 a.m.— of the 24th one diary states : " The infantry are done up after trying days without regular food and with little sleep." Later, the same diarist says : " The infantry are exhausted." [1] For thirty-six and even forty-eight hours many of the men had been under arms ; but, to their undying credit, there was no grumbling, no demoralization—only a dogged, grim determination to endure at all costs.

In one position, so sudden had been the retirement that 80,000 rounds of small-arm ammunition were left in the trenches ; there was no transport, and every man already carried three hundred rounds. For the same reason tools and supplies were also left behind. Many men had consumed their iron rations.

On the night of the 24th the 2nd Division lay on the line Bavai– La Longueville, the majority of the troops getting to their billets between the hours of 6 and 8 p.m. Divisional Headquarters were in Audignies, the Staff arriving at 7.30 p.m.

At 4.30 p.m. the retirement of the rearguard had begun, and that night the Guards Brigade bivouacked at Malgarni, just south of La Longueville.

---

[1] Official War Diary.

The 1st Division was on the right, La Longueville–Maubeuge, and the 3rd and 5th Divisions and the 19th Infantry Brigade on the left of the 2nd Division.

But the enemy was still pressing, and the position of the British force insecure. " The French were still retiring," said Sir John French,[1] " and I had no support except such as was afforded by the fortress of Maubeuge ; and the determined attempt of the enemy to get round my left flank assured me that it was his intention to hem me against that place and surround me. I felt that not a moment must be lost in retiring to another position."

In the early hours before dawn of the 25th the retirement was therefore continued. Divisional Headquarters left Audignies at 3.30 a.m. on the 25th. Bavai was blocked with vehicles, and as the German troops were only two miles north of the town, a portion of the column was diverted down the side roads through Audignies. The new position was to be the neighbourhood of Le Cateau.

Orders were issued to the 2nd Division to continue the march southwards, the 5th Infantry Brigade, XXXVIth Brigade R.F.A., 5th Field Company R.E., and 5th Field Ambulance to Noyelles ; 6th Infantry Brigade, XXXIVth Brigade R.F.A., 6th Field Ambulance, 11th Field Company R.E., and Divisional Troops to Maroilles ; 4th (Guards) Brigade, XLIst Brigade R.F.A., XLIVth (Howitzer) Brigade R.F.A., 4th Field Ambulance to Landrecies. The 6th Infantry Brigade was ordered to act as rearguard.

The three villages selected as billeting areas lay east of the Forêt de Mormal, a large, densely-grown forest, stretching ten miles from north to south and six miles wide, crossed only by rough tracks and quite unsuitable for the passage of heavy transport. And although it formed a barrier between the Ist Corps on the east and the IInd Corps marching west of the forest, no other direction was possible. For had the entire British force marched west of the forest a gap between Sir John French and de Lanzerac (Fifth French Army) would have been formed, offering an advantageous opening for the enemy's IXth and VIIth Corps then pressing Sir Douglas Haig. Moreover, the British left would have been pushed farther west into the oncoming German corps still endeavouring to envelop Sir John's left flank. To some extent also the line of the Sambre to the east of the forest offered a certain amount of protection to the tired and exhausted troops. Finally, the 81st French Territorial Division in Valenciennes had been forced to retire before the IInd German Corps, and was falling back along the line

1 Official Dispatches.

25TH AUG.

Valenciennes–Cambrai, which further congested the roads which the British left flank would have had to traverse had the whole force retired west of the Forêt de Mormal.

Thus Sir Douglas Haig had no choice but to move his corps east of the forest towards Le Cateau. The 4th (Guards) Brigade was the first to move.

The 3rd Coldstream, as advanced guard, set out shortly after 4 a.m., followed two hours later by the Artillery, Field Ambulances, and the three remaining battalions of the Brigade, in the order given. The cool air of the early morning somewhat revived the troops, but no sooner had the sun risen than thirst began to seize hold of the men. At Pont-sur-Sambre an opportunity occurred of refilling water-bottles, the battalion halting for twenty minutes. A little later a second halt was called, but here a Staff officer intervened, and gave orders that no more halts were to take place as the enemy was pressing in the rear. For nearly three hours the battalion trudged on, man after man falling out utterly done. "Between 9.15 and 9.45 a.m. no less than ninety-two men fell out utterly exhausted."[1] The marching pace was barely two miles an hour. At last Colonel Feilding, who commanded the battalion, in sheer desperation ordered a halt, during which stragglers were collected. About 1 p.m. Landrecies was reached, and the men went into billets in the barracks north-west of the Sambre. The 2nd Grenadiers arrived at 4 p.m., the Irish Guards and 2nd Coldstream about 4.30 p.m.

The 3rd Coldstream were detailed for outpost duty, and a post was placed at the level crossing north-west of the barracks. The Grenadiers were in the west of the village, the 2nd Coldstream south and east, whilst the Irish Guards were in reserve and were detailed for the defensive arrangements against attack.

In the meantime, the 5th and 6th Infantry Brigades were moving on their billets, Noyelles and Maroilles, with little inter- ference from the enemy. The 5th Brigade marched out of billets at Bavai at dawn on the 26th, assisted by the 5th Cavalry Brigade, covering its retirement. The march was uneventful until Chene- au-Loup was reached; but here a long halt took place, and the Brigade received orders to hold all the crossings over the Sambre at Pont-sur-Sambre, at Aymeries, Aulnoye, and Sassignies, the enemy[2] having opened fire on the rearguard after the 5th Infantry Brigade had left Bavai. On reaching the first-named place the

---

[1] War Diary.
[2] Von Kluck's IXth Corps.

2nd Worcesters prepared to defend the bridges, and the Connaught Rangers the northern exits of the village. As Divisional Headquarters entered Pont-sur-Sambre orders were received that the bridge was to be destroyed. This order was cancelled almost immediately, and the bridge ordered to be *prepared* for demolition only. The Oxford and Bucks went on to Aymeries, Aulnoye, and Sassignies, whilst the Highland Light Infantry were posted at the lock at Patignies. South of Pont-sur-Sambre a French Reserve Division was in billets, and later took over the defence of Aymeries and Aulnoye bridges from the Oxford and Bucks. But no attack was made, the enemy having fired only a few shells at the rear battalion of the 6th Infantry Brigade.

At 4.30 p.m. the 5th Infantry Brigade continued its march; but as the head of the Brigade reached the village of Leval, a galloping mass of artillery and transport wagons appeared on the road from Noyelles. An alarmist report had stampeded the artillery and transport of the Brigade back along the road towards Leval. The frightened horses were eventually stopped and the march continued, the Brigade, less the Oxford and Bucks, reaching Noyelles at 10 p.m. The battalion had been ordered to stay in Leval, and, after putting out outposts from Sassignies to Monceau, went into billets for the night.

At 7.30 a.m. the 6th Infantry Brigade withdrew from the line Bavai–La Longueville, the enemy's outposts advancing within 500 yards, but were driven off with the loss of 7 men and 1 officer (Lieut. C. J. Phipps) wounded.

At Pont-sur-Sambre the Brigade came up with the 5th Infantry Brigade, and, receiving orders to proceed to Maroilles, passed on through the village and continued its march without incident, save for the exhaustion of the men, who suffered from thirst and sore and blistered feet. Maroilles was reached about 6 p.m. There the Brigade was ordered to hold a bridge over the Sambre north-west of the town, at the southern exit of the Forêt de Mormal. The Divisional Cavalry had been sent out to hold the bridge until a company of the 1st Berks arrived.

Shortly after 6 o'clock another alarm was circulated: that the enemy had taken Landrecies from the 4th (Guards) Brigade, and were even then within a short distance of Maroilles. The troops fell in, only to be dismissed again—the rumour was false ! A thunderstorm broke over the town, and this, combined with the inky darkness and uncertainty of an unknown road, delayed the Berkshires in setting out for the bridge where they were awaited by the cavalry. Eventually the company started, but scarcely had the men taken the road, when they met the cavalry galloping towards Maroilles with information that the enemy in force[1]— the Hussars numbered only 12 rifles—with artillery, had taken the bridge. The Berkshires (Colonel Graham in command) hurried forward, with orders to retake the position at all costs. Two more companies of the Berks were ordered forward in support.

The approaches to the bridge were difficult. They led along a narrow causeway flanked on either side by ditches and marshes, and the enemy had placed a gun at the bridge end of the causeway. Deployment being impossible, a frontal attack had to be made. Almost before they knew, they were in touch with the enemy; the dark night was illumined by a sudden flash from the gun, and, before they had fired a shot, the Berkshires lost heavily. Rushing forward, however, they charged with the bayonet, firing wherever a target could be observed. The first assault was driven back. But in a second charge the enemy was driven to the farther side of the bridge. This was all that could be accomplished. Word had been sent back to Divisional Headquarters in Maroilles stating the position, and the 1st King's Royal Rifles were hurried up, and took over from the Berkshires just after midnight. The enemy then retired behind his barricade and did not again open fire.

In this affair the Berkshires lost Major A. J. Truman, missing; Captain H. H. Shott, D.S.O., killed; Lieut. V. Hopkins, wounded; and 61 other ranks killed, wounded, and missing.

The Officer Commanding Squadron 15th Hussars reported a gallant action which took place when the cavalry retired from the bridge. Lieut. Straker had gone forward with a small body of men to reconnoitre, and, unaware of his position, was cut off. Private Price, on his own initiative, swam a small canal, and reaching his officer safely, told him he was surrounded by the enemy. A sudden dash, however, brought the Hussars out of their dangerous position.

At midnight the 5th Infantry Brigade received orders to move out from Noyelles, and reoccupy the bridges at Pont-sur-Sambre and Aulnoye. This was followed by another order (unfortunately too late, as the troops had already started) ordering the Brigade to take up a line from the south-west exits of Noyelles along the high ground facing north-west. Eventually the battalions were collected, and finally received orders to march at 5 a.m. towards Le Grand Fayt *via* Marbaix.

[1] Portion of 5th Infantry Division of von Kluck's IIIrd Corps.

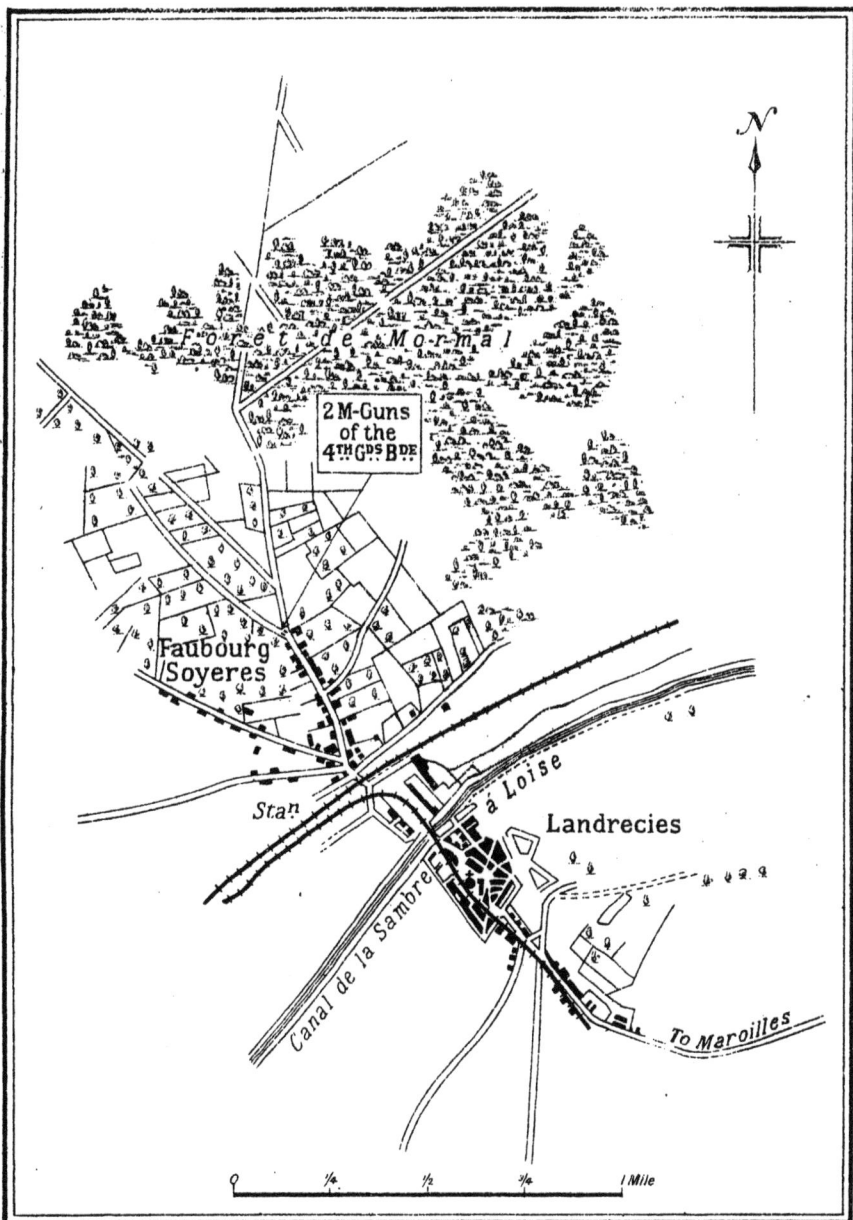

THE AFFAIR OF LANDRECIES, 25th August 1914.

(Facing p. 32.)

The Affair of Landrecies.

The receipt of frequent orders and counter-orders by the 5th and 25TH AUG. 6th Brigades on the night of the 25th was no doubt occasioned MAP. by the arrival at Divisional Headquarters of reports of the sudden attack on the 4th (Guards) Brigade at Landrecies. Here, between 4 and 5 p.m., the Guards were settling down to what promised a quiet night. But about half-past five civilians rushed into the town with the information that the enemy was moving from the north-west through the Forêt de Mormal, and was, in fact, at their very heels. The alarm was sounded, and after falling in and standing to arms, the men were dismissed, the enemy failing to put in an appearance. But one useful purpose was served, in that when later the enemy did appear, there was no confusion or rushing about for orders, as the battalions had all been allotted their posts and were prepared for any emergency. The 3rd Coldstream had gone into billets in the infantry barracks north-west of the town, but afterwards did outpost duty to the Brigade, and in consequence bore the brunt of the subsequent attack. To the north-west of the town there is a railway level crossing which runs across a narrow street—the Faubourg Soyères—leading directly to the Forêt de Mormal. At the end of this street No. 2 Company, under Captain C. Heywood, and the battalion machine-gun section, were placed on outpost duty. On the right was a turnip field rising to a sky-line, and on the left the edges of the forest; 200 yards along the road was a junction of two crossroads. The post was placed south of these crossroads with a machine gun facing down each road towards the forest.

Darkness hid the approaches from the forest. Soon after the outpost took up position, information was received that Uhlans were approaching, and behind them a body of the enemy with transport, estimated at 1,000 infantry, with two guns.

At 7 o'clock a German cavalry patrol appeared at the cross-roads and was fired on by the Coldstreamers; the patrol therewith withdrew, leaving two of their number lying on the ground. For a while all was quiet. No. 2 Company was now replaced by No. 3 Company. A report was spread by civilians that French infantry, marching to Landrecies, was expected along the road from the Forêt de Mormal. That French troops were in the vicinity was known, for they had evacuated Landrecies only that afternoon; moreover, French troops were south of Noyelles—they had been met along the crowded roads. When, therefore, the sound of infantry approaching the crossroads from the direction of the forest caught the ears of the British outpost, it was supposed they were French. The marching men came nearer ;[1] they were singing French songs, and they answered to the challenge : " Ne tirez pas ; nous sommes Français." A light was suddenly flashed into the face of Captain the Hon. C. H. Monck, who commanded No. 3 Company, by an officer who was leading the advancing infantry. A similar light flashed from the outpost. The order to fire was given immediately, but before it could be obeyed, the man working the Coldstream machine gun was bayoneted. The enemy made a rush, knocking over Captain Monck and Lieut. Bingham. In face of the sudden surprise, and in the confusion during the hand-to-hand fighting with revolver and bayonet which followed, the Guards fell back, losing a machine gun. Gradually, however, the enemy was pressed back and retired to the Faubourg Soyères, where, with a field gun, he took up a position. No. 3 Company was then reinforced by Major T. H. Matheson with three platoons of No. 1 Company under Captain E. Longueville. No. 2 Company and No. 4 were lining the village, and guarding all exits to the north-west. The 2nd Coldstream held one company in brigade reserve, whilst the remaining companies held the southern and eastern exits. The Irish Guards barricaded the streets, loopholed the walls of cottages, and generally placed the town in a state of defence.

The fight between the 3rd Coldstream and the enemy proceeded with intensity. Time after time the latter attempted a charge up the street, and was as often driven back by rifle and machine-gun fire. He then opened fire with the gun placed near the forest.

And here, for the first time on record during the Great War, the Germans used hand-grenades, which, a diarist says, " were of high-explosive, and had the same effect as shells."[2]

At the end of the street was a barn which had an exit leading to the forest. Down the narrow lane behind the barn the enemy tried to effect an entry and place a machine gun there ; but he was prevented. The barn was then shelled, and presently it burst into flames, disclosing the disposition of the defenders. But No. 5854 Private G. Wyatt, with fine presence of mind, extinguished the flames almost immediately. Again a shell fired the barn, and

[1] Portion of 7th Infantry Division of von Kluck's IVth Corps.

[2] War Diary. This is probably an isolated case, as grenades were not generally used until the beginning of trench warfare on the Aisne.

again, in face of a hail of bullets, Wyatt beat out the flames. For this act of gallantry, and later for conspicuous bravery when wounded at Villers-Cotterets, Wyatt was awarded the Victoria Cross.[1]

At length, at 1 p.m., Colonel Feilding brought up a howitzer of the XLIVth Brigade R.F.A., and, placing it in the firing line, indicated the direction of the flash of the enemy's gun. The howitzer fired three shots, the third evidently taking effect, for the hostile gun did not fire again. The attack then died down.

The 3rd Coldstream losses were heavy. Of the officers, Lieut. Viscount Hawarden and Second-Lieut. Hon. A. Windsor-Clive were killed, and Captain Whitbread, Lieut. Keppel, and Lieut. Rowley wounded. Other ranks : 12 killed, 105 wounded, and 7 missing. The 2nd Grenadiers, whose machine gun did excellent work, lost 1 officer (Second-Lieut. R. H. M. Vereker) killed, and 6 N.C.O's and men wounded.[2]

The official casualties were given as 200.

Very early in the morning, between 2 and 3 o'clock, the Irish Guards took over from the 3rd Coldstream, who, with the 2nd Coldstream and 2nd Grenadiers, retired, the Irish Guards covering the retirement. The Brigade was then ordered to march on Etreux, where it entrenched a position, the 2nd Coldstream acting as rearguard. | 26TH AUG.

A short distance from the village the Guards passed a number of ambulance wagons, belonging to the 4th Field Ambulance, wending their way back to Landrecies in order to pick up the wounded which had been left behind. With the exception of A Section, which escaped owing to its being out of position in the column, this ambulance was captured *en bloc* by the enemy, and the personnel subsequently sent as prisoners of war to Germany. The sections captured were B and C.

It was a mournful story.

The 4th Field Ambulance attached to the 4th Brigade had left Pont-sur-Sambre at 6 a.m. on the previous day to join up with the Guards in Landrecies. At 5 p.m. the ambulance arrived outside Landrecies, and was there met by a crowd of excited civilians, who were running about shouting " Les Allemands." An order was received by Major Collingwood, commanding the

---

[1] *London Gazette*, 18th November 1915.

[2] Landrecies is of historical interest to the 3rd Coldstream Guards, for here the battalion received its baptism of fire, not having been on active service previous to the Great War.

4th Field Ambulance, for all men who were lying in the ambulance, but fit to go into the firing line, to report at once with their rifles and ammunition to Headquarters.

" A corporal of the Irish Guards, whose feet were swollen and red like lobsters, went forward at the double on receipt of this order." [1]

The Field Ambulance halted in a field about a mile out of Landrecies. Early next morning, at 2.30, it moved from Favril. A Section joined up with the Guards in column, but B and C Sections had to wait until the long line had passed, and followed on behind with the wagons full of stragglers. The whole ambulance was soon after ordered back into Landrecies to collect the wounded, but only B and C Sections were able to return, and were in consequence captured by the enemy.

Besides stretchers, the light ambulance carts and (all but a very small proportion) the complete personnel of No. 4 Field Ambulance were captured. Only A Section, Major Falkner (O.C. Section), 30 men, 51 wounded, 6 ambulances, light carts—*i.e.*, water-carts and medical store carts, with horses complete—and (one excepted) all the heavy wagons escaped.

The officers captured were : Colonel H. H. Thompson, A.D.M.S.; Major F. S. Irvine, D.A.D.M.S. ; Major P. H. Collingwood (O.C. No. 4 F.A.) ; Captain J. P. Lynch, Captain A. A. Sutcliffe, Lieut. H. W. Hills, Lieut. J. W. Routh, Lieut. A. J. Brown, Lieut. M. Haltersbury, and Lieut. Lafayette Lauder.

During the 24th, 25th, and 26th the divisional dispatch riders—generally motor cyclists—did valuable work. Owing to the rapid movements of the British force, communication by field telephone was practically impossible, and had it not been for the dispatch riders " all communication would have failed." [2]

West of Landrecies, on the night of the 25th–26th August, the IInd Corps [3] had also been engaged. The 14th Infantry Brigade was attacked about the same time as the Guards in Landrecies, and suffered many casualties.

East of the 2nd Division, the 1st Division, then south-east of Maroilles, was also hard pressed by von Bülow's right flank, [4] and Sir Douglas Haig sent urgent requests to Sir John French for assistance to enable him to extricate the Ist Corps from its difficult

---

[1] Official Medical Diary.
[2] Official Diary R.E.
[3] The 14th Infantry Brigade, 5th Division.
[4] VIIth Corps.

position. With no reserves to call upon, Sir John had to ask for the co-operation of French cavalry, then in billets north and west of Avesnes. With this assistance the commander of the Ist Corps was able to draw off his 1st and 2nd Divisions, enabling the latter, early on the morning of the 26th, to continue its retirement southwards towards Etreux.

The Retreat resumed.

Sir John French had issued orders to his corps commanders to retire towards the line Vermand–St. Quentin–Ribemont. " Having regard to the continual retirement of the French army on my right, my exposed left flank, the tendency of the enemy's western corps (IInd) to envelop me, and more than all, the exhausted condition of the troops, I determined to make a great effort to continue the retreat till I could put some substantial obstacle, such as the Somme or the Oise, between my troops and the enemy, and afford the former some opportunity of rest and reorganization. Orders were, therefore, issued to the corps commanders to continue their retreat as soon as they possibly could towards the general line Vermand–St. Quentin–Ribemont." [1]

The 4th (Guards) Brigade moved out of Landrecies between 2 and 3 a.m. with the Irish Guards first, and later the 2nd Coldstream, as rearguards. The 5th Cavalry Brigade covered the retirement of the whole Brigade.

The 6th Infantry Brigade and Divisional Headquarters, which had billeted in the Maroilles area, marched out of billets at 3.30 a.m., taking an easterly route along the road to Marbaix, thence southwest to Le Grand Fayt, en route for Etreux. At Le Grand Fayt the Brigade met the 1st Division.

The 5th Infantry Brigade, some miles north of the 6th Brigade, was still scattered, and was in consequence late in assembling and setting out. General Haking had decided to take his Brigade *via* Taisnières and Prisches.

Nothing of interest happened to the Guards during the march to Etreux, which was reached just after midday, the battalions entrenching themselves immediately on arrival. But in the evening a German aeroplane flew over the trenches and dropped a bomb, which exploded harmlessly about twenty yards from the trenches of the Irish Guards. No. 3 Company of the 3rd Coldstream opened

[1] Official Dispatches.

fire with rifles, and, after flying a few miles, the machine dropped like a wounded bird, and the occupants were captured.

For the first time since the retirement from Mons began the troops bivouacked in the open.

Although Etreux was the destination of the 6th Infantry Brigade, supplementary orders were received for the Brigade to push on to Vénérolles, where the battalions entrenched, and, like the Guards, bivouacked in their trenches in a drenching rain. Before leaving Maroilles many men had discarded their packs, to enable them to carry more ammunition, and were in consequence without their greatcoats.

The 5th Infantry Brigade, scattered from Noyelles to Pont-sur-Sambre, succeeded eventually in assembling at Petit-Landrecies about 5 a.m., and marched out shortly afterwards along the road to Marbaix in the following order : 2nd Worcesters, advanced guard ; XXXIVth Brigade R.F.A., 2nd Highland Light Infantry, 2nd Oxford and Bucks Light Infantry, main body ; the 2nd Connaught Rangers, with one section of the XXXIVth Brigade R.F.A., as rearguard.

In retiring from Berlaimont, where the battalion was guarding the railway bridge, the 2nd Oxford and Bucks had two casualties. The French sappers blew up the railway bridge, and in the explosion Captain P. Godsal and Second-Lieut. G. T. Britton were injured, and had to be left behind in hospital, where they were eventually captured by the enemy.

The Worcesters having gone on as advanced guard, the head of the column—the Highland Light Infantry—reached the village of Les Cattiaux about 8.30 a.m. Here French troops had to use the same road as the Brigade, and there was considerable delay and confusion. The rearguard—the Connaughts—were then holding the ridge Bout du Diable. For a little over an hour the Brigade was halted, and, as subsequent events will show, this delay proved serious. At 9.45 a.m. the Brigade pushed on, but again, east of Chemin de Marbaix, another long halt was necessitated owing to the congested state of the road. In consequence, the Brigade was split up. The advanced guard (Worcesters), marching via the crossroads south-west of Marbaix, lost touch, and eventually reached Barzy at 7 p.m., where the battalion bivouacked, the Oxford and Bucks and one company of the Connaughts arriving soon after.

Similarly, General Haking, Brigade Headquarters, and the Highland Light Infantry, getting separated from the remainder of the Brigade, reached La Valles, and intended going on to Barzy; but it was found impossible. However, at 3.45 a.m., Brigade Headquarters, with the Highland Light Infantry, tracked across the boggy ground to Barzy, and there found that the Worcesters, Oxford and Bucks, and all that remained of the Connaughts—one company—had already left for Boué, where, at 5.30 on the morning of the 27th, the Brigade was once more assembled.

Meanwhile, the rearguard (Connaughts) under Lieut.-Colonel A. W. Abercrombie, owing to repeated delays in front, had been forced to hold on to their positions in the face of a rapidly advancing enemy. The battalion had moved out of Petit-Landrecies at 6.30 a.m., and had taken up successive positions until Taisnières was reached. Here one company was sent to the crossroads south of Taisnières, along the Maroilles–Marbaix road, and the remaining three companies followed the Brigade to Marbaix. At the latter place, the column was cut into by French troops passing from west to east. One of the three remaining companies of the Connaughts followed in the rear of the Brigade, and the other two went back along the Maroilles–Marbaix road to the crossroads where one company of the battalion had already been ordered to stand. Here also Battalion Headquarters were established. In the vicinity of the crossroads French infantry were entrenched, and French cavalry patrols were out along all the approaches. At 12.30 Colonel Abercrombie sent a message to Brigade Headquarters saying that unless he received orders to the contrary, he would hold on to the position until 3 p.m., and would then retire on Le Grand Fayt. But the Brigade had already left Marbaix for Le Grand Fayt. The French cavalry reported that the country round about was clear of the enemy; but at 3 p.m., just as the Connaughts were on the point of moving off towards Le Grand Fayt, French patrols galloped in with information that 200 of the enemy, with a machine gun, were quite close. Firing began almost immediately in the direction of Marbaix. Colonel Abercrombie immediately dispatched one platoon towards Marbaix, and followed with another platoon in reserve. The latter had gone 600 yards, when suddenly heavy firing from artillery and machine guns was opened on the roads. The remainder of the Connaughts, with the machine-gun section at the crossroads, were then ordered to the high ground south of and overlooking the road, with instructions to take up a position from which to open fire. Owing to the dense hedges and difficult nature of the ground, the machine gun could not be brought into action, and

platoons became mixed up. In an hour the fire ceased, and
Colonel Abercrombie sent a message to Le Grand Fayt (where he
imagined Brigade Headquarters to be) informing the brigadier
of the situation. But the message was never delivered ; Second-
Lieut. Denison, who took it, was unable to find Brigade Headquarters or where they had moved to. Between 5 and 6 p.m. the
company commander at the crossroads, having lost touch with
Colonel Abercrombie and his force, and thinking he had retired
on Le Grand Fayt, set off in that direction, but on arrival, save for
a few civilians, found the village deserted. The company then
pushed on to Barzy and bivouacked with the Brigade.

Meanwhile, Colonel Abercrombie, with the machine-gun section,
remained on the position until 6 p.m., when he, too, retired on Le
Grand Fayt, still in the belief that Brigade Headquarters were in
the village. At the entrance to the village he was met by a
civilian, evidently an enemy agent, who informed him that the
British troops had withdrawn and that there was no enemy.
But on continuing the march, the Connaughts were suddenly subjected to a heavy fire from the enemy concealed in the houses and
enclosures. Though fighting gallantly against superior forces and
retiring to the fields about the village, the Connaughts suffered
heavy casualties. What followed is not clear, but when night fell
Colonel Abercrombie, Captain W. W. Roche, and Lieuts. W. Leader,
G. Baker, J. L. Hardy, and C. Turner, with 284 other ranks, were
missing.[1]

During the day, as the 2nd Division retired southwards, furious
artillery fire could be heard in the direction of Le Cateau—Sir
Horace Smith-Dorrien was fighting his famous action in the face
of overwhelming numbers, later extricating his troops and withdrawing them safely, worn out and battered but unbeaten, to
Estrées, Hargicourt, and Vermand. Nor could the Ist Corps lend
him any assistance. When morning broke on the 26th, the 2nd
Division was scattered over a wide area : the 5th Brigade being,
when the Battle of Le Cateau began, about fifteen miles from the
scene of the action ; the 6th Brigade at least ten miles away, and
the 4th Brigade almost eight miles distant. The Ist Division was
even more remote. East of the 2nd Division, Sir Douglas Haig
had had great difficulty in withdrawing his troops from a dangerous
position. In this extremity the French lent him welcome assistance,
relieving the pressure put upon his tired troops by von Bülow's
VIIth Corps, which had even then begun to move westward with

[1] The Official Diary describing this mishap to the 2nd Connaughts is not clear.

the intention of following and harassing the Ist Corps in its retirement southwards.

On the early morning of the 27th August the 2nd Division held the line Barzy–Boué–Etreux–Vénérolles : at Vénérolles the 6th Brigade ; at Etreux the 4th (Guards) Brigade ; and at Boué and Barzy the 5th Brigade, still somewhat scattered ; the Highland Light Infantry, who were now acting as rearguard, being still in Barzy.

The Highland Light Infantry subsequently found their way to Le Nouvion, five miles east of Boué. It is probable that on leaving Barzy the battalion took the wrong road and then found itself a considerable distance from the 5th Brigade.

At 5.30 a.m. Brigade Headquarters had received information that the enemy " was close on our heels and that there was apparently nothing between the Highland Light Infantry and them."[1] A message was therefore got through to the battalion to proceed *via* Esqueheries, La Grande Rue, left of Lavaqueresse, Villers-les-Guise.

On the march between Etreux and Guise on 27th, under personal orders from Sir Douglas Haig to General Monro, the road was double-banked as it was very straight, and the column was thereby shortened. On arrival in Guise a French column also joined in on the same road, but went eastwards again on leaving the town. The checks were bad in consequence.

The 6th Infantry Brigade, leaving Vénérolles about 6 a.m., marched *via* Hannapes and Guise to Mont d'Origny, reaching the latter place about 5 p.m. without incident. The 4th (Guards) Brigade marched out of Etreux two hours later, and taking the Vénérolles–Tupigny–Vadencourt–Noyales road, reached Mont d'Origny at dusk. During the day the 4th Brigade shot down another enemy aeroplane.

The 5th Infantry Brigade reached Etreux at 7 a.m. and followed the route taken by the 6th Brigade, *via* Hannapes and Guise, but instead of billeting in Mont d'Origny went on to and entrenched a position at Neuvillette. Another false report having been received at Divisional Headquarters in Mont d'Origny stating that a strong German column was advancing east from St. Quentin, the Division took up defensive positions, but shortly afterwards the men were allowed to rest.

This information was given to the General Officer Commanding 2nd Division by an airman who landed on the roadside, and stated

[1] Official War Diary.

he had seen large columns of Germans away to the west moving southwards towards St. Quentin.

Soon after the 5th Brigade arrived in Neuvillette, the Highland Light Infantry with the transport marched in. The battalion was dead beat, having trudged thirty miles under exceptionally trying circumstances. The battalion was later complimented by the brigadier on its fine performance. Five hundred officers and men of the Connaughts also rejoined the Brigade, but Colonel Abercrombie, 5 other officers whose names have already been given, and 284 men were still missing. They had been captured by the enemy.

Hitherto, as far as Landrecies, the enemy's IXth Corps had harassed the 2nd Division, but from Landrecies von Kluck seems to have drawn off the IXth Corps to west of the Sambre and the Oise, leaving von Bülow's VIIth Corps to follow in pursuit of Sir Douglas Haig.[1]

28TH AUG. At 3 a.m. on the 28th August[2] the 2nd Division resumed the retirement on La Fère ; but by this time the enemy was also exhausted and the pursuit lacked vigour, though the cavalry of both armies joined action repeatedly.

The 4th (Guards) Brigade, the XXXIVth Brigade R.F.A., and the 1st Cavalry Brigade under Brigadier-General Horne, acting as rearguard, crossed the Oise at Mont d'Origny, and with the Irish Guards as advanced guard marched via Regny, Chatillon, Berthenicourt, and Moy to the crossroads west of La Fère. Here the Irish Guards took up a position as rearguard, whilst the Brigade, continuing its march to Deuillet, south of La Fère, went into billets. The Irish Guards then followed the Brigade via Beautor, and with the 3rd Coldstream eventually bivouacked near Bertancourt. One company of the Irish Guards (No. 2) went to guard the bridge at Beautor.

The main body of the Division (preceded at 3.30 a.m. by one company of the 6th Infantry Brigade and one platoon of the Divisional Cyclists Company) marched at 4 a.m. in the following order : Divisional Mounted Troops, 6th Infantry Brigade, 5th Field Company R.E., XXXVIth Brigade R.F.A., XLIVth (Howitzer) Brigade R.F.A., 35th (Heavy) Battery R.G.A., XLIst Brigade R.F.A., 11th Field Company R.E., 6th Field Ambulance, 5th Infantry Brigade, and Divisional Headquarters.

---

[1] Von Bülow's VIIth Reserve Corps was left behind to invest Maubeuge.

[2] Orders on 28th August announced that as Colonel Thompson, A.D.M.S., had not rejoined (the inference being that he had been captured at Landrecies with the 4th Field Ambulance), Lieut.-Colonel Copeland was appointed A.D.M.S.

Boussoit.
Havré
Bray
Obourg
Binche
Puissant
Rouveroy
Peissant
MONS
Villers St.Ghislain
Haumne
Point 93
Point 114
Havré
Ville
Ville-sur-
Haine
Grivry
Bethnies
MAUBEUGE
AVESNES
la Longueville
Frameries
Wasmes
le Petit
le Grand
Colignies
Pâturages
Bougnies
Aulnoy
Malgarni
Malplaquet
Bettignies
Feignies
Gognies
1ST DIV. AREA
Bachant
Monceau
Pont-sur-Sambre
Dour
La Bouverie
Sars la Bruyère
Blaregnies
Quévy-le-Grand
Bavay
Houdain
Amfroipret
Bermeries
Bavai
Bettrechies
Gommegnies
Jenlain
Potelle
Hargnies
Hon
Haisnieres
Marbaix
Point
Point
le Pt Fayt
Prisches
Quiévrain
Quaroble
Quarouble
St Waast
VALENCIENNES
Denlain
le Quesnoy
Englefontaine
Poix du Nord
Forest
Jolimetz
Ghissignies
Beaudignies
Salesches
Neuville
Fontaine
au Bois
Bousies
Preux
Croix
Forêt de Mormal
Bermerain
Landrecies
Robersart
St Python
Solesmes
Pommereuil
Fontaine
Le Cateau
Bazuel
La Groise
CAMBRAI
Conde
Condé - Mons Canal

Line held by 2nd Div. on
morning 24th August

Line held by 2nd Div. on
evening 24th August.

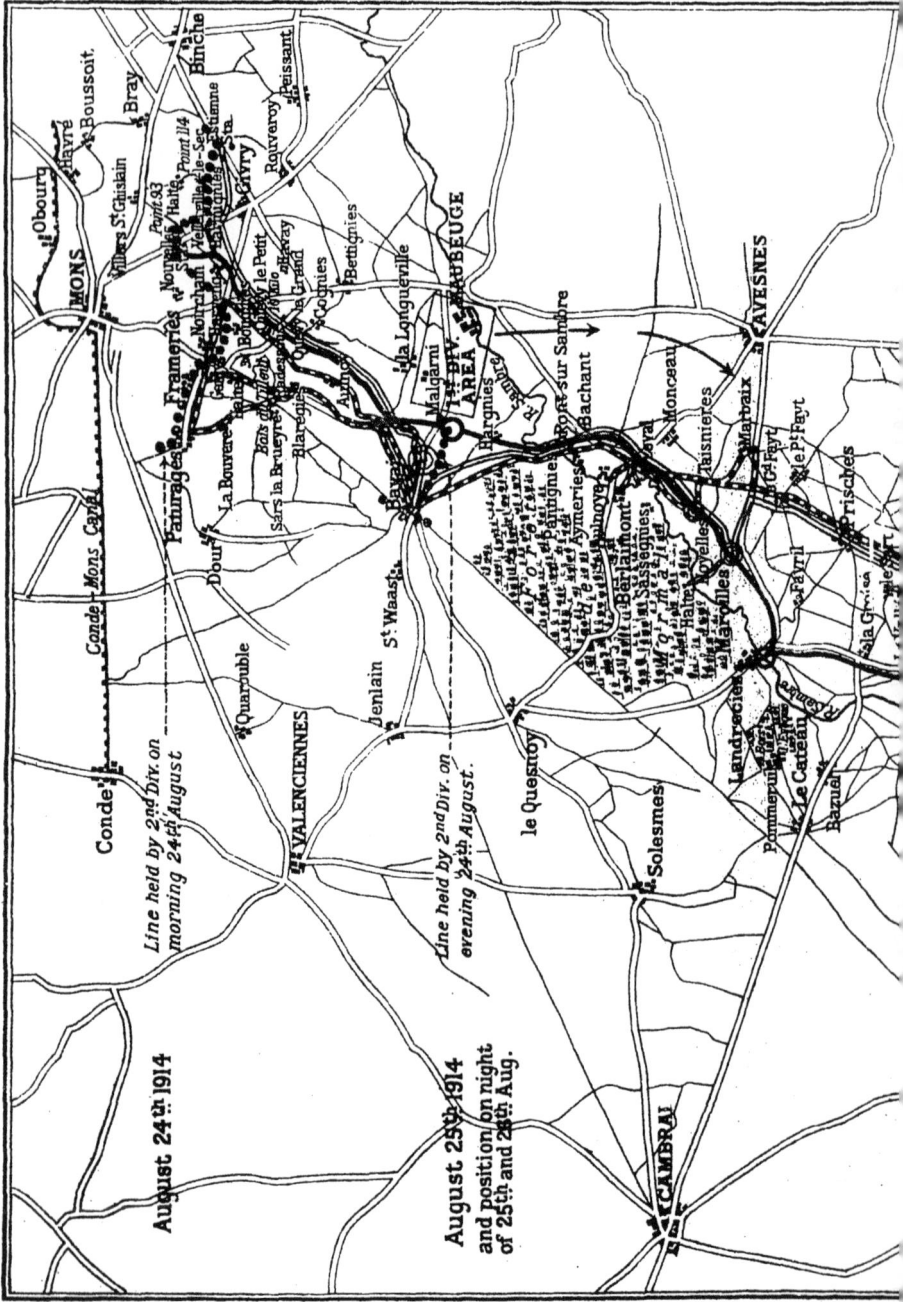

August 24th 1914

August 25th 1914
and position on night
of 25th and 26th Aug.

THE RETREAT. I.—24th–29th August 1914.

(Facing p. 42.)

August 27th 1914

August 28th 1914

August 29th 1914

R. Oise

R. Oise

Villers les Guise

Guise

R. Oise

Aubigny

le Gd Vary

Vadencourt

Longchamps

Noyales

Hauteville

Mont d'Origny

Neuvillette

Challes

Regny

Sissy

Chatillon

Ribemont

Berthenicourt

Moy

Chamégicourt

Vendeuil

Travecy

R. Oise

Beautor

Conarenne

Deuillet

Berlancourt

Servais

St QUENTIN

Junction Line A.B.

The Second Division rested in this area on 29th August 1914

The route selected was east of the Oise *via* Ribemont. The 6th Infantry Brigade area—Amigny–Rouy ; the 5th Infantry Brigade—Servais. Divisional Headquarters were also at Servais. One company (C) of the King's Royal Rifles (6th Infantry Brigade) was sent to hold the bridge over the Oise at Condren, and one company of the South Staffords the bridge at Sinceny.

The march was again without incident, but an acute stage in the sufferings of the troops had been reached. " The men felt the heat and length of the march very greatly ; straggling and falling out was very bad in all battalions." [1] " Though march discipline was greatly relaxed and though packs were in many cases thrown aside, rifles and ammunition were retained ; the hardships were borne with patient resignation, and there was a total absence of anything in the nature of insubordination or resentment." [2] A very eloquent tribute !

For nine days the men had been marching and counter-marching, covering in that time a distance of 143 miles. In great heat, with little sleep, scanty food, and a scarcity of water, carrying a greatly increased issue of rifle ammunition,[3] his feet swollen, blistered, and bleeding, the British soldier still " carried on ! "

At nightfall the whole Expeditionary Force extended from La Fère (2nd Division), Forêt de Gobain (1st Division), to Cuts, Carlepont, and Noyon (3rd, 5th, and 4th Divisions). On the right of the British force between Guise and La Fère was the Fifth French Army ; and the Sixth French Army, under Maunoury, was then forming up on the British left.

The night passed without incident but for the usual false alarms. The morrow—the 29th August—will never be forgotten by those who served in the Expeditionary Force from Mons to the Marne, for on this day the British army rested. Certain parties were detailed to dig trenches for defensive purposes, but even these, after a while, were ordered to rest.

29TH AUG.

Amongst the 2nd Division the casualties had not been excessive, the loss of the 4th Field Ambulance and the 6 officers and 284 men of the 2nd Connaughts being the most serious.[4] Up to the morning of 29th August the Division had lost : officers—4 killed, 8 wounded, 21 missing ; other ranks—25 killed, 167 wounded, 572 missing. The five casualties amongst the Irish Guards at

---

[1] Official War Diary.
[2] Official War Diary.
[3] 300 instead of 100 rounds.
[4] See Appendix II.

Harmignies do not appear in the lists ; it is probable the men were only slightly wounded and were able to remain on duty. The number of other ranks missing amongst No. 4 Field Ambulance are also unavailable.

During the 29th Sir John French was visited by General Joffre, and a discussion of the campaign took place. " I strongly represented my position to the French commander-in-chief," said Sir John, " who was most kind, cordial, and sympathetic as he has always been. He told me that he had directed the Fifth French Army on the Oise to move forward and attack the Germans on the Somme, with a view to checking pursuit. He also told me of the formation of the Sixth French Army on my left flank, composed of the VIIth Army Corps, four Reserve Divisions, and Sordet's Corps of Cavalry. I finally agreed with General Joffre to effect a further short retirement towards the line Compiègne–Soissons."

30TH AUG.   At 3 a.m. on the 30th, the 2nd Division was again on the move, and resumed the retirement in a southerly direction towards Soissons.

The bridges at Beautor and Condren were demolished by the sappers, and at various times from 3 to 4.45 a.m. the three brigades took the road. The route lay through the Basse Forêt de Coucy and the Forêt de St. Gobain *via* Barisis. But very little protection from the sun was afforded by the trees, and the day being exceptionally hot the men were very exhausted and numbers again fell out. As the distance to be covered was twenty-six miles, a very early start had to be made, and in consequence many men did not get their breakfasts or only a very scanty meal.

The 4th (Guards) Brigade, with the exception of one company of the Irish Guards (No. 2) which had been left behind to guard the bridge at Beautor, reached Pasly about 6 p.m. and bivouacked just north of the village. The belated company of the Irish Guards slept that night at Bois Roger, and rejoined the Brigade very early next morning.

The 6th Infantry Brigade set out at 4 a.m. and marched to Coucy-le-Château, where the troops settled down early. The 5th Infantry Brigade went on to Terny, and bivouacked shortly after 4 o'clock in the afternoon.

Divisional Headquarters were at Cuffies.

But for the very trying march the day passed without incident. At 11 p.m. " 2nd Division Operation Order No. 16 " was issued [1]—

---

[1] These Operation Orders are not without interest, for they show objectives which were often not reached owing to the condition of the troops.

i.e., Order of March for the 31st. The route to be followed was the Terny–Soissons road as far as the bridge of Pommiers, thence south across the river Aisne, through Pernant to billeting areas as follows :

4th Brigade area—Cœuvres-et-Valsery : 4th (Guards) Brigade, XLIst Brigade R.F.A., 4th Field Ambulance,[1] 11th Field Company R.E.

5th Infantry Brigade area—Cutry–Laversine : 5th Infantry Brigade, XXXVIth Brigade R.F.A., XLIVth (Howitzer) Brigade R.F.A., 35th (Heavy) Battery R.G.A., 5th Field Ambulance, Divisional Headquarters, Divisional Mounted Troops.

6th Infantry Brigade area—Pernant : 6th Infantry Brigade, XXXIVth Brigade R.F.A., 6th Field Ambulance, 5th Field Company R.E.

The Divisional Ammunition Column at Villers-Cotterets.

Instead of going into billets at Cœuvres-et-Valsery, the 4th (Guards) Brigade marched on to Soucy, where the battalions bivouacked at 4 p.m.

Of the 5th Infantry Brigade the Worcesters, Highland Light Infantry, and Oxford and Bucks bivouacked in Laversine ; and the Connaught Rangers in Cutry.

The 6th Infantry Brigade appears to have bivouacked in St. Bandry, a semicircular route having become necessary owing to the state of the roads about Pernant.

The Divisional Cavalry and Cyclists, who had received orders in Cuffies to push on to Soucy, got as far as Cutry ; but here the cavalry could get no farther. The cyclists were therefore sent on to Soucy, which they were able to reconnoitre before the Guards Brigade arrived.

The night of 31st August saw the British line as follows : Ist 31ST AUG. Corps (1st and 2nd Divisions) to the south-west of Soissons ; IInd Corps (3rd and 5th Divisions) between Villers-Cotterets and Crépy ; 4th Division and 19th Infantry Brigade west of Crépy and south of the Forest of Compiègne ; the cavalry was disposed partly in the gaps between the corps and partly on the left flank.

---

[1] The remaining section (A) and the wagons not captured at Landrecies.

The Rearguard Actions of Villers-Cotterets.

For four days the 2nd Division had not been attacked. This immunity was mainly due to the vigorous efforts of General Gough with the 3rd Cavalry Brigade, and General Chetwode, 5th Cavalry Brigade, who attacked two German cavalry columns moving southeast of St. Quentin. Moreover, the Fifth French Army had with some success attacked the enemy along the Oise. But on the night of 31st August the enemy was almost within striking distance of the 2nd Division,[1] and on the following morning (1st September) attacked the 4th (Guards) Brigade on the northern edge of the Forêt de Villers-Cotterets. This action, which began as an ordinary rearguard action, assumed later the nature of a running fight through the forest. Von Kluck had, on 31st August, changed direction. Thus, his IIIrd Corps, in carrying out the new movement, came into conflict, in the thickly wooded country about Villers-Cotterets, with the 2nd Division of Sir Douglas Haig's Ist Corps.

1ST SEPT.   On the morning of the 1st September, the 5th and 6th Infantry
MAP.   Brigades moved out of billets at Laversine and St. Bandry ; the 4th Brigade, Divisional Cavalry, and XLIst Brigade R.F.A., under Brigadier-General Scott-Kerr, at Soucy, acting as rearguard.

The bridges at Pommiers - and St. Bandry were demolished by the Royal Engineers.

The 5th Infantry Brigade took the Soucy–Villers-Cotterets–Ivors–Covergnon road at 2 a.m., and passed through the Guards, who were then holding the high ground at Point 158 north of Soucy. At Villers-les-Potees orders were received by the Brigade to move into billets at Betz. These orders were shortly afterwards supplemented, and the Brigade was ordered to halt at Covergnon and take up a position round the village as a rallying point for the 4th and 6th Infantry Brigades, who had been attacked in the woods about Villers-Cotterets. During the night the Highland Light Infantry and the Connaught Rangers, which had been late in reaching Betz, were ordered to move out southwards to a position south of Vincy-Manœuvre to assist in helping the rearguard back on the following day.

The 6th Infantry Brigade left St. Bandry at 3 a.m., and the march southwards *via* Cœuvres–Soucy–Rond de la Reine to just south of Villers-Cotterets was without incident. South of Villers-

---

[1] The IXth Corps was between one and two miles north-west of the 2nd Division.

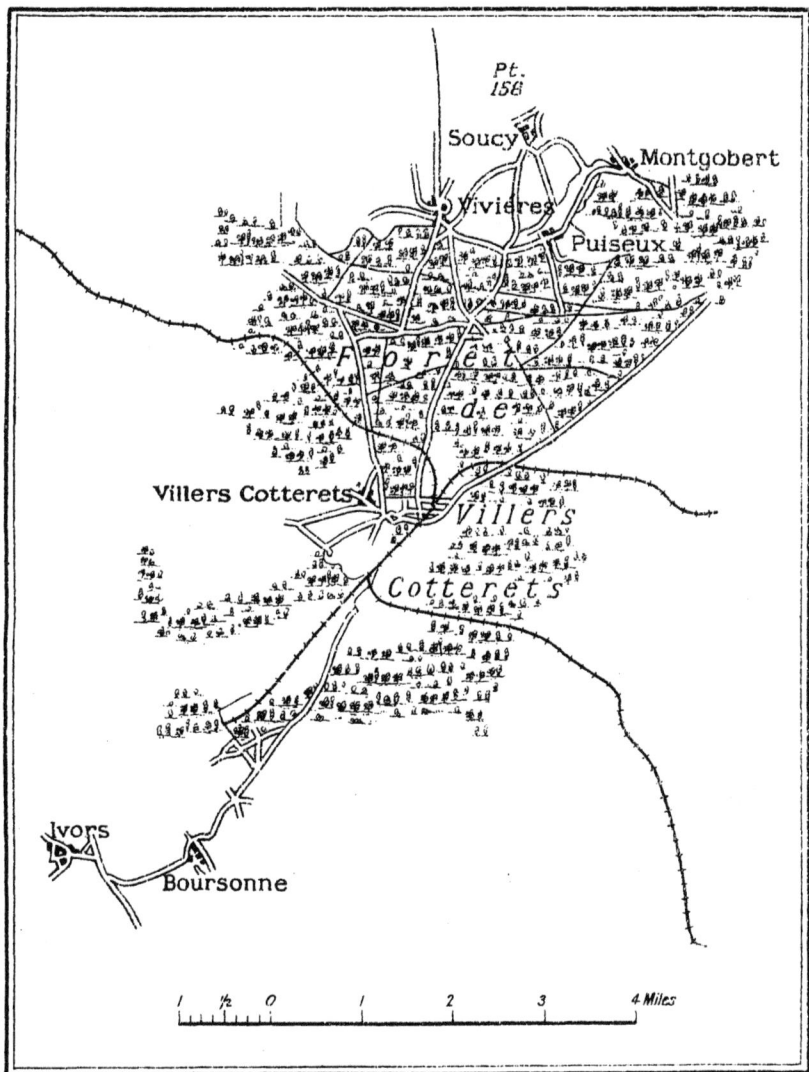

REARGUARD ACTIONS OF VILLERS-COTTERETS,
1st September 1914.

(Facing p. 46.)

Cotterets the Brigade halted.   Shortly afterwards [1] heavy firing was heard in the direction of the Rond de la Reine (in the forest) ; the Guards were in action.   At 2.45 p.m. orders were received by the 6th Infantry Brigade to let the Guards pass through the Brigade and then cover the retirement.

In order to facilitate the retirement of the 5th and 6th Infantry Brigades, the 4th (Guards) Brigade had been ordered to " arrest and delay the advance of the enemy with the greatest energy and stubbornness." [2]

As the enemy [3] advanced from the north-west he opened fire with his artillery.   His line of march was towards the south-east corner of the forest, for the right flank of his IIIrd Corps later came into action with the left flank of the Guards in the dense wood, before either had time to realize each other's presence.

The first position taken up was from Soucy to Montgobert. The 2nd Grenadiers were on the right with one company detached on the high ground about Montgobert, covering the right flank of the battalion.   The 3rd Coldstream were on the left : No. 1 Company on the right joining up with the left flank of the 2nd Grenadiers, No. 2 Company in the centre, and No. 4 Company on the left towards Viviers.   No. 3 Company was in reserve.   The retirement was to be carried out in succession by companies from the left.

Behind the 2nd Grenadiers and 3rd Coldstream there was a second position, from Puisieux to Viviers, occupied by the 1st Irish Guards (right) and the 2nd Coldstream (left) respectively.

Such was the position when, between 6 and 7 a.m., the 2nd Grenadiers and 3rd Coldstream with the 9th Battery of the XLIst Brigade R.F.A. received orders to retire through the Irish Guards and 2nd Coldstream.   Just as this order was received a few Uhlans appeared in front of Nos. 1 and 2 Companies of the 3rd Coldstream, and were immediately fired on.   The enemy thereupon withdrew, and the companies continued their retirement.   Before No. 4 Company retired a farm cart crossed the front of the company and was allowed to proceed, as it was thought to contain only refugees.   The cart, however, contained a machine gun, which opened fire at close range, but without doing any damage ; and both the 3rd Coldstream and 2nd Grenadiers retired in good order

---

[1] The action began about 10.30 a.m.

[2] This order seems to imply definite information of an impending attack, but during the retreat such orders were frequent.

[3] His strength was one complete corps (the IIIrd) and some cavalry of the IInd Cavalry Corps.

through the two other battalions of the Brigade to the Rond de la Reine, a long drive in the forest running from west to east.

Shortly after the retirement began orders were received announcing a " long rest " from 10 a.m. to 1 p.m., and as the Division intended halting in Villers-Cotterets, the 2nd Coldstream were sent back to Halte, at the southern exits of the forest. This left the Irish Guards holding a greatly extended front between Puisieux and Viviers, supported by the 2nd Grenadiers and 3rd Coldstream along the Rond de la Reine.

Exactly how the main attack began is not clear, but apparently the Germans attacked the Guards about 10 p.m. The Irish Guards was the first battalion attacked, and one company of the Grenadier Guards was sent forward to assist them. The Irishmen had already begun to fall back as ordered by companies, a retirement most difficult to carry out in the thickly wooded country which surrounded the battalion.

About 11 a.m. the enemy appears to have fallen heavily upon the left flank company of the 3rd Coldstream along the western end of the Rond de la Reine. There were gaps between the companies, and sooner or later it was inevitable that the enemy would penetrate them. " The enemy were in large numbers," said the diary of the 3rd Battalion Coldstream Guards, " and all that we could do was to fire at them whenever they were seen, and thus try to check their advance. In this the battalion succeeded, as did the Grenadiers and Irish Guards, though all three battalions lost heavily." Eventually the Grenadiers and Irish Guards worked back through the wood to a point where the Villers-Cotterets–Soissons road crosses the Villers-Cotterets–Corcy railway, whilst the 3rd Coldstream fell back on the 2nd Coldstream at Halte, at the southern exits of the forest.

The 2nd Grenadiers, Irish Guards, and 3rd Coldstream then took the road south towards Thury, followed by the 2nd Coldstream as rearguard.

South of Villers-Cotterets the 6th Infantry Brigade had been awaiting the order to cover the retirement of the Guards, and now, as the latter marched out of the forest, the Brigade moved forward with the 9th and 17th Batteries of the XLIst Brigade R.F.A.

The enemy seems to have reached the southern exits of the forest about the same time, for suddenly he opened fire with his artillery on the 6th Infantry Brigade, which—with the exception of two companies of the Berks, deployed one on either side of the 9th Battery, and two companies in reserve—was even then extended in column of route along the road. Gradually, however, the three other battalions (2nd South Staffords, 1st King's Royal Rifles, and 1st King's) were deployed. For two hours the Brigade and the artillery were subjected to an accurate and deadly shell-fire. The enemy's infantry were scarcely seen, but his artillery rained countless shells upon the devoted artillery of the 2nd Division, who served their guns until they were eventually driven to the protection of the gun-shields; whilst the infantry sheltered as best they could, having only artillery as targets.

Just as the attack died down, the 2nd Coldstream, who had followed the three other Guards battalions, reappeared ; they had been ordered to return and help the 6th Infantry Brigade out of its difficult position. Under cover of the Coldstream the Brigade was withdrawn, the enemy having broken off the attack.

The XLIst Brigade R.F.A. was specially mentioned in this action for bravery and steadiness, the 9th and 17th Batteries being heavily engaged. All guns were withdrawn most gallantly by the gun teams under a very deadly shell-fire. The Brigade's casualties were 1 other ranks killed, 12 wounded, and 4 missing. One limber only was lost.

South of Villers-Cotterets, in the Forêt Domanial de Retz, the Guards Brigade, before proceeding towards Thury, halted and called the roll. The day's fighting had been costly—20 officers and 471 other ranks killed, wounded, and missing.[1] The brigadier, General Scott-Kerr, was badly wounded in the thigh.

*   *   *   *   *   *   *

On arrival at Bousonne, the Guards Brigade (less the 2nd Coldstream, rearguard to the Division) was ordered to take up a position between the Ivors–Covergnon and the Ivors–Autheuil roads, the Irish Guards on the right and the 3rd Coldstream on the left, facing north-west to cover the retirement of the 6th Infantry Brigade.

Eventually the Guards (less the 2nd Coldstream) went into billets at Betz, arriving about 11 p.m.; whilst the 6th Infantry Brigade and the 2nd Coldstream (who in the darkness could not find their way to Betz) bivouacked round Thury-en-Valois.

At the end of the day the whole British army was once more united. The Ist Corps lay between La Ferte Milon and Betz, the IInd Corps between Betz and Nanteuil, the 4th Division and 19th Infantry Brigade west of Nanteuil, and the bulk of the cavalry operating on the left flank of the latter.

[1] See Appendix III.

On the night of the 1st September the Ist Corps received orders to resume its march upon Meaux at 2 a.m. next morning ; the 2nd Division by the road Betz–Acy-en-Multein–Vincy-Manœuvre–Barcy–Meaux station, by the right bank of the river Marne, to the bridge at Esbly.

2ND SEPT. At 4 a.m., therefore, the Irish Guards leading, the 4th (Guards) Brigade complete (the 2nd Coldstream having at 2 a.m. marched from Thury to Betz in time to form up in column) marched again southwards towards Meaux. The 6th Infantry Brigade followed very shortly afterwards. The 5th Infantry Brigade acted as rearguard, the Oxford and Bucks holding Betz until the Division was clear of the village. The two remaining battalions of the Brigade (Highland Light Infantry and Connaughts) had on the previous evening been sent on to Vincy-Manœuvre with instructions to hold the position until the Division had passed through it.

The day passed without incident, though the long march—24 miles in intense heat, and water practically unobtainable—tried the troops to the very utmost, and straggling was very prevalent.

Of the 4th (Guards) Brigade, the 2nd Coldstream bivouacked at Villenoy, the Irish Guards and 3rd Coldstream at Esbly, and the 2nd Grenadiers at Rolentier. The 6th Infantry Brigade bivouacked at Trilbardou, and the 5th Brigade at Chauconin.

3RD–5TH SEPT. The story of the next three days—3rd, 4th, and 5th September—is merely a repetition of the sufferings of weary, hungry, thirsty, and sleep-starved men, almost dropping from fatigue ; of miles trudged uncomplainingly along hot, dusty roads ; of broken nights and early morning startings before the sun had risen. Proud in the knowledge that whenever he had joined action with the enemy he had beaten him off, and had inflicted far heavier losses than he had suffered, the British soldier did not question the reason why he continually had to retire : it was an order, and, as such, to be obeyed. But the longing to turn about and fall upon the enemy was intense, and no commander ever made a greater mistake than von Kluck, who, having accomplished what he deemed a series of wonderful successes, appears to have imagined he had completely overthrown and disorganized Sir John French's little army.

So for three days more the retirement continued !

From their billets in the Meaux, Penchard, Chauconin, Villenoy, and Trilbardou area, the 2nd Division, setting out on the morning of the 3rd, crossed the Marne and marched through Trilport and Montceaux to Pierre-Levée, Petit-Courrois, and Grand-Bilbarteaux

September 1st 1914

August 30th 1914

August 31st 1914

Junction line A,B

SOISSONS

R. Aisne

R. Oise

R. Ourcq

Compiegne

Folembray

Coucy le Chateau

Behancourt

Terny

Clannecy

Cuffies

Pasly

Pommiers

Pernant

Fontenoy

Ambleny

St Bandry

Laversine

Coeuvres et Valsery

Vauty

Montgobert

Puiseux

Soucy

Vivieres

Haramont

Villers-Cotterets

Pisseleux

Boursonne

Autheuil

Thury-en-Valois

Antilly

Betz

Cuvergnon

Ivors

Villers les Potees

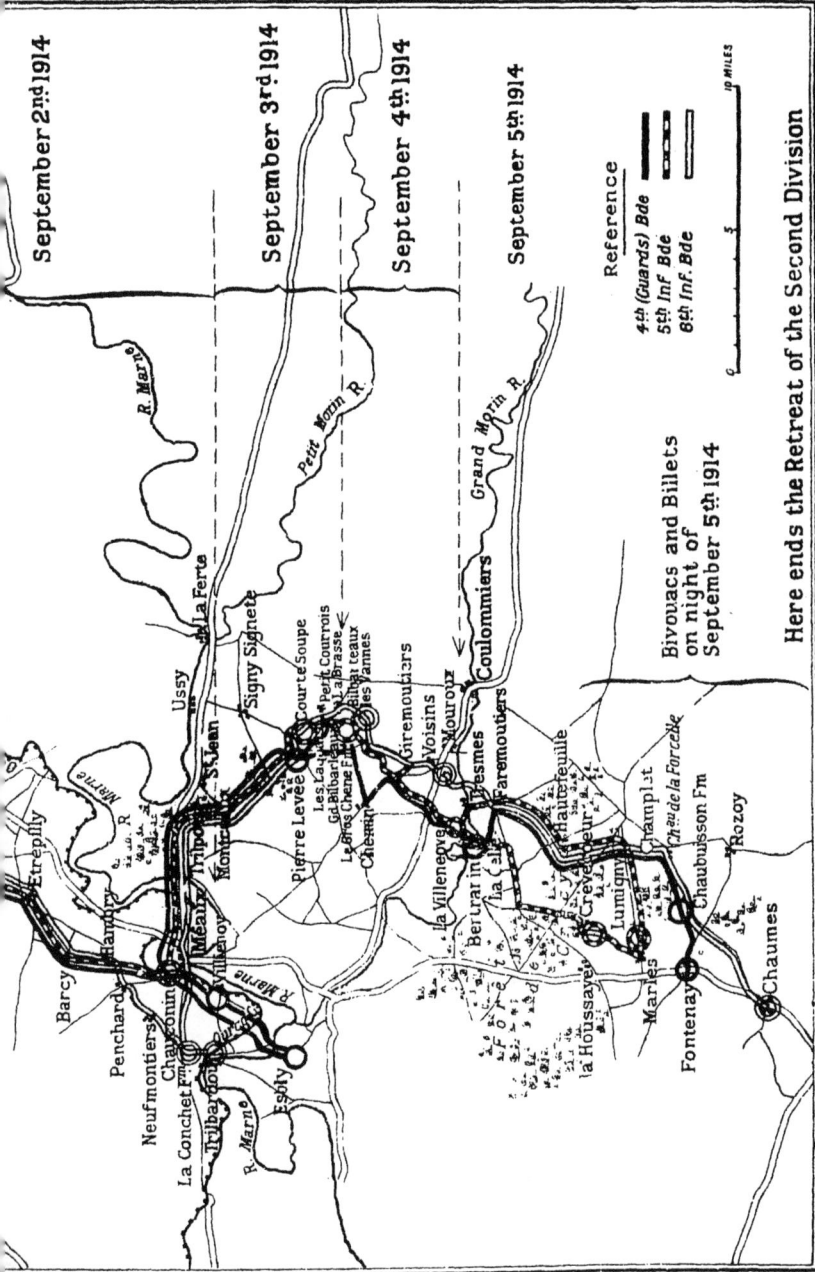

September 2nd 1914

September 3rd 1914

September 4th 1914

September 5th 1914

THE MAPPA CO LTD LONDON

Reference

4th (Guards) Bde
5th Inf Bde
6th Inf Bde

0   5   10 MILES

Bivouacs and Billets
on night of
September 5th 1914

Here ends the Retreat of the Second Division

THE RETREAT II —30th August–5th September 1914

(Facing p 50)

R. Marne

Petit Morin R.

Grand Morin R.

Coulommiers

Ussy
la Ferte
St Jean
Signy Signets
Courte Soupe
Pierre Levée
Montce
Meaux
Trilp
Villenoy
Penchard
Chauconin
Neufmontiers
La Conchet
Trilbardou
Esbly
R. Marne
Barcy
Etrepilly
Chambry

Les Laris
Ga Bibarle
Le Gros Chêne Fm
Chemin
Le Petit Courrois
La Brasse
Chateaux
des Vannes

Giremoutiers
Voisins
Tesmes
Mouroux
Faremoutiers
la Villeneuve
Berurain
la Haute Feuille
Champlat
Chu de la Forcelle
Rozoy
Chaubusson Fm
Crève cœur
la Houssaye
Marles
Lumigny
Fontenay
Chaumes

Fme. As the Division moved, the sappers blew up the bridges on the Marne from St. Jean to La Ferté.

Four o'clock on the morning of the 4th saw the Division again taking the road towards the areas Mouroux and Tresmes, just north of the Grand-Morin River, one of the shortest marches of the retreat. The first part of the march was across fields, and the wire fences had to be cut to allow the passage of wheeled traffic. The day was very hot and oppressive, and the short march was a great boon to the men.

On the 5th the Division crossed the Grand-Morin, and between 10 and 11 a.m. the heads of columns reached Chaumes, and there halted until 1 p.m.

" This halt turned into bivouacs for the night," said an official diarist, " and in the evening we were delighted to hear that the great retirement was over, and that we were to move forward next day to strike the enemy's right flank. It was good news for the men." [1]

The bivouac areas were as follows :—

4th (Guards) Brigade, Fontenay; 5th Infantry Brigade, Champlet station to north-west of Marles; 6th Infantry Brigade, Chaumes.

Divisional Headquarters were in Fontenay.

During the 4th and 5th September the Division received its first reinforcements from England.

Compared with the prodigious events which came after it to the close of the Great War, the retreat from Mons is a series of seemingly unimportant rearguard actions. But considered (as it always must be) in relation with the whole campaign, its significance cannot be overstated. The one thing the Allies needed at that momentous period was time in which to organize and regroup their armies ; whereas the enemy's one chance of success lay in striking a rapid, overwhelming blow before the Allies were ready. Two things denied the German Higher Command the success they had endeavoured to obtain : first the Belgian, and later the British resistance. These two armies, by their delaying tactics, completely disorganized the enemy's carefully laid plans.

For 236 miles, from 21st August to 5th September inclusive, the British Expeditionary Force had marched, counter-marched, and then retired—*always under orders, and not as a beaten and disorganized army*, as the German Higher Command sought to impress upon the world. A semi-official German report of 31st

[1] Official War Diary.

August said : " The English army is retiring on Paris in the most complete disorder, and its losses are estimated at 20,000." [1] Another report stated : " The reports of spies who had seen the enemy in retreat are very satisfactory. They are a disorganized and discontented horde, and there is no chance of their being able to do us any harm. The General [2] fears nothing from the direction of Paris." [3]

Von Kluck's refusal to recognize in Sir John French's army a striking force capable of inflicting defeat was very largely responsible for his subsequent discomfiture.

During the 5th September Sir John French met General Joffre at the request of the latter. " He informed me of his intention to take the offensive forthwith, as he considered conditions were very favourable to success. General Joffre announced to me his intention of wheeling up the left flank of the Sixth Army ; pivoting on the Marne and directing it to move on the Ourcq ; cross and attack the flank of the First German Army, which was moving in a south-easterly direction east of that river. He requested me to effect a change of front to my right, my left resting on the Marne, and my right on the Fifth Army to fill the gap between that army and the Sixth. I was then to advance against the enemy [4] in my front and join in the general offensive." [5]

These combined movements were to begin at sunrise on the 6th September.

[1] German Communiqué.
[2] Von Kluck.
[3] German officer's report.
[4] At nightfall on 5th September the position of the First German Army (von Kluck) was as follows :—

IInd Cavalry Corps : at Vaudoy, between Courtacon and Rozoy. ·
IXth Corps : at Esternay.
IIIrd   ,,   Montceaux–Sancy.
IVth   ,,   Choisy.
IInd   ,,   between Coulommiers and Crécy.

IVth Reserve Corps and 4th Cavalry Division were west of the river Ourcq and north-west of Meaux.

The Second German Army (von Bülow) was, on the night of 5th September, between Montmiral–Vertus, its line running from left to right as follows : VIIth, Xth Reserve, Xth, and Guard Corps.

[5] Official Dispatches.

ADVANCE TO THE AISNE.

THE BATTLE OF THE MARNE.
The Passage of the Petit-Morin.
The Passage of the Marne.

THE BATTLE OF THE AISNE.
Actions on the Aisne Heights and the Beginning of Trench Warfare.

THE BATTLE OF THE MARNE.

WHEN von Kluck changed direction from south-west to south-east there is no doubt that he committed a tactical blunder. His principal error seems to have been in considering Maunoury's Sixth French Army and the British Army incapable of arresting or seriously affecting his change of front. His intention evidently was to fall upon the Fifth French Army, roll up its flanks, and in conjunction with the Second and Third German Armies pierce the Allied centre. Von Kluck had attacked Maunoury during the time the latter was assembling his corps about Amiens, and had worsted him and forced him to retire on Paris. But the consistent manner in which he ignored the ability of the Allies to recover and reorganize after his onslaughts demonstrated how greatly at the beginning of the war the German military system lacked imagination. The machine was too perfect, it was over-certain ; it made no allowance for the entry into warfare of that great element " chance," which no wise commander in the field can afford to ignore. Otherwise von Kluck would never have marched across the front of an enemy without first making sure that his opponents were impotent and incapable of seriously interfering with his strategical plans. The vigour with which the British fought two rearguard actions at Néry and Villers-Cotterets on 1st September should have convinced him that Sir John French's army at least was anything but out of action. *But the machine had been ordered to change direction, and change direction it did.*

After Sir John French and General Joffre had met on 5th September and had discussed the coming offensive, the former issued orders (" Operation Order No. 17 ") to his corps commanders which not only detailed the change of front which was to take place but gave the troops some idea of what they were called upon to perform : " The enemy has apparently abandoned the idea of advancing on Paris, and is contracting his front and moving south-east.[1] The army will advance eastward with a view to attacking.

---

[1] This was obvious on 1st September.

Its left will be covered by the French Sixth Army, also marching east, and its right will be linked to the French Fifth Army marching north. In pursuance of the above the following moves will take place, the army facing east on completion of the movement :

> " Ist Corps: right, on La Chapelle-Iger; left, on Lumigny ; move to be completed by 9 a.m.
>
> " IInd Corps : right, on La Houssaye ; left in neighbourhood of Villeneuve ; move to be completed by 10 a.m.
>
> " IIIrd Corps: facing east in neighbourhood of Bailly ; move to be completed by 10 a.m.
>
> " Cavalry Division (less 3rd and 5th Brigades) : to guard front and flank of Ist Corps on the line Jouy-le-Châtel (connecting with French Fifth Army)–Coulommiers (connecting with 3rd and 5th Brigades).
>
> " The 3rd and 5th Cavalry Brigades will cease to be under the orders of the Ist Corps, and will act in concert under instructions issued by Brigadier-General Gough. They will cover the IInd Corps, connecting with the Cavalry Division on the right and with the French Sixth Army on the left."

These orders were issued between 5 and 6 on the evening of 5th September. At that period, it will be remembered, the 2nd Division occupied the line Fontenay (4th Guards Brigade)–Champlet–Marles (5th Infantry Brigade)–Chaumes (6th Infantry Brigade) : with Divisional Headquarters at Fontenay.

The line of the Ist Corps was to run from Lumigny to La Chapelle-Iger, the 2nd Division holding the northern (left) flank Lumigny to Rozoy (exclusive), and the 1st Division the southern (right) flank Rozoy (inclusive) to La Chapelle-Iger.

6TH SEPT.   Dawn of the 6th September broke warm and misty ; but long ere the sun had pierced the vapours hovering about their bivouacs the troops were astir. As yet they could hardly believe that after many days of retreating they were at last to advance. It seemed too good to be true. One thing was certain, that on that misty September morning Sir John French's army was in the very best of spirits, ready to go anywhere and do anything so long as an opportunity offered of joining action with the enemy.

At 7 a.m. the 4th (Guards) Brigade and XLIst Brigade R.F.A. moved out of Fontenay to take up the line Rozoy (exclusive)–Château de la Fortelle (inclusive) ; the 5th Infantry Brigade and XXXVIth Brigade R.F.A. took ground north of the Guards and prolonged the line to La Bectarderie Fme. The XLIVth (Howitzer)

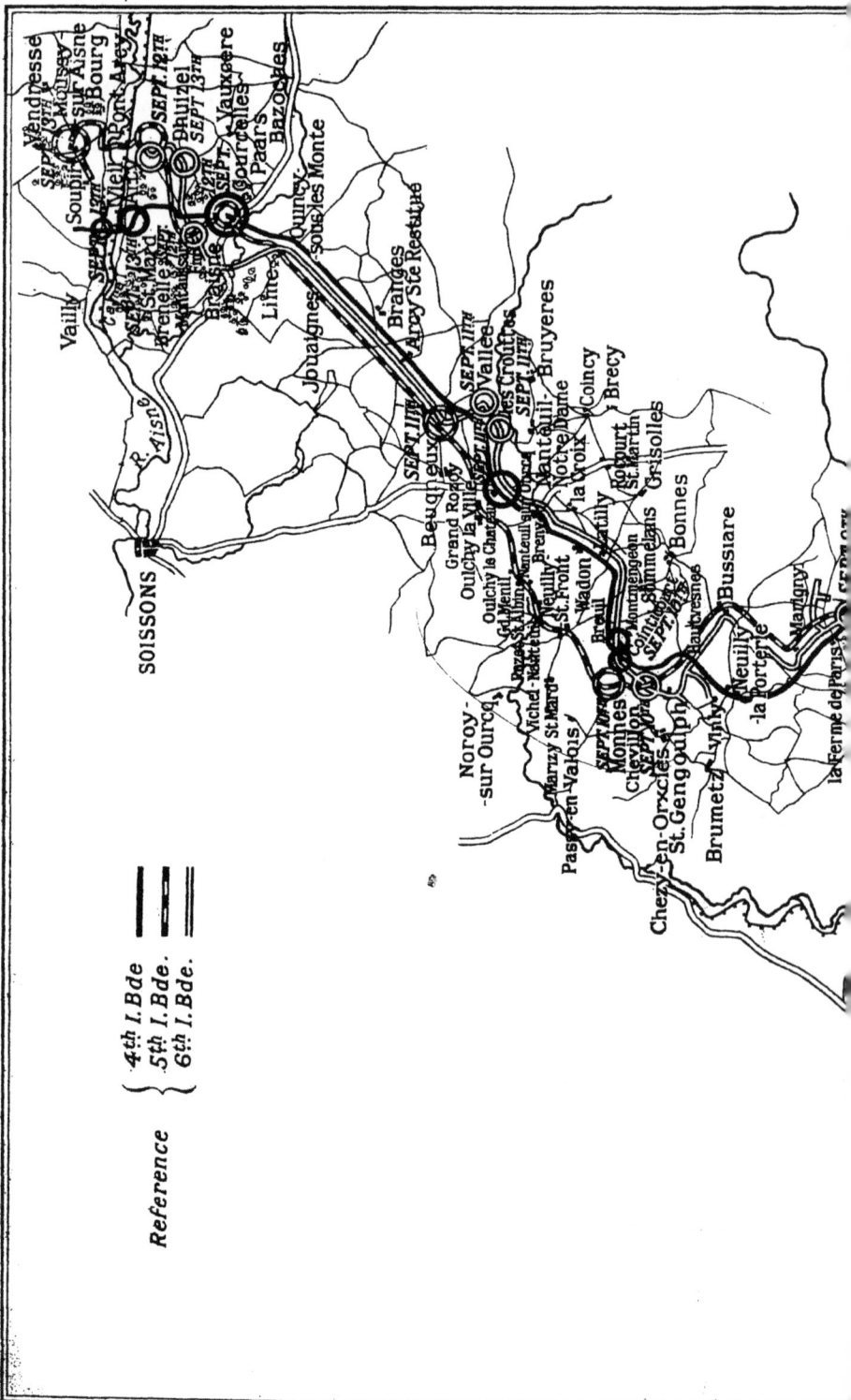

Reference
{ 4th I. Bde
  5th I. Bde.
  6th I. Bde.

SOISSONS

Vailly

R. Aisne

Vendresse
Moussy
Sur Aisne
Bourg
Pont Arcy
SEPT 12TH
SEPT 15TH
Soupir
Vieil
Braule
Baulzel
SEPT 13TH
Bourdelles
SEPT.
Paars
Vauxcere
Bazoches

Brenelle
Breuie
SEPT 13TH
SEPT
Acheule le ville

Quincy
Lihus
Jouaignes
Sous les Monte

Branges
Arcy Ste Restitue

Beugneux
Grand Rozoy
Oulchy la Ville
Oulchy le Château
St Menil
Mareuil sur Ourcq
Vichel Nanteuil
St Albin
Villers
Neuilly
Brény
St Front
Wadon
Breuil

SEPT 11TH
Vallée
Les Crouttes
SEPT 11TH
Nanteuil
Notre Dame
la Croix
Bruyères
Rocourt
St Martin
Grisolles
Brécy
Coincy
Bonnes
Bussiare

Noroy-
-sur-Ourcq

Passy-en-Valois

Marizy St Mard

SEPT 10TH
Monnes
Chevillon
SEPT 10TH
Montigny
Sommelans
Bussiare
Montagny
SEPT 7TH
Neuilly
-la Porterie
la Ferme de Paris
SEPT 7TH

Chézy-en-Oryxcles
St. Gengoulph
Brumetz
Licy
Beaubresne

THE ADVANCE TO THE AISNE, 6th–12th September 1914.

(Facing p. 54.)

The Mappa Co., Ltd., London

Scale

0   5   10   20 MILES.

Brigade and 35th (Heavy) Battery R.G.A. were ordered to take up positions at the junction of roads at Bourbeaudoin Fme. The 6th Infantry Brigade, XXXIVth Brigade R.F.A., and one troop Divisional Cavalry formed the reserve at Chaubuisson Fme. Of the two Field Companies Royal Engineers, the 5th was allotted to the 5th Infantry Brigade and the 11th to the 4th Brigade. The Field Ambulances were ordered to remain in their billets, but clear of the roads.

Divisional Headquarters were at Bourbeaudoin Fme.

These movements all took place at an early hour, and were made without opposition or incident. At 10.30 a.m., as ordered in "Operation Orders," the 2nd Division (in line with the remainder of the British army) faced east ready to attack. Before the advance began Sir John French issued an "Order of the Day":

"After a most trying series of operations, mostly in retirement, which have been rendered necessary by the general strategic plan of the Allied armies, the British force stands to-day formed in line with their French comrades ready to attack the enemy. Foiled in their attempt to invest Paris, the Germans have been driven to move in an easterly and south-easterly direction, with the apparent intention of falling in strength upon the Fifth French Army. In this operation they are exposing .their right flank and their line of communications to an attack from the combined Sixth French Army and the British forces.

"I call upon the British army in France now to show the enemy its power, and to push on vigorously to the attack beside the Sixth French Army. I am sure I shall not call upon them in vain, but that, on the contrary, by another manifestation of the magnificent spirit which they have shown in the past fortnight, they will fall on the enemy's flank with all their strength, and in unison with their Allies drive them back."

But in spite of high expectations, little happened on the 6th September on the front occupied by the 2nd Division. The Divisional Cavalry sent out a patrol very early in the morning, with instructions to penetrate the enemy's screen in the vicinity of Touquin. Hostile guns were located at Pézarches, and the enemy discovered in force behind Touquin. Here the Hussars eventually fought a dismounted action with the enemy, losing 6 men wounded and 6 horses wounded and killed. The Hussars then moved to the vicinity of Lumigny, where north-west in the Forêt de Crécy the 12th Lancers and 5th Cavalry Brigade were engaged with the enemy's cavalry.   They then retired south-west to Rigny and bivouacked.

Artillery duels took place during the early part of the day, the 2nd Worcesters being shelled, though without loss.   Both the XLIst and XLIVth (Howitzer) Brigades R.F.A. were in action, the former near La Fortelle and the latter near Nesles.

Generally, however, the 2nd Division stood to arms all day and waited orders, which came to hand during the late afternoon ; an advance was made, but only to billets for the night.

The 4th (Guards) Brigade, which had moved out to the line Rigny–Château de la Fortelle, entrenched along the road, its right flank being in touch with the 1st Division at Rozoy.   About 2.30 p.m. the enemy opened fire from Le Plessis and shelled the Brigade, the 1st Irish Guards and 3rd Coldstream sustaining casualties ; 3rd Coldstream losing Second-Lieut. W. de Winton killed, and the Irish Guards 4 men killed and 9 wounded.   At 3 p.m. the hostile battery was silenced by the XLIst Brigade R.F.A., and the Guards occupied Villeneuve without further opposition or loss, eventually moving north to Touquin, where the Brigade bivouacked at 9 p.m.

The 5th Infantry Brigade (less 2nd Highland Light Infantry) was ordered forward in support of the Cavalry Division, and held a position at Le Paradis ; the XXXVIth Brigade R.F.A. and 5th Field Company R.E. bivouacked at Pézarches.

The 6th Infantry Brigade, XXXIVth R.F.A., 35th (Heavy) Battery R.G.A., XLIVth (Howitzer) Brigade R.F.A., and the 5th Field Ambulance bivouacked at Château de la Fortelle.

Divisional Headquarters were at Rigny.

At the close of the day of 6th September the Battle of the Marne had opened, but, as far as the British army was concerned, very little more.

On Sir John French's right the Fifth French Army (d'Esperey) had advanced its front, and had obtained considerable success. Maunoury with his Sixth Army, on the British left, had progressed against von Kluck's IVth Reserve Corps posted along the Ourcq.

Von Kluck by this time,[1] appreciating the threat made on his right flank, had reinforced the IVth Reserve Corps on the Ourcq with the IInd Corps.   He had withdrawn his centre, and had interposed cavalry, under von Marwitz, between his retiring infantry and the British army.[2]

[1] About noon on 6th September.

[2] Von Kluck had apparently received orders from the German Higher Command

The position at nightfall of the various armies was as follows :

Sixth French Army : right at Meaux, left near Betz.

British Army : on the line Dagny–Coulommiers–Maison.[1]

Conneau's Cavalry Corps : between the British army and Fifth French Army.

Fifth French Army : about Courtacon, with its right on Esternay.

First German Army : IVth Reserve Corps and IInd Corps west of the Ourcq ; 2nd Cavalry Division north-east of Lumigny ; IVth Corps north of the Marne facing La Ferté and Nanteuil ; IIIrd and IXth[2] Corps south-west of Montmiral, on the line Sancy–Montceaux–Escardes– Chatillon.

About midnight (6th–7th) rumours of an enemy advance reached Divisional Headquarters, and in consequence the Divisional Mounted Troops were sent out in order to gain touch with the 3rd Cavalry Brigade, and obtain from the latter information of the movements of the enemy. At 1.15 a.m. an order was issued cancelling all moves in a forward direction until the situation had been cleared up. These orders were subsequently supplemented by the issue at 8.10 a.m. of more definite instructions—the Ist Corps was to advance to the line Mauperthuis–Amillis, the 1st Division on the right, the 2nd Division on the left.

7TH SEPT.

The advanced guard of the 2nd Division was composed of the 4th (Guards) Brigade, XLIst Brigade R.F.A., and 11th Field Company R.E. under the command of Lieut.-Colonel Feilding. Very early in the morning cyclist patrols of two men of the 2nd Coldstream had gone out to reconnoitre the road, and at La Moinerie came suddenly upon a German barricade across the road. Before the patrol could turn they were fired upon and wounded, though both men were eventually brought in. These were the first casualties suffered by the 2nd Coldstream Guards during the war. Though present at Mons, Landrecies, and Villers-Cotterets, the battalion had no casualties—a case of extraordinary good fortune.

to face the eastern exits of Paris—*i.e.*, to face west—and was to transfer his army north of the Marne to the line of the Ourcq.

[1] Maisoncelles or La Haute Maison : probably the latter. The line here given in the Official Dispatches is not quite accurate. At nightfall on the 6th September the British line was as follows :—Ist Corps : Vaudoy–Touquin (1st Division) ; Touquin–Pézarches–Le Paradis (2nd Division). IInd Corps, Faremoutiers (3rd Division) ; Montcerf (5th Division). IIIrd Corps : Villeneuve-le-Comte–Villers-sur-Morin. The cavalry, on the line Lumigny–Jouy-le-Châtel–Le Corbin.

[2] In the Official Dispatches this corps (IXth) is given as VIIth, but the latter belonged to the Second German Army.

The advanced guard having taken the road towards Epieds, was next ordered to push out patrols through Coulommiers towards Aulnoy, and through Mouroux towards Giremoutiers.

The main body was massed about Le Paradis with the Field Ambulances.

At 10.45 Order No. 164 was issued :

" The Ist Corps will move forward at once, general direction north-east. 1st Division, Amillis–L'Epauche–St. Remy–Le Jariel inclusive, and all roads to south. 2nd Division, north of the above road via Beautheil–La Touche–Chailly–St. Siméon–Launoy–Beaufort inclusive. Ist Corps will halt on reaching line Dagny–Coulommiers, and will await orders. 3rd and 5th Cavalry Brigades will protect the front. Cavalry Division will cover the right ; main body will resume its march about 11.30."

The enemy was still retiring, and the 2nd Division, though close on the heels of two large German columns, did not join action with them. A few isolated encounters took place with the enemy's cavalry,[1] which covered his retirement ; and to the immense delight of the British soldier, who at last began to feel he really was doing something else than retiring, some prisoners were taken. Everywhere as the British advanced there was evidence of the hurried flight of von Kluck's troops. There were also signs of drunken orgies. When the Division entered Chailly, it found most of the shops had been ransacked and the goods thrown on the floor. In addition, the chief wine merchant's shop had been burned down, and such wine as had not been drunk had been poured away before the Germans retired.

The 4th (Guards) Brigade had a hard day's march, and eventually went into billets at Voigny, north-east of the Grand-Morin, the passage of which the enemy had not disputed. During the day the enemy's cavalry came into contact repeatedly with the Guards, and the 2nd Coldstream killed 4 and captured 7 Uhlans.

A driver of a battery (48th) of the Field Artillery went to a haystack for feed for his horses, and found beneath the top layer of hay five drunken Germans, whom he promptly marched off as prisoners.

The 5th Infantry Brigade marched via Pézarches, Mauperthuis, Beautheil, La Touche, Chailly-en-Brie to St. Siméon, and there bivouacked.

The 6th Infantry Brigade as rearguard left Château de la Fortelle at 11.30 a.m., and marched via Pézarches, Touquin, La

[1] IInd Cavalry Corps.

Boissière, north, then east, Maillard, Courcelles, St. Eloi, and Chailly, then to bivouacs round Mondollot, at 7.30 p.m.

During the day several units received further reinforcements from England.

Cavalry actions chiefly summed up the day's fighting on other portions of the British front, though the 7th Brigade (3rd Division) had a stubborn fight with the enemy.

On the British right and left flanks the Fifth and Sixth French Armies respectively were heavily engaged, but were still making progress against von Bülow and von Kluck, the latter especially having perceived the danger threatening his corps, which for the time being was still spread out.

So far as Sir John French's army was concerned, the 6th and 7th September had practically been spent in following a retreating enemy; but the 8th September was to tell a different tale, for von Kluck had ordered his corps commanders to put up a resistance on the Petit-Morin, and delay the British advance as long as possible. If he could hold off Sir John French's corps a little longer, von Kluck evidently imagined he could beat Maunoury back from the Ourcq and free his army from the danger of envelopment to which he had exposed it. But Maunoury was not to be denied, and though he had at first reeled under the sledge-hammer blows poured upon him, he had been so well supported from Paris by General Galliéni that slowly but surely the enemy was giving way before him. The Fifth French Army also had thrown the enemy back to the line of the Petit-Morin, and had inflicted losses upon him.

At 10.15 p.m. on the 7th September, " Ist Corps Operation Order No. 11 " was issued :

" After fierce fighting the Fifth French Army on our right has won a considerable success, taking 1,200 prisoners.

" The Sixth French Army on our left has also made considerable progress.

" The 18th Hussars and 9th Lancers to-day engaged superior forces of the enemy with great success.

" The pursuit will be continued to-morrow at 6 a.m.

" The right of the Corps on Nogent.

" Ist Division : starting-point, Jouy-sur-Morin, 6 a.m., to Sablonnières–Hondevilliers–Nogent–L'Artaud.

" 2nd Division : starting-point, Voigny, 6.30 a.m., to Rebais–La Trétoire–Boitron–Charly.

" The Cavalry Division will be sending out patrols to the north and north-east at daylight, and will cover the front and flank of the Ist Corps during the march.

" The 3rd and 5th Cavalry Brigades will keep touch with the Sixth French Army on our left.

" The IInd Corps will advance on our left.

" Divisions will push out infantry patrols during the night, 1st Division towards St. Barthélemy and Le Jariel object, to make sure the enemy will not dispute the passage of the Petit-Morin."

The advanced guard of the 2nd Division was formed of the 4th (Guards) Brigade, XLIst Brigade R.F.A., 11th Field Company R.E., and the Divisional Cavalry, under Lieut.-Colonel Lushington, R.F.A.

The Passage of the Petit-Morin.

8TH SEPT.   The Guards moved out of Voigny at 6 a.m. on the 8th, the 3rd Coldstream leading, followed by the 1st Irish Guards and then the 2nd Grenadiers, the 2nd Coldstream acting as rearguard. Two companies (Nos. 3 and 4) of the 3rd Coldstream, under Major Bond, R.F.A., were detailed as advanced guard to the Brigade.

The Divisional Cavalry had already gone on ahead when the infantry and artillery formed up at the rendezvous. Orders were therefore issued to push on at once. On reaching Rebais the advanced guard found that the road was blocked by the 3rd Division and cavalry, and being unable to advance farther, had to halt. A change of route *via* the eastern side of the town was made, which necessitated the throwing out of a fresh advanced guard—*i.e.*, the two remaining companies (Nos. 1 and 2) of the 3rd Coldstream, under Major Matheson.

As the advanced guard approached La Trétoire, the Divisional Cavalry reported that the village was held by a small detachment of the enemy's cavalry, but the latter retired without putting up a resistance.

The village of La Trétoire lies at the top of a winding road which leads down to the Petit-Morin through a thickly wooded valley offering excellent cover for infantry with machine guns— cover of which the enemy was not slow in taking advantage.

As the advanced guard cleared La Trétoire the enemy's artillery opened fire from Boitron, a village high up on the hilly slopes north of the Petit-Morin. The first shell caused a number of casualties, for the advanced guard was marching in column of route. No. 2 Company was at once ordered down the hill to make good the crossing of the river, whilst No. 1 Company was sent through the wood on the left flank as support. But half-way down the hill the two companies came upon cleverly concealed machine guns and entrenched infantry, and were in consequence unable to advance farther. Nos. 3 and 4 Companies, having by this time reached the top of the road, were ordered to deploy through the wood with the same idea of making good the passage of the river. But they also were unable to proceed farther than about half-way down the hill, the machine-gun and rifle fire being deadly and difficult to locate.

Considerable confusion now reigned, platoons and companies, and even battalions, becoming very much mixed.

" The wood was very thick, and companies got somewhat disorganized, consequently platoons had to act on their own initiative."

In the meantime the XLIst Brigade R.F.A. had come into action, and had silenced the enemy's guns at Boitron. Guns were also brought forward down the hill towards the Petit-Morin, and opened fire on a farmhouse near the bridge of La Trétoire held by the enemy. Following considerable artillery preparation, the 1st Irish Guards were advanced to the left of the 3rd Coldstream, and together the two battalions made good the road leading down to another road running parallel with the river. Meanwhile the 2nd Coldstream and 2nd Grenadiers advancing on the right flank of the 3rd Coldstream had crossed the river at La Force, and had already gained the high ground on the enemy's flank at Boitron.

The 5th Infantry Brigade, which had left St. Siméon at 6 a.m., was waiting in support of the 4th (Guards) Brigade, formed up in two lines just south of La Trétoire ; on the left, the 2nd Worcesters with the 2nd Connaughts behind them, and on the right the 2nd Highland Light Infantry, supported by the 2nd Oxford and Bucks.

At noon the Worcesters were ordered forward to support the 3rd Coldstream and 1st Irish Guards, and by making good the passage of the river at Le Gravier work up stream and so assist the Guards. The Highland Light Infantry were likewise dispatched to help the 2nd Coldstream and 2nd Grenadiers at La Force, but the passage had been captured when the battalion arrived.

By 1.30 p.m. the Irish Guards and Worcesters had seized the bridge at Le Gravier, though they had not obtained it without a considerable struggle. In the farmhouse by the bridge 30 prisoners were taken, and the enemy retired leaving behind many killed and wounded and two machine guns.

The capture of the bridges at La Force and Le Gravier now opened the way for the advance of the Division. Small detachments then pushed forward, on the initiative of officers on the spot, up the slopes on the northern bank. They did not meet with much opposition, and eventually reached the line occupied by the German batteries earlier in the day. Here numerous dead Germans and dead horses, besides some abandoned limbers, testified to the severe handling they had received from the XLIst Brigade R.F.A. Thus the passage of the Petit-Morin had been won.

The 3rd Division on the left of the 2nd Division was hung up in front of Orly, the enemy contesting the crossings of the river with determination. A Company of the Connaught Rangers (2nd Division) was lent for co-operation with the 3rd Division, and at 4.45 p.m. the Oxford and Bucks supported the Connaughts. But the attack on Orly was not completed, as the enemy retired about 5 p.m., the advance of the 3rd Division having been greatly assisted by the Connaughts and Oxfords. The action which took place during the afternoon of the 8th was a sequel to the morning attack on the river crossing.

By 2.30 p.m. Boitron had been captured, and the 2nd Grenadiers and 2nd Coldstream were sent north to a point 800 yards short of the La Belle Idée road in order to protect the front of the Division. Two brigades of field artillery took up their positions and shelled the woods west of Boitron. The Highland Light Infantry were sent off towards Bussières in order to cut off the enemy's retreat, whilst the remainder of the 5th Infantry Brigade and A Company of the Connaughts worked northwards through the woods north-east of Becherelle road.

The concentrated fire of the two brigades of artillery on the woods west of Boitron had an almost immediate effect, for from the woods emerged enemy artillery and infantry, and the British gunners made fine practice as the Germans retreated in disorder, leaving many dead and wounded lying on the ground.

But the fight was not over, for a hostile battery of machine guns and some infantry still clung to the woods. These attempted a counter-attack, but although they fought gallantly they were eventually forced to surrender, and a complete machine-gun company of a Guards Schutzen Battalion, about 100 men with six machine guns, were taken prisoners.[1]

---

[1] There is some doubt as to which unit of the 2nd Division actually captured these machine guns and prisoners; but evidence points to the 2nd Coldstream (Captain Hardy's Company), for whilst Lieut. Lloyd of that battalion was taking over the

Action closed, the 4th (Guards) Brigade bivouacked at Petit-Villiers and the 5th Infantry Brigade at Le Petit-Bassevelle.

The 6th Infantry Brigade had a quiet day, having started at 6.40 a.m. from Mondollot. The route lay through St. Siméon, Voigny, Rebais, La Trétoire, Boitron, Petit-Villiers, and Le Petit-Bassevelle, where the Brigade, passing through the 5th Infantry Brigade, went on and bivouacked round La Noue, thus becoming advanced guard to the Division. The Brigade, with the XXXIVth Brigade R.F.A., was then pushed forward with its northern posts overlooking the Marne River, west of Pavant. The enemy, in unknown strength, was believed to be just north of the river, holding and preparing to destroy the bridges.

The 11th Field Company did good work during the day reconnoitring the bridges before the troops passed over them, one man especially (Corporal Hallet) being personally commended by the General Officer Commanding 4th (Guards) Brigade for the coolness and courage with which he went about his dangerous work.

The gunners of the 47th Battery (XLIVth Howitzer Brigade) had quite a little adventure. This battery crossed the Petit-Morin at 2 p.m. Later it came into action at Boitron, at 4 p.m. engaging hostile infantry and artillery to the west at 4,000 yards. Suddenly enemy infantry only 300 yards from the guns opened fire on the battery. Leaving one section to engage the enemy's artillery, the gunners seized their rifles, rushed into the woods and captured 9 Germans.

The passage of the Petit-Morin cost the 2nd Division 8 officers, and 169 other ranks killed, wounded, and missing.[1]

During the night the field ambulances were busy collecting the wounded from all parts of the field. Motor ambulances were badly needed, but not until later were they forthcoming. In the meantime the R.A.M.C. had to carry on as best they could under very great difficulties.

The Passage of the Marne.

On the night of the 8th September the whole British Expeditionary Force lay just south of the river Marne, on a line running (approximately) from La Ferté-sous-Jouarre to Viels-Maisons ;

prisoners, a shell from the British artillery unfortunately burst close at hand, knocking over and wounding that officer, and the Germans scuttled back to the woods, but were again captured.

[1] See Appendix IV.

the IIIrd Corps being on the left (west), the IInd in the centre, and the Ist on the right. The latter occupied the line La Noue (2nd Division)–Viels-Maisons (1st Division), both inclusive.

The Sixth French Army was still strenuously engaged west of the Ourcq, whence von Kluck had practically withdrawn all his corps [1] from the British front, leaving only von Marwitz's cavalry to prevent the too rapid advance of Sir John French's army.

The Fifth French Army away on the British right had experienced little difficulty in advancing until the line of the Petit-Morin was reached, for von Bülow had had to retire in order to conform with von Kluck's movements, though by now the gap between the two armies was becoming still more pronounced. At the Petit-Morin, however, von Bülow put up a big fight, and the French did not gain Montmirail without very severe fighting and heavy losses.

Von Bülow seems to have divided his attention between Sir John French's army and the Fifth French Army, for his Garde Corps was present at the passage of the Petit-Morin at La Trétoire, the prisoners captured by the 2nd Coldstream belonging to the latter corps. Von Kluck had none of the Garde Corps with his army.

9TH SEPT.   The 9th September was a critical day—not for the British force, which, opposed only by von Kluck's cavalry and the right of von Bülow's army, VIIth Corps, experienced little difficulty (excepting at one place, La Ferté) in forcing the passage of the Marne, but for the Sixth French Army on the left, and the Ninth French Army on the right of the Fifth French Army.

At 4.30 a.m. the 6th Infantry Brigade, as the advanced guard of the 2nd Division, moved off to force a passage at the bridge over the Marne south of Charly. "The 1st King's (Liverpool) Regiment moved through the wooded slopes above Pavant ; 1st King's Royal Rifles, followed by the 1st Royal Berks and 2nd South Staffords, moved on La Ferme Marie, supported by the XXXIVth Brigade R.F.A., and relieved the 1st Cavalry Brigade. The 1st King's Royal Rifles pushed on and demonstrated towards the bridge. A few of the enemy could be seen leaving the house by the bridge which was loopholed, and the bridge barricaded with carts and furniture. After a time a platoon of the King's, led by Lieut.

[1] In the " Orders of Battle " published by the German General Staff the German corps on the Ourcq are given as follows: IInd Active Corps (3rd and 4th Jäger Divisions), IIIrd Active Corps (5th and 6th Jäger Divisions), IVth Active Corps (7th and 8th Jäger Divisions), IVth Reserve Corps (7th and 22nd Reserve Divisions), IXth Active Corps (17th and 18th Jäger Divisions), IInd Cavalry Corps (2nd and 9th Cavalry Divisions).

Scott-Tucker, advanced across the bare and open ground leading to the bridge.

" Then in the fields below appeared a string of dots slowly advancing towards the bridge. They were a platoon sent forward to find out what there was in front of us. Every moment we expected to hear the stillness of the morning broken by the crackle of machine guns and rifle fire. They reached the bank and lay down ; nothing happened. Then a figure got up and started across the bridge ; surely it was mined ? No ! one by one they followed their leader, and started to throw the carts which formed the barricade into the river. And so we crossed absolutely unopposed ; we learnt from the inhabitants that the enemy had got everything ready for defending the bridge, and had then got hopelessly drunk." [1]

The barricades removed, the Divisional Mounted Troops pushed forward, followed by the Brigade.

In Charly evidence of the disorderly retirement of the enemy was abundant. Wanton ruin everywhere met the eye. Furniture and household goods smashed and thrown into the street, empty wine bottles by the dozen—all testified to the lack of discipline amongst von Kluck's cavalry and von Bülow's infantry.

In Charly the 6th Infantry Brigade had a long halt, for the IInd Corps was also passing through the town. About 10 a.m., however, the road was sufficiently clear to permit an advance, and the Brigade marched northwards *via* Villiers-sur-Marne and Domptin to Coupru. Here the Brigade bivouacked, the 2nd South Staffords finding the outposts (two companies) which were posted along the main chaussée from Point 201 to the crossroads at Ferme Paris, in touch on the right with the 1st Division, and on the left with the 3rd Division (IInd Corps).

The XXXIVth Brigade R.F.A. also bivouacked in Coupru.

The 5th Infantry Brigade, which had bivouacked at Le Petit-Bassevelle, marched out at 11.30 a.m., and on reaching Pavant was ordered to entrench a position on the south bank of the Marne ; but before the order could be carried out it was cancelled, and the Brigade ordered to continue its march. At 5 p.m. the river was crossed and Domptin was reached about 8 p.m., and here the Brigade bivouacked.

The Guards at Petit-Villiers were later still in setting out, the Brigade not leaving their bivouacs until 1 p.m. As there was only a single bridge at Charly, long waits and frequent checks caused

[1] *The Marne Campaign* (Whitton).

the delay. It was 10 p.m. before the Brigade marched into Villiers-sur-Marne and bivouacked for the night, the troops having great difficulty in the dark in finding suitable bivouacs.

The following story is related in the official Diary of the Divisional Mounted Troops (B Squadron, 15th Hussars) for 9th September. The diarist with his men had bivouacked at Coupru that night. " The tale told me by the inhabitants was that one Guardsman all by himself had come on and got into a farm—Ferme de Paris, where he hid. A party of eleven Germans came by ; he killed the first nine, wounded the tenth, and the other escaped. Six Germans were, I believe, buried at the Ferme de Paris, and I saw the graves of three more in a wood, which gives some support to the story." [1]

At 11.15 p.m. " 2nd Division Operation Order No. 24 " was issued. The 6th Infantry Brigade as advanced guard, with XXXIVth Brigade R.F.A., Divisional Mounted Troops, and 11th Field Company R.E. (under Brigadier-General Davies), was to set out at 4 a.m. on 10th September, the destination of the 2nd Division being Noroy-sur-Ourcq, *via* Marigny-en-Orxois–Bussiares–Hautevesnes–St. Gengoulph–Monnes and Passy-en-Valois. The 5th Infantry Brigade with the main body: the 4th (Guards) Brigade as rearguard.

10TH SEPT.   The advanced guard left Coupru at 3.45 a.m. on the 10th. The Divisional Cavalry went on ahead, and were followed by the 1st Royal Berks, with one battery (50th) of the XXXIVth Brigade R.F.A. acting as vanguard. Marigny and Bussiares were passed without incident, the enemy's cavalry retiring before the Hussars without offering any resistance. But just south of Hautevesnes a hostile column, composed mainly of transport, was seen moving along the road from Vinly to Chezy-en-Orxois in a north-westerly direction and parallel with the 6th Infantry Brigade.

The 1st Royal Berks were ordered to make good the northern exits of Hautevesnes, whilst the 50th Battery came into action immediately south-west of the village. The time was about 9.30 a.m. A second column of German infantry was then discovered moving northwards along the Vinly road, evidently acting as rearguard. The guns immediately opened fire at 1,500 yards, and the 1st King's Royal Rifles at the head of the main guard deployed to attack. " The enemy then lined the side of the road, which at this point ran through a cutting forming a natural trench. C Company was ordered to attack, starting with their left on the right

[1] 1st Royal Berks.

of 50th Battery, and advanced across an open stubble field to a position about 400 yards in front, on the slope of the hill. B Company was deployed on the left of C Company, and D Company kept in reserve in a sunken lane until another battalion was deployed on our right. As soon as our guns opened fire, the enemy brought four guns into action from high ground just north of Brumetz.[1]

" The XXXIVth Brigade R.F.A. having by now brought into action its two remaining batteries, the German guns quickly retired from the fight. It was evident that the enemy was offering some considerable measure of resistance, and the 1st Royal Berks was directed to move against them through St. Gengoulph on the right of the 1st King's Royal Rifles, while two companies of the 2nd South Staffords were thrown in on the extreme left. By 11 a.m. the hostile fire was observed to slacken considerably."

The 5th Infantry Brigade at this period was ordered forward to assist the 6th Infantry Brigade ; but reports having been received that the advanced guard of the 1st Division had been driven back at Courchamps, the Brigade changed direction and moved on Monnes. At Montmenjon the Brigade came under hostile artillery fire, but it was ineffective ; and the XXXVIth Brigade R.F.A. pushed forward and opened fire on the enemy's infantry then moving in column of route about Marizy St. Mard.

At 11.30 the 1st King's (Liverpool) Regiment was ordered to reinforce the King's Royal Rifles, but the battalion had hardly moved forward when the enemy surrendered all along the line. His position was quite untenable, as he was surrounded on three sides, and could not move to the rear on account of a deadly and accurate rifle and artillery fire which pinned him to his ground. In the early stages of the operation a portion of the enemy, about 500 men, made good their retreat over the hill towards Chezy, to fall eventually into the hands of the 3rd Division.

The official number of prisoners taken is given as 350, including 4 officers. One officer and 17 men were buried, and 30 taken into hospital with the British wounded. Two hundred and eighty rifles and 31,000 rounds of small-arms ammunition were also captured.

" Towards the close of the engagement the superiority of fire attained by our troops was very marked—the enemy themselves confessing that they were quite unable to move or aim, in spite of the fact that they had good natural cover, while the British

[1] War Diary, 1st King's Royal Rifles.

battalion that bore the brunt of the fighting (1st King's Royal Rifles) had to move over very exposed ground, without an atom of cover."

The casualties suffered by the 6th Infantry Brigade in this action were severe :

1st Royal Berks : 1 officer killed (Lieut. and Adjutant A. H. Perrott), 1 man killed and 23 N.C.O's and men wounded. 2nd South Staffords : 2 officers wounded (Captain R. Duckworth, Lieut. F. R. Birch), 1 man killed, 7 N.C.O's and men wounded. 1st King's Royal Rifles : 4 officers wounded (Lieut. and Adjutant R. H. Woods, Lieut. A. L. Bonham-Carter, Second-Lieut. R. A. Barrow, Second-Lieut. H. W. Butler), 10 N.C.O's and men killed and 60 men wounded.

At the close of this action the 6th Infantry Brigade marched on as far as Chevillon and there bivouacked for the night.

The 4th (Guards) Brigade had an uneventful day, though as the Guards marched north they could see the action at Hautevesnes, but were not called upon to join in. The Brigade bivouacked at Cointicourt and Breuil.

The 5th Infantry Brigade having guarded the northern flank of the 6th Brigade during the fight at Hautevesnes, marched on to and bivouacked in Monnes.

The 1st Division lay on the right of the 2nd Division, and the 3rd and 5th Divisions and the IIIrd Corps [1] continued the line on the left.

And here, in order that the advance of the 2nd Division may be more easily understood, it is necessary to give a brief general view of the left of the Allied line as it was on the night of 10th September 1914.

Von Kluck had given way on the Ourcq. He had recognized the danger in which he stood, for, notwithstanding the employment of practically all his infantry against the Sixth French Army, he was still unable to maintain his line, though at one period he came very near breaking Maunoury's advance. He was, therefore, in retreat towards the Aisne. Von Bülow, on the left of von Kluck, was involved in this retreat, and he too was withdrawing his corps towards the line of the Aisne, though as he moved northwards the distance between the two armies was becoming more pronounced.

From Soissons to Verdun the whole German line was on the move. The first German army bivouacked on the night of the 10th

[1] The IIIrd Corps at this period still consisted of the 4th Division and the 19th Infantry Brigade.

on a line running west (from just east of Crépy-en-Valois) to east
(just east of Grumilly), with the Cavalry Corps on its left flank—
i.e., north-east of Billy and facing south. A space of at least 25
kilometres lay between von Kluck's left (IInd Cavalry Corps) and
von Bülow's right, which was just north-west of Dormans on the
Marne River.

Maunoury's Sixth French Army lay along the line Raray–La
Ferté–Milon. There the line was continued by the British army
to Monthiers, a point about 5 miles north-west of Château-Thierry.
From the latter place to Epernay lay the Fifth French Army under
d'Esperey. Foch, with his Ninth French Army, occupied the line
Villeneuve–Vatry.

Briefly, such was the position of the Allied left on the night of
10th September.

A French official communiqué published on the evening of
the 10th gave an excellent survey of the fighting which had been in
progress since the 6th September :

" As already announced, a battle has been in progress since
the 6th September on the general line Paris–Verdun. Early in
the battle the German right wing (the army of General von Kluck)
realized that it must give way before the enveloping movement
which threatened it. By a series of rapid and skilful movements
this army managed to escape from the pressure by which it was
menaced, and threw itself with the bulk of its forces against our
enveloping wing north of the Marne and west of the Ourcq. But
the French troops operating in this region, powerfully assisted by
the bravery of our English allies, inflicted considerable losses on
the enemy, and gained time for an offensive to progress elsewhere.
As matters stand in this quarter of the field, the enemy is retreating
northwards towards the Aisne and the Oise, and has fallen back
75 kilometres in four days. Meanwhile, the Anglo-French forces
which were operating south of the Marne have continued their
offensive. Starting from the region south of Esternay, they have
crossed the Marne and are north of Château-Thierry. Severe
fighting took place from the beginning of the battle round La Ferté-
Gaucher, Esternay, and Montmirail. The left of General von
Kluck's army, as well as the army of General von Bülow, are retiring before our troops. In the region of the plateaux north of
Sezanne–Vitry-le-François the severest fighting has taken place.
There, the left of General von Bülow's army, the Saxon army,
and portion of the army commanded by the Duke of Würtemberg,
were engaged. By a succession of violent attacks the Germans

tried to break our centre, but in vain ; our success on the high ground north of Sezanne had enabled us in turn to pass to the offensive, and during the night the enemy has broken off the fight between the Marshes of St. Gond and the neighbourhood of Somme-sous so as to fall back to the region immediately west of Vitry-le-François."

11TH SEPT. The 2nd Division marched about 5.30 on the morning of the 11th in two columns, in a north-westerly direction, in the order given :

The Left Column (under Brigadier-General Haking) was formed of : Divisional Mounted Troops (less one troop), XXXVIth Brigade R.F.A., XLIVth (Howitzer) Brigade R.F.A., 35th (Heavy) Battery R.G.A., 5th Field Company R.E., 5th Infantry Brigade, XXXVIth and XLIVth Brigade Ammunition Columns. The route lay *via* Neuilly, Vichel–Nanteuil, Rozet–St. Albin, Grand Menil, Oulchy-la-Ville.

The General Officer Commanding was ordered to send out patrols towards Chouy and Billy, in order to make sure that the high ground north of the Ourcq was clear of the enemy.

The Right Column (under Brigadier-General Davies) was formed of :—Advanced Guard : one troop Divisional Mounted Troops, XXXIVth Brigade R.F.A. (less Ammunition Column), 11th Field Company R.E., 6th Infantry Brigade (less two battalions).

Main Body (in order of march) : Divisional Headquarters, two battalions 6th Infantry Brigade, XLIst Brigade R.F.A. (less Ammunition Column), 4th (Guards) Brigade, XXXIVth and XLIst Brigade Ammunition Columns, 5th and 6th Field Ambulances.

The route to be taken by the Right Column was through Breuil, Sommelans, Latilly, Wadon, Breny, Oulchy-le-Château, and Cugny.

The troops were ordered to move across country wherever possible, in order to conceal their movements from the enemy's aircraft and observers.

Excepting for a heavy rain which drenched the troops, the march was without incident. And even the discomfort of wet clothes was counteracted by the provision of billets instead of bivouacs—for the first time since the early days of the retreat the troops had a roof over their heads.

The day was tedious owing to the long wait about Oulchy, where divisions were changing positions and marching across one another's front. Eventually the Left Column reached Oulchy-la-Ville, but went on to Beugneux and billeted there for the night. Of the Right

Column the 4th (Guards) Brigade billeted in Oulchy-le-Château, and two battalions of the 6th Infantry Brigade (1st Berks and the 1st King's) in Les Crouttes, the two remaining battalions of the Brigade (South Staffords and King's Royal Rifles) in Wallee.

On 11th September an alteration was made concerning the Brigade Ammunition Columns—they were henceforth to march together in the rear of all the infantry of the Division, one officer being placed in command known as "Officer Commanding Brigade Ammunition Columns."

The morning of the 12th was showery, and in a drizzling rain 12TH SEPT the 5th Infantry Brigade with XXXVIth Brigade R.F.A., 5th Field Company R.E., and Divisional Mounted Troops, under Brigadier-General Haking, as advanced guard to the Division, marched out of billets in Beugneux at 5 a.m. *en route* for Pont Arcy. At 5.30 a.m. the Brigade reached Arcy St. Restitué, and all was reported clear in front and flank. At Quincy, however, a halt was ordered, as reports were received that some French cavalry had been driven back from Bazoches across the river Vesle, and that a brigade of German infantry held the southern banks of the river, disputing the passage. These reports were officially contradicted, and the 5th Infantry Brigade pushed on. General Haking had been ordered to cross the Vesle at Courcelles, but on reaching the river he found that the bridge had been blown up. He was therefore instructed to cross without horses and transport, using bridging expedients. The 5th Field Company and a half company of the 11th Field Company began work at once (2 p.m.). Bridging materials were scarce, but a large farm near the river supplied some good planks, and from these and a ladder a footbridge was made. By 3.15 p.m. the Brigade, covered by the guns of the XXXVIth Brigade R.F.A. firing from the neighbourhood of Lime, had passed over and had reached Monthussart Farm. Further progress was impossible, as the British shells were falling north of the farm ; the guns were searching the ground for the enemy's infantry known to be in the locality. At this period the Worcesters were leading the 5th Infantry Brigade, and were ordered to occupy Monthussart. The Oxford and Bucks were then pushed out towards the Braisne–Dhuizel road, the artillery having ceased firing. On passing Monthussart Farm, German infantry were discovered advancing from the west, across the front of the battalion. The latter at once extended, and D Company opened fire on the enemy, who, without putting up any defence whatsoever, hoisted the white flag and surrendered. The number of prisoners taken was 7

officers and 107 other ranks.   Shortly afterwards a small party
of German cavalry galloped out from the woods on the west
towards A Company, which had extended on the right flank of
D Company.   One was killed and two captured.

Both of these parties seem to have belonged to the force at
Braisne which had been driven out by the 1st Cavalry Brigade.
The infantry belonged to the Landwehr, and the cavalry were
Uhlans of the Garde Corps.

The 5th Infantry Brigade then marched on without further
incident to Vieil Arcy, where the battalion went into billets with
outposts pushed out towards Pont Arcy.

The main body, formed of Divisional Headquarters and the
6th and 4th Infantry Brigades, with Artillery, Engineers, and Field
Ambulances, set out at 6 a.m., marching *via* Beugneux, Arcy,
Branges, Jouaignes, Quincy, and Courcelles, and were to billet in
Pont Arcy, but on crossing the Vesle information was received
that the 3rd Division (on the left of the 2nd Division) could not get
beyond Brenelle owing to the opposition they were encountering.
In consequence the billeting areas were altered.   The 5th Infantry
Brigade had already gone on to Vieil Arcy ; the 6th Infantry
Brigade was therefore ordered to billet at Monthussart Farm,
whilst the 4th (Guards) Brigade, with Divisional Headquarters,
both Field Companies of Engineers, and the Artillery, billeted in
Courcelles.   The Field Ambulances were on the Braisne–Courcelles
road.

THE BATTLE OF THE AISNE.

The position on the afternoon of the 12th September is thus
described by Sir John French in his official dispatches: " From
the opposition encountered by the Sixth French Army to the west
of Soissons, by the IIIrd Corps south-east of that place, by the
IInd Corps south of Missy and Vailly, and certain indications all
along the line, I formed the opinion that the enemy had, for the
moment at any rate, arrested his retreat and was preparing to
dispute the passage of the Aisne with some vigour.   South of
Soissons the Germans were holding Mont de Paris against the
attacks of the right of the Sixth French Army when the IIIrd
Corps reached the neighbourhood of Buzancy, south-east of that
place.   With the assistance of the artillery of the IIIrd Corps
the French drove them back across the river at Soissons, where

they destroyed the bridges. . . . On this day the cavalry, under General Allenby, reached the neighbourhood of Braisne and did good work in clearing the town and the high ground beyond it of strong hostile detachments. The Queen's Bays are particularly mentioned by the General as having greatly assisted in the success of the operation. They were well supported by the 3rd Division, which on this night bivouacked at Brenelle, south of the river.

" The 5th Division approached Missy, but was unable to make headway. The Ist Corps (1st and 2nd Divisions) reached the neighbourhood of Vauxcéré without much opposition.

" In this manner the Battle of the Aisne commenced.

" The Aisne valley runs generally east and west, and consists of a flat-bottomed depression of width varying from half a mile to two miles, down which the river follows a winding course to the west at some points near the southern slopes of the valley, and at others near the northern. The high ground both on the north and south of the river is approximately 400 feet above the bottom of the valley, and is very similar in character, as are both slopes of the valley itself, which are broken into numerous rounded spurs and re-entrants. The most prominent of the former are the Chivres spur on the right bank, and the Sermoise spur on the left. Near the latter place the general plateau of the south is divided by a subsidiary valley of much the same character, down which the small river Vesle flows to the main stream near Sermoise. The slopes of the plateau overlooking the Aisne on the north and south are of varying steepness, and are covered with numerous patches of wood, which also stretch upwards and backwards over the edge on to the top of the high ground. There are several villages and small towns dotted about in the valley itself and along its sides, the chief of which is the town of Soissons."

After describing the characteristics of the Aisne valley Sir John continues : " The Aisne is a sluggish stream of some 170 feet in width, but, being 15 feet deep in the centre, it is unfordable. Between Soissons on the west and Villers on the east (the part of the river attacked and secured by the British forces) there are eleven road bridges across it. On the north bank a narrow-gauge railway runs from Soissons to Vailly, where it crosses the river and continues eastwards along the south bank. From Soissons to Sermoise a double line of railway runs along the south bank, turning at the latter place up the Vesle valley towards Bazoches. The position held by the enemy is a very strong one, either for a delaying action or for a defensive battle. One of its chief military characteristics is that from the high ground on neither side can the top of the plateau on the other side be seen except for small stretches. This is chiefly due to the woods on the edges of the slopes. Another important point is that all the bridges are under either direct or high-angle artillery fire. The tract of country above described which lies north of the Aisne is well adapted to concealment, and was so skilfully turned to account by the enemy as to render it impossible to judge the real nature of his opposition to our passage of the river, or to accurately gauge his strength ; but I have every reason to conclude that strong rearguards of at least three Army Corps were holding the passages on the early morning of the 13th.

"On that morning I ordered the British forces to advance and make good the Aisne."

The Ist Corps' Orders were as follows : " Patrols will be pushed forward by daylight—by the 1st Division towards Bourg, and by the 2nd Division towards Pont Arcy and Chavonne, with the object of finding whether the enemy is holding these crossings. Both divisions will close up their fighting troops on the heads of divisions, ready to act on the information obtained by the reconnaissances. This closing up to be commenced at 6 a.m. and to be carried out concealed from the enemy. In the event of the enemy seriously disputing the passage of the Aisne, orders for the attack will be issued from Corps Headquarters. In the event of the enemy continuing his retreat divisions will occupy points to secure the crossings with their advanced guards and push reconnaissances towards the enemy."

13TH SEPT.
MAP.

At 4.45 a.m. on the 13th the Divisional Mounted Troops moved out of Vieil Arcy to reconnoitre the canal and river bridges at St. Mard and Chavonne. The canal bridges (at St. Mard and Cys) were found intact, but the bridge at Chavonne had been blown up. At Pont Arcy also the bridge had been destroyed, but one girder remained in such a position as to admit the passage of troops in single file to the northern banks of the river.

At 5 a.m. the 2nd Connaughts, as vanguard of the advanced guard, formed of the 5th Infantry Brigade, 11th Field Company R.E., and the Divisional Mounted Troops, advanced to the river, and crossing by the girder took up a position with their right on the Oise and the Aisne Canals, north-west of Bourg, their left on the river west of Pont Arcy. This position was made good by 11.15 a.m., and the 11th Field Company immediately began work on the canal bridge at Pont Arcy, which had been partially destroyed. Wooden planking was laid across a gap from 6 to 8 feet

THE BATTLE OF

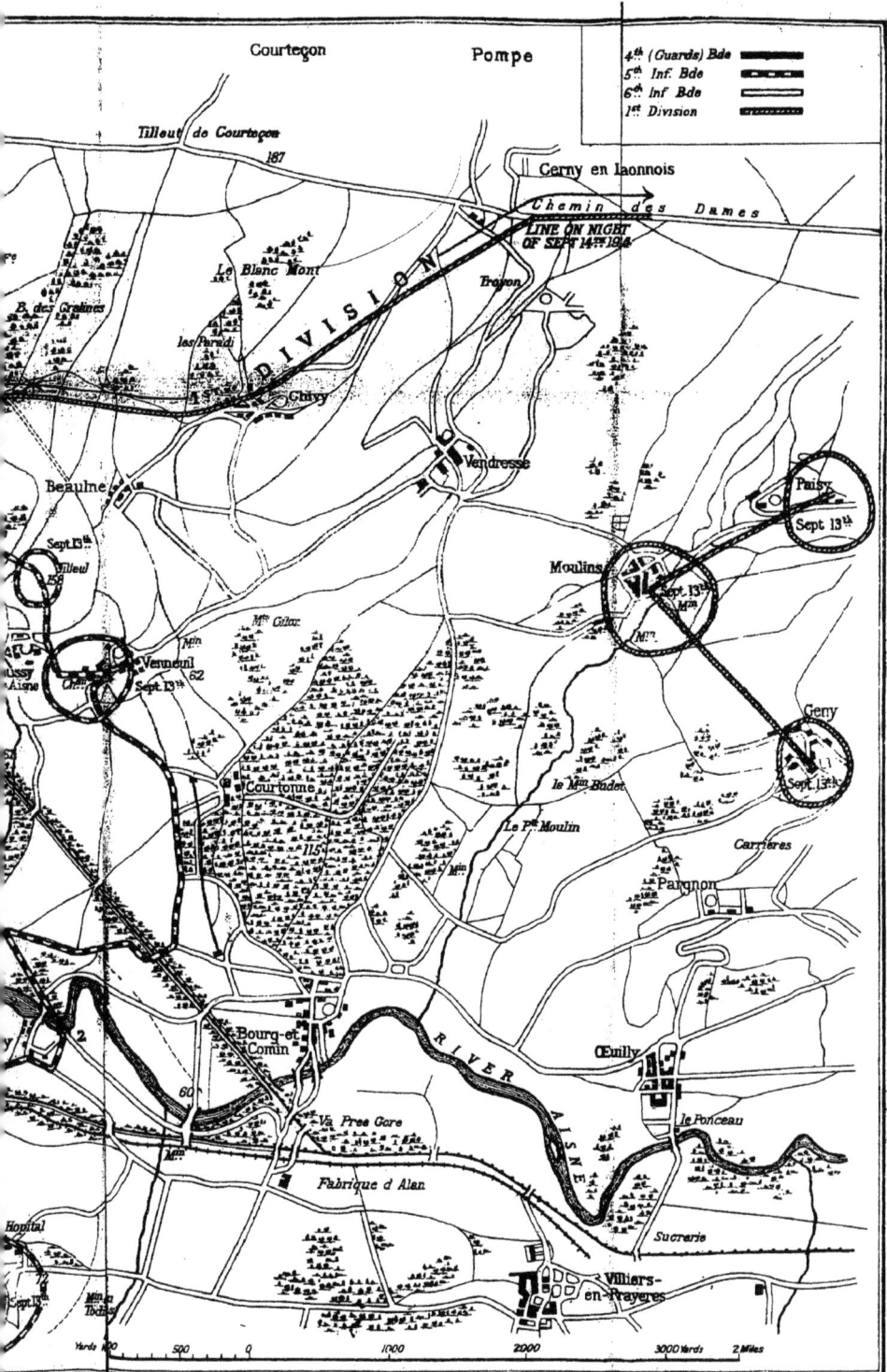

Courteçon   Pompe

4th (Guards) Bde
5th Inf. Bde
6th Inf. Bde
1st Division

Tilleul de Courteçon
187

Cerny en laonnois

Chemin des Dames

LINE ON NIGHT
OF SEPT 14TH 1914

Le Blanc Mont

Troyon

B. des Graines

les Paradi

DIVISION

Chivy

Vendresse

Beaulne

Paissy
Sept 13th

Moulins
Sept 13th
Mn

Sept 13th
Troyon

Troyon
58

Mn Gilor.

Venneuil
62
Sept 13th

Chau

ssy
Aisne

Mn

Cerny
Sept 13th

Courtonne

115

le Mn Budet

Carrières

Le Pte Moulin

Mn

Paignon

Bourg-et-Comin

60

RIVER   AISNE

Œuilly

le Ponceau

Vte Pres Gare

Mn

Fabrique d'Alan

Sucrerie

Hopital

Villiers-en-Frayères

Sept 13th

Mn du
Tourn

Yards 100   500   0   1000   2000   3000 Yards   2 Miles

THE MAPPA CO LTD LONDON

NE, 12th–15th September 1914

(Facing p. 70)

wide in the road, and with sleepers and road metalling a road sufficiently strong to take ordinary military traffic was completed by 4.30 p.m. The sappers then crossed the canal bridge and proceeded to select a site for the construction of a trestle bridge over the river. Trees growing close to the river were cut down for this purpose, but before work was properly begun information was received that the 1st Division was sending its pontoons. These arrived almost immediately afterwards and were thrown across the river, the 5th Field Company, which by now had arrived, assisting the 11th Field Company. The bridge was constructed of six barges and one trestle.

The three remaining battalions of the 5th Infantry Brigade then advanced, and having crossed the river, halted in a position of readiness about the Chavonne–Bourg road until dusk. The crossing was made under heavy shell-fire from the enemy's artillery, posted on the high ground north of the river. The movement forward was then continued to Verneuil. Here the Brigade halted for the night, the first line transport having crossed by the pontoon bridge at Pont Arcy. An outpost line was then formed from Moussy–Tilleul–Point 158–M^{in}-Brulé and Ferme de Metz to Soupir. The Connaughts occupied the latter village. Brigade Headquarters were on the Moussy–Soupir road. The Oxford and Bucks were on a line extending from Ferme de Metz to Soupir. The Worcesters were to the north-west of Moussy, and the 2nd Highland Light Infantry at Verneuil.

In the meantime the main body of the 2nd Division had set out from Monthussart Farm (6th Infantry Brigade) and Courcelles (4th Guards Brigade) with Chavonne as their destination.

The 6th Infantry Brigade marched at 6 a.m., and halted and closed up just south-west of Point 175 (about one mile west of Dhuizel). Here a very long halt was called, the Brigade eventually being ordered into billets, the King's and King's Royal Rifles in Dhuizel, and the South Staffords and Berks in Vieil Arcy.

At 8 a.m. the 4th (Guards) Brigade moved to the high ground south of St. Mard, and took up a position in readiness to seize the crossing of the Aisne at Chavonne. Here the Brigade came under a considerable artillery fire, and it was not until noon that the 2nd Coldstream could be sent forward to Cys-la-Commune in order to seize the bridge, which, like that at Pont Arcy, had been destroyed.

On approaching the bridge the scouts of the 2nd Coldstream were fired on by machine guns and rifles. No. 2 Company advanced and lined the canal banks about half a mile from the river.

From this position considerable bodies of the enemy's cavalry and infantry were seen retiring over the hills north of the river. A little later the hostile fire ceased. Sections of No. 2 Company were therefore pushed forward, but after a short advance machine-gun and rifle fire again impeded the advance, and the attack for a while was held up, it being apparent that the slope of the hill on the northern banks of the river and the village of Chavonne were strongly held. The machine guns belonging to the 2nd Grenadiers had been lent to the 2nd Coldstream, and these, in conjunction with the guns of the XXXIVth and XLIVth Brigades R.F.A., reduced the hostile fire across the river. A further retirement of the enemy then took place, and No. 3 Company was moved up to secure the bridge. It was now seen that the latter had been destroyed by the French, but a temporary structure had been built by the enemy, who had, however, failed to demolish it when he withdrew. Nos. 1 and 3 Companies were at once advanced to the line of the canal, No. 4 being in reserve.

Towards 4 p.m. it was apparent that the enemy was vacating his position, and No. 3 Company rushed forward and gained the bank of the river. This advance was not seriously contested, and the company was able to pass over in a ferry-boat which by extraordinary luck had not been discovered by the retiring enemy. The 11th Field Company then repaired the bridge sufficiently for the remainder of the battalion to cross over. On reaching the high ground north of Chavonne, however, the battalion was ordered to retire and re-cross the river and billet in Cys-la-Commune, one company (No. 1) being left to guard and hold the bridge. No reason was given for this retirement, and it was a disappointment to the gallant Coldstreamers, who had fought for it all day, having 23 men killed and wounded.

During the day columns of the enemy's troops had been observed moving from west to east along the roads north of Froidmont Farm, Braye-en-Laonnois, and Troyon, but they were out of range of the British artillery. The "Heavies" (35th Battery), however, had excellent targets on thick masses of the enemy[1] seen moving along the ridge of the hills overlooking the river, and came into action with good effect.

It must have been on or about the 13th September that the enemy first used his heavy howitzers, for the official diaries all contain references to the size and effect of his high-explosive shells. The probability is that the 13th was the first day of their use, for the ridges

[1] Probably the VIIth Reserve Corps arriving from Maubeuge.

beyond the river Aisne had already been put into a state of defence, the big howitzers being too cumbersome to move on the march. Or they may have recently arrived from Maubeuge, which place had capitulated on 7th September.

Sir John French's conjecture of the enemy's intention to stand and offer a determined resistance on the northern banks of the river Aisne was certainly well founded. The position was admirable for a defensive or a delaying action, and the enemy had selected and entrenched his position not only with the intention of offering a determined resistance, but to put an end to demoralization amongst his troops caused by the retreat from the Marne. He was also within touch of the prepared position on the Craonne plateau, where with considerable foresight he had constructed a very elaborate system of trenches of a kind new to field warfare, but in the time to come terribly familiar.

On the night of the 13th September, therefore, he had succeeded in arresting the progress of the British, though the crossings over the Aisne were in the possession of his opponents.

The 1st Division, in face of only slight opposition, had crossed by the bridge at Bourg, and with the cavalry had pressed forward, at nightfall occupying the area Moulins–Paissy–Geny, with posts at Vendresse: an excellent beginning. Indeed, Sir Douglas Haig's 1st Corps had done well, and although only the 5th Infantry Brigade of the 2nd Division bivouacked north of the river, the passage of the river had been made good, and the crossings at Chavonne, Pont Arcy, and Bourg were in his possession.

The IInd and IIIrd Corps were, roughly, along the line of the Aisne westwards from Chavonne to Soissons.

During the night of the 13th the field companies of Engineers were incessantly at work. Indeed, at this period the sappers showed splendid devotion to their duty. Eight pontoons and one foot bridge were thrown across the river under generally very heavy artillery fire, kept up incessantly on to most of the crossings, after completion. Even the terribly wet weather of the middle of September did not deter them, though, owing to the very heavy traffic continually passing to and fro, the approaches to the bridges were almost impassable, resembling quagmires. But the roads also were repaired.

" The operations of the Field Companies," said Sir John French, " during this most trying time are worthy of the best traditions of the Royal Engineers."

The 14th September 1914 was a day of more than ordinary 14TH SEPT.

significance. On the previous evening the position was still some-what obscure, for in his dispatches Sir John French says : " On the evening of the 14th [1] it was still impossible to decide whether the enemy was only making a temporary halt, covered by rear-guards, or whether he intended to stand and defend the position. With a view to clearing up the situation I ordered a general advance."

At this period the British Expeditionary Force occupied approximately the line of the Aisne from Venizel to Chavonne, thence through Soupir, Moussy, Moulins, and Paissy, though not all the crossings were in its possession ; the bridge at Condé, for instance, remained in the hands of the enemy during the whole of the Aisne operations. The Sixth French Army under Maunoury lay on Sir John French's left flank west and north-west of Soissons ; the Fifth French Army, under d'Esperey, on his right.

The 2nd Division was directed on the line Courtecon–Ostel.

With Courtecon as its objective, therefore, the 6th Infantry Brigade crossed the river at Pont Arcy at 5 a.m. on the 14th, passing through the 5th Infantry Brigade area (Moussy–Verneuil–Soupir), and moved up the valley towards Braye. The Brigade, accompanied by the XXXIVth Brigade R.F.A. and 5th Field Company R.E., was led by the 1st Berks and a section of sappers as vanguard. A force consisting of the 4th (Guards) Brigade and the XXXVIth Brigade R.F.A., first under Colonel Hall, R.F.A., and later commanded by Brigadier-General Perceval, was ordered to advance to Point 197 at Croix-sans-Tête (east of Ostel). Led by the 2nd Grenadiers as advanced guards, the Guards Brigade left St. Mard at 6 a.m., the 2nd Coldstream having joined from the Chavonne crossing at 5.30 a.m. and being in the rear of the column. The 3rd Coldstream were at the head of the main body, and were followed by the 1st Irish Guards. But the road at Pont Arcy was blocked with traffic, and it was not until 10 a.m. that the Brigade finally crossed the river and set out for Soupir.

The 5th Infantry Brigade, though spread out, was in reserve, with instructions to conform to the movements of the 4th and 6th Brigades.

The artillery positions were as follows : XXXIVth Brigade and one Howitzer Battery (60th) on or near the southern end of the Beaulne Spur ; 35th (Heavy) Battery and two Howitzer Batteries (47th and 56th) near Courtonne ; the XXXVIth Brigade, with the 4th (Guards) Brigade and the XLIst Brigade in reserve. On

[1] 13th (?).

the morning of the 14th there was a very thick mist and artillery observation was out of the question.

The Divisional Mounted Troops and Cyclists had been ordered to reconnoitre the high ground through which ran the Chemin des Dames, and for that purpose Courtecon, Braye, and Point 197 to Froidmont were the selected destinations. But none of the patrols reached these points. The first patrol stopped short at Chivry ; the second at Braye, where it was ambushed but suffered no casualties, though at one point within ten yards of the enemy ; the third could get no farther than Cour de Soupir Farm.

The result of these reconnaissances showed the enemy in possession of, and skilfully disposed on, all the high points north of the river.

The 6th Infantry Brigade, supported by the XXXIVth Brigade R.F.A., joined action with the enemy about 10 a.m. Two companies of the 1st King's Royal Rifles (A and D) were sent off as left flank guard towards La Bouvette Wood, where later they came into touch with the right of the Guards Brigade ; the remaining two companies (B and C) were moved up to Tilleul as right flank guard. Both parties were heavily fired on by hostile artillery just south of Braye, and by machine guns and infantry hidden in La Bouvette Wood and in a wood about 700 yards north of Tilleul. At the latter place the Rifles made a somewhat premature charge, and lost a machine gun as well as many killed and wounded (amongst the latter being Captain Maclachlan and Lieut. Lloyd), though they inflicted severe losses on the enemy. In the face of this opposition the two companies retired to Tilleul, where they were reinforced by companies of the Worcesters and Highland Light Infantry (5th Infantry Brigade).

The Berks, as vanguard of the 6th Brigade, passed through Moussy and advanced to M$^{in.}$-Brulé (Ecluse) via Ferme de Metz. On reaching the former place, however, the battalion came under heavy shell-fire, and was pinned to the ground and could not advance, the line then occupied running east and west through M$^{in.}$-Brulé (Ecluse). Casualties were : Lieut. R. G. B. Perkins killed, and Lieut. S. Hopkins and Second-Lieut. Y. R. D. Wigan wounded, with 39 other ranks killed, wounded, and missing.

The 1st King's were then (10.30 a.m.) pushed forward to support the right of the Berks, east of the canal through the wooded slopes west of the Beaulne Spur. Together these two battalions, though exposed to considerable fire from heavy howitzers and field guns, and also from nests of machine guns which the enemy had mounted in a series of tiers of trenches in front of Les Grelines Farm, advanced gallantly up the valley, the Berks reaching the southern end of the spur just east of Braye, and the King's the Moulin de Braye Farm. But the ground, won only after stiff fighting, had soon to be abandoned, for the enemy counter-attacked down the Beaulne Spur and from the Chivry Valley against the junction of the 5th and 6th Brigades. The King's in the Bois des Boules came under enfilade fire and lost very heavily, but pushing one company east to protect its right flank, the battalion gradually withdrew. The Berks, fighting all the way and attacked from three sides, also retired. At dusk these two battalions occupied a line from the southern edge of the Beaulne Spur to the canal (King's), the Berks continuing the line westwards from the canal in the direction of La Bouvette Wood. The right-flank guard, B and C Companies of the 1st King's Royal Rifles, had also to retire as the King's and Berks fell back, but the 5th Brigade (which at this period consisted only of the Worcesters and Highland Light Infantry) reinforced the Rifles, and the enemy was beaten off with very heavy losses.

In this action Private G. Wilson of the 2nd Highland Light Infantry gained the Victoria Cross.[1] After the two companies of the King's Royal Rifles retired and were reinforced by the Worcesters and the Highland Light Infantry, the latter with the Rifles moved forward again to attack a small wood in which the enemy had established himself with a machine gun. A charge was made which was only partially successful, for the left flank of the attackers then rested on the edges of the wood. From this wood the enemy's machine gun now began to take heavy toll of the Scotsmen and Rifles. Then it was that Private Wilson and a man from the Rifles (whose name was not mentioned) rushed forward. The rifleman fell dead immediately, but Wilson went on alone, killed the machine-gun team (consisting of 1 officer and 6 men) and captured the gun, together with two and a half cases of ammunition. In the charge mentioned the Highland Light Infantry lost heavily, Captain Sir A. C. Gibson Craig and Second-Lieut. R. C. Powell being killed, Captain C. T. Martin wounded, and 20 N.C.O's and men killed, wounded, and missing.

The 5th Infantry Brigade and Rifles then occupied the Beaulne Spur and dug in. The pressure on the right flank of the 2nd Division in the morning was fortunately relieved by the left flank of the 3rd Brigade (1st Division), then advancing towards Troyon.

[1] *London Gazette,* 5th December 1914.

The South Staffords were not engaged during the day, but were held in reserve in and near Moussy.

Meanwhile, west of the Aisne Canal and La Bouvette Wood the Connaught Rangers had engaged the enemy.

The battalion had on the previous night occupied the village of Soupir, and at 1 a.m. received orders from 5th Infantry Brigade Headquarters, which stated that the 4th (Guards) Brigade with the XXXVIth Brigade R.F.A., under Brigadier-General Perceval, had been ordered to cross the river at 6 a.m. and march *via* Soupir to Point 197 (Croix-sans-Tête). As soon as the Guards and Artillery had passed through Soupir the battalion was to close on Moussy. The Officer Commanding the Connaught Rangers decided to move up the valley to La Cour de Soupir Farm, from which position he could cover the advance of the Guards. The battalion arrived at the farm about 5.30 a.m., and immediately sent out pickets to Croix-sans-Tête and on both flanks. No signs of the enemy were found, and the inhabitants said they believed there were no Germans in the vicinity.

About 9.30 a.m. the 2nd Grenadiers, the advanced guard of the 4th (Guards) Brigade, arrived, but from this period what actually happened is not clear.[1] The accounts are conflicting, for, whereas the Battalion Diary of the 2nd Connaught Rangers relates the subsequent fighting which undoubtedly took place during the day, the Battalion Diary of the 2nd Grenadier Guards is too brief to permit of verification. It is very evident, however, that heavy fighting took place about La Cour de Soupir Farm, and that the Connaught Rangers and 4th (Guards) Brigade were heavily engaged, for the former battalion lost 4 officers killed, 4 officers wounded, and many other ranks killed and wounded ; the Guards also lost heavily, Lieut. J. R. Pickersgill-Cunliffe, who commanded the advanced guard of the 2nd Grenadiers, being killed, and many of his party. "When the advanced guard was checked everywhere, the 3rd Coldstream and Irish Guards were sent up, and reinforced the thin firing line of the Grenadiers, the firing line then becoming composed of a mixture of three battalions."[2]

At 5 p.m. the 2nd Oxford and Bucks (5th Infantry Brigade), having been on outpost duty all day between Moussy and Soupir village, were marched off *via* the latter to assist the 4th (Guards) Brigade. The battalion was however not required, and went into billets in Soupir.

---

[1] See Appendix for narrative of this action, taken from the Battalion Diary, 2nd Connaught Rangers.

[2] Major-General G. D. Jeffreys, C.B., C.M.G.

In the evening the Connaught Rangers also marched back to billets in Soupir. The valuable assistance rendered by the battalion cannot be passed over, though it is not mentioned in any of the official documents which deal with the Battle of the Aisne. The tactical effect of the unfortunate delay (owing to the blocking of the road about Pont Arcy) which held up the 4th (Guards) Brigade, so that it was only able to reach its destination several hours behind its scheduled time, was to expose the left flank of the 2nd Division. The occupation of La Cour de Soupir Farm, first by the Connaughts and later by the Guards, prevented an advance by the enemy, which might well have forced the left flank of the division back to the very banks of the Aisne.

The position won by the Connaughts and 4th (Guards) Brigade on the 14th September was held continuously until the 2nd Division moved from the Aisne to Ypres.

The right flank of the 2nd Division had been splendidly covered by the 1st Division, which at nightfall had gained ground just south of the Chemin des Dames—*i.e.*, about Troyon. Indeed, as Sir John French said,[1] the 1st Corps had on the 14th September won most valuable ground in the face of fierce opposition from an enemy whose infantry, strongly entrenched in carefully selected positions, was supported by powerful artillery and howitzers of large calibre, which poured an almost incessant fire of shrapnel and high-explosive upon the devoted troops of the 1st and 2nd Divisions under Sir Douglas Haig. At the close of 14th September the position of the 1st Corps extended from the Chemin des Dames on the right, through Chivry, to La Cour de Soupir Farm, with the 1st Cavalry Brigade extending to the Chavonne–Soissons road.

The British artillery on the 14th September was without heavy howitzers and siege batteries such as were possessed by the enemy. Neither had the use of " high-explosive " been exploited as it had been by the enemy. In consequence Sir John's field guns, though served with splendid devotion, and fired by men whose marksmanship was second to none, were often outranged and " smothered " by the infinitely superior weapons of his opponent. The Germans fired from a higher altitude, which hid their guns, whereas the British guns were easily discovered as they lay or moved about the valley of the Aisne.

---

1 " The action of the 1st Corps on this day (14th), under the direction and command of Sir Douglas Haig, was of so skilful, bold, and decisive a character that he gained positions which alone have enabled me to maintain my position for more than three weeks of very severe fighting on the north bank of the river."

Though lending valuable support wherever it was possible to locate targets and find suitable artillery fire-positions, the gunners of the 2nd Division on 14th September had a disappointing day, and were unavoidably prevented from giving the greatest assistance to the sorely tried infantry as they attacked or were counter-attacked by the enemy. The XXXVIth Brigade R.F.A., for instance, which accompanied the 4th (Guards) Brigade, found great difficulty in supporting the Brigade as it moved forward above Soupir, there being no positions suitable in that section. Only one Battery (71st) remained at Soupir, the remaining batteries being sent off to Moussy, where they might be of use ; the XLIst Brigade R.F.A., just south of the river, being ordered to lend what support was possible to the Guards. But the guns of the XLIst, though constantly shelled by the enemy, were outranged by him, and only fired some eighteen rounds during the whole day. The XXXIVth Brigade R.F.A., with the 6th Infantry Brigade, was subjected to very heavy fire from the enemy's heavy howitzers, and the 50th Battery especially suffered many casualties amongst its gun teams and horses. The XLIVth (Howitzer) Brigade R.F.A., which had moved *via* Bourg to Verneuil and Moussy, also came under heavy fire, one Battery (56th) losing 1 officer (Captain G. W. Blathwayt) and 6 men killed and 1 officer (Lieut. Tidmarsh) and 6 men wounded. The " Heavies " (35th Battery R.G.A.) fired only thirty-two rounds, and these at distant targets.

The constant hostile shell-fire both troubled and made arduous the work of the medical units. " Towards the front regimental medical officers and bearers had a share of it, while bearers of the field ambulances searching the slopes of the rising ground behind the front carried out their work under an unceasing rain of missiles." In spite of these conditions, advanced dressing stations were opened in some caves near Chivry, and near Moussy. There were two main dressing stations, one at Verneuil and the other at the Château de Soupir. On the southern banks of the river at L'Hôpital, close to Vieil Arcy, was a divisional collecting station. Only at night was it possible to evacuate the wounded to the divisional collecting station. Motor ambulances had not yet arrived, and evacuated cases were carried in the old horse-drawn ambulance wagons. The main dressing station at Verneuil was opened about midday on the 14th, and very soon wounded swarmed in, some walking, others carried by the bearers. Amongst those brought in was Lieut.-Colonel Dalton, the A.D.M.S. of the 2nd Division. He was wounded by shell-fire whilst himself carrying wounded into the château at Verneuil. At night he was taken to L'Hôpital, but succumbed to his injuries.

Instances of bravery and devotion to duty amongst the R.A.M.C. were many. An artillery sergeant who had been badly wounded was being carried to the rear. He was bleeding to death, but the bearers carrying him held the arteries until the dressing station was reached, thus preventing loss of blood in any large quantity : they saved the man's life. Lieut. Watson, R.A.M.C., medical officer of the Irish Guards, was wounded by the enemy at close quarters whilst he was attending a wounded man.

The passage of the Aisne had been won only after heavy costs, the casualties of the 2nd Division alone being :—Officers : 16 killed, 41 wounded ; other ranks : 89 killed, 516 wounded, and 515 missing.[1]

Actions on the Aisne Heights and the Beginning of Trench Warfare.

15TH SEPT.   On the morning of the 15th September Sir John French made a careful survey of the whole position along his front—*i.e.*, from Venizel to the right flank of the 1st Division (Ist Corps) just north of Troyon and south of the Chemin des Dames. The dispositions of his opponent's troops and the reports of his commanders confirmed him in the opinion that the enemy intended making a determined stand ; that the attacks of the 14th were not merely intended to delay his passage over the Aisne, but were the beginning of a concerted plan of action for arresting the progress of the left flank of the Allied armies from Rheims to Compiègne.

And yet Sir John had come within an ace of defeating this plan ! For on 12th September, owing to disagreement between the commanders of the First and Second German Armies, a dangerous gap had existed between von Kluck's left and von Bülow's right.

On the night of the 12th, von Kluck's left (2nd Cavalry Corps) lay at Vailly, whilst the right of von Bülow's army was at Châlons, some miles away. Only enemy cavalry operated between the two armies, but it should be remembered that a German cavalry corps in 1914 also included infantry and artillery. The gap continued after the Aisne was crossed, but the fortunes of war were with the enemy, for on the 13th the VIIth German Reserve Corps which had been investing Maubeuge came into line between the First

[1] See Appendix V.

and Second German Armies, and with the XVth Corps formed
the Seventh German Army, which on the 14th and the morning
of the 15th held a line approximately from the north-east of Vailly
through Ostel, Braye, Courtecon, Cerny, Ailles to Corbeny. On
this front, between the 13th and 20th September the enemy employed the 25th Landwehr Brigade, VIIth Reserve Corps, and
XVth Active Corps. These hostile formations faced the right flank
of the IInd Corps, the front occupied by the Ist Corps and the left
of the Fifth French Army (French Moroccan troops of the XVIIIth
French Corps). On Sir John's right, the Fifth French Army
operated from Corbeny to Rheims, and on his left the Sixth French
Army from Soissons to Compiègne, with cavalry operating in a
north-west and northerly direction.

On the morning of the 15th, therefore, the relative positions
of the opposing forces were as follows :

> Sixth French Army (Soissons to Compiègne) opposed by
> First German Army (Compiègne to north-east of Vailly).
> British Army (Venizel to just north of Troyon) opposed by
> left of First German Army and the Seventh German
> Army.
> Fifth French Army (Corbeny to Rheims) opposed by left of
> Seventh German Army and the Second German Army.

At daybreak the enemy's guns opened fire along the whole
line : the 1st and 2nd Divisions, being the most advanced of the
British army, suffered heavily. Throughout the day high-explosive
shells and shrapnel fell thick and fast amongst Sir Douglas Haig's
devoted troops, causing many casualties. Amongst the horses also
the losses were very heavy. No infantry attacks were, however,
launched against the 2nd Division, and the day was spent in making
good the positions won, though the work was often interrupted
by shell-fire and the activities of snipers. Little or no response
by the Divisional Artillery was possible owing to the difficulty
in finding suitable fire-positions and in locating targets. The
patient infantry had therefore to endure the enemy's shelling
without being able to reply, their only safety being in digging deep
into the ground and strengthening their " dug-outs " (as they
were then first called) with wooden planking or anything which
would afford shelter. Thus began the terrible system of living in
trenches, which, until the close of the Great War, was to be the New
Warfare. The infantry had lost most of their entrenching tools
during the retreat, and the country round about the Aisne had

to be scoured for agricultural implements with which to dig trenches.

For a month from this date the history of the 2nd Division is that of a series of attacks and counter-attacks, with very little change in the line as held on the night of the 14th September. A regular system of relief was introduced: some battalions went into the trenches, whilst others rested in reserve—change and change about. At times it was necessary to reinforce parts of the line threatened by the enemy; battalions were therefore moved from one place to another in support. But descriptions of these moves are unnecessary, as from the 15th September onwards the tactical position of the British army remained the same practically throughout the whole course of the operations on the Aisne.

The period, however, was not without interest.

On the 15th the Commander-in-Chief sent a message of congratulation to Sir Douglas Haig : " I wish to express my warmest appreciation of the conduct of the Ist Army Corps under General Sir Douglas Haig, throughout the last two days' battle (13th and 14th) on the Aisne. It is owing to the intrepid advance and splendid resistance of all counter-attacks that we are now able to secure the passage of the river. I heartily congratulate Generals Lomax (1st Division) and Monro (2nd Division) and their gallant Divisions upon their splendid behaviour."

During the 14th and 15th the Royal Engineers continued their work on the bridges over the river and the canal behind the 2nd Division's front. Hastily contrived structures were either strengthened or rebuilt. With the advance of the Division it was essential to provide bridges which would stand heavy traffic, and at the same time secure the lines of communication should a retreat become necessary. For the first few days the trenches in the front lines were dug and strengthened by the infantry, but later both field companies sent sections to all three infantry brigades for the purpose of erecting barbed-wire entanglements, trip wire, and making them generally secure from surprise attacks. The work could only be carried out at night, as the enemy was extremely vigilant ; indeed, it is recorded in the Official Diaries that by day and by night, whenever troops were moving up to or from the trenches, they were fired upon by hostile artillery. The hours during which the infantry in the front line trenches were relieved were continually changed, nevertheless the enemy never failed to shell the moving troops. The woods and all buildings in the rear of the front line were thoroughly searched, and several persons arrested on suspicion of giving information to the enemy, but the informers were never found. It was one of the mysteries of the Aisne operations.

The trenches at this period were mostly dug deep and narrow. The Guards' trenches, for instance (or " pits " rather), held one man apiece ; these were then connected up with narrow communication trenches which led back to the support trenches, thence to the caves, or woods, or village where the billets were situated. The condition of the trenches was horrible. The wet weather had turned them into regular water channels, and in one part of the line the troops were standing in water up to their knees all the time they were in the trenches.

Sapping had hardly begun, and mines were only being thought about, though later, before the British army moved from the Aisne, both " saps " and mines were in use. The energies and powers of endurance of the " Sappers " were tested to the utmost, for not only were they called upon to perform their ordinary functions, but they were frequently used as infantry in the trenches, and on one occasion the 5th Field Company took 23 prisoners.

On the 16th the enemy's heavy howitzers (8-inch, with a range of 10,000 yards) caused much damage in the trenches and behind the lines. One shell fell on a building in Verneuil which had been occupied by two companies of the King's Royal Rifles, with the result that 12 men were killed and 56 wounded. After this tragedy troops were ordered not to billet in large numbers in buildings open to the enemy's shelling. These shells were known as " Black Marias," but they soon lost their terrors.

Brigadier-General Haking, commanding the 5th Infantry Brigade, was slightly wounded on this day, and the command devolved upon Lieut.-Colonel Westmacott of the 2nd Worcesters.

*   *   *   *   *   *   *

On the 18th, Brigadier-General the Earl of Cavan arrived and assumed command of the 4th (Guards) Brigade, *vice* Lieut.-Colonel G. Feilding, 3rd Coldstream, who rejoined his regiment. Lieut.-Colonel Lord Ardee also arrived and took over command of the 1st Irish Guards.

Colonel R. Whigham as G.S.O.I. joined, *vice* Colonel the Hon. F. Gordon, D.S.O., who left the Division on 6th September to take over the command of the 19th Infantry Brigade (IIIrd Corps). Colonel M. P. C. Holt, D.S.O., R.A.M.C., arrived as A.D.M.S., *vice* Colonel Dalton (killed), and Major Davidson took up his duties as D.A.D.M.S. in succession to Major Irvine, who was captured at Landrecies.

*   *   *   *   *   *   *

Attacks on the 2nd Division were numerous. They were often pressed with great vigour and persistence, but without weakening the line in any one place. Day and night attacks were repulsed, with great loss to the enemy. On the 19th and 20th the Division repulsed two very determined attacks.

The 2nd Division on the morning of the 19th held the following line :

> From Chavonne to La Cour de Soupir Farm (exclusive): 2nd Coldstream, 1st Irish Guards, and 2nd Grenadiers.
>
> From La Cour de Soupir Farm (inclusive) to west of the canal (exclusive) : Oxford and Bucks, 3rd Coldstream, two companies of the 1st King's Royal Rifles, 1st Berks.
>
> From east banks of canal through Maison-Brulé across the valley and up the wooded slopes of the Beaulne Spur to Tilleul : 1st King's, 2nd Worcesters.
>
> Behind the Worcesters in support were the 2nd Connaughts ; and behind the latter, in the village of Moussy, the 2nd Highland Light Infantry.
>
> In reserve : two companies of the King's Royal Rifles, and the South Staffords in Soupir.

Artillery positions were :

> XLIVth (Howitzer) Brigade R.F.A.: 60th Battery just north of Soupir ; 47th and 56th Batteries just south of Tilleul. XXXIVth Brigade R.F.A. : 70th and 22nd Batteries south-west of Beaulne Spur ; 50th Battery west slope of Beaulne Spur. XXXVIth Brigade R.F.A.: 71st Battery and 48th Battery south-east corner of château at Soupir; 15th Battery just north of Moussy. XLIst Brigade R.F.A. at Vieil Arcy in reserve ; 35th (Heavy) Battery R.G.A. in the vicinity of Vieil Arcy and Brunelle.

At 1.30 p.m. heavy shell-fire opened on the 4th (Guards) Brigade and Oxford and Bucks at La Cour de Soupir ; the attack spread along the 6th Brigade line (King's Royal Rifles and Berks) as far as the western banks of the canal. Later, heavy infantry attacks were launched against this part of the front, but were repulsed.

At 7 p.m. in the evening the enemy again attacked, but without success of any kind.

The attack on the 20th was directed principally against the King's, and on the 5th Infantry Brigade on the Beaulne Spur just east of the King's. The accounts of this action in the official diaries are interesting, and they are given *in extenso :*

" Raining hard ! The Germans made an attack on both flanks and brought two machine guns close up against the right (flank). Just before daylight they attacked across the open and through the woods against C and D Companies. The enemy got within eighty yards of the trenches, but were finally driven back with heavy losses, leaving a large number of dead outside the wood. The attack on the right (flank) at this time was not pressed home.

" A second attack started about 9 a.m. Two companies of the Highland Light Infantry and two platoons of Worcesters were sent out to clear the wood in front of our right and the ridge above. They charged the Germans, but were driven back, losing all their officers, and returned . . . through our lines. This (retirement) carried part of B Company with them, and whilst B Company were being rounded up the Germans came on close up. A Company, who were on the right of the line under Captain J. H. S. Batten, held on splendidly, although very heavily employed against superior numbers. B Company were re-formed, and the attack was by that time well in hand. At this time a message was received that the Connaught Rangers, who were holding the high ground on our right, had had to retire. This left the right of our line in the air. Major Stevenson then went up on the high ground on our right and re-formed all the odds and ends of the other regiments which he could find. The right of A Company was thrown back, A Company keeping up a heavy fire the whole time, which was eventually too much for the Germans, and they gradually retired. The situation in this attack was always critical, but was rendered more so owing to the retirement of the troops holding the high ground, and to the fact that a message was received during the attack that the Royal Berkshires on our left were retiring. It was ascertained afterwards that the Berks had not retired." [1]

The casualties of the King's in this attack were : Lieut. L. Sweet Escott, killed ; Captains A. K. Kyrke-Smith (died of wounds, 23rd September 1914), F. Marshall, and R. G. Tanner ; Lieuts.

[1] 1st King's (Liverpool) Diary.

P. C. Snatt and L. E. L. Horton wounded; 21 N.C.O's and men killed and 38 wounded.

The 2nd Worcesters' account of their charge with two platoons of the Highland Light Infantry throws further light on this attack: "A and B Companies, under orders received from Officer Commanding 1st King's Regiment, advanced from Moussy to attack some Germans on the right front of the King's. With great difficulty they pushed through a dense wood, suffering from shrapnel, machine-gun, and rifle fire. Together with a small party of the Highland Light Infantry they charged, driving back a party of Germans entrenched, but were then taken in flank by considerable numbers of the enemy well concealed. The losses were heavy, and the companies got scattered in the wood, all the officers being either killed or wounded. Killed: Lieut. A. W. Hudson and 6 other ranks; wounded: Captains C. G. Porter, R. W. Pepys, Lieut. H. S. Lowe, Second-Lieut. O. C. Summers, and 51 other ranks; 16 men were missing." [1]

On the same afternoon at 1.30 the 4th (Guards) Brigade ordered two companies of the South Staffords to proceed to the bridge, ¼ mile north-west of Chavonne, to help the 7th Infantry Brigade (3rd Division), which had been driven back; the 15th Battery (XXXVIth Brigade R.F.A.) was also moved to St. Cys. The Staffords, with one gun of the 15th Battery, moved up in close support of the Wiltshires, who were hard pressed, and relieved the situation. Indeed, so effective was the support given that on the 25th the General Officer Commanding IInd Corps (General Sir Horace Smith-Dorrien) sent the following message to Sir Douglas Haig: "About five days ago a section of Field Artillery of the 2nd Division, and part of the South Staffordshire Regiment, gave very material assistance to the 3rd Division from the north-west of Chavonne, when the latter was being attacked. General Hamilton (General Officer Commanding 3rd Division) tells me that he sent a verbal message of thanks to Brigadier-General Perceval (General Officer Commanding 4th Infantry Brigade), but I should like to add my own written thanks. The section of artillery was very boldly handled."

During the night of the 19th–20th, B and C Companies of the King's Royal Rifles in reserve at Verneuil had marched off to the north-east corner of La Bouvette Wood, where they relieved A and D Companies, who were sent back to Soupir to billets. Later, the South Staffords went forward to the wood and relieved B and C Companies of the Rifles, and the battalion as a whole

---

[1] 2nd Worcesters' Diary.

then marched back to Moussy and Verneuil, two companies in each village.

On the 16th the 6th Division had arrived from England. It was kept in general reserve, and used for the purpose of relieving the troops in the front-line trenches, who badly needed rest. On the 21st and 22nd, therefore, both the 5th and 6th Infantry Brigades were relieved and brought back to Œuilly, Bourg, and Dhuizel for rest and refitting ; but the 4th (Guards) Brigade held their front without relief, though each battalion kept two companies in the trenches and two in reserve, thus affording the men some measure of relief.

The gradual evolution of the trenches lent security and gave considerable more comfort to the troops, but the discomforts were still very trying. The situation was admirably described in a Brigade Diary which may be taken as descriptive of the whole front line : "During the period 14th–21st September the weather had been consistently bad, and the troops were continually wet through. Very few had greatcoats. It was found impossible to carry out any cooking, or even to get hot tea at night up to the trenches. In spite of these privations, however, the health of the troops remained wonderfully good, but diarrhœa was commencing to spread about the time the men were relieved. The men's spirits appeared in no way damped, notwithstanding the enemy's incessant shell - fire. The hostile 8½-inch howitzers (" Black Marias ") expended a vast amount of ammunition round and in Moussy, Verneuil, and the road junctions and roads in the vicinity ; luckily with very little result, except for the shell on the 16th amongst the men of the King's Royal Rifles (already mentioned). The château at Verneuil was used as an advanced dressing station, and the sick and wounded were evacuated with wonderful precision every night. Horses and transport were eventually kept right back near the Aisne, and rations, etc., were brought up and issued at night." [1]

On the 23rd Brigadier-General R. H. Davies, C.B., who had commanded the 6th Infantry Brigade since it landed in France, left for England. Brigadier-General R. Fanshawe succeeded General Davies.

On the same date, to the unbounded satisfaction of both "gunners " and infantry, the long-desired heavy howitzers, which would enable the artillery to reply to the enemy's "Black Marias," arrived.[2]

---

[1] 6th Infantry Brigade Diary.
[2] No. 1 Siege Battery, R.G.A.

They were of 6-inch calibre, and from the very first day they were used—they came into action by the Chavonne bridge on the 24th—good results were reported by Sir John's aerial observers. On this occasion the enemy's trenches were shattered to bits, and for a while the intense shelling to which the first-line troops and even the back areas had been subjected died away. A section of anti-aircraft "pom-poms" also arrived on the same day, and their fire considerably worried hostile aeroplanes, which before had flown over the British lines almost with impunity.

The gallantry and devotion of the artillery during the Aisne operations were deservedly extolled. The following instances of the good work of the gunners are from the official diaries :

" On the 15th September 1914 and following days the battery under my command [1] was in action near the village of Verneuil, with an observing station on Tilleul ridge between Moussy and Tilleul, about 800 yards from the battery. The battery was connected with the observing station by telephone ; but as the wires were constantly being broken by the enemy's shell, a chain of orderlies and signallers was established in addition. On the 15th September, No. 19107 B.-S.-M. G. Walby and No. 44935 Corporal H. W. Hinds were at the observing station. No. 58690 Corporal S. Beckett and No. 33906 Bombardier F. Morris, and No. 31745 Gunner A. Clarkson and No. 69730 Corporal Huston, were acting as connecting files and signallers. In spite of very heavy shelling from the German heavy howitzers, the signallers and connecting files continued to get orders down to the battery. Corporal Huston and Bombardier Morris were both wounded. B.-S.-M. Walby attended to their wounds, and then proceeded to send the messages. himself by semaphore, although the shells were falling all round at the time. On 15th September and on the succeeding days the telephone wires were constantly cut by hostile fire, and were as constantly repaired, generally under shell-fire." [2]

The second gallant action took place south of the Aisne, and was to the credit of the " Heavies "—the 35th Battery R.G.A. In this affair officers and men were concerned. " I have the honour to report that on the 24th September, near Vieil Arcy, one of the ammunition wagons of the Battery was ignited by a shell. It immediately blazed furiously, and the conflagration was carried by the wind to another wagon, which also caught fire. As soon as it was possible to approach the wagons the fire was partially

[1] 47th Battery R.F.A.
[2] Report by Major H. W. Newcome, R.F.A., commanding 47th Battery R.F.A.

subdued, and it was thought no more danger would ensue. Owing
to the strong wind, however, the burning wagons became practically
red-hot, and one of the limbers exploded with a terrific report.
As the gun appeared to be in imminent danger of being destroyed,
it was necessary to remove the shell and cartridges from the remaining wagons. This was done at great personal risk by Lieut. Paris,
assisted by Sergeant Weatherhead and certain men of the Left
Section. The shells at the time were so hot that they had to be
wrapped in cloth in order to handle them. Bombardier Cooper
and Gunner Heywood did well on this occasion." [1]
    The shell which exploded near the wagons set some straw
alight which had been used as " cover " for the gun—*camouflage*
had not then been invented.
    Major Wilkinson himself and Captain Mowbray were also com-
mended for their part in this affair.
    From the 20th September onwards a period of stagnation
set in ; but the Allied commanders were not idle. General
Joffre had communicated to Sir John French a new scheme—to
bring up the Seventh French Army under de Castelnau, and the
Tenth French Army under Maud'huy. These two armies were to
prolong the left of the Sixth French Army under Maunoury (then
situated between Soissons and Compiègne) and endeavours were to
be made to turn the right flank of the German armies. De Castelnau
was to occupy ground from Roye to Chaulnes, and Maud'huy from
north of the Somme near Albert to Arras, and beyond.
    On the 23rd, as Sir John French said, " The action of General
de Castelnau's army on the Allied right developed considerably,
and apparently withdrew considerable forces of the enemy army
from the centre and east. I am not aware whether it was due
to this cause or not, but until the 26th it appeared as though the
enemy's opposition in our front was weakening." Orders were
indeed issued by the Ist Corps for the Division to be ready to advance.
But later these were cancelled, as night patrols, sent out to test
the strength of the hostile forces, came back with reports that no
retirement had taken place ; the enemy's trenches were as strongly
held as ever.
    The enemy again continued his attacks on the 27th and 28th,   27TH–28TH
but did not succeed in gaining any advantage. Thenceforward   SEPT.
only desultory attacks took place, each side seemingly bent upon
making its position as secure as possible. " Sapping " began,

    [1] Report by Major A. C. Wilkinson, R.G.A., commanding 35th (Heavy) Battery
R.G.A.

and hand-grenades were brought into use by the Germans, who at this period used the " hairbrush " pattern. The British army had no grenades on the Aisne, nor trench-mortars. The latter were first described as follows : " *27th September*—1st Division reports new form of projectile, which emits dense black smoke and bursts into very small fragments. Estimated that they were thrown 800 yards." [1]

Three Victoria Crosses were won by the 2nd Division on the Aisne : One by Captain H. S. Rankin, R.A.M.C. ; [2] another by Private Dobson [3] of the 2nd Coldstream Guards ; the third by Private Wilson, 2nd Highland Light Infantry (already mentioned).

Captain Rankin was medical officer to the 1st King's Royal Rifles. On the 18th September, during an attack on La Bouvette Wood, he was severely wounded, his thigh and leg being shattered by a shell as he was attending wounded men. He refused to leave the trenches, and even went on treating the stricken men until he was carried away by the stretcher-bearers. On former occasions this gallant doctor had " carried on " under shell and rifle fire, refusing to take cover as long as a wounded man lay within his reach. He died a few hours after his leg was amputated, the Victoria Cross being awarded him posthumously.

He was only one of many doctors killed and wounded whilst gallantly carrying on their deeds of mercy. Lieut. J. L. Huggan, the medical officer of the 3rd Coldstream, was killed on the 16th. His death was a splendid example of devotion to duty—for he was killed not only in attending to British, but to German wounded. A barn in front of the 3rd Coldstream in which a number of German wounded were lying was set on fire by enemy shells. At great risk to himself, Lieut. Huggan, accompanied by some officers of the 3rd Coldstream, rushed out and removed every one of the men in danger. They were placed in a quarry behind the lines ; but a high-explosive shell burst there also, killing Lieut. Huggan, 11 men, and wounding 50 others. On the 18th Lieut. R. Walker, R.A.M.C., medical officer of No. 6 Field Ambulance, was wounded ; on the 20th, Lieut. J. T. O'Connell, R.A.M.C., medical officer to the 2nd Highland Light Infantry, and on the 26th Lieut. W. O. W. Ball, R.A.M.C., medical officer to the South Staffords, were killed.

The second V.C., won by Private Dobson, was also for personal bravery. The story is as follows : " On the 26th September,

---

[1] General Staff Diary, 2nd Division.
[2] *London Gazette*, 16th November 1914.
[3] *London Gazette*, 9th December 1914.

at La Cour de Soupir Farm, a patrol from the trench tunnel had one man killed and two wounded ; one of them got back with only a graze. Corporal Brown and Private Dobson volunteered to go out and see to the man who had been hit. They crawled out under heavy fire, and found that one man was dead and the other wounded ; they rendered first aid, and then they came back for a stretcher, and Dobson went out a second time and brought him in."[1]

From the 21st to the 26th September, de Castelnau's Seventh French Army was attacked heavily all along the line from Lassigny and Roye to Péronne ; the enemy had brought up fresh forces— the Sixth German Army.[2] De Castelnau had alternate gains and losses, and General Joffre saw that if the new turning movement was to be successful another army would be necessary. On the 27th, 28th, and 29th, the Sixth German Army gradually moved northwards and attacked the French at Ervilliers, Courcelles, and Achiet-le-Petit. De Maud'huy's Tenth French Army was then moved up north of de Castelnau, but again the enemy lengthened his line until Amiens, Arras, and Béthune were successively reached by both armies.

The race to the coast had begun !

Along the British front on the Aisne the position was that approximating a stalemate. " Futile attempts were made all along our front up to the evening of the 28th," said Sir John French, " when they died away and have not since been renewed."

The losses of the 2nd Division from the 16th September to 14th October were heavy. In the aggregate they totalled :—Officers : killed 19, wounded 27, missing 2—48 ; other ranks : killed 148, wounded 649, missing 155—952.[3]

---

[1] War Diary, Colonel Pereira, 2nd Coldstream Guards.

[2] The date of the arrival on the Somme of the Sixth German Army is given as 23rd September. It was formed of the following : Ist Bavarian Active Corps, IInd Bavarian Active Corps, XIVth Reserve Corps (26th and 28th Reserve Divisions), XVIIIth Active Corps, XXIst Active Corps, 1st Cavalry Corps with Guards Cavalry Division and 4th Cavalry Division, IInd Cavalry Corps with 2nd, 7th, and 9th Cavalry Divisions.

[3] See Appendix VI.

OPERATIONS IN FLANDERS, 1914.

THE BATTLES OF YPRES, 1914:
    THE BATTLE OF LANGEMARCK.
    THE BATTLE OF GHELUVELT.
        Fighting from 1st to 10th November 1914.
    THE BATTLE OF NONNE BOSSCHEN.
        The Operations of Lord Cavan's Force—30th
        October to 17th November 1914.

THE BATTLES OF YPRES, 1914.

By the end of September it had become evident to Sir John French and General Joffre that open warfare, so far as the Compiègne-Verdun front was concerned, had ceased. Both Allied and enemy troops were living a life closely resembling that of cave-dwellers. The opposing trenches were gradually pushed forward towards one another, but as the distance between the lines lessened the defences increased in strength. A new kind of warfare had taken the place of the old. The German Higher Command had foreseen, and had partially prepared for it; but to the Allies it came as a surprise. Artillery duels assumed a new significance: to batter down the opposing trenches and disperse the barbed-wire entanglements became the tasks of the gunners; there were other innovations later. The infantry sat in their trenches all day and slept there at night, taking shelter in their dug-outs. The old shallow trenches were superseded by deep, strongly built shelters, which shell-fire could not demolish unless by a direct hit. Snipers had become a terror; to expose a head meant certain death. Neither side made any appreciable advance or retirement.

The impossibility of obtaining a decision, combined with other events, determined Sir John French that efforts to turn the enemy's flank and press him back must be made. In his fourth dispatch he says : " Early in October study of the general situation strongly impressed me with the necessity of bringing the greatest possible force to bear in support of the northern flank of the Allies, in order to effectively outflank the enemy and compel him to evacuate his positions. At the same time the position on the Aisne . . . appeared to me to warrant a withdrawal of the British force from the positions they then held. The enemy had been weakened by continual abortive and futile attacks, whilst the fortification of the position had been much improved. I represented these views to General Joffre, who fully agreed."

But there were other considerations.

The enemy was gradually withdrawing men from the stagnated front and extending his right flank until the line reached the vicinity of Arras. Lille was still held by French Territorials, and Antwerp sheltered the remnants of the Belgian army. The position of the British Expeditionary Force on the Aisne was very awkward also from the point of view of supply. The British line of communication cut right across the French communications. A position in Flanders would automatically shorten the train movements between the Channel ports and the British army.

The 3rd Cavalry Division and the 7th Division under Sir Henry Rawlinson had landed at Ostend, and were already operating in support of the Belgian army and assisting its withdrawal from Antwerp. In the event of the success of Sir John's plans Sir Henry Rawlinson would be available to co-operate as soon as circumstances would allow. " In the event of these movements so far over-coming the resistance of the enemy as to enable a forward move-ment to be made, all the Allied forces to march in an easterly direction. The road running from Béthune to Lille was to be the dividing line between the British and French forces, the right of the British army being directed on Lille."

3RD OCT.   Arrangements for withdrawal and relief were made with the French General Staff, and on the 3rd October the 2nd Cavalry Division set out by road for the new theatre of operations *via* Compiègne.

The operations of the British army were to be as follows : " The IInd Corps to arrive on the line Aire–Béthune on the 11th October, to connect with the right of the French Tenth Army pivoting on its left, to attack in flank the enemy who were opposing the Xth French Corps in front. The cavalry to move on the northern flanks of the IInd Corps and support its attack until the IIIrd Corps, which was to detrain at St. Omer on the 12th, should come up. They were then to clear the front and to act on the northern flank of the IIIrd Corps in a similar manner, pending the arrival of the Ist Corps from the Aisne."

The IInd Corps detrained at Abbeville on 8th October, and on the 11th, covered by the 2nd Cavalry Division, moved forward. After considerable fighting it had by the 18th reached the line Givenchy–Villaines–Lorgies–Herlies.

The IIIrd Corps completed its detrainment at St. Omer by the evening of the 11th, and moved east to Hazebrouck. On the morning of the 13th the corps moved forward, and by the night of the 18th the line ran through Radingham–Lavalles–Ennetières–

Capinghem–Premesques railway line–L'Epinette to a point half a mile east of Le Ghier.

Conneau's French cavalry operated between the IInd and IIIrd Corps.

On 9th October Antwerp fell, and later, on the 12th, Lille was surrendered to the enemy. The IVth Corps was therefore available to co-operate in the new movement, and Sir Henry Rawlinson was ordered to make good the line Zandvoorde–Gheluvelt–Zonnebeke, which was occupied by the 7th Division, with the 3rd Cavalry Division on its left towards Langemarck and Poelcappelle.

The 2nd Cavalry Division operated between the IVth and IIIrd Corps.

The 87th French Territorial Division in Ypres and Vlamertinghe, and the 89th French Territorial Division in Poperinghe, supported the left of the IVth Corps.

The Belgians occupied a line from Dixmude to the coast town of Nieuport.

It will be observed that the Ist Corps had not yet arrived from the Aisne.

Sir John French's operations were at this period directed against the Sixth German Army, which held the line Menin–Lille–La Bassée. He knew that the enemy's IIIrd Reserve Corps was operating in a south-easterly direction from Ostend, but does not seem to have been aware of the formation of a new Fourth German Army under Duke Albert of Würtemberg. This army on the evening of the 18th October held the following line :

IIIrd Reserve Corps: St. Pierre Capelle–Schoore–Leke–Keyem.
XXIInd Reserve Corps : Aertrycke–Thourout.
XXIIIrd Reserve Corps : Lichtervelde–Ardoye.
XXVIth Reserve Corps : Emelghem–Iseghem.
XXVIIth Reserve Corps : Lendelede–Courtrai.

The first corps (the IIIrd) was formed of three divisions, 5th and 6th Reserve Divisions and 4th Ersatz Division. Up to the 18th the IIIrd Reserve Corps acted as a screen in order to mask the concentration of the new Fourth [1] Army from the Allies.

In the meantime the British Ist Corps on the Aisne was in the

[1] At various times from 10th October to 16th November the Fourth Army had operating with it on the Ypres front the 9th Reserve Division, 6th Bavarian Reserve Division, a Marine Division, 38th and 37th Landwehr Divisions, 2nd Ersatz Brigade, and a Guard Cavalry Division.

process of being railed up to St. Omer. Early in the month—October—the corps had received warning of the change over and had seen the IIIrd Corps withdrawn, and had in fact with the 16th Infantry Brigade extended the line to cover the positions held by the two other corps.

11TH OCT.

On the afternoon of 11th October the 2nd Division received the following order :

" The 2nd Division must be in readiness to move at short notice at latest to-morrow night.

" All preliminary arrangements must be made forthwith, and all surplus ammunition and impedimenta removed to-night.

" Battalion and company guides must be ready to meet relieving troops. These guides should have prepared sketches showing the exact position of the trenches into which the relieving troops are to go. The nearest hostile positions should be shown in these sketches and the ranges thereto : artillery units should show the position of hostile batteries as far as located, and the zone and objectives engaged by our gunners by day and by night.

" Details as to time and procedure to be adopted as well as of the place of assembly for the 2nd Division troops will be notified later. The guns dug in will be removed to-night."

The relief is thus described in the 2nd Division General Staff Diary :

" 11th October, 5.30 p.m.—The French General Officer Commanding 69th Brigade arrived with some Staff officers. He was apparently under the impression that his Brigade (six battalions and six batteries) was to take over the whole line, but realizing the impossibility of this he returned to his Corps Headquarters. It was subsequently decided that the 69th Brigade would take over the line held by the 16th Infantry Brigade and 4th (Guards) Brigade on the night of 12th–13th. It was stated that seven more French battalions, with two batteries, would be available on the 13th to extend up to the line of L'Oise and L'Aisne Canal. This position might be taken over on the night 13th–14th. The pontoon bridges at Bourg and east of the railway bridge east of Vailly were dismantled during the night 11th–12th.

" 12th October.—Quiet night. The French Divisional Staff officer arrived at Bourg at 6 a.m. in order to go round the line of trenches of 4th (Guards) Brigade and 16th Infantry Brigade. French regimental officers had been ordered by 1st Corps to Chassemy by 5 a.m., and found out the trenches their battalions would occupy. It was necessary for both French and British to move over high

ground south of river Aisne only during hours of darkness. Ist
Corps Operation Order No. 15 arrived about 9.45 a.m.   It detailed
Fismes, Fère-en-Tardenois, and Neuilly-St.-Front as entraining
stations on the 13th and early hours of 14th for 16th Infantry
Brigade, the battalions of the 4th (Guards) Brigade, one (No. 4) Field
Ambulance, and the XXXIVth, XXXVIth, and XLIst Brigades
R.F.A.

" The intention was to relieve the three battalions of the 4th
(Guards) Brigade in the trenches, keeping the Irish Guards as a
reserve on the left of the 5th Infantry Brigade.   The 3rd Coldstream on the left had to be considered as part of the 16th Infantry
Brigade line, as they formed its right flank.

" By midday the French officers had visited trenches up to the
3rd Coldstream inclusive ; but by 5 p.m. none had gone over the
line occupied by the 2nd Grenadiers and 2nd Coldstream, the next
in order from left to right.   At 7 p.m. a general Staff officer of the
2nd Division arranged with the 69th Brigade that only the line held
by the 3rd Coldstream and 2nd Grenadiers would be taken over
to-night, the remaining 4th Brigade battalions being relieved
to-morrow evening.

" The French crossed at Vailly, and the relief took place without
trouble or confusion.   The 3rd Coldstream and 2nd Grenadiers
marched off to billets at Perles at 2.15 a.m. by the Chavonne Bridge.
The battalions had arranged representatives to meet the French
units ; they guided them through the woods, and the French filed
in as our men filed out.   There was no interruption from the enemy.

" The artillery withdrew across the river in the darkness and
marched off to billet or entrain as ordered.

" 13th October. — The intention for the night of 13th – 14th
was to relieve the 2nd Coldstream in the trenches and the Irish
Guards of the 4th Brigade, the whole of the 5th Infantry Brigade
and that portion of the 6th Infantry Brigade which extended up to
L'Aisne and L'Oise Canal.   The battalion of the 6th Brigade east
of the canal was to remain, whilst the rest of the Brigade moved
into billets at Bourg and Œuilly, forming corps reserve.

" The French regimental officers arrived at Bourg at 12 noon.
They were taken to Soupir, and conducted over the trenches by
representatives of the 4th, 5th, and 6th Infantry Brigades.

" The whole French column (seven battalions and two batteries)
crossed at Pont d'Arcy, having been billeted up to dusk at Longueval and Dhuizel.   They had travelled 120 kilometres the previous
evening in motor buses from the west.   All, except one battalion

bound for Ferme de Metz, marched to Soupir, where they were led by battalion representatives to the trenches.

" The relief of the 2nd Coldstream was completed by 5.45 p.m.

" *14th October.*—The relief of the 5th Infantry Brigade was finished at 2.10 a.m., and the 6th Infantry Brigade at about 3 a.m. The battalions of the 4th (Guards) Brigade marched to Perles, and the 5th Brigade to Vauxcéré, those of the 6th Brigade to Bourg and Œuilly.[1]

" The entrainment of the 2nd Division proceeded according to time table. Divisional Headquarters entrained at 5 p.m. at Fère-en-Tardenois.

" *15th October.*—The Division reached St. Omer about midnight 15th–16th, where it stopped the night.

" *16th October.*—Divisional Headquarters moved to Hazebrouck. The Division was detrained and billeted in the area Hazebrouck–Ebblinghem–Blaringhem."

The 4th and 6th Infantry Brigades billeted in Hazebrouck, the 5th Infantry Brigade in Morbecque.

19TH OCT.   The 17th, 18th, and 19th were spent by the 4th (Guards) Brigade at Boeschepe. The 5th Infantry Brigade was billeted for two days (17th and 18th) at Godewaersvelde, and moved on the 19th to Poperinghe ; the 6th Infantry Brigade, which had been billeted at Hazebrouck on 16th, 17th, and 18th, taking over the billets vacated by the 5th Brigade at Godewaersvelde.

During the 19th most of the battalions received reinforcements from England.

Thus on the evening of the 19th October the left flank of the Allied line to the coast was complete, though in places woefully thin. Indeed, the position was serious. Just as the German Higher Command had planned to turn the left flank of the Allies, so the attempt of the Allies to outflank the enemy's right wing had failed, and a deadlock similar to that on the Aisne was the result.

The enemy regarded these operations as of vital importance. " All the more therefore were the hopes of Germany centred in the Fourth Army, which was fighting farther northwards, for in its hands lay the fate of the campaign in Western Europe at this period." [2]

In Sir John French's own words : " A question of vital impor-

[1] The strength of the 2nd Division when it left the Aisne was approximately :
    Fighting troops : Officers, 401 ; other ranks, 15,357.
    Non-fighting troops : Officers, 52 ; other ranks, 881.
[2] *Ypres 1914*, by the German General Staff.

tance now was for decision. I knew the enemy were by this time in greatly superior strength on the Lys, and that the IInd, IIIrd Cavalry, and IVth Corps were holding a much wider front than their numbers and strength warranted. Taking these facts alone into consideration, it would have appeared wise to throw the Ist Corps in to strengthen the line; but this would have left the country north and east of Ypres and the Ypres Canal open to a wide turning movement by the IIIrd Reserve Corps and at least one Landwehr Division which I knew to be operating in that region. I was also aware that the enemy was bringing large reinforcements [1] up from the East, which could only be opposed for several days by two or three French Cavalry Divisions, some French Territorials, and the Belgian Army.

" The Belgian Army was in no fit condition to offer much resistance to a turning movement by the enemy, and unless the Allied left flank was strongly reinforced there was a danger that the Channel ports would be laid bare to the Germans. I judged that a successful movement of this kind would be fraught with such disastrous consequences that the risk of operating on so extended a front must be undertaken; and I directed Sir Douglas Haig to move with the 1st Corps to the north of Ypres.

" From the best information at my disposal I judged at this time that the considerable reinforcements which the enemy had undoubtedly brought up during the 16th, 17th, and 18th [2] had been directed principally on the line of the Lys and against the IInd Corps at La Bassée; and that Sir Douglas Haig would probably not be opposed north of Ypres by much more than the IIIrd Reserve Corps, which I knew to have suffered considerably in its previous operations, and perhaps by one or two Landwehr Divisions."

The importance of the above quotations cannot be overstated, for here are given the Commander-in-Chief's reasons for the Ypres operations, which began on the 20th October and ended in the creation of the famous, but terrible, Ypres Salient.

The orders given to Sir Douglas Haig were to advance with the French Corps through Thourout, with the object of capturing Bruges and if possible driving the enemy towards Ghent.

[1] This seems to indicate that the formation of the new German Fourth Army was known to Sir John French, but this view is contradicted later in Sir John's words : " Sir Douglas Haig would probably not be opposed north of Ypres by much more than the IIIrd Reserve Corps." The enemy claimed to have hidden the formation of this new army behind a screen formed by the IIIrd Reserve Corps.

[2] This cannot refer to the new Fourth German Army.

On the afternoon of the 19th October General Monro, commanding the 2nd Division, motored to Bailleul (General Headquarters Report Centre), and was there informed that orders (through 1st Corps) were on the way to him to move north-east on the morning of the 20th. The 1st Division was to move on Poperinghe and the 2nd Division on Ypres.

At 1.30 on the morning of the 20th final orders were received : " Hostile columns are reported to be moving west and south-west from Menin, Roulers, and Thourout. The Ist Corps will advance to-day, general direction Thourout, and will drive the enemy back wherever met. The road Steenvoorde–Poperinghe is to be left clear for the 1st Division.[1]

" The Division (2nd) will march as follows :—Advanced Guard (General Lord Cavan) : Two troops 15th Hussars, one platoon Divisional Cyclists, XLIst Brigade R.F.A. (less Ammunition Column), 4th (Guards) Brigade, one Bearer Sub-division, 4th Field Ambulance ; will march from Boeschepe at 6 a.m. via Reninghelst, Vlamertinghe, north side of Ypres to St. Jean.

" Main Body (in order of march) : One troop 15th Hussars, one battalion 6th Infantry Brigade (2nd South Staffords), XXXIVth Brigade R.F.A. (less Ammunition Column), XLIVth Brigade R.F.A. (less Ammunition Column), 6th Infantry Brigade, 11th Field Company R.E., 35th (Heavy) Battery R.G.A. ; will march from the north-east end of Godewaersvelde at 6 a.m. and will follow the same route as the advanced guard.

" Flank guard (Lieut.-Colonel Westmacott) : One troop 15th Hussars, two platoons Divisional Cyclists, XXXVIth Brigade R.F.A. (less Ammunition Column), 5th Field Company R.E., 5th Infantry Brigade, one Bearer Sub-division, 5th Field Ambulance ; will march from Poperinghe via Elverdinghe to Boesinghe. The Brigade Ammunition Columns will follow the main body, and will assemble under orders from Major Cotton with their head at Reninghelst. The Field Ambulance will march at 7.30 a.m., and form up in column of route with their head at Heksken, one mile south-west of Reninghelst. The train will march at 8 a.m., and assemble along the road Boeschepe–Inn (one and three-quarter miles north-west of Heksken).

" On arrival on the line of the canal the 4th and 5th Brigades will cross the canal, and hold the high ground with their main bodies about Wieltje and Pilkem. The flank guard will also be responsible for the crossing over the canal at Steenstraate."

---

[1] Then in billets in Cassel and area.

THE BATTLES OF YPRES 1914.
Approximate Positions of the Allied Armies and the German Armies
on 19th October.

(*Facing p. 108.*)

The IInd and IIIrd Corps were to assume a defensive *rôle*; the IVth Corps was to conform generally to the movements of the Ist Corps.

Thus the preliminary dispositions for the desperate and prolonged operations which followed.

At 6 a.m. on the 20th the advanced guard set out, led by the 4th (Guards) Brigade in the following order: 2nd Coldstream (as vanguard), 2nd Grenadiers, 3rd Coldstream, and 1st Irish Guards. The Divisional Mounted Troops and the XLIst Brigade R.F.A. followed. The route taken was *via* Mt. Kokereele–Reninghelst–Vlamertinghe–Ypres. At the latter place, however, the Brigade halted for some hours. The 2nd Coldstream and 3rd Coldstream were sent forward to Point 37 between Langemarck and Zonnebeke, and gained touch with the left of the 22nd Infantry Brigade (7th Division). Here they entrenched themselves, and although heavy firing was heard coming from a north-easterly direction, they were not attacked. The 2nd Grenadiers and Irish Guards billeted in St. Jean.

The 6th Infantry Brigade at the head of the main body marched out of Godewaersvelde also at 6 a.m. Divisional Headquarters led, followed by the 2nd South Staffords, XXXIVth and XLIVth Brigades R.F.A., 1st Royal Berks, 1st King's Royal Rifles, and 1st King's. The route lay *via* Boeschepe, Westoutre, Reninghelst, Vlamertinghe, north of Ypres to the crossroads immediately south of Kaai. Here the main body halted until about 3.30 p.m., when the Brigade went into billets in the north-eastern suburbs of Ypres. "Artillery fire was heard to the east and south-east until after dark. French Territorial troops were met on the northern exits of the town, and crowds of Belgian refugees passed through the town all the afternoon. A very sad sight." "Very comfortable bed, also some very nice attics full of straw, above asylum. Lunatics harmless, dangerous one locked up." Another battalion of the same brigade billeted in a diamond factory! The flank guard (5th Infantry Brigade), under Colonel Westmacott, on reaching its destination, found that the crossings over the canal at Streenstraate and the high ground about Pilkem were already held by French Territorials. The Brigade, however, entrenched on the line Pilkem–Streenstraate and bivouacked for the night, which, barring the rain, passed without incident.

Divisional Headquarters were at Ypres.

At nightfall on the 20th the Division had reached all its objectives, and there are no records of casualties having been suffered on this day.

THE BATTLE OF LANGEMARCK.

21ST–24TH
Oct.
MAP.
During the night 20th–21st (at 1.30 a.m.) 2nd Division Operation Order No. 26 was issued : the Ist Corps was to advance towards Thourout and drive the enemy back wherever met. The 3rd Cavalry Division was about Langemarck and St. Julien.

The 7th Division held the line Zonnebeke–Kruiseecke. French cavalry were reported to be holding the line Clercken–Langemarck west of the Forêt de Houthulst. The 1st Division was ordered to reach Langemarck by 7 a.m., and attack thence in the direction of Poelcappelle.

The 2nd Division was to cross the Zonnebeke–Langemarck road when the 1st Division left Langemarck, and attack in the direction of Passchendaele, keeping touch with the 1st Division.

The right flank of the Ist Corps—i.e., the right flank of the 2nd Division—was protected by the IVth Corps (22nd Infantry Brigade), and the left flank by French troops under General Bidon.

At 6 a.m. a Divisional conference took place, and the infantry brigadiers, and Officers Commanding the R.A. and R.E., were given verbal orders for the attack.

The 2nd Division was ordered to be disposed as follows:—At Point 37 on the west side of ridge north-west of Zonnebeke : 4th (Guards) Brigade, XLIst Brigade R.F.A., 11th Field Company R.E., one troop B Squadron 15th Hussars, and a bearer sub-division of the 4th Field Ambulance.

At a point just west of the crossroads north of St. Julien : 5th Infantry Brigade, XXXVIth Brigade R.F.A., 5th Field Company R.E., two platoons of Divisional Cyclists and a Bearer Sub-division 5th Field Ambulance ; troops to be concealed as much as possible from the eastward.

At each side of the road at Wieltje : 6th Infantry Brigade, XXXIVth and XLIVth Brigades R.F.A., and 35th (Heavy) Battery R.G.A. ; the artillery placed close to the road in readiness to move forward at short notice.

These moves were ordered to be completed by 6.30 a.m.

The attack was timed for 7 a.m., but the 1st Division was delayed on the road between Boesinghe and Langemarck by French troops, and in consequence the general advance did not begin until 9.20 a.m.

The Hussars (attached to the 4th (Guards) Brigade) had received special instructions from Lord Cavan (commanding 4th Brigade)

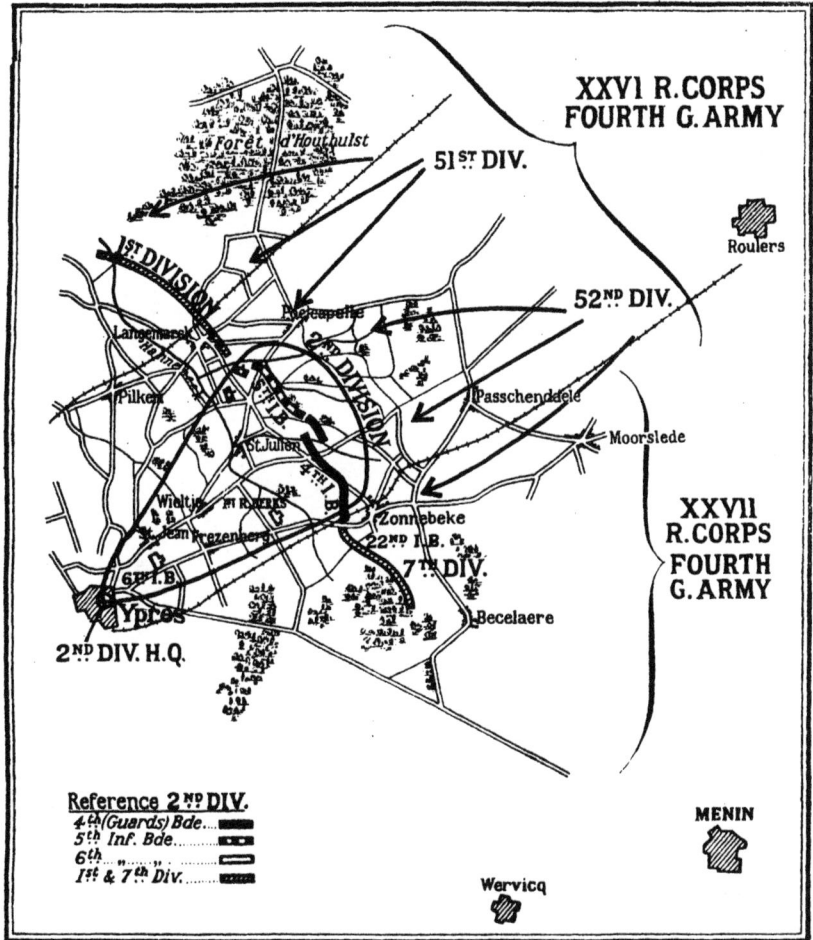

XXVI R. CORPS
FOURTH G. ARMY

Forêt d'Houthulst

51ST DIV.

Roulers

1ST DIVISION

52ND DIV.

Langemarck

Poelcapelle

2ND DIVISION

Pilken

Passchendaele

St. Julien

Moorslede

Wieltje

1ST R. BDE.

St. Jean

Frezenberg

Zonnebeke

22ND I.B.

XXVII
R. CORPS
FOURTH
G. ARMY

6TH I. B.

7TH DIV.

Ypres

Becelaere

2ND DIV. H.Q.

MENIN

Reference 2ND DIV.
4th (Guards) Bde....
5th Inf. Bde......
6th ,, ,, ...
1st & 7th Div......

Wervicq

THE MAPPA CO., LTD., LONDON.

THE BATTLE OF LANGEMARCK,
21st–24th October 1914.

(Facing p. 110.)

to close up any gaps between the right of the 2nd Coldstream, who were on the extreme right of the 2nd Division, and the left flank of the 22nd Infantry Brigade (7th Division) at Zonnebeke.

At 8 a.m. the 2nd Coldstream started off with instructions to make good the Zonnebeke–Langemarck road, and get into touch with the 22nd Infantry Brigade, whose left flank rested on the railway station at Zonnebeke : Nos. 1 and 4 Companies were in the firing line, and Nos. 2 and 3 Companies in support.

The 3rd Coldstream, who had assembled just south of St. Julien, were engaged in a converging attack, and had received orders to advance in line and in touch with the 2nd Coldstream. No. 2 Company formed an advanced guard to the battalion, and, when clear of the village, advanced in extended order ; No. 3 following in close order, and Nos. 4 and 1 in reserve.

Both battalions came under heavy artillery fire almost at once.

The 2nd Coldstream, advancing in artillery formation up the reverse slope of the hill, suffered little damage. But on reaching the high ground about Point 37 the enemy's infantry was encountered in considerable strength, and the companies were forced to deploy under heavy rifle-fire at comparatively short range. Gradually, however, the Guardsmen advanced, forcing the enemy back. By 11.30 a.m. the line of the Zonnebeke–Langemarck road was gained, but here the attack was held up. The two supporting companies (2 and 3) had by now been ordered into the firing line, but further advance was checked ; a halt was therefore called.

The 3rd Coldstream joined action with the enemy about Point 20, the latter being in considerable strength. A farm on the right front of the battalion was full of hostile infantry ; also a small wood on a ridge running east and west. In the face of this opposition the battalion checked its advance. Scouts were sent forward to ascertain if the Hanebeek, a small river, was fordable. The scouts were supported by an advance of the right half of the line. But owing to heavy rifle-fire from the farm and woods this half company swung slightly to the right. Again, however, at 100 yards, from a fence which surrounded the farm, the advanced guard was held up, and sent back a request for support. By now the battalion was in advance of the 2nd Coldstream on the right, and the Connaught Rangers (5th Infantry Brigade) on its left, and in fact at this period held the foremost position of the 2nd Division. But this advance was justified, as the ground held was a ridge. Beyond the ridge, however, Lieut.-Colonel Feilding would not go.

One company of the 2nd Grenadiers was ordered up in support, but, whilst on its way, No. 2 Company of the 2nd Coldstream had come under an enfilade fire from a small party of the enemy in occupation of a ridge slightly to the right rear. This necessitated an attempt to throw back the right flank of the company; but owing to a mistaken order the whole firing line retired, though in good order and not losing a single man in the retirement.

The company of 2nd Grenadiers arrived too late to be of any material assistance.

Thus up to 2 p.m. steady progress had been made. The 4th (Guards) Brigade had gained ground across the Hanebeek stream as far as a point 2,300 yards east of St. Julien.

At 2 p.m. Colonel Feilding (commanding 3rd Coldstream) was wounded, and handed over the command to Major Matheson.

The Irish Guards and the remainder of the 2nd Grenadiers were during this period in reserve about Wieltje and St. Julien.

East of the 2nd Coldstream, the 22nd Infantry Brigade of the 7th Division in Zonnebeke had been subjected to continual heavy attacks. The enemy had concentrated his artillery upon the line of thinly held trenches about the town, and they were almost untenable. Colonel Pereira of the 2nd Coldstream sent a half company of his men along the light railway and through the trenches north-west of the town, but there was still a dangerous gap. Household Cavalry and the 2nd Divisional Mounted Troops were put in to close up the gap, until during the afternoon No. 4 Company of the Irish Guards arrived and took over the position. Later, the remainder of the battalion moved up and relieved the cavalry between the 2nd Coldstream and the left of the 22nd Brigade.

In the meantime the 5th Infantry Brigade, which had occupied a position covering the crossings of the Yser Canal at Boesinghe and Steenstraate, had at 6 a.m. set out for the point of assembly half a mile north of St. Julien. Here orders were received to advance on Passchendaele, keeping touch with the 3rd Infantry Brigade (1st Division) on the left flank, and the 4th (Guards) Brigade on the right.

The Brigade advanced in two lines :—First line : left, Oxford and Bucks ; right, 2nd Worcesters. Second line : left, 2nd Highland Light Infantry ; right, 2nd Connaught Rangers.

A violent rifle and machine-gun fire opened on the Brigade soon after the advance began. This caused the 3rd Brigade (1st Division) to draw off to the left, which in turn necessitated a slight change of front to the left by the 5th Brigade. One company of the Highland Light Infantry reinforced the left of the Oxford and Bucks, and the pressure on that flank was thus somewhat relieved. The Brigade at this period was in a line which extended from a point just north of the seventh kilometre stone on the Ypres–Poelcappelle road—east, along the southern banks of the Stroonbeek.

Word was passed along the line by the South Wales Borderers, who were on the right of the 3rd Infantry Brigade, that the latter was held up at Langemarck and could get no farther. A halt was therefore ordered until the right flank of the 1st Division was able to advance level with the 5th Infantry Brigade. Owing to this enforced halt, during which the Brigade was exposed to heavy rifle, machine-gun, and artillery fire, serious casualties were incurred. The Oxfords in particular suffered heavily. Subjected to a severe oblique rifle-fire which came from its left front (in front of the South Wales Borderers) the battalion pushed on just short of the Hanebeek stream. Here the thick hedges, which had been cunningly interwoven with barbed wire, brought the advance to a standstill. But a gate in the hedge had been left unprotected. A rush was made for the gate, but immediately a murderous machine-gun fire was opened upon it, and officers and men tumbled over one another—killed or wounded. Captain A. H. Harden, Lieutenants G. M. R. Turbutt and C. F. Murphy, and Second-Lieutenants J. S. C. Marshall and L. A. Filleul (all of the Oxfords) were killed, and five other officers wounded. Still losing heavily, the battalion pressed on, and eventually captured the position and dug in along the southern banks of the stream. But the cost had been terrible ! In a few minutes the total in killed and wounded numbered over 200 all ranks, many being killed outright.

As no advance could be made by the 1st Division the fight became stationary, and the 5th Infantry Brigade set to work to entrench the position. "The enemy's trenches could be seen in front, the nearest being about 300 yards off along the track which leads from near the junction of the Stroonbeek and Hanebeek towards Langemarck. Men could be seen running into these trenches to occupy them or reinforce them, and many were shot here by our front line."

The Brigade entrenched in the following order :—Front line : two companies Highland Light Infantry, Oxford and Bucks, Worcesters, two companies Connaughts. Second line : two companies Highland Light Infantry (left), two companies Connaughts (right).

The attack of the 5th Brigade, like that of the 4th (Guards) Brigade, was thus brought to a standstill. The situation appears to have been caused by the sudden retirement, about 2 o'clock in the afternoon, of the French cavalry corps which had been operating on the left of the Ist Corps, and in conjunction with which Sir Douglas Haig had attacked the enemy on the line Poelcappelle–Passchendaele. The retirement of General Mitry's troops uncovered the left flank of the Ist Division, with the result that the leading brigade, which had nearly reached Poelcappelle station, had to fall back nearer to Langemarck. This retirement brought the 5th Infantry Brigade to a standstill.

At 6 p.m. on the 21st the situation of the 2nd Division was as follows :

Irish Guards, Zonnebeke station, connecting on their right with the 22nd Infantry Brigade (7th Division), and on their left with the 2nd Coldstream. On the left of the 2nd Coldstream and slightly echeloned, owing to the nature of the ground, were the 2nd Grenadiers, and beyond them the 3rd Coldstream, who had maintained their position 2,200 yards east of St. Julien. The 5th Infantry Brigade was in touch with the left of the 4th, and had the Worcesters, Oxford and Bucks, and Highland Light Infantry in the front line, with two companies of the Connaughts in close support of the right of the Worcesters, and the remainder of the Connaughts in Brigade reserve. The 6th Infantry Brigade had remained in Divisional reserve all day about Wieltje and St. Jean, though the 1st Berks were ordered up to Frezenberg in close support of the right of the 4th Brigade.

During the day artillery support was given as follows : to the 4th (Guards) Brigade, by the XLIst Brigade R.F.A., and one Battery of Howitzers XLIVth Brigade R.F.A. ; to the 5th Infantry Brigade, by the XXXVIth Brigade R.F.A., and one Battery of Howitzers from the XLIVth Brigade R.F.A. The 35th (Heavy) Battery was in action near Wieltje; and the XXXIVth Brigade R.F.A. in reserve with the remaining battery of the XLIVth Brigade R.F.A.

The 9th Battery belonging to the XLIst Brigade was heavily engaged, the battery firing 1,400 rounds at ranges rarely exceeding 1,200 yards, and although heavily shelled by the enemy with high-explosive, the gallant gunners stood fast throughout the day : 1 man was killed and 11 wounded in the battery. " For their work on this day the battery received the thanks of Lord Cavan commanding the 4th (Guards) Brigade."

The 21st October was a busy day for the doctors. The Bearer

Sub-divisions of the 4th Field Ambulance with the Guards Brigade, and the Bearer Sub-divisions of the 5th Field Ambulance with the 5th Infantry Brigade, had advanced dressing stations at St. Julien. The remaining Bearer Sub-divisions of these field ambulances were in reserve at Wieltje. The Tent Divisions of the 4th and 5th Field Ambulances, with the whole of the 6th Field Ambulance, remained in Ypres, where a dressing station was opened. The Divisional collecting station was at St. Julien.

At dusk the enemy's attacks for a while died down, but the Ist Corps had not reached its objective. Sir Douglas Haig, owing to the demands made upon him by the 7th Division, which had borne the attack of at least a whole corps, had been forced to halt and bivouac on the line Zonnebeke–St. Julien–Langemarck–Bixschoote instead of Passchendaele–Poelcappelle.

A conference took place in Ypres between Sir John French, Sir Douglas Haig, Sir Henry Rawlinson, General de Mitry (commanding the French cavalry), and General Bidon (commanding the French Territorials). As a result of this conference the French generals undertook to move their troops out of Ypres to the left flank of the Ist Corps. Sir John French also informed the commanders of the Ist and IVth Corps that he had interviewed the French commander-in-chief, General Joffre, who had told him that " he was bringing up the IXth French Corps to Ypres, that more French troops would follow later, and that he intended, in conjunction with the Belgian troops, to drive the Germans east. General Joffre said he would be unable to commence this movement until the 24th."

A defensive rôle was then enjoined on the commanders of the Ist and IVth Corps. " I directed the General Officers Commanding the Ist and IVth Corps," said Sir John, " to strengthen their positions as much as possible, and to be prepared to hold their ground for two or three days until the French offensive movement to the north could develop."

Thus the troops billeted or bivouacked for the night in their fighting areas.

Divisional Headquarters were still at Ypres.

The casualties in the 2nd Division on the 21st were : Officers, 25 ; other ranks, 578—killed, wounded, and missing.[1]

For a while, at dusk, the attack died down, but about 12.45 a.m. a message was received at Divisional Headquarters from the 4th (Guards) Brigade to the effect that the 22nd Infantry Brigade

[1] See Appendix VII.

would withdraw its left at 1 a.m. to the level crossing on the Ypres–Zonnebeke road, three-quarter mile west of Zonnebeke, with its right flank on the northern borders of the Polygone Wood, and that the 4th (Guards) Brigade would have to conform by throwing back its right flank to keep touch on the left.

This move being sanctioned by Divisional Headquarters, the Irish Guards, who were then occupying the right of the line of the 4th (Guards) Brigade (about the railway crossing south of Zonnebeke), and half the battalion of the 2nd Coldstream, retired at 1 a.m. from their positions. The former took up a new line with its right on the level crossing, one kilometre south-west of Zonnebeke, its left resting on the lower slope of the hill at Point 37 in touch with the right company of the 2nd Coldstream, which had bent back its line to conform with that of the Irish Guards.

Immediately the 22nd Infantry Brigade evacuated Zonnebeke, the town was occupied by the enemy, who also obtained possession of about one kilometre of the Zonnebeke–Langemarck road.

Apart from the advance made by the Ist Corps on the 21st the fighting was not without advantage to the Allies, for it disclosed the presence of the very considerable forces which the enemy was then engaged in rushing up to the front in feverish haste. The IIIrd Reserve Corps which had acted as a screen was now engaged only with the Belgians and the left of the French, whilst the remainder of the new Fourth German Army—*i.e.*, XXIInd, XXIIIrd, XXVIth, and XXVIIth Reserve Corps—had already joined action with French troops and the Ist British Corps from Dixmude to Zonnebeke. That the 1st and 2nd Divisions were able to advance in the face of enemy corps of fresh troops, double their strength, backed by superior artillery, is an eloquent tribute to the fighting qualities of the British Expeditionary Force.

On the afternoon of 21st October, Sir John French must have realized what he had been unable to find out before—that he was opposed by very considerable enemy forces, and that the original plan for turning the right flank of the enemy was impossible. " I discussed the situation," he says, " with the General Officers Commanding the Ist and IVth Corps, and told them that in view of the unexpected reinforcements coming up of the enemy, it would probably be impossible to carry out the original rôle assigned to them." And, as already stated, they were enjoined to strengthen their positions and hold on for two or three days until the French had attacked on the north-west flank.

During the night of the 21st–22nd the Division dug itself in more securely and prepared for more strenuous fighting.

But in the morning the enemy, although considerably active on the right (2nd Division) and left (1st Division) flanks, did not launch any infantry attacks against the 2nd Division. The trenches of the 4th and 5th Infantry Brigades were, however, heavily shelled, though the casualties were light.

The IVth Corps was still hard pressed, and the 1st Royal Berks lent support to the 22nd Infantry Brigade at Frezenberg. On the left of the 2nd Division the 1st Division, heavily engaged, retired its left flank to Steenstraate.

About midday, a section of the 56th Howitzer Battery (XLIVth Brigade R.F.A.) was dispatched to Verbranden-Molen to support cavalry operations in the direction of Messines and Houthem.

At 3.30 p.m. Ist Corps Headquarters reported hostile columns were advancing from Comines and Wervicq towards Zandvoorde and Hollebeke (south-east of Ypres). Brigadier-General Fanshawe was therefore ordered to take two battalions of infantry (1st King's and 1st King's Royal Rifles, 6th Infantry Brigade), with two batteries of the XXXIVth Brigade R.F.A. and the 56th Howitzer Battery, less one section already sent to Verbranden-Molen, to Hollebeke, and there support the right of the 7th Division.

It was evident that the enemy was making or about to make desperate efforts to capture Ypres. Between Zonnebeke and Comines at this period, he must have had considerably more than an Army Corps,[1] with cavalry and artillery, operating against the now greatly weakened 7th Division supported only by whatever forces Sir Douglas Haig could spare from his 1st and 2nd Divisions.

Arrangements were therefore made by the 2nd Division to organize a Divisional Reserve, which now consisted of 2nd South Staffords (at St. Jean), 1st Royal Berks (at Frezenberg), and one Battery XXXIVth Brigade R.F.A. (at St. Jean). To these were added, on instructions from Ist Corps Headquarters, the 1st Loyal North Lancashires from 2nd Infantry Brigade, 1st Division, in Corps Reserve.

The Berks were ordered to remain at Frezenberg still supporting the left of the 7th Division : the South Staffords and Loyal North Lancashires, under the command of Lieut.-Colonel Davidson (of the South Staffords), remained in readiness at St. Jean.

---

[1] Probably a portion also of the Sixth German Army, as the left of the Fourth German Army (XXVIIth Reserve Corps, 53rd and 54th Reserve Divisions) was between 21st and 31st October operating on the line Becelaere–Gheluvelt.

Soon after 5 p.m. the enemy made an attack on the Oxford and Bucks near the St. Julien–Poelcappelle road. His troops advanced in massed formation, covered by artillery fire. But although the grey lines got within twenty-five yards of the Oxfords' trenches the attack was everywhere repulsed with heavy losses: many dead were counted in the morning and a large number of wounded had been removed during the night. The Oxfords' casualties in this attack were only two other ranks killed and one wounded.[1]

Amongst the remaining battalions of the 5th Infantry Brigade only a few casualties were suffered from shell-fire during the 22nd, though the troops passed through a very trying ordeal, the enemy plastering the ground with high-explosive and shrapnel.

The 4th (Guards) Brigade continued to strengthen its position with the loss of only a small number of men from shell-fire : no infantry attacks were launched against the Brigade.

Late at night the 1st King's Royal Rifles were recalled from Hollebeke, and the battalion reached its old billets in St. Jean very early on the 23rd, not having been in action, though heavy firing had broken out along the front of the 3rd Cavalry Division at Klein Zillebeke. The battalion continued in Corps Reserve.

At midnight the 2nd South Staffords and 1st Loyal North Lancashires were ordered to march at 2.30 a.m. to Pilkem, where on the previous afternoon the enemy had succeeded in breaking through the thin and widely extended line of the 1st Cameron Highlanders, pressing them back south of the Langemarck–Bixschoote road and capturing the Korteken cabaret.

At 8.30 a.m. on the 23rd the South Staffords and Loyal North Lancashires reached Pilkem, where they joined up with the 2nd King's Royal Rifles of the 2nd Infantry Brigade. During the morning the 1st King's Royal Rifles were sent up to a farm one mile south-east of Pilkem, also in support of the 1st Division.

A counter-attack was launched against the enemy, which was completely successful, over 500 prisoners being taken. Very heavy losses were also inflicted on the enemy, who resisted stubbornly the attacks of the Northamptons, Queen's, South Staffords, and King's Royal Rifles, the attack necessitating frequent bayonet charges. The Korteken cabaret was retaken.

In this attack two companies of the South Staffords (A

---

[1] " The French, who relieved us here during the night, reported officially that 740 dead Germans were counted near the trenches next morning."—Official Diary, 2nd Oxford and Bucks Light Infantry.

and D) were in the firing line with the Queen's Regiment, the remaining two companies being in reserve. At 4 p.m. the whole battalion was withdrawn into reserve just north of Pilkem. The Staffords' losses were : 1 officer killed (Second-Lieut. B. J. H. Scott), 3 officers wounded, and 45 other ranks killed, wounded, and missing. The 1st King's Royal Rifles did not join action with the enemy, and at night billeted in Pilkem. The two remaining battalions of the 6th Infantry Brigade—i.e., 1st Berks and 1st King's—billeted in Frezenberg and St. Jean respectively.

In the meantime the enemy along the front of the 4th and 5th Brigades had during the day shown considerable activity.

The night of the 22nd had for the 4th Brigade been one of comparative quietude, but the 23rd opened with a terrific hostile shell-fire along the whole line, which continued with great vigour throughout the day. Under cover of this bombardment the enemy's infantry in considerable strength could be seen assembling, apparently for another heavy attack. But the Brigade had orders merely to hold on, as the 17th French Division and two divisions of French cavalry were going to attack at noon in the direction of Roulers, through the 2nd Division.

During the afternoon the 2nd Coldstream lost their second-in-command, Major R. A. Markham, who was hit in the head by a stray bullet and died two days later.

The 1st Irish Guards, on the left of the 22nd Infantry Brigade, at the railway crossing on the Zonnebeke–Ypres road were subjected not only to shell-fire but to constant machine-gun fire almost the whole day. The battalion attempted an outflanking movement which was partially successful, but later the enemy counter-attacked and the ground won was lost again.

French troops passed through the battalion at 5 p.m. and retook Zonnebeke.

The heaviest attack on the 23rd fell on the 5th Infantry Brigade. During the day the trenches were held only under heavy shelling, which at one period blew in a portion occupied by the Oxford and Bucks. At 5.30 p.m., as on the previous evening, the enemy's infantry advanced in dense masses : they came on singing and shouting. They reached a point only twenty-five yards from the Oxfords' trenches, but here the accurate rifle-fire was too much for them, and they were hastily drawn back, leaving the ground littered with killed and wounded men. They retired to a hedge about 150 yards off, but did not advance again. The attack was supported by shell and rifle fire on other portions of the trenches held by the Oxfords, whose casualties were almost all in that part of the line not directly attacked.

Similarly the Worcesters, Highland Light Infantry, and Connaughts were shelled and had casualties. The former battalion seems to have suffered more severely than any other of the 5th Brigade, the casualties being 6 officers wounded, and 48 other ranks killed, wounded, and missing. The Highland Light Infantry lost 22 other ranks and the Connaughts 24 other ranks killed, wounded, and missing.

The Divisional Artillery from the 20th to the 23rd did excellent work. On the latter date it was particularly effective. " Our artillery did wonderful shooting to-day. A German line was advancing over a bare field in single rank in close order ; they plastered the line with a bunch of shrapnel. A few bolted back, but the majority were killed and wounded. A platoon dug in just in front of our observation post had about twenty howitzer shells up and down the line ; in places the hedges behind which the trenches were dug were stripped clean of leaves and twigs. When the shelling was over I went down, expecting to find any amount of casualties. Not one man had been hit ; one was buried but uninjured, and they dug him out, but never recovered his equipment. Deep and narrow rifle-pits afford the most wonderful protection." [1]

At 7.10 on the night of the 23rd October, orders were received for the relief of the 2nd Division by the 17th French Division.

" Second Division troops will be relieved by French 17th Division commencing from the right of 4th Brigade,[2] so that relief is completed by 11 p.m. The 114th French Regiment will take over from the right of 4th Brigade. On its left will be 90th, 68th, and 125th in the order named." [3]

On relief the troops of the 2nd Division were ordered to billet in the following areas :

6th Infantry Brigade : Headquarters and 1st King's in St. Jean ; 1st King's Royal Rifles and South Staffords, Pilkem ; 1st Berks, just north of the main road at Frezenberg. The latter battalion was ordered to act as escort to the XXXIVth and XLIVth Brigades R.F.A.

5th Infantry Brigade : in bivouacs about Halte, two kilometres on Ypres–Menin road ; Headquarters at Halte station.

[1] War Diary.
[2] 22nd Infantry Brigade at the railway crossing on the Zonnebeke–Ypres road.
[3] French battalions.

4th (Guards) Brigade and 11th Field Company R.E., Zillebeke.
Divisional Mounted Troops, Verbranden-Molen.

The 4th and 5th Infantry Brigades, on being·relieved by 17th French Division, were each to send a battalion as escort to the guns left in the areas vacated by them.

Brigade Ammunition Columns and Divisional Ammunition Column, Field Ambulances, and the Divisional Train were to remain in their former positions.

Divisional Headquarters still in Ypres.

In order to support the French attack, the howitzer batteries of the 2nd Division were to remain in position until 12 o'clock noon on 24th; they were then to be withdrawn.

From 20th to 23rd October the Allied line from Zandvoorde (the right of the 7th Division) to the Belgian coast town of Nieuport had been in the greatest danger. At times the position was critical. The necessity of detaching portions of the Ist Corps to lend assistance to the sorely tried 7th Division had robbed Sir Douglas Haig of the advantage he had gained at the outset of his advance from Ypres, and he had been forced to abandon his offensive action against the enemy and act on the defensive. The enemy also was compelled to abandon his attempt to turn the left flank of the Allies, though for this purpose he had brought up the newly formed Fourth German Army. The failure of the latter to break through the Allied front was frankly admitted in a book issued by the German General Staff on the Ypres operations of 1914: " With the failure of the 46th Reserve Division [1] to gain a decisive victory between Bixschoote and Langemarck on 22nd and 23rd October the fate of the XXVIth and XXVIIth [2] Reserve Corps was also settled. For the time being any further thought of a break through was out of the question. The troops up till now had met the enemy full of a keen fighting spirit, and had stormed his position singing 'Deutschland, Deutschland über Alles' regardless of casualties, and had been one and all ready to die for their country; but they had suffered heavily in the contest against a war-experienced and numerically superior opponent [3] entrenched in strongly fortified positions."

[1] XXIIIrd Reserve Corps operating against the Belgians and French.
[2] Operating against the Ist and IVth Corps.
[3] A typically German excuse for failure, for both in men and guns the enemy outnumbered the Allies. The "numerically superior forces " were non-existent. The Belgian, French, and British forces in the Ypres area had all been much weakened by constant fighting, whereas the Fourth German Army was a new formation. The "strongly fortified positions " were likewise a fable. They really consisted of makeshift trenches dug in soft soil which often crumbled away under shell-fire and were unprotected by barbed wire or any other obstacle.

With the arrival of the Ninth French Army on 23rd October, the Ypres operations entered on a new phase.

At 6.30 a.m. on the 24th October the General Officer Commanding 2nd Division visited the General Officer Commanding 7th Division at the Headquarters of the latter situated five kilometres east of Ypres on the Ypres–Menin road : the General Officer Commanding IVth Corps was also present. During the conference orders were received from Sir Douglas Haig that the 2nd Division was to relieve the 21st and 22nd Infantry Brigades of the 7th Division on the line Poezelhoek (exclusive)–Zonnebeke (exclusive). The relief of the 7th Division was to begin at 11 a.m. The General Officers Commanding 4th, 5th, and 6th Infantry Brigades were warned, and at 9.30 the three brigades moved off to carry out the reliefs. The 5th Infantry Brigade was ordered to Westhoek to gain touch with the 21st Infantry Brigade ; the 6th Infantry Brigade to advance by Frezenberg and gain touch with the 22nd Infantry Brigade south of Zonnebeke ; the 4th (Guards) Brigade and other troops in the same area to Westhoek and remain there in Divisional Reserve. And at 12.30 the 2nd Division was ordered to attack through the 21st and 22nd Infantry Brigades.

At 9.20 the 5th Brigade had moved forward towards the southern corner of the Polygone Wood in the following formation : 2nd Worcesters on the left, 2nd Highland Light Infantry on the right ; the Oxford and Bucks and Connaughts were in reserve.

Owing to the wood being somewhat wedge-shaped the right of the Worcesters and the left of the Highland Light Infantry overlapped, and in consequence the latter battalion followed in echelon. A stiff fight ensued, but the enemy, who on the night 23rd–24th had made an attack on the 21st Infantry Brigade with overwhelming numbers[1] and had succeeded in gaining a portion of the latter's trenches, was driven out of the wood at the point of the bayonet. Here the Worcesters joined up with the right of the Scots Guards (1st Brigade, 1st Division). The Worcesters, upon whom the brunt of the fighting fell, lost heavily in officers and men. Major Sweetman and Lieuts. Gilson, Heyman, Pope, and Smythe-Osborne were wounded, and 75 other ranks killed, wounded, and missing : Lieut. C. M. Pope died later of his wounds. The Oxfords and Highland Light Infantry lost only a very few men. The Connaughts had been ordered to the ninth kilometre stone on the Ypres–Menin road, to fill a gap in the line of the 7th Division

---

[1] The 21st Brigade had been opposed by the 53rd Reserve Division (Fourth German Army).

which had been broken by the enemy ; their casualties were 37 other ranks killed, wounded, and missing.

At nightfall the 5th Infantry Brigade entrenched along the eastern edge of the Polygone Wood ; Worcesters on the left, Highland Light Infantry in the centre, and a composite company of Worcesters, Warwicks, and Queen's (the two last named belonging to the 21st Infantry Brigade) on the right. The Brigade was supported during the day by the XXXVIth Brigade R.F.A.

The 6th Infantry Brigade (which consisted only of Brigade Headquarters and 1st King's when it set out from St. Julien) marched *via* Frezenberg, linking up with the 1st Berks in that place. The South Staffords and 1st King's Royal Rifles were still on their way to rejoin the Brigade. The Staffords did not come up until midday, whilst the Rifles did not report till 7 p.m.

The Brigade was ordered to advance and to maintain close touch with the 17th French Division, whose right was on the level crossing west of Zonnebeke whilst supporting the 22nd Infantry Brigade, which at this period held a line running almost north and south between the level crossing west of Zonnebeke and the northeast edge of Polygone Wood. The Brigade's objective was the ground from Noordemhoek to the sixth kilometre stone on the Becelaere–Passchendaele road.

The enemy was already in part possession of Polygone Wood, and in consequence the right flank of the 22nd Infantry Brigade was in considerable danger when the Berks and King's arrived. One company of the King's was pushed along the northern edges of the wood to keep line with the left of the 5th Infantry Brigade, which was then advancing and pressing back the enemy to the eastern exits of the wood.

About 2.30 p.m. the Berks began to take over the trenches occupied by the 22nd Brigade from the level crossing west of Zonnebeke, southwards. At 3.30 p.m. the attack was ordered, and the Berks and King's moved forward, the former keeping touch with the 17th French Division, who were advancing on Zonnebeke.

The Berks had B and D Companies in the firing line, and A and C in reserve ; the King's A, B, and C in the front line, and D in reserve.

Heavy rifle and shell fire met the advance, but the two battalions advanced with great gallantry, only A Company of the King's being held up in front of a number of houses strongly fortified by machine guns. The houses were eventually cleared at the point of the bayonet, and the battalion occupied them, thus obtaining their objectives. The line of the King's was slightly bent back from the fifth kilometre stone, to the left of the 5th Infantry Brigade at the north-east corner of the Polygone Wood. The advance of the 6th Infantry Brigade had not been made without considerable loss. The Berks had 5 officers and 48 other ranks wounded. The King's unfortunately lost their commanding officer, Lieut.-Colonel W. S. Bannatyne, a very gallant leader, killed, two other officers wounded, and 27 other ranks killed, wounded, and missing. Colonel Bannatyne was shot through the heart just about dusk. The South Staffords, who were late in arriving and were moved up in support of the King's, had no casualties.

During the advance of the 6th Infantry Brigade the XXXIVth and XLIVth (Howitzer) Brigades R.F.A. lent great assistance, and effectively covered the Berks and King's as they pressed on.

The 4th (Guards) Brigade did not come into action. The Brigade was held in Divisional Reserve at Westhoek, though earlier in the day the 1st Irish Guards were sent off to assist the 20th Infantry Brigade in the Zandvoorde area. They were, however, not required, and subsequently returned to Westhoek.

The Berks and King's entrenched during the night ; the former had a strange experience in finding that at one point a trench full of the enemy's troops was only six yards distant, though the British and German trenches were separated by a hedge. During the following day the Berks captured this trench, with 1 officer and 70 men ; those of the enemy who tried to escape were shot down.

*   *   *   *   *   *   *

25TH OCT.   During the evening orders were issued to the 2nd Division to continue the attack on the morning of the 25th : " The General Officer Commanding intends to continue the advance to-morrow, keeping touch with the French right—first objective, Becelaere. When that place has been captured the advance will be continued—general direction, centre on Terhand. This attack will be carried out by the 2nd Division. The 1st Division, after being relieved, will remain in corps reserve south of the Ypres–Menin road in the neighbourhood of Zillebeke. The 2nd Division will make an active reconnaissance of the enemy's position, beginning at daylight. The infantry will be in readiness to advance at 11 a.m., but will not actually attack until orders to do so are received from General Officer Commanding Ist Corps."

During the night of the 24th–25th the 1st Division was relieved by French Territorial troops and concentrated about Zillebeke.

The attack was to be made in conjunction with the 17th and 18th French Divisions north of the Berks; but, as the former were not sufficiently advanced at 11 a.m., " Zero " was postponed until the afternoon.   At 1.30 p.m. orders were given to attack at 3 p.m.

The 5th Infantry Brigade in reserve was to hold its present position; the 4th (Guards) Brigade was to advance through the 5th Brigade, having as its objective the Reutel Spur; the 6th Infantry Brigade was to assist the attack of the 4th Brigade by co-operating on the left of the latter, whilst keeping touch with the French, who were advancing from Zonnebeke.   The 7th Division, on the right of the 2nd Division, was to advance in line.

The general advance was to be on Ledeghem, and not on Ter-hand as previously ordered.   On account of shortage of ammunition the preliminary bombardment was mostly confined to the heavy and siege artillery.[1]

At 3 p.m. the attack was launched, the 6th Brigade advancing as the French on its left gained ground towards Passchendaele–Moorslede.   The French passed just south of Zonnebeke and through the left flank of the Berkshires, who succeeded in capturing a gun and a few prisoners.   But the attack was made too late in the day, and further progress was stopped by darkness, the Berks being then several hundred yards east of the Becelaere road ; the King's were, however, unable to move from their trenches, and their advance from the Polygone Wood could not be carried out.

Meanwhile the 4th (Guards) Brigade, advancing through the 5th Brigade, came under a very heavy fire when debouching from the wood towards Reutel, which was strongly held by the enemy posted in force on the high ground north of the village.   At 5 p.m. the Irish Guards on the left, with the 3rd Coldstream in support, had succeeded in getting within 200 yards of the northern exits of the village, but came under rifle-fire from concealed enemy trenches on the right.   The Grenadiers on the right, with the 2nd Coldstream in support, had been held up earlier by a German trench on their left, and touch was therefore lost between the two battalions.   A patrol was sent out by the Irish Guards to

---

[1] The German General Staff in their monograph *Ypres 1914* continually refer to the superiority of the British in personnel and material : " Thanks to his good observation posts, the enemy was able to keep our roads of advance and communication under artillery fire.   As the roads were already broken up by the constant rain, the ammunition supply of our artillery, *inferior in any case to our opponents, failed.*"   At this period every round of artillery ammunition had to be counted, and Sir John French's infantry were often held up because artillery support was impossible owing to shortage of ammunition.

find the Grenadiers, but only the German trenches between the two battalions could be found. Darkness was almost complete, and the thick wood added to the difficulty. The Commanding Officer and the adjutant of the Irish Guards went back to Brigade Headquarters and explained the situation, but were ordered to hold on to their position at all costs. The battalion was finally disposed in a " P " position, with a double row of men back to back extending from the tail of the " P " back to the trenches of the Worcesters in the wood. In this position the night was passed, heavy rain and the activities of snipers causing considerable discomfort.

The gap between the left of the Irish Guards and the King's was filled during the early hours of the morning by two companies of the 1st King's Royal Rifles, with the remaining companies in reserve.

Captain O. Steele of the Berks, and Captain J. H. S. Batten and Lieut. H. B. Wallace of the King's, were killed during the fighting on the 25th.

At 4 a.m. on the 26th the Commanding Officer of the Irish Guards received a message to report at Brigade Headquarters, and later returned with information that the 2nd Coldstream were coming up on the right of his battalion, and that the 6th Infantry Brigade would attack on the left. The 2nd Coldstream arrived at 5.30 a.m. " As soon as touch with the right of the Irish Guards had been obtained, the battalion (2nd Coldstream) swung back its right on a line running south south-west through the woods, till it finally linked up with the left of the Grenadiers; though in order to effect this, the point of junction with the Irish Guards had to form almost a right angle, which exposed our left companies to serious enfilade fire from the German trenches opposite the Irishmen on the eastern edges of the wood. This line was immediately entrenched under heavy rifle-fire from the enemy in the wood about 200 to 300 yards to our front, as well as from the trenches already mentioned, clear of the wood on our left flank. But although digging had in consequence to be done as best we could, lying down, by evening we were well dug in, with a line of fairly deep if not very elaborate trenches." At 10 p.m. the enemy counter-attacked, but was easily repulsed.

The Irish Guards lost heavily during the day. Lieut. H. J. S. Shields, R.A.M.C., attached to the battalion, was killed as he was attending to some wounded men near a farmhouse in the firing line; other ranks casualties numbered 51 killed and wounded.

The pressure on the 4th (Guards) Brigade was somewhat relieved by the 6th Infantry Brigade, which had received orders at 9.15 a.m. to push forward where possible towards Point 27 (Keiberg). The 5th Brigade was also ordered to advance towards the fifth kilometre stone on the Becelaere–Passchendaele road and join in the attack.

Under a heavy shell-fire, which extended all along the ridge and line of the Becelaere road, the South Staffords moved forward at 11.30 a.m. through the lines of the Berks, who were withdrawn into reserve. The battalion made steady progress, though suffering severe casualties, and by 4.30 p.m. had reached the edges of the wood just east of the fifth kilometre stone. Here, in the woods, the battalion came on to a wide ride at the farther end of which were some 200 to 300 German infantry. These pretended to surrender by waving white flags; but when a party of the Staffords went forward to take them, they threw down their flags and opened fire with rifles and machine guns. The Staffords then proceeded to dig themselves in on the gound won.

Meanwhile, at 7.15 a.m. a French battalion, which had been sent on the previous night to fill a gap between the Berks and King's, moved north towards the crossroads at Broodseinde.

At 3.30 a.m. the King's received orders to attack Noordemhoek village, which had not been cleared of the enemy, and the trenches on the Becelaere Ridge. The attack was to begin at 5.30 a.m. Two companies of the 1st King's Royal Rifles were placed under the command of the Officer Commanding 1st King's, and were to advance on the right of the battalion and join up with the left of the 4th (Guards) Brigade in Polygone Wood.

As soon as the advance began, the King's came under heavy fire; D Company rushed forward and gradually cleared the village, working through as far as the exits on the Becelaere road, within 300 yards of the enemy's trenches. C Company (on the right of D) reached the Reutel track. A Company moved along level with C, but B Company was slightly thrown back owing to the Rifles not coming up into line. A little later, however, B Company charged the enemy's trenches and occupied them. The battalion was then ordered to dig in on the ground won.

A feature of the King's attack was the valuable assistance given by the 11th Field Company R.E. No. 1 Section advanced with D Company of the King's in an assault on some houses supposed to contain enemy machine guns. Four houses were taken by the sappers. A little later No. 2 Section advanced to the support of No. 1. The sappers held on to the houses all day, though losing heavily, and at night were relieved by the South Staffords and King's. Major P. T. Denis de Vitre of the 11th Field Company was wounded in both legs during the attack, and 12 N.C.O's and men were killed and wounded. On relief, the sappers dug and strengthened trenches.

The King's Royal Rifles had, as ordered, started off to fill the gap between the King's and Irish Guards at 5.20, but in the dim morning light could not see very far ahead. D Company moved forward followed by C, and A and B were for the time being in support. As soon as D Company had crossed the wood and had emerged 100 yards beyond, a heavy enfilade fire from rifles and machine guns was opened from the hostile trenches, and the Rifles were brought to a standstill. The left of the company succeeded in getting into some old French trenches in a turnip field; but the right was unable to move, and had to dig themselves in as best they could, lying amongst the turnips. During the morning it was discovered that a considerable gap still existed between C Company and the left of the Irish Guards. C Company was therefore sent forward to fill it. A and B Companies remained in support all day, for, although later in the afternoon orders were received to support the left of the brigade, the two companies did not come into action.

The Rifles maintained their positions during the night.

Both the King's and the Rifles suffered heavily. Two companies of the former battalion lost all their officers, but the vigour of the attack was not suspended: " This was due to the splendid work of the N.C.O's who were left, the two companies in question being re-formed and kept going, although under a very heavy rifle and artillery fire from the enemy." Of the King's, Lieuts. P. T. Ferneaux and E. B. Baker were killed, 5 other officers wounded, and 54 other ranks killed and wounded. The King's Royal Rifles lost 1 officer (Second-Lieut. G. Cronk, 3rd Buffs, attached) and 12 other ranks killed, and 2 officers and 32 other ranks wounded. The South Staffords' losses were 4 other ranks killed and 1 officer and 22 wounded; the Berks had 17 other ranks killed and wounded.

During the night of the 26th–27th the Irish Guards took over the trenches dug by the Rifles, who were relieved.

From prisoners taken on the 26th and other official German sources information was obtained that the line Becelaere–Broodseinde was held by the whole of the 53rd Reserve Division of the XXVIIth Reserve Corps. The British troops were therefore outnumbered.

On the 26th the 1st Division came up into line, and took over the front from Poezelhoek to Zandvoorde from the 7th Division.

At 6.30 a.m. on 27th October orders were again issued to the 4th, 5th, and 6th Infantry Brigades to be in readiness to take the offensive. The 6th Brigade was directed towards Keibergmolen Spur ; the 5th Infantry Brigade was ordered to be in readiness to support the 6th.

The attack of the 6th Brigade progressed well. This brigade had fought with great gallantry during the very strenuous period which followed its arrival between the Polygone Wood and Zonnebeke on the 24th.[1]

At 7.15 a.m. the South Staffords, pressing on with the King's Royal Rifles on their left, occupied without opposition the German trenches from which the white flag had been treacherously shown on the previous afternoon.

At 7.50 a.m. the 36th French Brigade (on the left of the 6th Infantry Brigade) attacked eastwards up the Moorslede road, this attack being the signal for the advance of the 2nd Division. But unfortunately the 135th French Regiment was checked in its advance, and at 12.45 the Staffords, reaching the eastern edge of the wood, reported the high ground about Keiberg strongly held and entrenched, and they could get no farther. Two companies of the Berks were filling the gap between the King's and Staffords, the King's having been ordered to remain stationary, as their front was too strongly held and they could not advance without incurring heavy casualties. Meanwhile A Company of the King's Royal Rifles had pushed on north of the Staffords, though losing heavily, with D Company in support and the remaining companies in reserve. As A Company advanced, the distance between

---

[1] The operations of the 2nd Division and the IXth French Corps on the left of the 2nd Division during the 25th, 26th, and 27th are especially commendable. The German General Staff in their monograph, *Ypres 1914*, admit forces which show considerable superiority : " The fighting was especially severe on the front of the XXVIth and XXVIIth Reserve Corps on 25th, 26th, and 27th October. In this section the British and French troops made a series of attacks in the direction of Poelcappelle–Passchendaele and east of Zonnebeke. The 37th Landwehr Brigade and the 2nd Ersatz Brigade had to be sent up to the fighting line, in addition to detachments of the Marine Division and of the 38th Landwehr Brigade." The 37th Landwehr Brigade was on the 26th in the Broodseinde area, and the 38th Landwehr Brigade at Becelaere. Both the 53rd and 54th Reserve Divisions (the complete XXVIIth Reserve Corps) were on 27th October east of Molenaarelsthoek—*i.e.*, operating against the thinly held line of the 2nd Division.

the right of the French and left of the Staffords was so great that B Company was ordered up to extend the line ; later C and D were absorbed into the line. The battalion at this period had reached a road which runs north and south 1,400 yards due west of Keiberg, but here a terrific shell and rifle fire played havoc with the Riflemen. Lieut. H. H. Prince Maurice of Battenberg and Captain W. N. Wells (attached) were killed outright and 4 other officers wounded, and 147 other ranks killed, wounded, and missing. Further advance being impossible, the battalion made good the position, though under shell-fire for the remainder of the day.

The South Staffords in their advance lost 2 officers (Lieuts. F. E. Robinson and D. T. F. Fitzpatrick) killed, 3 officers wounded, and 115 other ranks killed, wounded, and missing. The casualties of the 1st King's were 38 other ranks killed and wounded ; and the 1st Berks, 1 officer and 13 other ranks wounded.

The 5th Infantry Brigade was at 3.30 p.m. at the fifth kilometre stone on the Becelaere–Broodseinde road in readiness, three-quarters of a mile in the rear of the 6th Infantry Brigade ; but owing to the lateness of the hour and strength of the enemy an attack in force was postponed until the following day, and at dusk the Brigade, less the Connaughts who remained at Molenaarelsthoek at the disposal of the 6th Brigade, returned to bivouacs.

The 4th (Guards) Brigade had a quiet day and maintained their original position in front of the Becelaere plateau. The Irish Guards were relieved in the trenches by the 3rd Coldstream. Major Stepney of the former battalion was wounded during the evening of the 27th.

During the day, about 1.30 p.m., the Commander-in-Chief visited Headquarters of the Ist Corps and personally investigated the condition of the 7th Division. " Owing to constant marching and fighting this Division had suffered great losses and was in fact very weak." Sir John French therefore decided temporarily to break up the IVth Corps and place the 7th Division with the Ist Corps under Sir Douglas Haig. The 3rd Cavalry Division was also detailed for duty with the Ist Corps.

Sir Douglas Haig then disposed the line held by the Ist Corps thus :

7th Division from château east of Zandvoorde to the Menin–Ypres road ;

1st Division from the Menin–Ypres road to a point immediately west of Reutel village ;

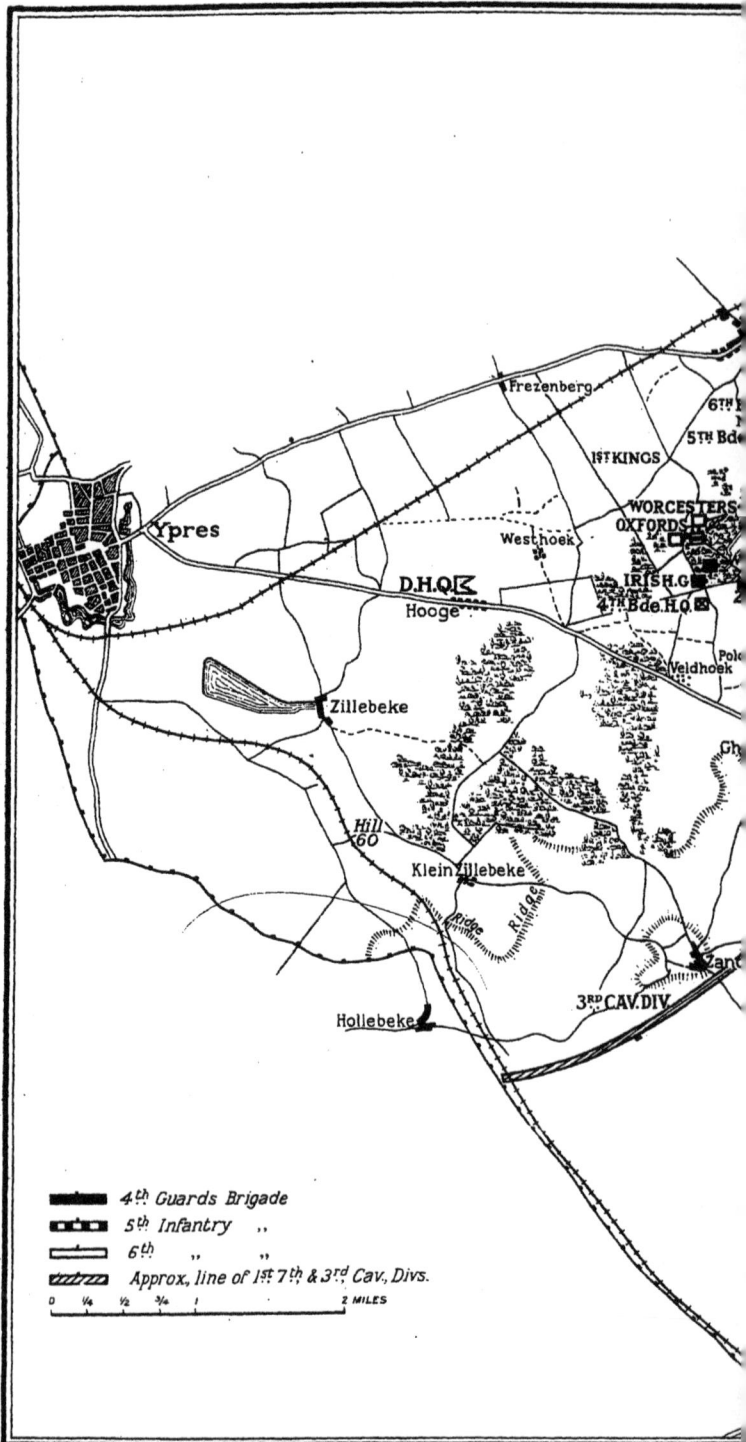

Frezenberg

6ᵀᴴ
5ᵀᴴ Bde

1ˢᵀ KINGS

WORCESTERS
OXFORDS

Westhoek

IRISH G.
Bde. H.Q.

DHQ

Hooge

Poe

Veldhoek

Ypres

Zillebeke

Ch

Hill
60

Klein Zillebeke

Ridge

Ridge

Zant

Hollebeke

3ᴿᴰ CAV. DIV.

▬▬▬ 4ᵗʰ Guards Brigade
▭▭▭ 5ᵗʰ Infantry ,,
▭▭▭ 6ᵗʰ ,, ,,
▨▨▨ Approx. line of 1ˢᵗ 7ᵗʰ & 3ʳᵈ Cav., Divs.

0   ¼   ½   ¾   1   2 MILES

THE BATTLE OF GH
I. Position

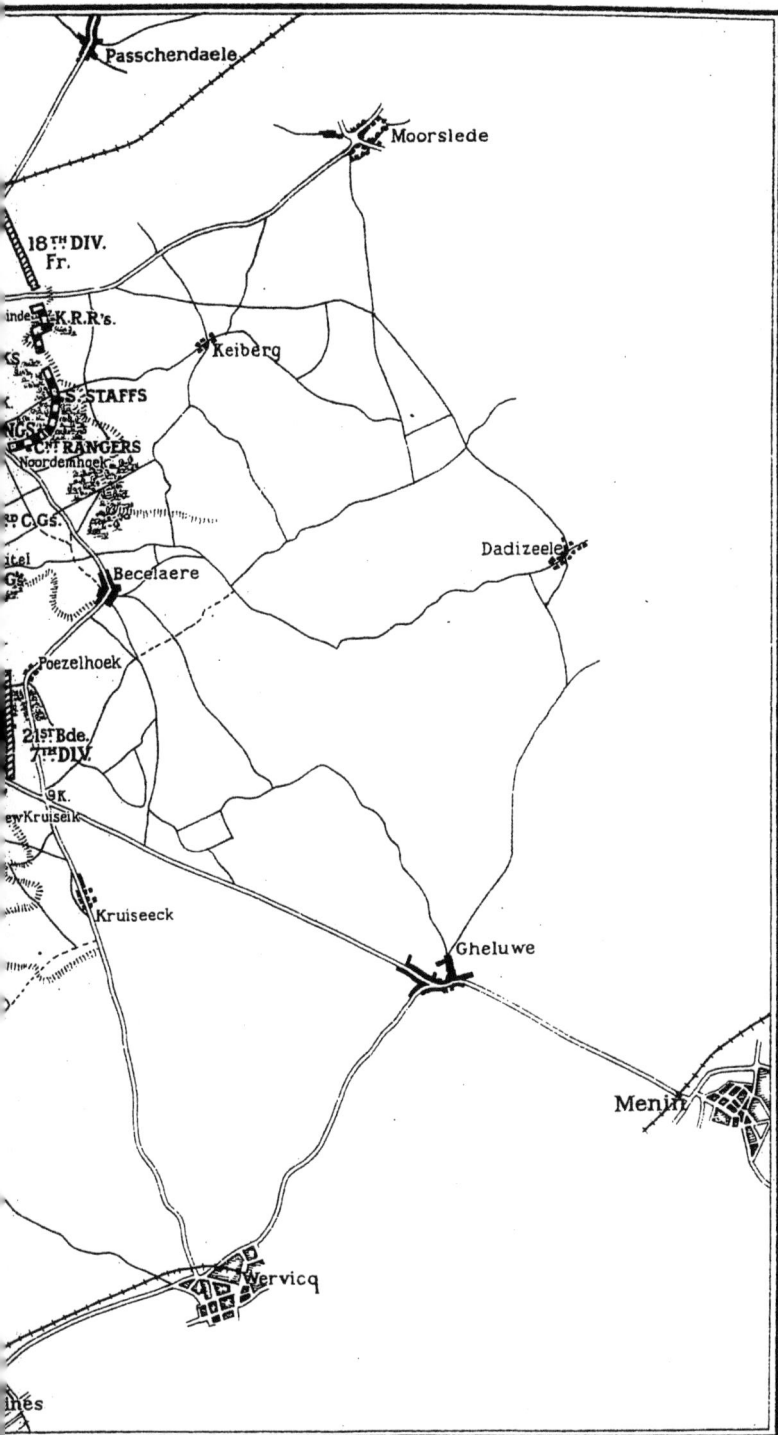

.T, 29th–31st October 1914.
29th October.

(Facing p. 130.)

2nd Division from west of Reutel village to near the Moor-slede–Zonnebeke road.

During the night of the 27th–28th the enemy attacked all along the line, but was everywhere repulsed.

On the 28th the 5th and 6th Infantry Brigades were ordered to attack at 9.30 a.m., the 4th (Guards) Brigade being warned to give support on receipt of orders. But although the 6th Brigade began an advance, it was held up almost immediately by shell-fire. The 5th Brigade for the same reason found advance impossible. Another attempt was made later, and by 5 p.m. the South Staffords and King's Royal Rifles (6th Brigade) had gained a little ground towards the east, whilst the Connaught Rangers (5th Brigade) had made good the edge of the wood facing the northern slopes of the Becelaere plateau.

At 9.30 p.m. General Headquarters having received information that the enemy (XXVIIth Reserve Corps) intended making a heavy attack on Gheluvelt and Kruiseecke at 5.30 a.m. on the following morning, the 5th and 6th Infantry Brigades were instructed to press their attacks in order to pin the enemy to his ground and prevent any advance between Poezelhoek and Moorslede.[1]

From the 25th to the 28th, north of the Menin–Ypres road on the front held by the 7th Division, the fighting had been of a very severe nature. On the night of 27th–28th the enemy penetrated Kruiseecke, but the village was recaptured by one company of the 2nd Scots Guards, who took over 200 prisoners of the 242nd Reserve Infantry Regiment (XXVIIth Reserve Corps). On the next day, however (28th), the enemy again counter-attacked with the whole of the 53rd Reserve Division, and succeeded in dislodging the 20th Infantry Brigade, which immediately formed a new line behind the village, and with the aid of the 1st Division maintained its position.

THE BATTLE OF GHELUVELT.

About 8 on the morning of the 29th 2nd Division Head-quarters received a report from the 1st Division that enemy troops were massing near the crossroads south-east of Gheluvelt—*i.e.*, opposite the line of junction of the 1st and 7th Divisions. Under

29TH–31ST
OCT.
MAP.

---

[1] During the 28th the 6th Bavarian Reserve Division had arrived at Dadizeele as Army Reserve.

cover of an early morning mist, the enemy, whose strength was estimated at an army corps, attacked the crossroads where the right of the 1st Division joined up with the left of the 7th Division, and broke through, rolling up the inner flanks of the two divisions. The resistance of the troops in the front line had, however, delayed the enemy in his advance, and during this delay the divisional reserves were able to come up and close the gap. The enemy occupied a short line of advanced trenches in front of the crossroads, but could get no farther.

Meanwhile further reports had reached the 2nd Division Headquarters that the enemy was also massing in the château grounds west of Poezelhoek. The Brigade Reserve of the 4th (Guards) Brigade was moved off hurriedly to the southern exits of the Polygone Wood.

A Divisional Reserve, under Brigadier-General the Earl of Cavan, was then formed of the Oxford and Bucks and the Worcesters from the 5th Infantry Brigade, and 2nd Grenadiers and Irish Guards from the 4th (Guards) Brigade. The troops of the 6th Infantry Brigade and the two remaining battalions (Connaughts and 2nd Highland Light Infantry) of the 5th Infantry Brigade already deployed, were placed under the command of Brigadier-General Fanshawe (General Officer Commanding 6th Infantry Brigade), who was ordered to maintain his position at all costs. The 2nd and 3rd Coldstream Guards, who were holding the eastern edges of the Polygone Wood facing the Reutel Spur, were placed under the command of Colonel Pereira (2nd Coldstream), who was similarly ordered to maintain his position.

At 1.10 p.m. the Earl of Cavan was ordered to send the 1st Irish Guards to assist the 1st Brigade (1st Division) in driving the enemy from the woods north-west of Poezelhoek.

The 1st King's were then placed in Divisional Reserve.

The attacks of the 1st and 3rd Brigades, assisted by the Irish Guards, were successful, the enemy being driven eastwards, and nearly all the trenches occupied by him in the early morning were recaptured.[1]

The 6th Infantry Brigade and the Connaughts and Highland Light Infantry of the 5th Brigade held to their trenches all day, and by keeping up a continuous fire upon the enemy pinned him to his position and prevented any movement of his troops either

---

[1] The distribution of the 2nd Division on the afternoon of the 29th is as shown on the sketch map, but the positions of the 1st and 7th Divisional troops are approximate only.

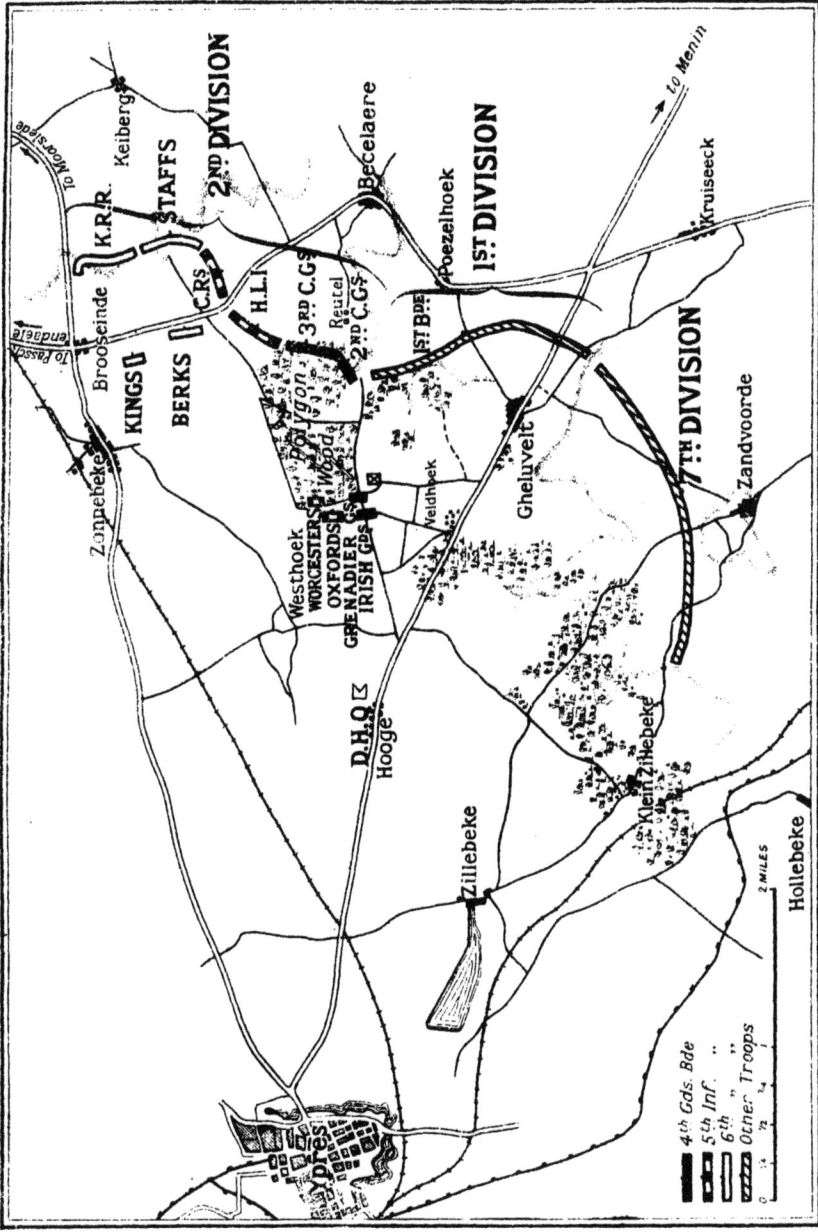

THE MAPPA CO. LTD. LONDON.

(Facing p. 132.)

THE BATTLE OF GHELUVELT, 29th–31st October, 1914.

II. Position at 4 p.m., 30th October.

To Menin

1ST DIVISION

2ND DIVISION

7TH DIVISION

Keiberg

K.R.R.

STAFFS

Becelaere

Poezelhoek

Kruiseeck

C.R.s

H.L.I

3RD C.GS

Reutel

2ND C.GS

1ST BDE

Broodseinde

To Pass—

To Moor—slede

Zonnebeke

KINGS

BERKS

Polygon
Wood

Gheluvelt

Zandvoorde

Westhoek

WORCESTERS

OXFORDS

GRENADIER

IRISH GDS

Veldhoek

D.H.Q.

Hooge

Klein Zillebeke

Zillebeke

Hollebeke

YPRES

4th Gds. Bde
5th Inf. "
6th " "
Other Troops

2 MILES
0 ¼ ½ ¾ 1

in a forward direction, or as reinforcements to his attack on Gheluvelt farther south. The 2nd and 3rd Coldstream of the 4th Brigade likewise held their trenches, though under heavy artillery fire and the annoying activities of enemy snipers.

Throughout the 29th the position of the 2nd Division was practically unchanged, but the 1st and 7th Divisions had undergone attacks of extreme violence, the enemy greatly outnumbering the troops of the two divisions. Moreover, his artillery was vastly superior, even though the guns of the 2nd Division were turned southwards in order to assist the two sorely tried divisions whose troops held the right and centre of the Ist Corps line. Nor is it to be wondered at that ground was given : for three months these British troops had fought hard, and their ranks had been much depleted in officers and men, whereas the enemy opposed fresh troops and always superior numbers. On one occasion the enemy outnumbered the British by eight to one. Yet to their eternal glory the latter held the trenches, dying where they stood rather than surrender. In all the military history of the nation there is nothing more grand or noble than the stand of the British soldier during the Battles of Ypres, 1914.

During the night of the 29th–30th close touch was maintained on the Divisional front by means of active reconnaissances ; under cover of darkness the troops improved their positions by erecting barbed wire, placing machine guns in houses, and digging trenches, and in the latter operation the Royal Engineers did splendid work.

On the morning of the 30th, about 6 o'clock, the enemy opened a violent artillery and rifle fire against the trenches of the 6th Infantry Brigade. Half an hour later he launched a strong attack against the South Staffords and King's Royal Rifles and against the French troops whose right joined up with the Rifles. On the right of the Staffords the enemy came right up to the barbed wire, a German officer being killed whilst actually engaged in cutting the wire. The attack was beaten off, but D Company of the Rifles lost heavily ; 1 officer (Lieut. J. Casey) was killed, another officer wounded, and 14 other ranks were killed and wounded. The only reinforcements needed by the Staffords and Rifles were a single platoon of the Berks.

At 11.20 a.m. the enemy again attacked, but was stopped by wire entanglements and driven off.

About midday Brigadier-General Fanshawe took over command of the 5th Brigade section of the line (Connaughts and Highland Light Infantry), as the enemy again showed signs of launching an attack. The attack, however, did not develop, but the Connaughts had many casualties from shell-fire, 1 officer being wounded and 63 other ranks killed, wounded, and missing. One company of the Berks was sent to reinforce the Connaughts, and did excellent work clearing the enemy out of several houses on the Becelaere road, and establishing an advanced post in one of them.

At 1.30 p.m. orders were received from Ist Corps Headquarters that three battalions of the Divisional Reserve under Lord Cavan were to move immediately towards Klein Zillebeke to a position of readiness one mile south of Hooge. The 2nd Grenadiers, 1st Irish Guards, and the Oxford and Bucks were dispatched and reached the position about 3.15 p.m. The 1st King's moved down to the southern face of the Polygone Wood, linking up with the 2nd Coldstream ; the Worcesters remained in their old position in the north-west corner of the wood. The King's now came under the orders of Colonel Pereira, who commanded the southern and eastern exits of the Polygone. The 2nd and 3rd Coldstream were shelled throughout the day and suffered casualties, Lieut. Nigel Legge-Bourke of the former battalion being killed.

The King's and the King's Royal Rifles were congratulated by the brigadier on their good work in holding their positions under exceptionally trying circumstances. The fire of the XXXIVth and XLIVth Brigades R.F.A. was exceptionally effective, the gunners lending splendid support to the infantry in the front-line trenches. The former brigade fired over 1,000 rounds, with excellent results.

At this period the rain and mud began seriously to affect the arms of the troops. The rifles, almost choked with mud, would not properly eject the cartridge cases. Rifle oil was unobtainable, and it was practically impossible to keep the weapons clean.

From and including the morning of the 29th the attacks of the enemy had been pressed with greater vigour. The German Kaiser had come into the Ypres area and had told his troops that Ypres must be taken at all costs. South of the 2nd Division the 1st and 7th Divisions had not only been violently attacked but pressed back, though fighting valiantly against superior numbers. Nor did the attacks show signs of diminishing. Late on the night of the 30th the forward battalions of the 2nd Division were warned to hold on to their positions during the coming day no matter how severe their losses. No reinforcements could be sent up, as all the reserve troops of the Division would most probably be required to help the 1st and 7th Divisions, who were being (and most certainly would be) attacked in great strength during the next few days.

When, therefore, the morning of the 31st October broke, there were numerous signs of a further imminent and terrible struggle. The enemy not only held all his trenches fully, but was collecting in strength along the various positions of the Ist Corps. Opposite the 6th Infantry Brigade and south-east of Gheluvelt he was massing troops preparatory to launching an attack. Saving the attack by the Prussian Guard on 11th November this attack was destined to be the most violent of all his efforts to break through to Ypres, and although most of the fighting took place between Poezelhoek and Messines (the shortest way to Ypres from the south-east), there can be no doubt that the 2nd Division, by its tenacious hold of the north-east corner of the salient, saved the whole line of the Ist Corps from crumpling up.

Mainly owing to the devotion of the artillery the 6th Infantry Brigade was not attacked in force, the enemy having apparently filled his trenches in order to contain his opponents and prevent reinforcements being sent south where the main attack was to fall. If such were his intentions they failed, for during the morning troops were gradually withdrawn and placed in reserve. The Connaughts, however, suffered some casualties. An attack by one and a half platoons of C Company under Captain F. H. Saker, in support of a company of the Berks advancing along the Becelaere road, was heavily counter-attacked, and as a result Captain Saker was killed, 30 men were captured, and 36 N.C.O's and men killed and wounded. The line nevertheless was held intact, though the trenches, owing to hostile artillery fire, were in a terrible condition. Through all, the devoted infantry of the 5th and 6th Infantry Brigades hung on with splendid tenacity.

About 11.30 a.m. the Connaughts asked for reinforcements, but were told none were available. They also reported " a sort of howitzer 300 yards in front of their right which was dropping shells into their trenches." [1]

The 70th Battery (XXXIVth Brigade R.F.A.) man-handled a gun up to near the fifth kilometre stone on the Passchendaele–Becelaere road, and opened fire with high-explosive from behind a hedge. The first shot blew the enemy gun up into the air and killed 15 German infantrymen who were at that moment lining the trench to attack the Connaughts. The enemy's trenches were also bombarded and reduced to silence. An interesting note concerning this incident is contained in the Official Diaries of the 70th Battery : " Twenty-five rounds of high-explosive had been issued

---

[1] This was probably a trench mortar or minenwerfer.

to the battery a few days previously, and this was the first issue to British Field Artillery."

The attacks south of the 2nd Division—*i.e.*, on the front of the 1st and 7th Divisions—are thus described in the official dispatches : " After several attacks and counter-attacks during the course of the morning along the Menin–Ypres road, south-east of Gheluvelt, an attack against that place developed in great force, and the line of the 1st Division was broken. On the south the 7th Division and General Bulfin's detachment, consisting of the 1st Queen's (3rd Brigade), 2nd King's Royal Rifles and 1st Northamptons (2nd Brigade), were being heavily shelled. The retirement of the 1st Division exposed the left of the 7th Division, and owing to this the Royal Scots Fusiliers, who remained in their trenches, were cut off and surrounded. A strong infantry attack was developed against the right of the 7th Division at 1.30 p.m."

At 12.45 General Lomax (1st Division) and General Monro (2nd Division), with their respective staffs, met at the Headquarters of the latter, at Hooge Château. A few minutes later two high-explosive shells struck the building in which the two staffs were assembled : General Lomax was wounded ; Colonel F. W. Kerr, G.S.O.1 1st Division, Lieut.-Colonel A. J. Percéval, G.S.O.2 2nd Division, Major G. Paley, G.S.O. 1st Division, Captain R. Ommaney, G.S.O.3 2nd Division, Captain F. M. Chenevix Trench, Brigade-Major R.A., 2nd Division, were killed ; and Lieut. G. P. Shedden, R.G.A., died later of wounds. Lieut.-Colonel R. H. H. Boys,[1] D.S.O., C.R.E., 2nd Division, Lieut. H. M. Robertson, A.D.C., R.A., 2nd Division, and Major I. W. Forsett, were wounded ; Lieut. R. Giffard, A.D.C. to General Lomax, was also wounded, and died later. General Monro had a most fortunate escape—with Colonel R. Whigham, G.S.O.1 2nd Division, he had just gone into an adjoining room to examine a map when the first shell struck the building ; he was rendered unconscious, but unwounded. There were also casualties amongst the N.C.O's and men attached to the Headquarters Staff of the 2nd Division.

The period between 2 and 3 p.m. on the 31st, when the 1st Division was retiring, was the most critical stage of the Battles of Ypres, 1914. But " the 1st Division rallied," says the dispatch, " on the line of the woods east of the bend of the road, the German advance by the road being checked by enfilade fire from the north. . . . The attack against the right of the 7th Division forced the 22nd

---

[1] Lieut.-Colonel H. P. Scholfield, C.M.G., R.E., succeeded Colonel Boys as C.R.E., 2nd Division.

Brigade to retire, thus exposing the left of the 2nd Brigade.   The General Officer Commanding 7th Division used his reserves already posted on his flank to restore the line ; but in the meantime the 2nd Brigade, finding the left flank exposed, had been forced to withdraw.   The right of the 7th Division thus advanced as the left of the 2nd Brigade went back, with the result that the right of the 7th Division was exposed, but managed to hold on to its trenches till nightfall."

In the meantime the enemy on the Menin road had captured Gheluvelt.   But not for the present was the possession of the village to be of much use to him.   For a counter-attack was organized, in which the 2nd Worcester Regiment of the 2nd Division, splendidly supported by the XLIst Brigade R.F.A., advanced, and with the bayonet drove the enemy back and denied him the value of his position.

Gheluvelt was the key of the Ist Corps line.   Its long, straight road led westwards to Ypres—the goal of the German armies in Flanders.   The possession of Gheluvelt and the road to Ypres was essential to the plans of the enemy, and to get them he had launched against two battalions of the 3rd Infantry Brigade, with details from other battalions of the 2nd Brigade (about 2,000 troops in all, which held the village on the morning of 31st October), a force approximating four times the strength of that of the defenders.[1]

The Ypres–Menin road was also the junction of the XXVIIth and XVth German Corps, the latter belonging to the newly formed Army Group Fabeck [2] which had been brought up between Gheluvelt and Menin for the attack on Ypres.   The right of the XVth Corps and the left of the XXVIIth Corps joined up on the road just east of Gheluvelt.   That the British troops were able to put up any fight at all in the face of these overwhelming numbers is extremely creditable, and when later the gallant Worcesters charged the enemy north of the village and forced him back, they achieved what must have appeared impossible.   For by midday the Welch Regiment and South Wales Borderers of the Ist Division, who held the northern flank of the village and a line running north, though fighting with extraordinary gallantry, had, owing to the retreat of

---

[1] Two battalions of 105th Infantry Regiment, 1 battalion 143rd Infantry Regiment, a strong mixed detachment from the 54th Reserve Division, mainly belonging to 245th Reserve Regiment and 26th Reserve Jäger Battalion ; the 99th Infantry Regiment—in all about 8 battalions.

[2] This formation consisted of XVth Corps (General von Deimling), IInd Bavarian Corps, and the 26th Würtemberg Infantry Division.   The 6th Bavarian Reserve Division, which had arrived at Dadizeele a few days previously, was also in the line.

the 7th Division on the south, been forced back. Assistance was therefore asked from the 2nd Divisional Reserve, and the Worcesters were dispatched with instructions to restore if possible the line lost by the two battalions. The XLIst Brigade R.F.A. admirably supported this counter-attack.

It was at this period (between 2 and 3 p.m., the official reports state) that the position was most critical : Sir Douglas Haig had decided to withdraw his line, when information was brought to him that the Worcesters had charged and had recaptured the line.

MAP.

On receipt of orders the Worcesters, who had been waiting in reserve in the south-west corner of the Polygone Wood, set off under the command of Major Hankey.[1] One company—A—had already been dispatched earlier in the day to a point north-west of Gheluvelt in order to catch any Germans emerging from the village ; only B, C, and D Companies were therefore available. In a small wood west of Polderhoek Château the Worcesters deployed—D and C in the front line, B in reserve. With irresistible *élan* they charged through the château grounds on the northern outskirts of Gheluvelt and bore down upon the temporarily lost trenches of the South Wales Borderers and Welch Regiment, and with the bayonet cleared the enemy from them, forcing him to evacuate his dearly won position. Command of the village was practically assured the battalion by this success, for the enemy could not advance his troops along the Ypres–Menin road because of the danger to his flanks. So fine was this performance of the Worcesters that the attacks in this part of the line—a point upon which the enemy had concentrated his frantic endeavours to break through to Ypres—wavered, and finally broke down. The effect of this gallant charge was enormous : the 1st Division gradually re-formed and took up the old line again, and the 6th Cavalry Brigade, which had been sent up to help, was relieved for action farther south. By the evening practically the whole of the position lost earlier in the day had been rewon. But during the night it was found that the 1st Division would have to withdraw the right of its line slightly westward in order to connect up with the left of the 7th Division, which had lost ground during the day. The left of the 1st Division at nightfall connected up with the right of the 2nd Division at the south-west corner of the Polygone Wood.

The Worcesters were later relieved and again drawn into Divisional Reserve ; also A and B Companies of the Berks, who

---

1 The order was given by Brigadier-General Fitzclarence, V.C., the troops having been disposed to meet this possible contingency on the 29th.

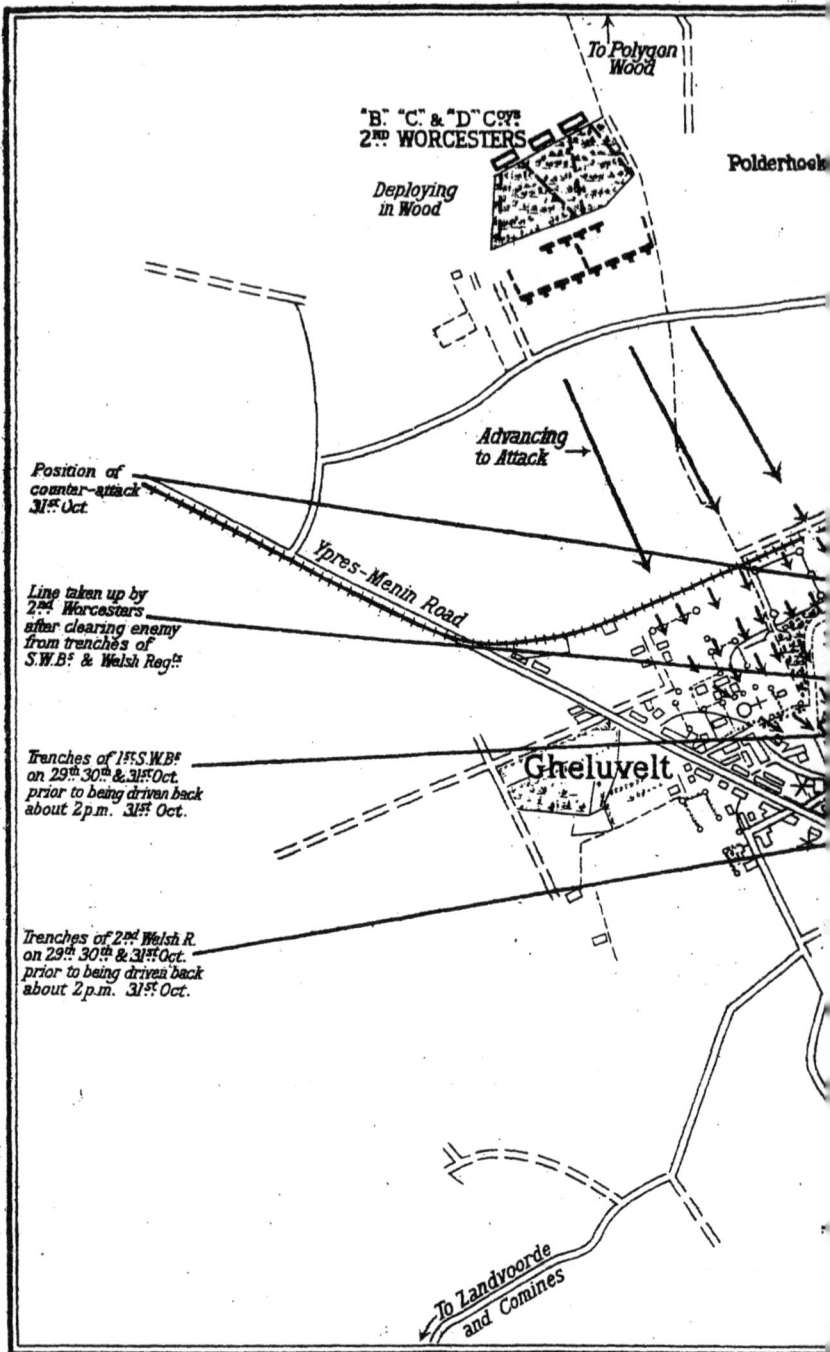

To Polygon Wood

"B." "C." & "D" C⁰ᵧˢ
2ᴺᴰ WORCESTERS

Polderhoek

Deploying
in Wood

Advancing
to Attack →

Position of
counter-attack
31ˢᵗ Oct.

Ypres-Menin Road

Line taken up by
2ⁿᵈ Worcesters
after clearing enemy
from trenches of
S.W.B⁵ & Welsh Reg⁵ᵗˢ

Trenches of 1ˢᵗ S.W.B⁵
on 29ᵗʰ 30ᵗʰ & 31ˢᵗ Oct.
prior to being driven back
about 2 p.m. 31ˢᵗ Oct.

Gheluvelt

Trenches of 2ⁿᵈ Welsh R.
on 29ᵗʰ 30ᵗʰ & 31ˢᵗ Oct.
prior to being driven back
about 2 p.m. 31ˢᵗ Oct.

To Landvoorde
and Comines

THE BATTLE OF GH
III. Charge of the

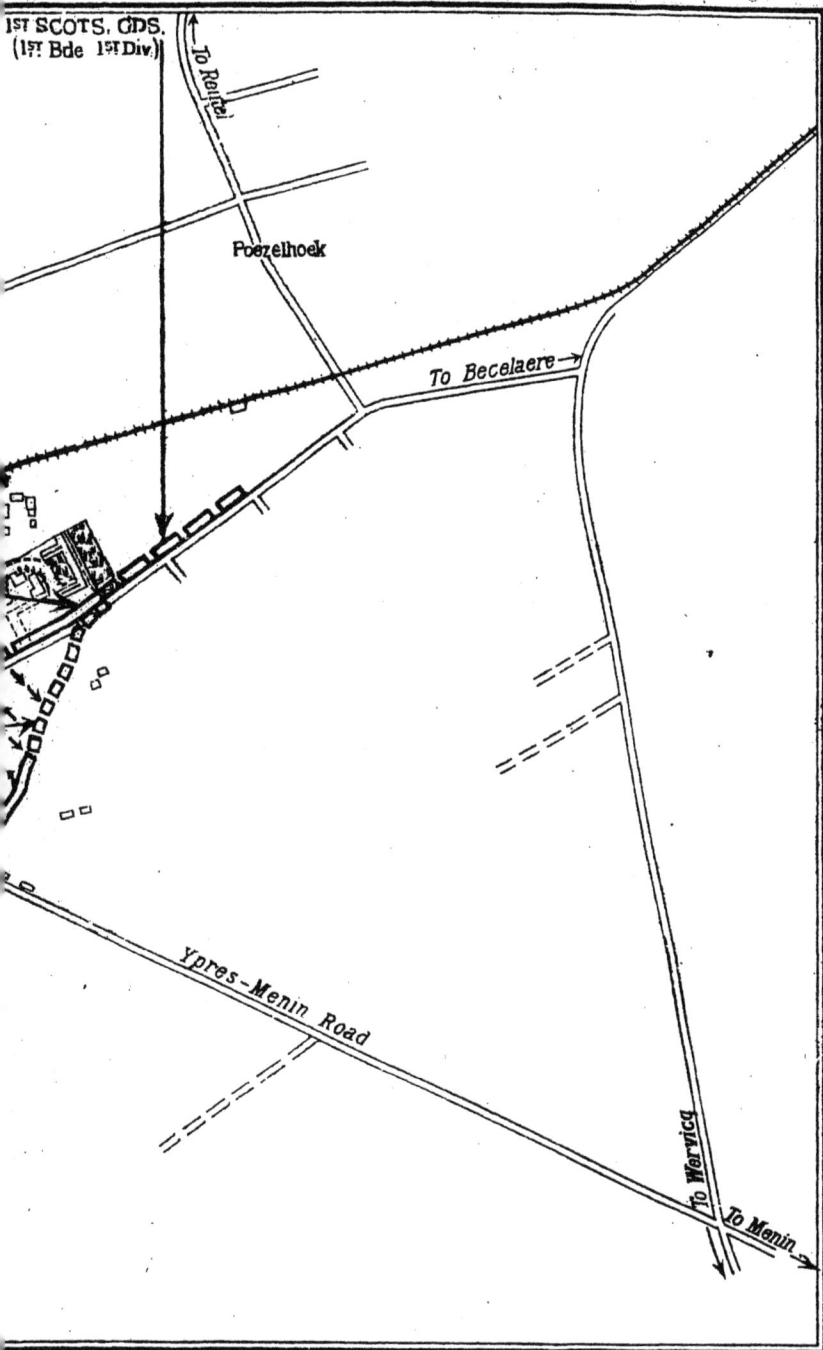

.T, 29th–31st October 1914.
ters on 31st October.

(*Facing p. 138.*)

at 4 p.m. had been hurriedly dispatched to the south-west corner of Gheluvelt, where the enemy had attempted to debouch from the village. The Worcesters' casualties were 3 officers wounded, and 120 other ranks killed, wounded, and missing.

During the night (at 10 o'clock) the 6th French Cavalry Division took over the trenches occupied by the King's Royal Rifles (6th Infantry Brigade), the latter passing into Divisional Reserve near Brigade Headquarters.

Fighting from 1st to 10th November 1914.

In the early days of the Battles of Ypres the Divisional Troops, Royal Engineers, and Royal Artillery " carried on " under extraordinary difficulties. The frequent rains had turned the ground into quagmires; whilst the terrific and constant bombardments to which the enemy subjected the trenches, and even the ground far behind the lines, made the passage of guns, the digging of trenches, and the movement of supply wagons possible only under the most trying conditions.

1ST–10TH Nov.

The artillery often man-handled their guns from place to place, at times moving them up to the front-line trenches through a sea of mud. The XXXIVth Brigade lent splendid support to the 6th Infantry Brigade during the time the latter was advancing north of Becelaere, and later in repelling counter-attacks—the work of the 70th Battery being especially brought to the notice of the General Officer Commanding. The 15th Battery of the XXXVIth Brigade also assisted the 6th Infantry Brigade, and shelled the enemy with excellent effect. The XLIst Brigade and XLIVth (Howitzer) Brigade were also commended for their work. On 26th October Major Newcome of the 47th Battery was wounded whilst observing for the battery. Both in officers, N.C.O's, and men, the "gunners" had many casualties. The fire of the howitzers whilst the infantry were advancing between Reutel and Becelaere was very effective.

The work of the " gunners " was, however, much hampered by the restrictions governing the expenditure of ammunition, which during the early period of the war was quite inadequate to meet the demands of the Army.

In addition to their ordinary functions of digging trenches, making and erecting barbed-wire entanglements, and generally preparing defences, the Royal Engineers often undertook the duties of infantrymen. On more than one occasion they successfully charged the enemy's trenches and fortified houses, and cleared them out with the bayonet. Their work went on day and night unceasingly. The following is an example of the strenuous duties undertaken by the Sappers : " 10 a.m.—No. 4 Section was ordered to dig second line of trenches . . . but work interrupted by shell-fire; completed 6 p.m. Night work: 6 p.m.–5 a.m.—No. 1 Section, overhead cover for machine guns; No. 2 Section, improvement of communications in front; also wire. Wire obstacles erected here as usual on previous night were very effective in checking the German attack to-day. General Officer Commanding greatly appreciated the work of the company in this direction. No. 3 Section, wire obstacles; settled in new billets 10.30 p.m. No. 4 Section made new track. At 4 p.m. orders for company to stand by as reserves for infantry." During the erecting of wire entanglements out in front of the British trenches the Sappers were constantly sniped and suffered many casualties. Captain Skipwith, commanding No. 11 Field Company R.E., was wounded by shrapnel on 27th October, and on the same day Captain Scott of the 5th Field Company R.E. was killed whilst reconnoitring.

The Divisional Mounted Troops were used mostly for liaison purposes, their work in this direction being keenly appreciated.

The R.A.M.C. and the Army Service Corps[1] carried on their work in the face of many dangers and difficulties. To the former a signal honour fell during the strenuous days of the fighting round Ypres. Lieut. Arthur Martin Leake, R.A.M.C., who was awarded the Victoria Cross on 13th May 1902, gained a clasp to his Cross for conspicuous bravery and devotion to duty throughout the campaign, especially during the period 29th October to 8th November 1914, near Zonnebeke, in rescuing, whilst exposed to constant fire, a large number of the wounded who were lying close to the enemy's trenches.[2]

If the doctors and ambulance bearers faced danger and death in tending their wounded comrades in the field (and many were killed and wounded), the Supply services suffered no less from the long-range shelling and bombarding of their supply dumps and depots—little protection was possible in those early days.

Throughout the terrific struggle round Ypres in 1914 the 2nd Division was so split up (brigades very seldom being intact—having lent battalions here and there to strengthen various parts

[1] Now the Royal Army Service Corps.
[2] *London Gazette*, 18th February 1915. One of the only two instances in the British Army of the Victoria Cross being won twice.

of the line) that only with difficulty is it possible to follow the operations.

*   *   *   *   *   *   *

A thick mist lay over the countryside during the early morning of the 1st November, and the British and German guns were silent.

At 1.45 a.m. 2nd Divisional Headquarters had received from Ist Corps Headquarters instructions to interview the French commander, General Bernard, who proposed to attack Becelaere from the north-west at 6.30 a.m. on the morning of the 1st, with four battalions of infantry. Orders were accordingly issued to the 5th and 6th Infantry Brigades, to Colonel Pereira commanding the two Coldstream battalions of Guards, and to Colonel Westmacott commanding the 1st King's and 5th Field Company R.E., east, south-east, and south of Polygone Wood. The 6th Infantry Brigade was to protect the left flank of the attack ; the Highland Light Infantry and 2nd and 3rd Coldstream were to co-operate in the attack when the French troops had reached the line held by the Highland Light Infantry. Heavy rifle and machine-gun fire was to be maintained against the hostile troops holding the Reutel Spur. As the French attack developed, the 6th Infantry Brigade was to press the enemy in front. The 35th (Heavy) Battery R.G.A., and XLIVth (Howitzer) Brigade R.F.A., with the siege howitzers, were also ordered to co-operate in the attack, particularly against the Keiberg and Becelaere spurs.

At 6.30 a.m. the leading French troops passed through the line of the 4th and 6th Infantry Brigades, and got into the trenches occupied by the Highland Light Infantry and 3rd Coldstream. The mist delayed the opening of the attack, as the guns were unable to locate their targets until the atmosphere cleared.

In the meantime the Worcesters, King's Royal Rifles, and two companies of the Royal Berks, who had spent the night in some dug-outs just east of the wood at Veldhoek, were drawn into Divisional Reserve. The first-named battalion was ordered at 9.30 a.m. to report to Hooge Château and remain at the disposal of the 1st Division, and was later sent to a position east of Zillebeke to be attached to the 7th Division under General Capper. One company of the Berks relieved one company of the South Staffords, and Colonel Graham took command of the section. None of the brigades of the 2nd Division on the 1st November were therefore intact, some battalions being lent to the 1st and others to the 7th Division.

About 10.30 a.m., the mists having dispersed, the French advanced to the attack, which was almost immediately brought to a standstill by intense hostile artillery fire. Their right was on the eastern exits of Polygone Wood, and their left on the Passchendaele–Becelaere road.

The enemy also advanced his troops to the Polderhoek Château, which had been vacated on the night 31st October–1st November, owing to the withdrawal of the line on the loss of Gheluvelt. He had on this day the whole of two divisions—53rd Saxon Reserve Division and 54th Würtemberg Reserve Division, *i.e.*, XXVIIth Reserve Corps—operating between the Menin–Ypres road and Broodseinde. The XVth Corps under von Deimling operated between Gheluvelt and Klein Zillebeke, its right on the first-named place and its left towards the latter.

By noon the French attack had made no further progress, the intense artillery fire of the enemy making advance impossible ; the operation was therefore postponed until night, when the attack under cover of darkness was to be resumed.

On account of very heavy attacks on General Bulfin's troops near Klein Zillebeke, the 1st King's Royal Rifles and three companies of the Royal Berks were also sent to Hooge Château under orders of the 1st Division.

At 4.20 p.m. a hostile infantry attack developed against the line of trenches held by the South Staffords, Berks, and Connaughts north-east of the Becelaere–Passchendaele road, but was repulsed with very heavy loss to the enemy. The Connaughts were congratulated by General Fanshawe on the tenacity with which they clung to their trenches and repulsed the determined efforts of the enemy.

Arrangements were made for the French to take over the Highland Light Infantry's trenches, in view of a possible French advance. This move was carried out during the night, and three companies of the Highland Light Infantry were placed in Brigade Reserve, one company being left in support trenches in rear of the right of the Connaughts.

At 3 p.m. the line of the Ist Corps was as follows : the 18th French Division was astride the Zonnebeke–Moorslede road, their right occupying the trenches lately held by the 1st King's Royal Rifles ; then came the South Staffords along the eastern edges of the wood east of the fifth kilometre stone on the Becelaere–Passchendaele road. The right of the Staffords connected up with the Connaughts ; one company Highland Light Infantry was in

THE POSITION AT 3 p.m., 1st November.

(*Facing p. 142.*)

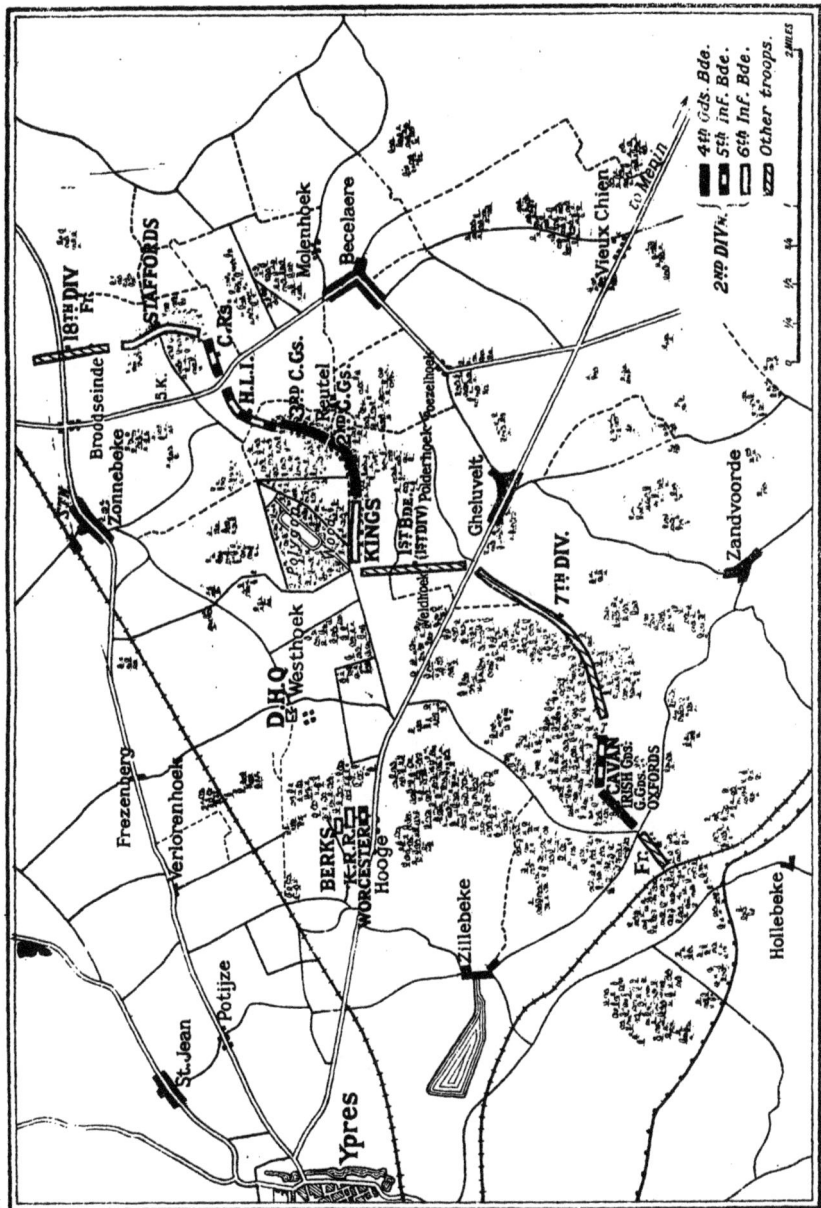

THE MAPPA CO. LTD. LONDON.

2 MILES

2ND DIVN. { 4th Gds. Bde.
            5th Inf. Bde.
            6th Inf. Bde.
            Other troops.

St. Jean
Potijze
Frezenberg
Verlorenhoek
Ypres
Hooge
Westhoek
D.H.Q.
BERKS
K.R.R.
WORCESTER
Zillebeke
Hollebeke
Zonnebeke
Broodseinde
18TH DIV Fr.
STAFFORDS
C.Rs.
H.L.I.
KINGS
1ST Bde.
(1ST DIV) Polderhoek
Reutel
2ND C.Gs.
3RD C.Gs.
Gheluvelt
Veldhoek
7TH DIV.
CAVAN
IRISH Gds.
G.Gs.
OXFORDS
Fr.
Molenhoek
Becelaere
Vieux Chien
to Menin
Zandvoorde

support between the right of the Connaughts and the left of the
3rd Coldstream Guards, whose trenches faced east from the Polygone Wood ; the 2nd Coldstream joined up with the right of the
3rd Coldstream, and faced south-east from the Polygone Wood ;
the 1st King's faced direct south from the southern exits of the
Polygone Wood ; here the line of the 2nd Division ended. One
company of the Berks was in reserve in the north-west corner of
Polygone Wood. Almost at right angles to the left of the King's
trenches, facing Polderhoek and occupying a line north and south
to the Menin–Ypres road, was the 1st Brigade (1st Division). The
7th Division joined up with the right of the 1st Brigade, thence
through the south-eastern exits of the Herenthage Wood with its
right connecting up with Lord Cavan's force, whose left was in
Shrewsbury Forest and whose right rested on the Zandvoorde–
Zillebeke road. South of the latter were more French troops
under General Moussy.

Divisional Headquarters were now at Westhoek.

During the day Major C. N. North, of the 5th Field Company
R.E., was killed by a sniper.

The morning of the 2nd November opened with plans for
another French attack—this time on Gheluvelt—with eight battalions of infantry and four groups of French artillery. The attack
was timed for 10 a.m., the French issuing from the south-west
corners of the Polygone Wood. An artillery preparation by French
artillery was timed to begin at 9 a.m. The 6th Infantry Brigade,
and troops under Colonels Westmacott and Pereira, were informed
that the attack would be made. The 3rd Cavalry Brigade was
ordered to the road junction one mile south of Hooge ; the 1st
Divisional Reserves were south of the Ypres–Menin road, and 7th
Divisional Reserves in rear of the right flank of the Division.

The orders issued to the 2nd Division were to bring a gradually
increasing rifle and machine-gun fire to bear on the enemy's trenches
from daylight to 10 a.m. The 2nd Divisional Artillery was to
co-operate by engaging hostile targets north of the Ypres–Menin
road, particularly the enemy's trenches. At 10.45 a.m. 2nd Divisional Headquarters were at the road junction half a mile west
of Frezenberg on the Ypres–Zonnebeke road.

At 1 p.m. the 71st Battery (XXXIVth Brigade R.F.A.), which
had taken up a position just north of the fifth kilometre stone on
the Ypres–Menin road, reported that the enemy had broken through
the 1st Division line south of Veldhoek. At this period the French
attack had not developed farther than the trenches held by the

1st King's on the southern exits of the Polygone Wood and the 1st Brigade between the wood and the village of Veldhoek.

Shortly before this, at 12.45, the South Staffords reported that on their left the French were being driven back, which exposed the battalion's left flank in the wood. Captain Kilby (South Staffords), however, twice advanced his company, and after some stiff fighting eventually turned the enemy out of the wood, and later French reinforcements arrived and restored the left flank of the Staffords. The Connaughts, too, were heavily attacked and asked for support, as they feared they would be unable to hold the enemy, who at one period had penetrated the trenches of the Irishmen, but were cleared out. The battalion, however, managed to hold on, though sorely pressed and losing heavily. Lieuts. A. T. C. Wickham and C. J. O. Mallins were killed, Captains Brooke and Whyte were wounded, and 27 other ranks killed and wounded. At night the Highland Light Infantry relieved the Connaughts, who were withdrawn into Brigade Reserve. When the reliefs were completed the line in this section from left to right ran as follows: French, three companies of South Staffords, one company Royal Berks, the Highland Light Infantry, and one French battalion who occupied the old Highland Light Infantry trenches connecting up with the 3rd and 2nd Coldstream Guards.

Again, on the 2nd November no brigade of the 2nd Division was intact, for while the South Staffords and one company of the Berks of the 6th Brigade, the Highland Light Infantry and Connaughts of the 5th Brigade, and the two Coldstream battalions of the 4th Brigade had been engaged with the enemy in line, the remaining battalions of the Division were marching, countermarching, and fighting, or entrenching west and south-west between the left of the 1st Brigade (which linked up with the right of the 1st King's along the southern exits of the Polygone Wood) and the right of the 7th Division in the vicinity of Klein Zillebeke. And upon one of these battalions at least—the 1st King's Royal Rifles—disaster had fallen! For on this day the gallant Rifles lost 9 officers and 437 other ranks (three companies, B, C, and D) captured by the enemy.

The battalion had received orders at 9 p.m. on the 1st November to take over a section of a partially dug trench running south from the Hooge–Menin road. One company of Berks (D) had also been sent to occupy trenches on the right of the Rifles. The latter had relieved the remnants of several

different battalions—South Wales Borderers, Gloucesters, etc.—
and the left of the line was held by all that remained of the 1st
Coldstream, about 200 men under Captain Christie Miller. " That
portion north of the road was occupied by Captain H. Adeane (who
was killed the following day), and south of the road by myself.
The greater part of the night was spent in trying to improve the
trenches, which were not and never were continuous.   There was
a barricade across the road, and a farm and some cottages which
were not in a state of defence divided the position.   The field of
fire and observation was bad.   Some cottages and a wood about
150 yards immediately in front were occupied by the enemy and
overlooked our trenches." [1]

At dawn on the 2nd November the position was as follows :
the 1st Coldstream were just north and just south of the Ypres–
Menin road about midway between Gheluvelt and the Herenthage
Wood ; the right of the Coldstream was supported by half of B
and the whole of D and C Companies of the King's Royal
Rifles ; D Company of the Berks joined up with C of the
Rifles.   Two companies of Berks were in support at the crossroads about 300 yards in rear of the trenches.   A Company of
the Rifles and Battalion Headquarters were in the wood.   What
followed is not clear, no authentic account being in existence,
but soon after 11.30 a.m. the Berks reported that the Coldstream
had been attacked and driven from their trenches and their officer
killed.   The Berks also reported having seen in the distance a
number of men of the Rifles surrendering to the enemy.   It is
probable that the enemy broke through the Coldstream line and
then, pushing along the trench, surrounded the three companies
of Rifles.   This could never have occurred had a system of
trenches in depth been in existence.   A counter-attack launched by
the two companies of Berks, assisted by A Company of the
Rifles and later by the 2nd King's Royal Rifles and weak battalions of Welsh, South Wales Borderers, Loyal North Lancashires,
and Gloucesters, restored part of the line, though the trenches taken
from the Coldstream were not immediately recovered.   At nightfall an astonishingly alternating line of Berks and Gloucesters,
Germans, Berks, Germans, lay north and south of the Ypres–
Menin road.   Finally the remaining portion of the line was recaptured, and the Berks' position ran north and south-east along the
eastern exits of the Herenthage Wood at Veldhoek, with A Company of the 1st King's Royal Rifles in the wood in close support.

[1] Statement by Captain Christie Miller, 1st Coldstream Guards.

In addition to the losses already given, the King's Royal Rifles lost (of A Company) 3 other ranks killed and 1 officer (Second-Lieut. Collins) and 9 other ranks wounded. The Berks' casualties were Major Finch and Second-Lieut. Frizell and 3 other ranks wounded.

At 8.30 p.m. on the 2nd November a short summary of the day's fighting was issued : " We have maintained our line against very severe attacks throughout the whole day. On the right [1] the French, after a series of attacks, made some progress, and report having taken over 100 prisoners. On our left the IXth French Corps has maintained its line.[2] Our IIIrd Corps (General Pulteney) was also attacked unsuccessfully by the enemy. General Foch, commanding the French armies in Belgium, is satisfied with the general situation. The line will be maintained to-morrow at all costs." [3]

Imperative orders were now issued to form reserves. From the already depleted thin line troops were to be withdrawn, so that if at any moment the line gave way it could be reinforced. Two companies of the King's were accordingly withdrawn late on the night 2nd–3rd November and placed in reserve, the French taking over that part of the line held by them—*i.e.*, the southern exits of the Polygone Wood. Nos. 1 and 4 Companies of the 2nd Coldstream were also ordered into reserve and were to move on the following day. On the 2nd November Lieut. R. C. Graves-Sawle (2nd Coldstream Guards) was killed.

The four companies thus placed in reserve were sent to the north-west corner of the Polygone Wood.

Throughout the 3rd November the enemy contented himself with vigorously shelling the front-line trenches and in making small attacks, all of which were repulsed.

Certain changes took place in the trenches occupied by the Division. The Connaughts took over the old Highland Light Infantry line which had been occupied by a French battalion. Of the 5th Infantry Brigade, B Company Highland Light Infantry was ordered forward to the small wood on the left of their line ; the Worcesters were still with the 7th Division, as were also the Oxford and Bucks. Of the 6th Infantry Brigade, the three companies of Berks and all that remained of the King's Royal

---

[1] The right of the 2nd Division. This refers to the attack by eight French battalions.

[2] From Dixmude to the left flank of the 6th Infantry Brigade.

[3] General Staff Diary, 2nd Division.

Rifles were still entrenched on the eastern exits of Herenthage Wood. The South Staffords held on to their position, one company remaining in the support trenches and the remainder in the front line ; and the King's moved their two companies back to the southern exits of the Polygone Wood, again taking over that portion of their trenches which had been given up to French troops.

Orders were issued to begin the construction of " small closed works, a short distance in rear of our front trenches, to cover points where there is a danger of the enemy breaking through. These works need not necessarily be larger than to accommodate ten rifles each . . . wired all round . . . as invisible as possible. The works should form the basis of the defences, and should be capable of extension and reinforcement by the addition of zig-zag communication trenches and wing trenches. . . . Cover must be got by digging deep and not by erecting parapets." These first defensive posts were but experimental ; soon parapets were found essential, and, when sandbags became more plentiful, formed the best protection.

An interesting commentary on the enemy's methods of making warfare is contained in a Royal Artillery Diary for 3rd November : " Germans habitually use British uniforms, especially kilts, and use English commands, etc. All ranks warned." These devices, however, recoiled upon their originators, for the German gunners often fired on their own comrades, mistaking them for British troops.

On the 4th the two Coldstream companies which had been placed in reserve were returned to Colonel Pereira.

During the night of the 3rd–4th, the 11th Field Company R.E. constructed several defensive posts. Two were made in the rear of the Staffords' wood ; two in rear of the line held by the Connaughts (i.e., between the Highland Light Infantry and the 3rd Coldstream) ; one behind the trenches of the Highland Light Infantry ; one in the south-east corner and another in the south-west corner of the Polygone Wood, whilst one section of the Field Company was moved off to Klein Zillebeke to put up redoubts for Lord Cavan's force. During the following night these " forts " were wired and communication trenches dug. They proved of great value.

Heavy shelling characterized the 4th, the Berks (at Veldhoek) having 21 casualties, including 1 officer wounded. A strong hostile demonstration was made against the Grenadiers' trenches at dusk, but it was easily repulsed. Two batteries, the 15th

(XXXVIth Brigade R.F.A.) and the 6oth (XLIVth (Howitzer) Brigade R.F.A.), did good work, several houses and a redoubt occupied by the enemy in front of the Highland Light Infantry's trenches being totally destroyed.

The 5th opened quietly, though the enemy as usual searched the trenches with his artillery, to which the guns of the 2nd Division replied. On the 6th Infantry Brigade front nothing happened until dusk (about 6.30 p.m.), when two attacks were launched. The first was against a company of Berks between the Highland Light Infantry and Staffords, but was easily repulsed, the support lent by the 70th Battery (XXXIVth Brigade R.F.A.) being very effective. The second attack was more serious ; it was directed against the Connaughts. The Highland Light Infantry and Staffords immediately manned the new redoubts in the rear of the Connaughts, whilst the Signal Section and orderlies of Brigade Headquarters, with grooms, police, servants, and whoever could be collected, were hastily dispatched to the threatened point. The enemy succeeded in establishing himself ten yards from the Connaughts, but the line was never broken. The Berks lost 32 other ranks, and the Connaughts Second-Lieut. A. Winspear, killed, Lieut. Foote and Second-Lieuts. Cheadle and Montgomery wounded, and 34 other ranks killed, wounded, and missing.

On the 4th (Guards) Brigade front—2nd and 3rd Coldstream— bombs and snipers took a heavy toll, the former battalion losing 10 other ranks killed and 19 wounded.

All that remained of the 1st Coldstream Guards were on this day attached to the 4th Brigade. " The remnants of the poor old 1st Coldstream joined us to be attached for the time being. They were in a dreadful state, about 180 rank and file with not a single officer, no senior N.C.O's, no rations, hardly any ammunition, and deficient of the greater part of their equipment." This gallant battalion had belonged to the 1st (Guards) Brigade of the 1st Division, and, though adding lustre to its glorious record, had suffered terribly in the heavy fighting about Ypres. Colonel Pereira, who already commanded the 2nd and 3rd Coldstream, thus had the unique experience of having the whole regiment (two of the battalions temporarily) under him. The 1st Coldstream were replaced in the 1st Brigade by the London Scottish, the first Territorial battalion to be attached.

Two batteries of the XXXVIth Brigade R.F.A. (48th and 71st), and one of the XLIVth (Howitzer) Brigade R.F.A., were on this day ordered to St. Omer and left the Divisional area.

The French attack on Gheluvelt was resumed, but little progress was made. Since these attacks began on the 2nd November little or nothing had been accomplished in the way of an advance, though they had created a diversion, relieving the sorely pressed troops north and south of the Ypres–Menin road.

At 9 p.m. Divisional Headquarters issued a statement that "the general situation remains satisfactory."

From 1st November to the night of the 5th–6th the 2nd Worcesters, who had been sent to be attached to the 7th Division east of Zillebeke, were mostly held in reserve. On the 2nd one company (A) was sent forward to the attack and turned the enemy out of some trenches he had taken, and restored the line. The battalion was thanked for this by General Capper. From 3rd to 5th November they were relieved, and were engaged in strengthening the defences. Their casualties during this period were 32 other ranks killed, wounded, and missing. At midnight on the 5th–6th they were relieved by the West Riding Regiment and marched back to the Polygone Wood. The battalion was shelled en route and lost a further 20 men.

The 6th November also was comparatively quiet, excepting for the now inevitable heavy intermittent shelling and sniping.

At 11 a.m. the remnants of the 1st King's Royal Rifles rejoined the Division and were placed in reserve.

The three companies of Berkshires which had been lent to the 1st Division were relieved by the 1st Loyal North Lancashires in Herenthage Wood, and returned to the Division, arriving at Brigade Headquarters about 4 p.m.

The 5th Field Company R.E. and the Divisional Cyclists were placed at the disposal of the 6th Infantry Brigade, the enemy having shown signs of attacking the trenches on the right flank of the brigade—i.e., the Connaughts.

About 4.40 on the morning of 7th November the enemy made a determined attack on the trenches of the Highland Light Infantry, B Company (Captain Buist) then holding the particular portion of the line attacked. Owing to the heavy morning mist, and the enemy's trenches being only a few yards away (from fifteen to fifty), there was no time to open fire on the attacking party. A hand-to-hand fight ensued, in which the enemy lost heavily, though he succeeded in gaining a small portion of the trench held by B Company. Fifty-four Germans were taken prisoners, and 80 were killed and wounded. The Highland Light Infantry lost Lieut. Dalrymple wounded, and 44 N.C.O's and men killed, wounded, and missing.[1] Owing to the conformation of the ground and the open space to be crossed, it was not possible to counter-attack and turn the enemy out of the trench by day ; the Highland Light Infantry line was therefore modified, though in one place the Scotsmen and the enemy were only separated by a barricade across the trench.

A troop of the 15th Hussars was sent off to assist Lord Cavan during the day.

At 4 p.m. another attack was made on the Connaughts. This attack was made after heavy hostile artillery and rifle fire, during which the Connaughts temporarily vacated their trenches, but were immediately replaced by a detachment of Berks in support. The 5th Field Company R.E. were also ordered up to support the Connaughts. In front of, and only five yards from the centre of, the latter's trenches was a fortified house which had given a great deal of trouble. During the night the 15th Battery (XXXVIth Brigade R.F.A.) man-handled a gun near to the trenches, and at daybreak opened fire and dislodged the enemy. The Connaughts' casualties were 50 killed, wounded, and missing.

On 7th November Major L. R. Vaughan, G.S.O.2 (vice Lieut.-Colonel Perceval killed), Brevet-Major C. Watson, G.S.O.2 (vice Captain Ommaney killed), and Captain Mowbray, R.A., appointed Brigade-Major R.A. (vice Captain C. Trench killed), joined the 2nd Division and took up their duties.

During the night of the 7th–8th, as a result of the attacks on the Highland Light Infantry and Connaughts, a slight readjustment was made in the line held by the 6th Infantry Brigade. No attack was made on the Division this day, and just before dusk the 2nd Worcesters went into the line and relieved the Connaughts, who were withdrawn to the north-west corner of the Polygone Wood in Divisional Reserve. The battalion had had a hard gruelling, its ranks being terribly thinned day after day through heavy artillery and rifle fire ; their portion of the line was most vulnerable to attack, hence the frequent attempts made upon it by the enemy.

During the 6th and 8th November the heaviest attacks had fallen on the 1st Infantry and 3rd Cavalry Divisions—i.e., from the left flank of the 1st Brigade (held by the Black Watch), at the south-west corner of the Polygone Wood, to Klein Zillebeke. At one

[1] Lieut. W. L. Brodie, 2nd Highland Light Infantry, was awarded the Victoria Cross for his gallantry in this action. "He called on the men near him, bayoneted four Germans himself, shot four or five others, and mounted a machine gun on a traverse and fired down the trench."—London Gazette, December 12, 1914.

period two French Zouave battalions filled a gap in the 1st Division line, and took a prominent part in the fighting near Veldhoek.

The Oxford and Bucks, who were still with Lord Cavan's force, were on the night of the 8th–9th relieved by the London Scottish (1st Division), and went into bivouac just west of White Farm; but the Irish Guards were not relieved until the night of the 9th, when this battalion also went into bivouac west of White Farm; the 2nd Grenadiers remained with Lord Cavan.

At 5.30 p.m. the Berks and King's Royal Rifles took over the trenches held by the Highland Light Infantry, and the line at this period from left to right ran as follows: South Staffords, Berks, King's Royal Rifles, Worcesters, 3rd Coldstream, 2nd Coldstream, King's—*i.e.*, from the right of the French 18th Division to the left of the 1st Black Watch at the south-west corner of the Polygone Wood.

The 9th was a quiet day generally.[1]

On the morning of the 10th the Oxford and Bucks and 1st Irish Guards again came under the orders of the 2nd Division. The latter battalion after their hard fighting near Zillebeke was in a terribly weak state, and with a freshly arrived draft could only number 296 rank and file. The battalion was therefore organized into two companies, each of 148 men.

During the night 10th–11th the 2nd Grenadiers were relieved by the Welsh and the Munsters, and marched at.1 a.m. to Belle-waarde Farm, for rest in Corps Reserve.

THE BATTLE OF NONNE BOSSCHEN.

On 8th November Ist Corps Headquarters had issued a comment on the operations: " Information from all sides points to the fact that the German offensive in this neighbourhood (from Zillebeke to Broodseinde) is breaking down."

The truth of the matter was that the German Higher Command had been organizing for another violent attempt to break through to Ypres and Calais. According to the views set forth

---

[1] " It is interesting to note the low number of casualties incurred by the Staffords during this period ; they were holding the most advanced line of the whole army and were constantly being heavily shelled, but having dug excellent trenches they suffered extremely little loss."—*6th Infantry Brigade Diary*. The casualties amongst the Staffords for the period 1st–9th November were 29, though the hostile trenches were only from forty-five to a hundred yards away.

by the German General Staff, the non-success of their heavy attacks during the latter days of October and in the first week of November forced them to conclude that even with the newly-formed Army Group Fabeck, which had been operating on and south of the Ypres–Menin road, a break through was impossible. The great superiority of the enemy in personnel and material had given him no success; not even though some of Sir Douglas Haig's battalions were pitifully weak.[1]   More guns and men might batter down and break through the British and French defences; so the German General Staff imagined. Thus during the "comparatively quiet" days along the northern section of the Ist Corps line there had been going on considerable organization of new forces—for the German Prussian Guard were being brought up to accomplish what their comrades had failed to do.

IITH Nov. The blow fell on the morning of the 11th November, when the enemy from Messines to Zonnebeke launched no less than six and a half corps against the British and French, who held the line somewhat intermixed. The XXVIIth Reserve Corps still operated between Becelaere and Broodseinde; the newly-formed Guards Division, consisting of the 1st and 4th Guards Infantry Brigades (called Winckler's Division, from the name of its commander), operated from opposite the centre of Herenthage Wood to the southwest corner of the Polygone Wood. Next came another new group— the Army Group Linsingen, consisting of the 4th, 39th, and 30th Infantry Divisions, operating from the left of the Guards Division to Zillebeke; from Zillebeke to Messines, in the order given, 4th and 3rd Bavarian Infantry Divisions, 6th Bavarian Reserve Division, 25th Reserve Division, 3rd Infantry Division, 26th Infantry Division, and 11th Landwehr Brigade—i.e., the Army Group Fabeck, also reinforced. The latter group was also given more heavy guns and "all the artillery ammunition allotted to the German Sixth Army."

The Fourth German Army—i.e., the northern flank of it— operated against the French and Belgians from Zonnebeke to Nieuport, and the Sixth German Army, south of the Army Group Fabeck, were to co-operate in this huge converging attack on Ypres.

Many of these formations consisted of perfectly fresh troops, and so far as numbers were concerned there could be no question

---

[1] On the 10th November the 1st King's Royal Rifles numbered about 180 men and officers; the 1st Irish Guards 296, and 1st Coldstream 180 men, with no officers; whilst the whole of the 1st Infantry Brigade numbered only about 800 bayonets.

of their superiority over Sir Douglas Haig's war-worn, though withal cheerful troops.   Even with the French troops the enemy outnumbered the Allies.   And the German Kaiser had come to see his famous Guard break through to Ypres !

At 7.30 a.m. the enemy's artillery opened with a roar ! It seemed as if he had brought every available gun in his possession to bear upon the British line.   Shortly afterwards the Prussian Guard advanced.   Their centre line was directed against Verbeek Farm ; their left on and south of the Ypres–Menin road.

About 10 a.m. a Black Watch Highlander suddenly appeared at the Headquarters of the 5th Infantry Brigade, which were then in the north-west corner of the Polygone Wood, and stated that under intense artillery fire the battalion had been forced to evacuate its trenches on the right of the King's, and that the Germans were occupying them.

Under very heavy pressure the Black Watch, Camerons, some of the 9th Infantry Brigade, and some Zouaves had fallen back from the line held on the night of the 10th–11th—*i.e.*, from the north-eastern exits of the Herenthage Wood to the south-west corner of Polygone Wood—and had been pressed back to the western exits of the Nonne Bosschen Wood.

The brigadier of the 5th Infantry Brigade went off himself for reinforcements, and in the meantime ordered up the Highland Light Infantry (who lined the western exits of the Polygone), and the Connaughts and 5th Field Company R.E., who continued the line to the north-western corner of the Nonne Bosschen Wood.

The Oxford and Bucks, with the Irish Guards in support, were moved up from Divisional Reserve near White Farm to Westhoek.   Here the former battalion received orders from the 5th Infantry Brigade to clear the Nonne Bosschen Wood and then join up with the Highland Light Infantry, who were at the western exits of the Polygone.   A and B Companies of the Oxfords [1] immediately advanced at the double from the north-west, with direction south-east into the wood, and drove the Prussian Guard before them, killing and capturing many.   As the survivors of the enemy rushed out from the wood the Highland Light Infantry, who were lying in wait for them, opened fire, killing many more.   The Oxfords, on emerging from the wood close on the heels of the Prussians, joined up on the right with some men of the Northampton Regiment, and on the left with the Connaughts and 5th Field Company R.E., who had also with them a hastily collected group

[1] At this period the Oxford and Bucks numbered less than 400 bayonets.

of orderlies, servants, cooks, transport men, and stragglers from the 1st Brigade. A combined charge was then made on the enemy, who, though standing bravely to meet the attack, again lost heavily in killed and wounded, besides many prisoners. The Prussians thereupon fell back to the trench they had captured earlier in the day from the Black Watch and Camerons.

The 1st King's, lying next to the Black Watch, had also suffered many casualties from the heavy shelling of the early morning, 30 other ranks being killed and wounded. But on the left of the battalion the Coldstream Guards, and battalions of the 5th and 6th Infantry Brigades who continued the line to Broodseinde, were not seriously attacked. A number of Prussian Guards rushed towards the trenches of the 2nd Coldstream, but were speedily dealt with and did not attempt a second attack on this part of the line.

The greatest and heaviest attacks had been made on and south of the Ypres–Menin road ; but there the line held fast, the enemy being mowed down in hundreds as he advanced in massed formation. The Kaiser's famous troops could not prevail against men who fought with the courage of lions, undismayed though vastly outnumbered. Seldom in the whole history of the Great War was the courage of the British soldier put more severely to the test than at this final attempt of the enemy to smash his way through to Ypres.

Alas, that only a very few of those who fought on that November morning survived the Great War ! But the traditions the dead left behind them will for ever remain glorious.

The 5th Field Company R.E., who took a gallant part in counter-attacking the enemy, lost heavily. Major A. H. Tyler, Captain A. E. J. Collins, and Lieut. H. F. T. Renny-Tailyour were killed, another officer was wounded, and 15 sappers were killed and wounded. The Oxford and Bucks lost 1 officer (Second-Lieut. J. Jones) killed, 1 officer wounded, and 25 N.C.O's and men killed, wounded, and missing. The Connaughts' losses were Captain Gilliat wounded, and 61 other ranks killed and wounded. The Highland Light Infantry lost 1 officer (Second-Lieut. J. W. Mears, who had been commissioned the previous day) killed, and 14 other ranks killed and wounded.

When night fell, the stretch of ground won by the Prussians was only 500 yards in length. Their losses were very heavy, for although they advanced with great gallantry in close formation they were decimated by the accurate and rapid rifle-fire of Sir.

John French's infantry, combined with the splendid practice made by the Divisional Artillery. When the Prussians broke through the northern exits of the Nonne Bosschen Wood they came within a hundred yards of the 9th, 16th, and 17th Batteries of the XLIst Brigade R.F.A., and within rifle fire of the gunners of the 35th (Heavy) Battery. Here again they suffered considerably from rifle fire, the gunners of the four batteries using their rifles with excellent effect.

From the Ypres-Menin road to Klein Zillebeke the enemy's attack made no progress. Thus far the attacks of the Prussian Guard, upon which the German General Staff had set such store, had failed. But the action was not concluded.

A counter-attack was arranged to take place at 1 a.m. when the moon had risen, with the object of recapturing the trench lost by the Black Watch and Camerons. The Oxford and Bucks, and the Highland Light Infantry under Colonel Davies, were ordered to reconnoitre the enemy's trenches, but found them strongly held and impossible to take without a considerable force. Another attempt later was made by the 1st Irish Guards, 2nd Grenadiers, and Munster Fusiliers under Brigadier-General·Fitz-Clarence, V.C. The following description of what happened during that fateful attempt is taken from the Diary of the Irish Guards: "At 2.30 a.m. the battalion in following order marched to the point of rendezvous, west of the Polygone de Zonnebeke (Wood): Irish Guards, Grenadiers, and Munsters. The march formation was 'fours' well closed up, and the route down a muddy lane which ran on (the) south side of the Nonne Bosschen—i.e., the small road leading from Hooge–Gheluvelt road to Reutel village. Open ground was reached after the lane one-eighth of an inch[1] north of the 'V' in Verbeek. As soon as the leading platoon of No. 3 Company, which was the leading company, had passed the farm here on the road, the enemy opened a heavy rifle fire on to the right flank of the platoon, presumably near the trench which was to be taken by General FitzClarence's troops. In addition to this fire some troops lining the south-west corner of the wood, Polygone de Zonnebeke, also began to fire at us, but were soon stopped. The whole column was sheered off to its left, and some of it eventually arrived and halted at the 'Z' in Polygone de Zonnebeke[1] (i.e., in the wood). It was almost as soon as the enemy began to open fire that General FitzClarence was killed. He was leading the column, and was one of the first to come under fire. At the same

[1] Map reference: 1/100,000. Ypres.

time also Major Webber and Lieut. Harding (both of the Irish
Guards) were wounded, besides about 12 men of the leading company.
Colonel Davies commanding the Oxfords (and Highland Light
Infantry) now arrived on the scene and consulted with Colonel
Smith (Grenadier Guards).   He (Colonel Davies) had already made
a reconnaissance, as ordered, with the idea of taking this particular
trench, but found that the enemy was not actually occupying it,
but one dug in rear of it, and so would have shot down any men
advancing down the abandoned trench."

Eventually Colonel McEwan of the Camerons at 1st Brigade
Headquarters, whither the force had returned, took over command,
and one company of Grenadiers was left to dig trenches in a sap
which was found to be in the line between Nonne Bosschen Wood
and the Menin road, whilst the remainder of the Grenadiers, with
the Irish Guards and Munsters, went back to the woods near the
Hooge Château, arriving at 6 a.m.   The Irish Guards now numbered
only 160 bayonets with 4 officers.

At 4 a.m. the 1st Herts (Territorials) had reported to 1st Corps
Headquarters and went into bivouac just west of Hooge, and were
later attached to the 4th (Guards) Brigade.

*   *   *   *   *   *   *

At dawn on the 12th and throughout the day the Prussian
Guards continued their violent attacks upon the 1st Brigade (1st
Division) but were everywhere repulsed.

Just after it was light, about 6 a.m., a strong attack was made
by the enemy against the left of the 6th Infantry Brigade and the
right of the French 36th Brigade (18th Division) and the latter
fell back just west of the crossroads north of Broodseinde.   This
retirement uncovered the left flank of the Staffords, who reported
that the enemy was now almost behind the battalion's left rear.
The French had no reserves in this part of the line.   The Divisional
and French artillery opened fire, and were able to check any further
advance of the enemy : but the position was still critical.   The
5th Infantry Brigade could send no reinforcements, but eventually
all that remained of the 1st Coldstream Guards, whose strength
was about one company, were rushed up.   These, with two sections
of the 11th Field Company, and later two companies of the Highland
Light Infantry, were all the supports the Division could spare.
But it was obvious the Staffords could not for long maintain their
hold unless the French re-established their position, for the pressure
of the enemy was increasing, and the Staffords up to this period
had already lost 60 killed, wounded, and missing.   Eventually

the Staffords were ordered to conform to the new front the French had taken up, and the battalion had reluctantly to withdraw from the line—a line held with great gallantry and splendid fortitude for nearly three weeks. This was done at 3 on the morning of the 13th without opposition from the enemy, the Staffords passing into Brigade Reserve. This left the Highland Light Infantry with the Berks on their right and 1st Coldstream on their left, slightly drawn back and connecting up with the French along the line of the Passchendaele–Becelaere road.

At 2 p.m. another attack was made upon the Highland Light Infantry and Berks, and the two battalions were again forced to withdraw their line slightly.

No attacks were made on the Division west of the Reutel Spur—i.e., on the 2nd and 3rd Coldstream, King's, or Oxford and Bucks—during the day.

On the 14th November 1st Corps Headquarters received orders that " all troops east of Ypres under Sir Douglas Haig were to be relieved by the French, commencing on the night of 15th–16th November."

The Battles of Ypres, 1914, were over !

The terrific struggle through which the British army from early in October to the 17th November had passed and emerged with its glories enhanced and its battle honours augmented, had taken very heavy toll of the gallant troops, who with their French and Belgian allies held the Ypres salient against enemy attacks often pressed with savage ferocity and with greatly superior numbers in men and artillery. The fall of Antwerp had been the grave of the Allies hopes of turning the right flank of the enemy. Similarly the Belgian, French, and British resistance had robbed the German Higher Command of the possession of Ypres and the Belgian and French coastal towns. The necessity for preventing the German outflanking movement was evidently discussed by General Joffre and Sir John French early in October before the British army moved north from the Aisne, for the following passage occurred in the French *Official Review of the First Six Months of the War* : " It was clearly specified that, on the northern terrain, the British army should co-operate to the same end as ourselves, the stopping of the German right. In other words, the British army was to prolong the front of the general disposition without a break, attacking as soon as possible, and at the same time seeking touch with the Belgian army." And a little later : " Thus the co-ordination decided upon by the General-in-Chief attained its end. The barrier was established. It remained to maintain it against the enemy's offensive. That was the object and the result of the Battle of Flanders, which lasted from 22nd October to 15th November."

But at what a cost was it maintained! So weak was the line held by Sir John French's indomitable troops that the enemy could not believe that the thinly lined trenches held all of the British army in France and Flanders. "A German Staff officer when captured said to his escort, as he was being marched off: 'Now I am out of it, do tell me where your reserves are concealed? In what woods are they?' And he refused to believe we had none!"

The enemy's main attacks were made south-east and south of Ypres, not only because that way was the shortest to the city, but because he thought that the British army's reserves were near St. Jean. The British trenches were taken by the enemy to be merely outposts. He was obsessed by the thought that somewhere behind them Sir John French had important concealed forces, and had prepared a trap.

The horrors of those terrible four weeks are indescribable. Lord Cavan, addressing the 2nd and 3rd Coldstream Guards after they had left their terrible trenches behind them, said: "The trenches dug on a hill full of natural springs have been undrainable, and constantly full of water above the knees for twenty-three days. The gale of about 2nd November cleared the wood in which they (the Guards) were of every particle of cover, the trees having all been pierced through by shrapnel and bullets." Similar conditions obtained in almost all parts of the line. Seas of mud covered the dead and drowned the wounded as they fell : verminous and ragged, often sleep-hungry and utterly worn, shelled night and day, yet withal stout-hearted and noble in his suffering, the British soldier took all as part of his duty, looked Doubt in the face, and did not flinch.

In the Battles of Ypres, 1914, the enemy introduced his minenwerfer (trench mortars). Hand and rifle grenades were used by both sides with deadly effect. Aerial observation for artillery became general.

Sir John French, writing on this period, said: "Throughout this trying period Sir Douglas Haig, ably assisted by his Divisional and Brigade commanders, held the line with marvellous tenacity and undaunted courage. Words fail me to express the admiration I feel for their conduct, or my sense of the incalculable services they rendered. I venture to predict that their deeds during these days of stress and trial will furnish some of the most brilliant chapters which will be found in the military history of our time."

The casualties of the 2nd Division from 21st October to 21st November were in killed, wounded, and missing: 227 officers, and 5,542 other ranks.

During the night of the 15th–16th November the IXth French Corps took over the area occupied by the 6th Infantry Brigade and attached troops, from the north-east corner of the Polygone Wood—*i.e.*, the 1st King's Royal Rifles, South Staffords, Worcesters, Berks, 1st Coldstream, and two sections of 11th Field Company R.E. These units then marched to bivouac north-west of Hooge in Corps Reserve. On the morning of the 16th, arrangements were made with the General Officer Commanding XVIth French Army Corps to take over the trenches between the Menin road and the north-west front of the Reutel spur. During the night of the 16th–17th the relief took place, and the Connaughts, King's, and Herts Territorials joined the 6th Infantry Brigade in Corps Reserve north-west of Hooge. The 2nd and 3rd Coldstream were ordered to rejoin the 4th (Guards) Brigade (1st Irish Guards and 2nd Grenadiers, under Lord Cavan) near Zillebeke. 15TH–16TH Nov.

The 6th Infantry Brigade marched to billets north-west of Ypres, being joined there by the Oxford and Bucks and Highland Light Infantry on their relief by the French.

At 6 p.m. on the 17th, 2nd Division Headquarters moved to Poperinghe, and at 4 a.m. on the 18th the 6th Infantry Brigade left Ypres to take up billets in the area allotted to the Division. The 6th Brigade marched to Caestre, and the Oxford and Bucks and Highland Light Infantry to Bailleul, the 5th Infantry Brigade area. On 21st November the 4th (Guards) Brigade complete and the Herts Territorials, arrived at Meteren, the 4th Brigade area. 17TH Nov.

Thus on 21st November the 2nd Division was once more complete, drawn out of the line for rest, re-fitting, and training, in the following areas: 21ST Nov.

Divisional Headquarters and Divisional Mounted Troops: Hazebrouck.

6th Infantry Brigade, XXXIVth Brigade R.F.A., and 6th Field Ambulance: Caestre.

XXXVIth Brigade R.F.A., XLIVth (Howitzer) Brigade R.F.A., 35th (Heavy) Battery R.G.A., Brigade Ammunition Column: Fletre.

4th (Guards) Brigade, XLIst Brigade R.F.A., 11th Field Company R.E., 4th Field Ambulance : Méteren.

5th Infantry Brigade, 5th Field Company R.E., 5th Field Ambulance : Bailleul.

The Operations of Lord Cavan's Force—30th October to 17th November 1914.

Elsewhere it has been stated that for many days during that terrible period from 24th October to 17th November no single brigade of the 2nd Division was intact.　In order to meet the urgent demands for relief from the constant pressure on the sorely tried and worn-out 1st and 7th Divisions, Sir Douglas Haig was forced to employ the reserve battalions of the Ist Corps wherever they were required.　Thus it came about that on the morning of 30th October, when the 3rd Cavalry Brigade was attacked by the German XVth Army Corps, and with the 7th Division on its left fell back from the Zandvoorde ridge towards Zillebeke, it became necessary to call upon the battalions in reserve belonging to the 2nd Division. Three battalions, 2nd Grenadier Guards, 1st Irish Guards, and the 2nd Oxford and Bucks Light Infantry, were lying at the western exits of the Polygone Wood when instructions were received from Ist Corps Headquarters that three battalions under the command of Lord Cavan were to move off at once towards Klein Zillebeke to support the 3rd Cavalry Brigade and the right of the 7th Division. At 3.15 p.m. a position was reached about one mile south of Hooge, and here a halt was called to await developments and for reconnaissance of the situation ; but at 5.30 p.m. the 7th Division and the 3rd Cavalry Brigade were still hard pressed.　Lord Cavan, therefore, moved his force to Klein Zillebeke, where the three battalions took up a position and came under the orders of Brigadier-General Bulfin, commanding the 2nd Infantry Brigade (1st Division), who had also been sent with reinforcements to relieve the pressure on the right of the Ist Corps.

Having reached their destination the Guards and Oxford and Bucks proceeded to dig themselves in.　The line taken up was approximately on and from the Klein Zillebeke–Zwartelen road to the railway line and from the former to Groenenburg Farm held by A and B Companies of the Oxfords ; the left of the Oxfords joined up with the right of the 2nd Gordons, who were on the south-east exits of the wood east of the farm.　On the right

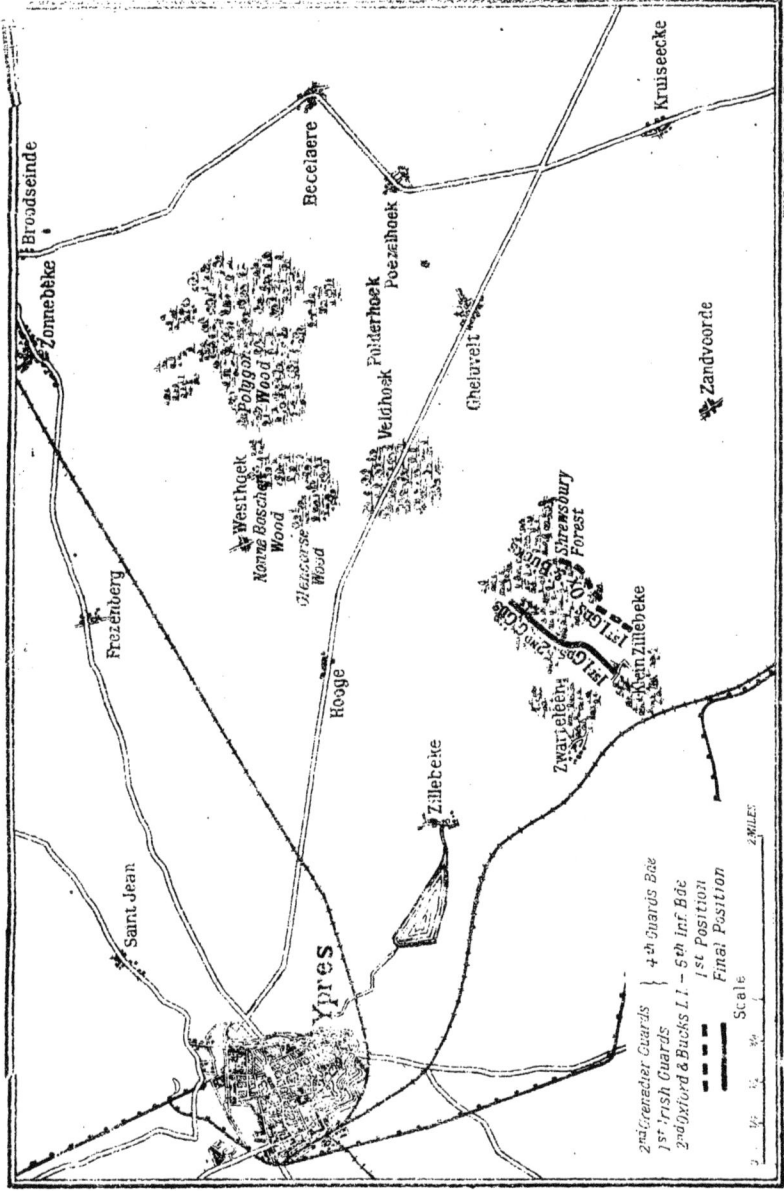

THE OPERATIONS OF LORD CAVAN'S FORCE,
30th October–17th November 1914.

(Facing p. 160.)

Key:
2ⁿᵈ Grenadier Guards — 4ᵗʰ Guards Bde
1ˢᵗ Irish Guards
2ⁿᵈ Oxford & Bucks L.I. — 5ᵗʰ Inf. Bde
1ˢᵗ Position
Final Position

Scale

of the Oxfords were the Irish Guards ; the Grenadiers were in support, but later took up a position on the left of the Irish Guards.

On the morning of the 31st the enemy opened a heavy shell-fire on Lord Cavan's force, particularly against the Irish Guards. It lasted for four hours, and was evidently designed to hold the troops to their trenches whilst the heavy attacks on the centre of the Ist Corps about Gheluvelt developed. An infantry attack which developed later south of the Ypres–Menin road pierced the line held by the Gordons, who were forced to retire. Their retirement uncovered the left rear of the Oxfords, who were bound to conform ; and Lord Cavan withdrew his line through the woods. Here, in a long drive, the Oxfords had a hand-to-hand fight, but finally pressed the enemy back to the eastern exits of the woods after killing and wounding many Germans. By nightfall the line was re-established, the French taking over the trenches of the Grenadiers at 3 a.m., and the Northamptons replacing the Gordons on the right of the Oxfords. Again heavy casualties had been incurred. The Grenadiers lost 1 officer (Lieut. I. St. C. Rose) wounded, and 40 other ranks killed, wounded, and missing ; the Irish Guards, 1 officer (Lieut. L. G. Coke) killed and 3 officers (Captain Lord Francis Scott, Lieut. the Earl of Kingston, and Lieut. R. Ferguson) wounded; the Oxfords lost 45 other ranks killed, wounded, and missing. Almost all these casualties were the result of shell-fire.

The 1st November opened with the now daily heavy shelling, the enemy bringing up light field guns, which were fired at very close range ; heavy guns being employed for searching the ground in the rear of the trenches to keep back reinforcements, which the enemy imagined were at hand in considerable numbers. A platoon of No. 3 Company Irish Guards had its trenches completely blown in, only a few escaping. But amongst the latter was Lieut. G. Maitland, who with a few survivors gallantly held the wreckage, until orders were received to retire with three platoons of No. 2 Company and take up a position which had been prepared 200 yards in the rear as a second-line defence.

The retirement of the left of the Irish Guards exposed the right of the Oxfords, and the inner flank company of the latter drew back in conformity. The Northamptons were the next to fall back, and this involved the whole line of the Oxfords, who retired to a road running north-east through the middle of the wood north-west of Klein Zillebeke. The position was now roughly : Irish Guards joining up with the French on their right ; then, in the order given, the Grenadiers, Oxfords, Northamptons, and Gordons. The line was approximately the shape of an arrow-head with the point of the arrow away from the enemy. A quarter-of-a-mile had been lost, but the new position was stronger. The losses on 1st November were very heavy. Of the Irish Guards, Lieut. K. R. Mathieson was killed; Lieut.-Colonel Lord Ardee, Captain Mulholland (who died later in the day in Ypres Hospital), Captain Vesey, Lieut. Gore-Langton, and Lieut. Alexander wounded; Lieut. G. Maitland was missing; amongst the rank and file (which figures include the casualties of 31st October) the losses were 44 killed, 205 wounded, and 88 missing. The Grenadiers likewise had severe losses: 10 killed, 29 wounded, and 8 missing. The Oxfords' losses were 64 killed, wounded, and missing. The day's fighting was one long struggle, involving advance, retreat, marching and counter-marching; but with the exception of the small loss of ground already mentioned the enemy was everywhere held.

From the 2nd to the 5th November Lord Cavan's force was subjected to violent artillery bombardments, machine-gun fire, and the persistent activities of snipers; but all attacks were repulsed.

The enemy advanced with gallantry, but was always met with a devastating fire, and his attacks were very costly indeed. On the night of 3rd November a party of Germans began digging a trench in front of a part of the line held by the Oxford and Bucks. Second-Lieut. Pepys, on his own initiative, and accompanied by Second-Lieut. Pendavis, with Privates Merry and Hall, crawled out to a small knoll in front of the line enfilading the German trench. Five Germans were shot, and the remainder came running down the trench in single file towards the British party, as this was the only way out. Twenty-five Germans were accounted for, and the trench abandoned by the enemy. For this exploit the two officers were awarded the D.S.O., and the two men the D.C.M.

On the 6th the enemy again attacked with violence. The morning was comparatively quiet, but at 1 p.m. heavy shelling began and lasted for an hour. Hostile infantry then advanced, chiefly against the French troops on the right of the Irish Guards. The former, who had suffered very heavy casualties and had no supports available, vacated their trenches. This opened the right flank of the Irishmen to an enfilade attack, and the position being untenable, the right company (No. 2) retired to support trenches. No. 1 Company, on the left of No. 2, was therefore isolated, and though sticking grimly to their trench, by the end of the day had almost disappeared. The Grenadiers who joined up with the Irish

were hard pressed, but managed to hold on until some Household
Cavalry who were in reserve were sent up, and strengthened the
line. The Oxfords were now reinforced by two companies of the
Sussex, but their front was not attacked, the enemy's object
apparently being to break through the right flank of the line held
by the French and British troops. The enemy used a Division[1]
in this attack.

At night a new line was formed : Irish Guards, Sussex, Oxfords
(one company), Grenadiers, Oxfords (three companies), in the order
given, from right to left. The Grenadiers' losses were 2 officers
and 75 other ranks killed and wounded. The Oxfords' casualties
were light (7), though Second-Lieut. J. E. G. Ward was killed.
The Irish Guards lost heavily in officers, Lieuts. W. E. Hope and
N. Woodroffe being killed, and Captain Lord John Hamilton[2] and
Lieut. E. King Harman missing.

On the 7th the 3rd and 22nd Brigades made a counter-attack
to regain the lost ground, but it was only partially successful.
At 6 a.m. the Irish Guards were ordered to keep up a heavy fire
when the counter-attack was launched. This was done ; but the
enemy was too strong, and in the woods many casualties were
incurred. Major H. A. Herbert-Stepney of the Irish Guards was
killed during the day. The Grenadiers were again attacked, but
gallantly maintained their line, though many men were lost—the
day's total being 68 killed, wounded, and missing.

The 8th was a quiet day. At night the Oxfords were relieved
by the London Scottish, and about 4 a.m. marched back into the
2nd Division Reserve area and bivouacs, in some trenches a little
south-east of Verlornhoek. On the night of the 9th, at 9 o'clock,
the Irish Guards were relieved by the South Wales Borderers, and
marched to bivouacs near the White Farm, just south of the Ypres–
Zonnebeke road, also in Divisional Reserve. The battalions'
losses from 31st October to 7th November had been terrible ; no
less than 613 in killed, wounded, and missing—of which 16 were
officers.

The night of 10th November brought the Grenadiers (who were
still at Klein Zillebeke) a terrible gruelling with high-explosive.
Trenches were blown in and many men buried amidst the debris,
and it was impossible to dig them all out. Major Lord B. C.
Gordon-Lennox, Lieut. M. E. Stocks, and Lieut. Lord Congleton
were killed ; Captains E. F. H. Powell and E. D. Ridley, and Lieut.

[1] 39th Jäger Division, XVth Corps, Army Group Fabeck.
[2] Afterwards reported killed.

Tudway wounded ; besides 74 N.C.O's and men killed, wounded, and missing. At 1 a.m. the battalion was relieved by the Welsh and Munsters, and marched to Bullewarde Farm for rest in Corps Reserve. But little rest was possible, for the battalion was sent off at 9 a.m. as support against the attack of the Prussian Guards, which by that time had been launched against the 1st Brigade (1st Division) from the Polygone Wood to the Menin–Ypres road.

The night of 14th November saw the Grenadiers again marching back to Klein Zillebeke to their ill-fated trenches, occupied by the Munsters, which battalion they relieved during the 14th–15th. Nothing of importance happened until the 17th, when the enemy once more opened first with a terrific shelling and then a powerful infantry attack, which was, however, repulsed with very heavy loss to the attackers. Some idea of the terrible execution done on the enemy may be gathered from the fact that over 24,000 rounds of small-arms ammunition were fired by the Grenadiers on this day. Captain C. Symes-Thompson and Lieut. J. H. G. Lee-Steers were killed, and 17 N.C.O's and men killed, wounded, and missing. On the 18th the 3rd Coldstream relieved the Grenadiers, who marched to St. Jean and there bivouacked.

On the 21st the 4th (Guards) Brigade, with the 1st Herts Territorials, was complete in billets in Méteren.

The gallant defence of the right of the 1st Corps from 31st October to the middle of November was an achievement of which the force under Lord Cavan might well be proud. Not all the violent attacks hurled against it by an infuriated and baulked enemy could break through the splendid defence put up by those three battalions, aided by reinforcements from other brigades of the corps. Vastly superior forces were launched against them ; yet even though the enemy came on with bands playing to hearten his troops he could not break through ; the indomitable pluck of the British soldier fighting under adverse circumstances came through unbeaten. The part of the line attacked (Klein Zillebeke) was considered by the German Higher Command to be next in importance to the possession of the Ypres–Menin road, which would open the way to the town itself.

II.

TRENCH WARFARE, 1914–1916.

WINTER OPERATIONS.
November 1914 to March 1915.

Trench Warfare, 21st November 1914 to 28th January 1915.
Affairs of Cuinchy, 29th January, 1st and 2nd February.
Trench Warfare, 20th February to 9th March 1915.

Trench Warfare,
21st November 1914 to 28th January 1915.

THE fighting strength of the 2nd Division on the 21st November was 272 officers and 11,213 other ranks; but as reinforcements are included, these figures do not give an accurate idea of the losses of the Division during the battles of Ypres of 1914. Some battalions which had left the Aisne not far short of full strength had been reduced to a third of their establishment.

But their weakness was only temporary, for they were soon made up to strength on arrival in the rest area. Refitting began immediately, and with such luxuries as bathing and haircutting, the troops gradually lost much of that drawn but grim expression on their faces produced by desperate fighting under terrible conditions. " Our men are beginning to look very different now they are washed and have had their hair cut," said one commanding officer in his diary. To the average soldier it was positive agony not to be properly washed and shaved. The cleanliness of the British soldier is proverbial ; but it is impossible for a human being to imitate the life of a rabbit without getting dirty !

On the 24th November the 9th Highland Light Infantry (Glasgow Highlanders), commanded by Lieut.-Colonel W. G. Fleming, arrived at Bailleul from Hazebrouck and joined the 5th Infantry Brigade. The battalion had arrived at St. Omer on the 7th November, and had been in training. The 9th Highland Light Infantry replaced the 2nd Connaughts, who left the 2nd Division to join the Ferozepore (Indian) Brigade.

Orders were received on the 23rd by Divisional Headquarters 23RD Nov for one brigade to proceed to Kemmel and there take over a portion of the trenches of the IInd Corps ; the 5th Infantry Brigade was detailed, and the relief completed on the 25th. The 26th witnessed the departure from the Division of one of its howitzer batteries, the 56th, from the XLIVth Brigade R.F.A., which left to join the Meerut (Indian) Division.

The 5th Infantry Brigade was relieved on the 27th, and marched back to Bailleul. During the brief period it was in the trenches at Kemmel the brigade was not attacked, but snipers were busy night and day, the enemy's trenches being quite close. The Oxford and Bucks, and the 9th Highland Light Infantry suffered a few casualties—*i.e.*, two officers wounded and 16 other ranks killed and wounded. This was the 9th Highland Light Infantry's baptism of fire.

Between 21st November and 22nd December (when the Division left the Bailleul–Méteren–Flêtre–Caestre–Hazebrouck area) " no troops of the 2nd Division were called upon to assist the attacks of the IInd Corps." But on 29th November orders were received for a brigade of infantry, with an artillery brigade and divisional troops, to be held in readiness each day to move at short notice should they be required. Short leave to England was introduced during this period.

On 3rd December H.M. the King, accompanied by H.R.H. the Prince of Wales, arrived at Méteren and Bailleul, and inspected the 2nd Division.

Sandbags were issued to the troops on 12th December. " One bag issued to each soldier for tactical purposes. The bag to be carried on the soldier, and in very cold weather permission is given for these to be used as foot muffs." [1]

21ST DEC.   On 21st December H.R.H. the Prince of Wales was attached to the 2nd Division for two days, and moved about amongst the troops. It is recorded that His Royal Highness was very eager to go up into the trenches.

The 22nd December saw the Division once more on the move. Orders had been received by the Ist Corps to take over the line held by the Indian corps on the 22nd: [2]

" *Ist Corps Operation Order No. 56, 21st December* 1914.—During the fighting yesterday the line of the Indian corps was broken between Givenchy and La Quinque Rue. About 3 p.m. to-day our 1st and 3rd Brigades (1st Division) delivered a counter-attack

[1] General Staff Diary, 2nd Division.
[2] " The 1st Brigade was advanced to Béthune, and reached that place at midnight on 20th–21st December. Later in the day Sir Douglas Haig was asked to send the whole of the 1st Division in support of the Indian corps. The 3rd Brigade reached Béthune between 8 a.m. and 9 a.m. on the 21st, and on the same date the 2nd Brigade arrived at Locon at 1 p.m.
" The 1st Brigade was directed on Givenchy, *via* Pont Fixe, and the 3rd Brigade through Gorre and the trenches evacuated by the Sirhind Brigade. The 2nd Brigade was directed to support. . . ."

against the enemy in this area.   The attacks made good progress, and at 9 p.m. Givenchy had been secured.   East of Festubert a lodgment had been made in the original trenches, and both attacks were sending out flanking parties to gain touch with one another. The Ist Corps will continue to take over the line from the Indian Corps[1] to-morrow.   The 2nd Division will send the following troops to Béthune : 6th Infantry Brigade, 4th (Guards) Brigade, XLIVth (Howitzer) Brigade R.F.A., with section of Divisional Artillery Column and proportion of Small Arms Ammunition wagons, Field Company and Divisional Mounted Troops.   Motor-buses will be at Caestre at 6.30 a.m. to convey the 6th Infantry Brigade to Béthune : route Hazebrouck–Morbecque–St. Venant-Lillers.   After reaching Béthune the brigade will arrange to take over from the right of the Lahore Division[2] to about Givenchy.   Details will depend upon situation."

The remaining troops of the 2nd Division were to await further orders before moving.

On the morning of the 22nd, however, some of the motor-buses carrying the 6th Infantry Brigade broke down, and the brigade did not begin to reach Béthune until noon.   Divisional Headquarters had already arrived and had opened in Béthune.

The 6th Infantry Brigade had completed the relief of the Lahore Division by 6.30 p.m., but owing to the activity of the enemy the whole of the 1st Brigade (1st Division) could not be relieved, and at nightfall only two companies of the 1st Berks were in the line east and north of Givenchy.   The 1st King's Royal Rifles occupied the trenches held by the 1st Connaught Rangers from the Beuvry–La Bassée road to the La Bassée Canal ; the 2nd South Staffords took over the line from the 57th (Wilde's) Rifles and one company of French Territorials, from the northern banks of the canal to east of Givenchy where they joined up with the Berks : the 1st King's were in reserve at Cambrin.   Opposite the King's Royal Rifles the enemy's trenches were 300 yards away on the right, and from 80 to 150 yards away near the canal.   The distance between the South Staffords and the hostile trenches varied from 600 yards by the canal (very open ground) to 150 yards on their left ; the Berks, about 100 to 150 yards.

The 4th (Guards) Brigade arrived at Béthune at 4.30 p.m. and

---

[1] Lahore Division : Ferozepore, Jullundur, and Sirhind Brigades.   Meerut Division : Dehra Dun, Garhwal, and Bareilly Brigades.

[2] The right brigade of the Lahore Division rested on the La Bassée–Beuvry road where it joined up with the French, whose left was just west of Auchy-lez-La-Bassée.

went into billets in the town. Between 10 a.m. and noon on the 23rd the 5th Infantry Brigade reached the area Locon–Le Lobes–La Couture, and went into billets and remained there throughout the 23rd, 24th, 25th, and 26th of December.

Two battalions of the 4th (Guards) Brigade, who were to relieve the 2nd Infantry Brigade, and the right of the Meerut Division, whose trenches lay east of Rue de l'Epinette (north and east from Richebourg l'Avoué to the La Quinque Rue–Festubert road), moved forward at dusk from the vicinity of Ghatignes, where they had been waiting all day, to take over. The first part of the relief was carried out by the 2nd Grenadiers and 2nd Coldstream (in the order given from south to north), who took over the 2nd Brigade line from La Quinque Rue–Festubert road to just east of Rue de l'Epinette. The 2nd Infantry Brigade then went into Corps Reserve. The 1st Herts (Territorials), Irish Guards, and two companies of the 3rd Coldstream were in support in Le Touret, the remaining companies of the 3rd Coldstream acting as supports in the right rear of the Meerut Division.

The trenches were in a terrible condition ; the water in some places was up to the men's waists, and several had to be dug out of the mud before the relief could be completed.

During the period when the Ist Corps was resting and training in the Hazebrouck area the troops had received their first instruction in bomb-throwing. It was a new kind of warfare to them, for hitherto they had been unable to reply to the hand grenades and rifle grenades hurled and fired into their trenches by the enemy. But during the battles of Ypres tests had been made from the Ist Corps' trenches with a new rifle grenade and also behind the lines with hand-bombs or grenades. On 7th December the Royal Engineers of the 2nd Division were making hand grenades. On the 23rd December, as the 2nd Division went into the line, the General Officer Commanding Division (General C. C. Monro) issued a letter in which instructions were given for the co-ordination of bomb-throwing and bayonet attack by assaulting parties on the enemy's trenches.

The salient points in these instructions were : " To avoid the losses entailed by a direct frontal attack against a length of hostile trench the flanks of the portion to be cleared should be assaulted. . . . The assaulting bodies are headed by ' bomb-throwers,' followed by a bayonet party. Having gained the trench these bodies work inwards towards one another, clearing the enemy out of his trench from traverse to traverse. A bomb is thrown over a traverse and then the bayonet men rush in, finish off those of the enemy between that traverse and the next, and so on. . . . As soon as a length of trench is gained every effort should be made to widen the breach, but no time must be lost in barricading any communicating trenches leading towards the enemy. Similarly, when no more ground can be made to right and left barricades must be erected. For these duties, as well as to reverse the parapet, wire entanglements, etc., a party of Royal Engineers should be in readiness. . . . Machine guns should at once be got into the captured trench, and artillery covering fire brought to bear on the hostile supports and reserves. Whenever practicable, pack or field guns should be brought up in close support of the attacking infantry. . . . The capture of a portion of the hostile trench should be the signal for immediate further efforts, both to take other portions of the same line and assault the enemy's second line. For this purpose and to meet possible counter-attacks fresh bodies are required. The original assaulting party must re-form and hold the ground it has gained. Fresh bodies must therefore be in readiness organized as above.''

The 24th December—Christmas Eve—was spent by the Division principally in taking stock of its surroundings, and by the battalions in strengthening their positions by building up the trenches, which everywhere were in a very poor condition and much dilapidated. Orders had been given that a defensive attitude was to be taken up, designed to place distance between the two opposing forces in order to prevent the enemy from using his grenades and trench mortars to the fullest advantage. Sapping was also ordered all along the line, and this operation started in earnest on the 24th. The enemy was also active in this respect, for he had observed the destruction caused by his grenades and minenwerfer ; also that the British troops had little with which to reply effectively to these new weapons of destruction. 24TH DEC.

The 2nd Grenadiers, in the front line east of Rue de Cailloux, suffered terribly from wet and cold. Their trenches were in a deplorable condition, the water being from two to three feet deep, whilst every now and then the enemy's trench-mortar bombs burst on the parapet and blew it to pieces. Snipers were busy, and the enemy had at two points sapped up to within ten yards of the Grenadiers. About 11 a.m. on the 24th the end of No. 2 Company's trench was blown in, and the enemy attacked immediately. No 2 and No. 3 Companies were then ordered to withdraw to the second-line trench, which was held securely, the enemy being driven off with severe losses. The Grenadiers' casualties were heavy : Captain

Sir M. A. R. Cholmeley, Bart., and Second-Lieut. J. H. G. Nevill were killed ; Second-Lieut. C. G. Goschen was wounded and missing, and Second-Lieut. Mervyn-Williams slightly wounded, besides other ranks 15 killed, 29 wounded, 5 wounded and missing, and 4 missing—total, 4 officers and 53 N.C.O's and men. During the night of 24th–25th the Grenadiers dug a new line of trenches just behind their second line, and these were drier and more comfortable.

At 6 p.m. the relief of the Indian troops in front of the 3rd Coldstream began, and was completed by 9 p.m. The line of the 4th (Guards) Brigade was then from right to left : 2nd Grenadiers, 2nd Coldstream, 1st Irish Guards, and 1st Herts ; the 3rd Coldstream were in support.

On the 6th Infantry Brigade front nothing happened of note. The weather was bitterly cold, and between the 24th and 27th hard frosts abounded. The result was numerous cases of " frost-bite." In three days the 2nd Grenadiers alone (probably owing to the terrible condition of their first trenches) had 47 casualties from this horrible affliction.

Apart from the attack on the Grenadiers on the morning of 24th December, the enemy from 25th to the end of the year, and practically throughout the whole of January 1915, contented himself with sniping, bombing, and shelling with minenwerfer and howitzers the front-line trenches of the Division. No infantry attacks were launched, though alarms were frequent. The line held by the Division at the end of December extended from the crossroads south-west of Les Brulots, thence just east of the Rue du Bois, through Richebourg l'Avoué, in a southerly direction to La Quinque Rue–Béthune Road. Divisional Headquarters were in Locon.

It was a period of gestation !

The British forces were reorganized on the 26th. The original British Expeditionary Force, the Indian Corps, and the 27th Division were divided into two Armies : First Army—Sir Douglas Haig : Ist, IVth, and Indian Corps. Second Army—Sir H. Smith-Dorrien : IInd and IIIrd Corps, and 27th Division.

General C. C. Monro, who at (and from) Mons had commanded the 2nd Division, assumed command of the Ist Corps, and with him went Colonel R. Whigham, G.S.O.1, 2nd Division Headquarters. Brigadier-General Fanshawe (6th Infantry Brigade) assumed temporary command of the 2nd Division, and Colonel Davidson temporary command of the 6th Infantry Brigade. On 31st December Brigadier-General A. A. Chichester arrived and took over command of the 5th Infantry Brigade, as Brigadier-General

GENERAL, THE LORD HORNE, G.C.B., K.C.M.G., A.D.C.,
COMMANDED THE 2ND DIVISION FROM 1ST JANUARY 1915
UNTIL 4TH NOVEMBER 1915.

Haking (who had recovered from his wound) had on 20th December been posted to temporary command of the 1st Division.

The gunners were busy during the latter part of December testing a new 5-inch trench howitzer, which, however, did not come up to expectations. The French had reported that greater accuracy could be obtained by attaching cord to the bomb.[1] This was tried and found effective, but unfortunately the range of the new howitzer was only about 250 yards, and also the breech mechanism was not good, and therefore it was practically useless.

The 2nd Siege Battery and the 114th Heavy Battery joined on the 26th December, and were a very welcome addition to the heavy guns of the Division.

A few casualties occurred during the latter part of December : Captain G. Spencer Churchill of the 2nd Grenadiers was wounded on the 25th ; Lieuts. G. P. Gough and F. H. Witts of the 1st Irish Guards were wounded on the same day. Captain Eric Gough (also of the Irish Guards) was killed on the 30th. The 3rd Coldstream lost Captain A. Tritton, and the 1st Berks Captain C. R. Wyld (3rd Wiltshire Regiment attached) on the 26th ; both these officers being killed. On the 30th Major Hankey of the 2nd Worcesters was wounded.

On January 1, 1915, Major-General H. S. Horne assumed command of the 2nd Division *vice* General C. C. Monro, appointed to the command of the 1st Corps ; Brigadier-General Fanshawe returned to the command of the 6th Infantry Brigade.[2] 1ST JAN. 1915

With the exception of the usual shelling and sniping, no infantry attack was made on the 2nd Division throughout January ; but the brigades and battalions were constantly on the move in and out of the front-line trenches. A regular system of reliefs was introduced which ensured the troops adequate rest in billets. The terrible condition of the trenches, which were feet deep in water, necessitated constant work and the rebuilding of parapets. Indeed, the position was so impossible that the front line was held only by

---

[1] " Liaison officer 10th French Army reports that the French find that by using a cord attached to French bombs of moderate weight thrown from mortars, accuracy is secured. After a few trial shots the exact length of cord is discovered, and about ten bombs are launched simultaneously. The cord tautens above the trench and checks the bomb, which falls perpendicularly into the trench." General Staff Diary, 2nd Division.

[2] The various commands in the 2nd Division were held as follows : Major-General H. S. Horne, G.O.C. 2nd Division ; Brigadier-General Fanshawe, D.S.O., G.O.C. 6th Infantry Brigade ; Brigadier-General Chichester, G.O.C. 5th Infantry Brigade ; Brigadier-General the Earl of Cavan, G.O.C. 4th (Guards) Brigade ; Brigadier-General Perceval, C. R.A. ; Lieut.-Colonel Schofield, C. R.E.

small posts, the bulk of the troops being placed in the support trenches. Redoubts or strong-posts were constructed behind the front line. Gradually as trench warfare evolved new weapons were invented, constructed, and tested, and whilst some produced excellent results, others were failures. As regards trench mortars the first troops to use these machines were the Indians, to whom must be given the credit. Flares and Véry lights for illuminating positions at night began to be used by both sides. Searchlights mounted on mobile carriages were also used first by the enemy. But the British profited day by day, though experience was often dearly bought. A certain number of rifles with telescopic sights were issued, and these proved invaluable in sniping operations. A Divisional Mortar officer and Brigade Mortar officers are first mentioned on 23rd January, while for the first time battalions and brigades are reported as having obtained excellent results with " their howitzers " : the 1st Irish Guards had in use a gun called the " gas-pipe " gun !

It was, as already stated, a period of gestation, each side preparing and devising new means of overcoming their opponents.

On the 1st January the 1st East Anglian Field Company R.E. (Territorials) arrived and joined the Division. The 2nd Battalion Royal Inniskilling Fusiliers (Lieut.-Colonel C. A. Wilding) reached Robec on the 26th to join the Division, and were posted to the 5th Infantry Brigade. Both the 4th and 5th Infantry Brigades were now each five battalions strong.[1]

25TH JAN. On the 25th the enemy made a demonstration along the front of the 2nd Meerut and 8th Divisions, which took the form of shelling and rifle fire, the 8th Division being subjected to a heavy bombing attack. Farther south the enemy pressed an attack on Givenchy, and the line of the 1st Division south of the La Bassée Canal. The artillery of the 2nd Division lent support, and put down a curtain of fire east of Givenchy ; the " heavies " also fired on La Bassée. In the afternoon, however, the 3rd Infantry Brigade, which had been driven out of Givenchy, again attacked, and the Welch Regiment and South Wales Borderers succeeded in recapturing the town and 35 prisoners, whilst casualties estimated at 600 were inflicted on the enemy.

South of the La Bassée Canal, however, the counter-attack was

---

1 4th (Guards) Brigade : 2nd Grenadiers, 2nd Coldstream, 3rd Coldstream, 1st Irish Guards, 1st Herts (Territorials).

5th Infantry Brigade : 2nd Worcesters, 2nd Oxford and Bucks, 2nd Highland Light Infantry, 2nd Royal Inniskilling Fusiliers, 9th Highland Light Infantry.

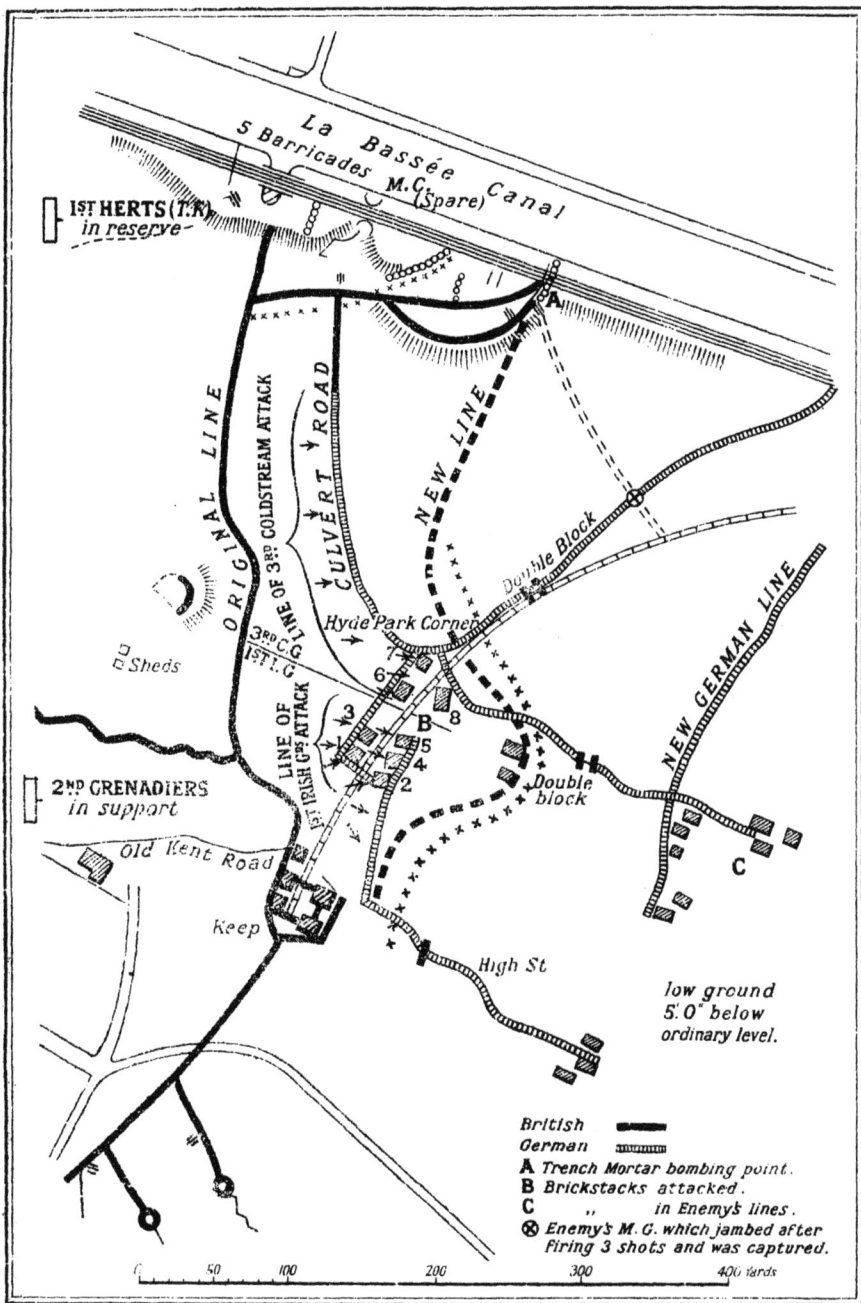

La Bassée Canal

5 Barricades M.C. (Spare)

1ST HERTS (T.F.)
in reserve

A

ORIGINAL LINE

NEW LINE

CULVERT ROAD

LINE OF 3RD COLDSTREAM ATTACK

3RD C.G.
1ST I.G.

□ Sheds

Double Block

Hyde Park Corner

7

6

LINE OF 2ND IRISH G.DS ATTACK

3

B

8

5

4

2

Double block

NEW GERMAN LINE

2ND GRENADIERS
in support

Old Kent Road

C

Keep

High St

low ground
5' 0" below
ordinary level.

British
German
A Trench Mortar bombing point.
B Brickstacks attacked.
C   „   „   in Enemy's lines.
⊗ Enemy's M.G. which jambed after
   firing 3 shots and was captured.

0   50   100   200   300   400 Yards

THE MAPPA CO., LTD., LONDON.

THE AFFAIRS OF CUINCHY, 29th January and
1st and 6th February 1915.

(Facing p. 176.)

held up and progress could not be made, the enemy having obtained a lodgment in the " Triangle," a position formed by a juncture of railway lines, and in the later stages of the war of terrible renown.

* * * * * * *

On the 26th January, Brigadier-General E. M. Perceval, D.S.O., commanding 2nd Division Artillery, left the Division to take over the duties of Sub-Chief of the General Staff. He was replaced by Brigadier-General W. H. Onslow.

The Affairs of Cuinchy.

"The British line south of the canal formed a pronounced salient from the canal on the left, thence running forward towards the railway triangle and back to the main La Bassée–Béthune road, where it joined the French. This line was occupied by half a battalion of the (1st) Scots Guards and half a battalion of the (1st) Coldstream Guards of the 1st Infantry Brigade. The trenches in the salient were blown in almost at once, and the enemy's attack penetrated the line. Our troops retired to a partially prepared second line running approximately due north and south from the canal to the road, some 500 yards west of the railway triangle. This second line had been strengthened by the construction of a 'Keep' half way between the canal and the road. Here the other two half-battalions of the above-mentioned regiments were in support. These supports held up the enemy, who, however, managed to establish himself in the Brickstacks and some communication trenches between the Keep, the road, and the canal, and even beyond and west of the Keep on either side of it." [1]

A counter-attack was only partially successful. "The result was that the Germans were driven back far enough to enable a somewhat broken line to be taken up, running from the culvert on the railway almost due south to the Keep, and thence southeast to the main road." [1]

The paragraphs given above, though describing the operations of the 1st Infantry Brigade on 25th January, are of interest, for it was this position that was later taken over by the 4th (Guards) Brigade, and the two actions of 1st and 6th February mentioned in Sir John French's dispatches were fought by the Guards in this particular part of the line.

29TH JAN. AND 1ST AND 6TH FEB. MAP.

---

[1] Official Dispatches.

A further attack took place from this section of the front on 29th January, but without affecting the position of the 1st Infantry Brigade, which, however, inflicted heavy losses on the enemy. The Brigade was later relieved by the 2nd Infantry Brigade.

On the morning of the 30th the 4th (Guards) Brigade marched from Locon to Béthune to take over the trenches at Cuinchy—*i.e.*, the 2nd Brigade's trenches south of the La Bassée Canal to the La Bassée–Béthune road. The 2nd Coldstream relieved the Sussex and Northamptons, and were extended in the following order from right to left : No. 1 Company on the La Bassée–Béthune road ; then No. 2 and No. 3 Companies. No. 4 Company was on the extreme left of the battalion on the south side of the canal. The 1st Irish Guards (Headquarters in Cuinchy) were in support, 3rd Coldstream in Annequin, 1st Herts in Beuvry, and the 2nd Grenadiers in Béthune. French troops (XXIst Corps of the Tenth French Army) continued the line south from the La Bassée–Béthune road.

The relief was successfully accomplished without casualties. The position held by the 2nd Coldstream was well described by the commanding officer of that battalion: "An almost dead flat, poplar-lined, and cobbled road breaks off at Beuvry one and a half miles from our Béthune billets, and runs for four miles to a crossroad known as the Pont Fixe road, which runs north to Givenchy, past the ruined distillery, the tall chimney of which was pierced by many German shells, and at last after many weeks was brought crashing to the ground by a final hit, towards the end of our occupation of the Cuinchy trenches. Immediately east of the Pont Fixe road there is a distinct rise in the ground to a semicircular road in which is Cuinchy village, which consists of a church, some villas and cottages, all roofless and shattered by the continual shelling of many weeks. The church is a mere ruin, but curiously a large statue of a saint still stands intact, the only unbroken thing in the general wreck. A short distance from the church are the two battalion Headquarters, both in the very large, roomy cellars which so many of the houses possess. To the north runs the La Bassée Canal with a broad tow-path on either side, and immediately south of it runs the railway on an embankment about sixteen feet above the general level. East of the village lie the famous brickfields, still [1] littered with British corpses from the fighting of 25th January, bounded on the north by the railway and on the south by the La Bassée road ; all a dead level except where the soil has

[1] February 1915.

been moved to get clay for the bricks. In the middle of the plain lie the Brickstacks, in two groups of almost a dozen, each lying from 80 to 100 yards apart, the stacks being much bigger than the stacks we see at home.

"The German right rested on the railway triangle, and this afforded them cover from rifle-fire and view. About 200 yards west of the point of this triangle was known as 'the Hollow,' formed by an embankment which carries no rails, and the railway meeting at an acute angle, near the point of which was a large bank of dumped earth of the same level as the embankment. At the end of the Hollow, which was about a hundred yards in length, was a small canal lock, which the railway crossed by a girder bridge; about midway was a brick culvert. The left of the first position we held rested on the culvert, and ran through a small depression on the embankment behind the bank of dumped earth, and at this point the Germans held the other part of the trench, which ran in a south-east direction towards the Brickstacks and had originally been a British trench." [1]

Such was the position during the night 31st January–1st February.

Before it was light on the morning of the 1st, the enemy attacked the 2nd Coldstream. About 2.30 a.m. a lot of bombs were thrown into that part of the trench held by No. 4 Company, the other end of which was German. The Coldstream had to retire to a barricade of sandbags in the Hollow between the railway embankment and the siding embankment. Here they still had command of the tow-path and could prevent the enemy coming out of it. No. 4 Company of the Irish Guards, in support, now arrived, and a counter-attack was organized, which took place about 4 a.m. The attack was made in three lines. The first line, which consisted of 10 men of No. 4 Company 2nd Coldstream, was directed up the tow-path. The second line, of 40 men of the Coldstream, was to advance up the Hollow and on top of the siding embankment. The third line consisted of 40 men of No. 4 Company of the Irish Guards, with 40 more to hold the first barricade along the canal bank.

The counter-attack suffered heavily, and stopped about thirty yards from the second barricade; the men on top of the embankment had to vacate it owing to machine-gun fire, and those who advanced across the Hollow found a depression in the middle and the ground much cut up with communication trenches and dug-outs,

[1] Diary of Lieut.-Col. C. Pereira.

which brought them to a narrow front and prevented a rapid charge, thus forming a fine target for the enemy. The sky was cloudy, but the moon was full and the light good. The 40 men of the Irish Guards at the first barricade were then advanced, but were held up. At 6.30 a.m., as it was getting light and further losses would be incurred, the attacking parties were withdrawn. Command of the tow-path and the second barricade had, however, been obtained, thus making a further German advance impossible.

Just before 7 a.m. instructions were received from Brigade Headquarters directing an attack on the position with bombs. A bomb party was formed, but Colonel Pereira, commanding 2nd Coldstream, and temporarily in command of No. 4 Company of the Irish Guards, lent for the attack, pointed out that such an attack was impracticable, as the losses would be very heavy.

Between 8 and 9 o'clock Lord Cavan issued orders for another attack, preceded by a ten minutes' bombardment by siege guns and howitzers. The actual time of starting was, however, 10.15 a.m. The gunners made splendid practice : " They poured high-explosive shells into a comparatively small area with astounding accuracy and enormous effect. The word 'awful' describes it when it pictures men in a perfect hell of explosives. I saw one body lifted on to the embankment ; another, evidently fearfully mangled, was hurled right over the embankment and tow-path into the canal, a sight which would sicken one in cold blood ; but our losses had been heavy and the place had to be retaken, and the relief of seeing the effect of the bombardment, which made it impossible that our losses in the next attempt on the position would be anything but slight, made one pleased, horrible though it may seem."

The new attack was organized as follows : 50 men of the 2nd Coldstream (10 for the tow-path and 40 for the first line up the Hollow, followed immediately by 4 bomb-throwers of No. 3 and No. 4 Companies), to be followed at a short distance by 30 men from No. 1 Company Irish Guards carrying filled sandbags, spades, and two boxes of bombs with which to build up the barricade near the railway bridge.

"At 10.15 by the watch I launched the attack, and they streamed up to the first barricade. A few gallant Germans still showed fight and were shot down. (Captain A.) Leigh-Bennett seeing the advantage of pushing on to the apex of the Hollow, and so advancing on our original front lost this morning, urged that the Irish Guards holding the second barricade should be pushed in (which was done). He then led the first line, strengthened by them, up to the end of the Hollow. Our bomb-throwers did most excellent work ; they were cool and plucky and most effective, and greatly assisted in overcoming the last resistance of the Germans."

It was during the advance of the Coldstream and Irish Guards that Lance-Corporal M. O'Leary of the latter regiment gained his Victoria Cross.[1] " He rushed ahead on to the railway embankment, and shot five Germans behind the first barricade. Then he dashed on to the next barricade, about sixty yards ahead, and shot three more, two of whom were trying to work a damaged machine gun, and took them prisoners." [2]

The result of this attack was that not only the whole of the ground lost in the morning was retaken, but the enemy's position for a length of sixty yards (including two trenches) was also captured, with 32 prisoners and two machine guns. It was a brilliant little exploit, and the Coldstream and Irish Guards received well-deserved praise for their gallant conduct.[3]

The artillery preparation was described by the General Officer Commanding as " splendid, the high-explosive shells dropping in the exact position with absolute precision." In forwarding his report on this engagement, the General Officer Commanding First Army gave special credit to the General Officer Commanding 4th Brigade (Lord Cavan) " for the thorough manner in which he carried out the orders of the General Officer Commanding the Division," and " to the regimental officers, non-commissioned officers, and men of the 2nd Coldstream Guards and Irish Guards, who with indomitable pluck stormed two sets of barricades, captured three German trenches, two machine guns, and killed and made prisoners many of the enemy." [4] When darkness had set in, the 2nd Coldstream and Irish Guards were relieved by the 3rd Coldstream and one company of the 2nd Grenadiers.

Captain Viscount Northland of the Coldstream was killed by a stray bullet just before the battalion was relieved.

On 4th February the 2nd Division took over command of the Festubert (C) and Givenchy (B) sections, the Cuinchy (A) section being already held by the 4th (Guards) Brigade, though hitherto under the command of the 1st Division. The 5th Infantry Brigade occupied Festubert, and the 6th Infantry Brigade Givenchy. The reliefs were carried out without incident.

---

[1] *London Gazette*, 18th February 1915.
[2] Diary, 1st Irish Guards.
[3] See Appendix IX. for casualties.
[4] Official Dispatches.

The system of holding the line was altered, two battalions being placed in the line in each section and finding their own supports; companies relieved companies, the usual method being to put two companies in the front line, one in support and one in billets. This system worked satisfactorily.

The following units joined the Division on this day: No. 1 Siege Battery R.G.A., 26th Heavy Battery R.G.A., No. 7 Mountain Battery R.G.A., 1st Motor Machine-Gun Battery, the Armoured Train (" Jellicoe "), No. 11 Section Anti-Aircraft, 26th Field Company R.E., a Lowland Company R.E. and a detachment of the 1st Queen's (Royal West Surrey Regiment) as a working party.

Since the brilliant action by the 4th (Guards) Brigade south of the La Bassée Canal on 1st February, the centre of the British line (the " Keep ") had formed an undesirable salient; it was a vulnerable point for enemy machine guns and snipers, who from the Brickstacks lying north and north-east were able to bring a destructive and worrying fire upon the Guards. Moreover, the French XXIst Corps, under General Maistre, was anxious to re-establish its old line east of the quarries just south of the La Bassée–Béthune road, which had been lost on 25th January. On 3rd February, therefore, a scheme of attack was proposed which would not only straighten out the line by the capture of the Brickstacks, but by lending support to the French would enable the latter to obtain their objective, if not immediately, in a very little while after the capture of the Brickstacks, should the attack succeed. The new 9.2-inch howitzer belonging to the 8th Siege Battery had arrived, and was to be used for the first time in the artillery preparation before the attack developed. Very strict instructions had been issued that on no account was this gun to be fired until the day of attack; it was thus hoped to spring an unwelcome surprise upon the enemy.

At 4 p.m. on 5th February orders for the attack were received by the General Officer Commanding 4th (Guards) Brigade. As a preliminary step the commanding officer of the 1st Irish Guards (then holding the line from opposite the Brickstacks to the Keep and southwards to the left flank of the French) pushed forward a small party at 9 p.m. and gained a portion of the enemy's trenches north and east of the Keep; it was a good move, for it greatly facilitated the big attack which took place on the following day.

Very explicit instructions were issued to all concerned by the General Officer Commanding 4th Brigade, and commanding officers and company commanders were taken round and shown their objectives and carefully rehearsed in their orders.

The morning of the 6th passed quietly, but at 2 p.m. the bombardment began. A siege howitzer battery and a field gun battery opened on the Brickstacks, and kept up a very heavy fire for fifteen minutes, the last five minutes being intense. The 9.2-inch fired on the Brickstacks behind the enemy's line and on the eastern front of the Triangle. The hostile artillery was engaged by another heavy battery, whilst a field howitzer shelled the German trenches, and two 18-pounder batteries the ground in front of the enemy's trenches and the Brickstacks.

At 2.15 fire on the enemy's trenches ceased, and the range was lengthened to a line between the two groups of Brickstacks.

The assault was formed of a bombing party, a bayonet party, and sandbag and engineer parties with a supporting party of machine gunners.

Meanwhile the 5th and 6th Infantry Brigades north of the La Bassée Canal, the Irish Guards south of the Keep, and the 3rd Coldstream on the left of the line immediately south of the canal, opened with bursts of rifle and machine-gun fire in order to contain the enemy and prevent him launching counter-attacks if the main attack on the Brickstacks proved successful.

The French were not ready to attack on the 6th, but lent valuable support by opening an oblique artillery fire on the enemy's support trenches and communications.

The 3rd Coldstream were allotted the north-western group of three stacks and the 1st Irish Guards the south-western group of five stacks—eight in all. The line of objective was the enemy's trenches in the rear of the Brickstacks. The latter were protected by front-line trenches which ran to north-east and south-west of the two groups, thence falling back south-east to a line just east of the Keep.

The ground over which the attack moved forward was somewhat broken by small pits dug in the soil by the brickmakers, though work had ceased many weeks before.

As the guns ceased firing the assaulting parties, each consisting of 30 men under an officer, and followed by more men with sandbags, and engineers, rushed forward, and in four minutes (the recorded time being 2.19 p.m.) had obtained their first objectives— the front line of stacks. This astonishing feat was made possible only by the splendid artillery support ; the fire of the guns having completely overpowered the enemy. The Irish Guards captured three stacks in their first stride, the 3rd Coldstream two : the former had still two more to capture and the latter one. They pressed on, leaving the captured stacks to be put in a state of defence by the supporting parties. The second line of stacks captured, the Irish Guards on their own initiative, quickly seeing that the possession of the Brickstacks did not offer a very good field of fire upon the enemy's position, pressed forward another seventy yards and captured the enemy's second-line trench also. The Coldstream then had to conform, and moving forward abreast of the Irishmen, succeeded also in establishing a line much in advance of the first objective. Here the engineers of the 11th Field Company, under Major Foulkes, performed a brilliant feat, for not only did they follow with sandbags and put the stacks into a state of defence immediately, but erected a line of wire entanglements 340 yards long and 10 yards wide in full view of the enemy, with only 8 casualties, of which but one man was killed. The German trenches north-east, east, and south-east of the Brickstacks, used as communication trenches by the enemy, were also double-blocked and barricaded with sandbags.

In the assault the Irish Guards lost Lieut. T. Musgrave, killed : he was first on the German parapet. Father Gwynn, the chaplain, was also wounded, and 6 men were killed and 25 wounded. The 3rd Coldstream lost Second-Lieut. C. M. Cottrell-Dormer, D.S.O., wounded (died of wounds, 8th), and 11 other ranks killed and 26 wounded—a total of 70 casualties in all.

The General Officer Commanding 4th Brigade and the two battalions were congratulated by the commander-in-chief, Sir Douglas Haig, and the General Officers Commanding 2nd and 1st Divisions.

Material help was given by the 5th and 6th Infantry Brigades north of the canal by their containing fire ; also by the troops on both flanks of the attacking parties, who compelled the enemy to keep to his trenches instead of counter-attacking immediately. In the evening the Irish Guards were relieved by the 2nd Grenadiers, and the 3rd Coldstream by the 2nd Coldstream.

The 9.2-inch howitzer (promptly christened " Mother ") lent splendid assistance and was very effective.

The enemy counter-attacked on the 7th, but was easily repulsed ; his troops advanced shouting: " Don't shoot ! we are engineers ! "

On the 8th the French 58th Division (XXIst Corps), supported by the 2nd and 1st Divisional Artillery, made a successful attack and pushed forward so as to conform to the right flank of the 4th Guards Brigade.

Trench Warfare, 20th February to 9th March 1915.

The 6th Infantry Brigade on 20th February carried out a care-   20TH FEB.
fully planned attack on a portion of the enemy's trenches opposite
the "Duck's Bill" (Givenchy section), where the German and
British trenches were only eighty yards apart.   The attack was organized to discover whether the enemy was driving a mine gallery
beneath the trenches of the brigade, and if so to destroy it.

The troops detailed for the attack were parties of the 2nd
South Staffords, 1st Berks, 9th Highland Light Infantry, and the
1st East Anglian Field Company R.E.   There were two storming
parties, each followed by an R.E. party carrying sandbags, shovels,
etc., followed by a demolition party and finally a support party.
The two assaulting parties were named the Right and Left Columns.
The Right Column numbered 1 officer and 10 men of the South
Staffords and 9th Highland Light Infantry, 20 in all ; and the Left,
1 officer and 20 men of the Berks.

The attack took place at evening, in a somewhat uncertain
light which favoured the operation.

At 5 p.m. the 17th Battery R.F.A. opened fire on the enemy's
wire entanglements, and five minutes later the 47th Battery opened
on the hostile trenches.   The artillery preparation was excellent,
the wire being breached whilst the trenches of the enemy were in
places blown in.

5.15 p.m.—Covering fire was opened by the troops on both
flanks of the trenches being attacked, thus preventing the enemy
firing on the attackers.   The assaulting parties left their trenches
at 5.20 p.m., and under the command of Captain Hill, D.S.O.,
advanced rapidly across " No Man's Land " : " The Right Column
as it started was partially buried by the explosion of a large shell,
and nearly the whole storming party was knocked down and a
good many casualties caused.   Lieut. Harris of the South Staffords, seeing the confusion caused by the shell, led his supports
forward too, and was seriously wounded at the enemy's trench.
The men entered the trench, and pushed to the right up to where a
communication trench came in.   About five or six Germans retired before them, and more opened fire from a trench said to be
about 200 yards in rear.   Captain Preedy, 11th Field Company
R.E., and Lieut. A. G. Langley of the East Anglian Field Company (the latter in charge of the demolition party), searched the
trench for a mine-lead but could find none.

"The Left Column stormers, led by Lieut. Burney of the Royal Berkshire Regiment, reached the enemy's parapet and found a small party of Germans retiring, leaving their rifles and equipment behind them, and two or three more stopping to shoot. These last were bayoneted, and it is reported some of the others were hit. This party pushed north about fifty yards up the trench, and were preparing to block the trench and the communication trench there, which led east, when the signal was given that all were ready to retire. Sergeant E. Burgess, Royal Berks, who had been wounded in the head as he entered the trench, now assumed command of the Left party as Lieut. Burney had also been wounded, and conducted the withdrawal in an orderly manner. . . . The withdrawal was unmolested."

The operation was quite satisfactory and was over by 5.50 p.m., the losses being comparatively light : the South Staffords lost Second-Lieut. L. T. Despicht wounded, Second-Lieut. J. St. C. G. Harris [1] missing, and 6 other ranks killed, wounded, and missing ; the Berks' losses were Lieut. E. E. N. Burney wounded and 10 other ranks killed, wounded, and missing ; the 9th Highland Light Infantry lost 3 other ranks wounded and missing ; and the 1st East Anglian Field Company 1 officer wounded (Second-Lieut. C. H. Humphreys), and 11 men killed, wounded, and missing.

No other attack of importance was made by or on the 2nd Division during the remainder of February.

H.R.H. the Prince of Wales arrived in the evening of 22nd February on being attached to the 2nd Division as extra G.S.O. (3rd Grade).

* * * * * * *

The 5th King's (Liverpool) Regiment joined the Division on the 22nd February and was posted to the 6th Infantry Brigade, the strength of which was now five battalions—i.e., 1st King's (Liverpool) Regiment, 1st King's Royal Rifles, 1st Royal Berks, 2nd South Staffords, and 5th King's (Liverpool) Regiment.

On 5th February the 22nd Battery of the XXXIVth Brigade R.F.A., which had been with the 2nd Division since the British Expeditionary Force landed in France in August 1914, was, with a proportion of the Brigade Ammunition Column, transferred permanently to the 28th Division.

Several changes took place in the 1st Corps area towards the end of February : the 1st Division took over the Festubert section, the 3rd Brigade replacing the 5th Infantry Brigade which

[1] Reported killed on 22nd February 1915.

moved into Béthune in reserve ; the 1st Brigade prolonged the left of the 3rd Brigade, relieving the right Brigade of the Meerut Division. On the 28th the 4th (Guards) Brigade in the Cuinchy section were relieved by the 5th Infantry Brigade and moved into Béthune as reserve. The 6th Infantry Brigade still held the Givenchy section.

There were numerous Staff changes in the Division during January and February. Lieut.-Colonel Gogarty (*vice* Colonel R. Whigham, to 1st Corps as Brig.-Gen. G.S.) joined as G.S.O.1 on 4th January; he left for England on 21st February and was replaced by Lieut.-Colonel L. R. Vaughan, D.S.O. Major F. A. Buzzard joined as G.S.O.2 on 24th February; Captain M. O. Clark, G.S.O.3, joined on the same date. Lieut.-Colonel C. D. Jebb, D.S.O., assumed the duties of A.A.Q.M.G. on 7th February (*vice* Lieut.-Colonel Conway Gordon, D.S.O.). Major H. E. Smythe relieved Major J. Baker on 27th January as D.A.D.O.S., and Captain G. W. R. Stackpool, D.S.O., relieved Captain G. A. Sullivan on 13th February as D.A.P.M.

SUMMER OPERATIONS, 1915.
March to October.

THE BATTLE OF NEUVE CHAPELLE:
The Second Division delivers a "Holding Attack" at Givenchy.

Trench Warfare, 14th March to 30th April 1915.

THE BATTLE OF FESTUBERT.

Trench Warfare, 21st May to 24th September 1915.

THE BATTLE OF LOOS:
Actions of the Hohenzollern Redoubt.

Trench Warfare, November 1915 to July 1916.

THE BATTLE OF NEUVE CHAPELLE:

The Second Division Delivers a " Holding Attack " at Givenchy.

THE winter campaign of 1914–1915 ended with the last day of February. Early in March the weather became brighter, and fair winds dried up the ground in and around the trenches, to the general satisfaction of the troops. It is not desirable to dwell upon the horrors of that first winter in the trenches, but it is doubtful whether Hannibal's legions crossing the Alps, or Napoleon's veterans trudging across the snow-covered plains of Russia in the retreat from Moscow, fared worse than those gallant men who stood for days in water reaching half-way up their benumbed bodies, suffering intense agonies from cold and exposure, to say nothing of the constant shelling and sniping which by day and by night went on almost without ceasing.

Vivid pictures are contained in some of the Official Diaries : " A man of . . . was killed in one of the communication trenches, and the mud is so deep they couldn't get him out and he has sunk out of sight. . . . The rain, which has never ceased since we came into this part of the line, washes away the parapet, the work on which has to go on continually as pieces keep collapsing. It is quite impossible for the men to get any rest owing to the water, and one can't dig owing to the water rising. . . . The man killed in the communication trench has disappeared in the soft mud, and it is quite impossible to get him out as he has sunk quite five or six feet. . . . The trenches are in an awful state. . . . Everything which falls into the bottom of the trench disappears in the mud and sludge. . . . Our Headquarters trenches are full of water to the top ! "

And then the battalion was relieved, and this is what happened subsequently : " Started getting the men cleaned up ; they are in an awful mess. Got up a load of presents and issued them. Have started a laundry to wash the men's blankets—they have got into such an awful state, and are alive ! We have got an old copper and some tubs, and are washing them (the blankets presumably) in creosol and then drying them in drying rooms. In another farm we have opened up baths, and are giving the men a hot bath and ironing their clothes to kill the vermin. The men undress and get into the tubs with hot water and permanganate ; another man takes away their clothes, and irons them to kill the vermin. In lots of cases the clothes are so bad it is impossible to clean them of vermin, and new clothes and underclothes have to be issued." After some days in billets the battalion is back again in the trenches undergoing the same torture : " The trenches are in a dreadful state, and full of water. Parapet has fallen in, in most places." So it went on !

And yet the official diaries of that period breathe also a wonderful spirit of cheerfulness and an indomitable determination to see the worst through to the end—despair was not for the British soldier !

In paragraph 4 of his dispatch dated 5th April 1915, Sir John French gives the reasons which resulted in the opening of a vigorous offensive.

" About the end of February," he said, " many vital considerations induced me to believe that a vigorous offensive movement by the forces under my command should be planned and carried out at the earliest possible moment. Amongst the more important reasons which convinced me of this necessity were :

(1) The general aspect of the Allied situation throughout Europe, and particularly the marked success of the Russian army in repelling the violent onslaughts of Marshal von Hindenburg ;

(2) The apparent weakening of the enemy on my front, and the necessity for assisting our Russian allies to the utmost by holding as many hostile troops as possible in the western theatre ;

(3) The efforts to that end which were being made by the French troops at Arras and Champagne ;

(4) And, perhaps the most weighty consideration of all, the need of fostering the offensive spirit in the troops under my command after the trying and possibly enervating experiences which they had gone through of a severe winter in the trenches."

But Sir John need not have feared for the " offensive spirit " of his troops. A diary kept by a brigade of the 2nd Division

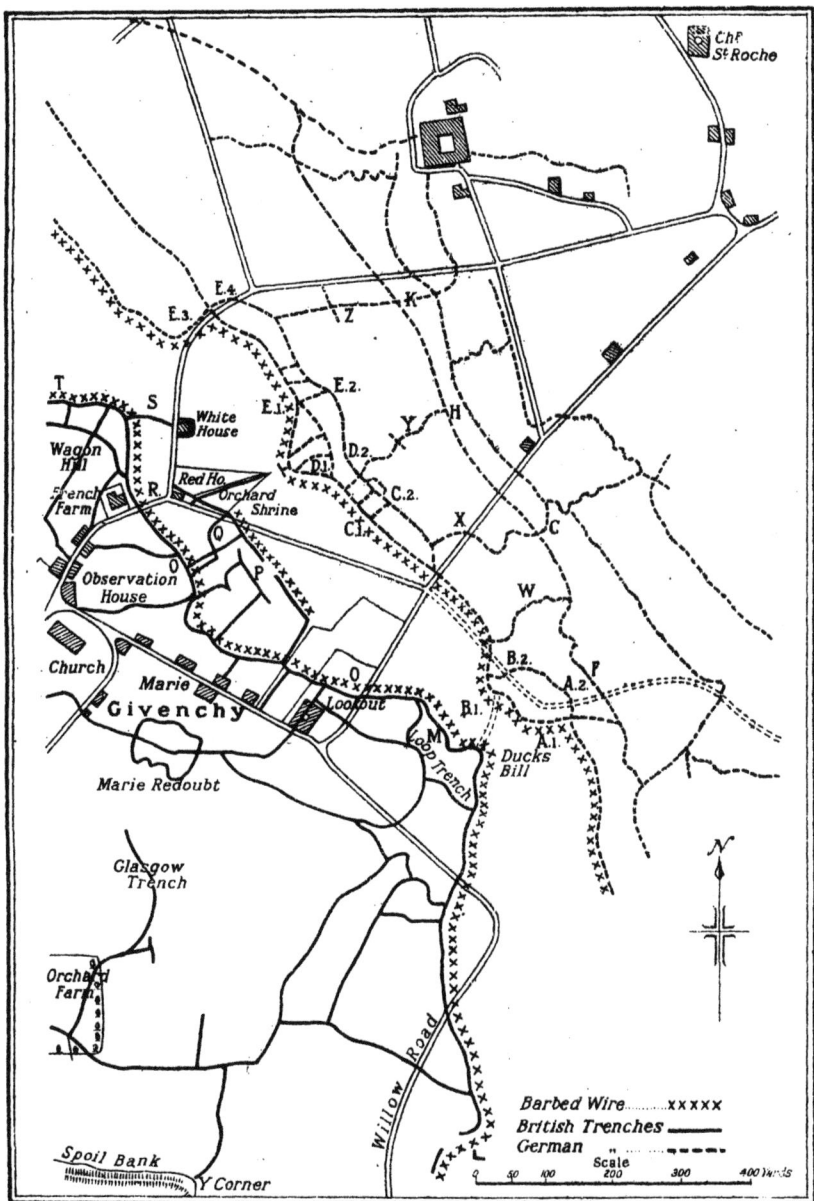

Ch St Roche

E.4.

E.3.

Z K

E.2.

T

S White House

E.1.

Y H

Wagn Hll

D.2.

Trnch Farm

Red Ho.

D.1.

R Orchard Shrine

C.2.

Q C.1.

X C

Observation House

O P

W

Church

Marie

B.2.

A.2.

Givenchy

Lookout

B.1.

A.1.

Marie Redoubt

Loop Trench

M Ducks Bill

Glasgow Trench

N

Orchd Far

Willow Road

Spoil Bank

Y Corner

Barbed Wire..........×××××
British Trenches ——
German ▪ ▪ ▪ ▪ ▪

Scale
0   50   100   200   300   400 Yards

THE MAPPA CO., LTD., LONDON.

HOLDING ATTACK BY THE 2ND DIVISION AT GIVENCHY, 10th March 1915.

(Facing p. 192.)

records: " The spirit of the brigade remains excellent "; and this was typical of the whole British force in France and Flanders.

As a result of these considerations an attack by the First Army on Neuve Chapelle was made. An offensive farther south was also launched from Givenchy against 700 yards of trenches, the capture of which was not only desired, but was designed to hold the enemy to his ground and prevent him sending reinforcements to assist in resisting the principal attack against his line at Neuve Chapelle; secondary and holding attacks were likewise made along the front of the Second Army. Of the First Army the IVth and Indian Corps bore the brunt of the attack, which took place on the 10th, 11th, and 12th of March. The 2nd Division of the Ist Corps, in an attack launched from Givenchy, contributed largely to the success at Neuve Chapelle.

This attack was made by the 6th Infantry Brigade, then holding the Givenchy section. For almost four months this brigade had sat in the trenches without any excitement in the way of attack or counter-attack. But on 9th March orders were received that on the morning of the 10th the brigade would attack and capture the enemy's trenches over a front of 700 yards. Details of the attack were then given.

9TH MARCH. MAP.

There were to be three points of attack—the first immediately north-east of the " Duck's Bill " (B1, B2, A1, A2); the second east and north-east of the " Shrine " (C1, C2, D1, D2); and the third east and north-east of " White House " (E1, E2, E3, E4). The distance between the British and enemy trenches varied from 70 to 300 yards, and from the Duck's Bill ran in a north-west direction; there were to be three assaulting parties, termed the Right, Centre, and Left Columns.

The 5th Infantry Brigade (south of La Bassée Canal) had also received orders to open bursts of rifle and machine-gun fire on the hostile trenches in front of their section—Cuinchy.

The 4th (Guards) Brigade were in reserve in and around Le Preol.

The 1st Division was to co-operate by a fire attack all along the line, and the 58th French Division, on the right flank of the 5th Infantry Brigade, had also undertaken to lend assistance by artillery fire.

The assaulting parties were formed as follows :

> *Right Column :* Three companies 2nd South Staffords, with two machine guns ; two sections East Anglian Field Company R.E., under the command of Lieut.-Colonel

Routledge, South Staffords. Objective—B1 and B2, and to push left until meeting Centre Column.

Centre Column : Three companies 1st King's (Liverpool), with two machine guns ; one section 5th Field Company R.E., under Lieut.-Colonel Carter, 1st King's. Objective —German trenches C1 to D1, then push to right and gain touch with Right Column and left to connect up with Left Column.

Left Column : Three companies 1st King's Royal Rifles, with two machine guns; one section 5th Field Company R.E., under the command of Major Shakerley, 1st King's Royal Rifles. Objective—German trenches E1 to E3, pushing to right to gain touch with the Centre Column.

10TH MARCH. On the morning of the 10th the artillery opened fire at 7.30, and for ten minutes poured shell on to the 700 yards of trenches to be assaulted. At 7.40 the first bombardment ceased ; at 7.50 the second bombardment opened, and was continued until 8.5, when it became " intense." Five minutes later the range was lengthened to the second-line trenches and to both flanks.

As the guns lengthened their range (at 8.10) the three assaulting parties simultaneously rushed from their trenches towards the enemy's position. They went forward most gallantly. The South Staffords, forming the Right Column, had only 80 yards to cover ; but no sooner had the troops left their trenches than they came under a very severe cross-fire from machine guns, and men began to fall quickly. A mere handful reached the hostile trenches, only to find that the wire entanglements had hardly been touched, and nowhere were there wide gaps through which a rapid attack could be made. Second-Lieut. Hewat with 15 men attacked one of the machine guns—" But," the Diary states, " none of them returned." Second-Lieut. Wood with 12 men did succeed in getting into a German trench, but he and his party were bombed out again. He then formed another party and returned to the attack. Second-Lieut. Richardson next led a party of C Company forward, but a permanent lodgment could not be made, and eventually the attack ceased.

The Centre Column fared no better. Here the 1st King's assaulted in two columns, B Company (under Lieut. Snatt) moving forward over the 300 yards which divided them from the enemy's trenches under a perfect hail of bullets; and A Company (under Captain Feneran) attacking a trench some 100 yards from their own trenches. Of B Company the foremost man did not get farther than 150 yards, and by this time all the officers of the company had been killed or wounded. A Company got as far as the barbed wire, but here the men of the leading section were all shot down and some actually fell across the wire. With the exception of Lieut. Miller all the officers of this company also were killed or wounded ; Lieut. Miller was slightly wounded.

The Left Column (1st King's Royal Rifles), which had also been divided up into two assaulting parties—Right and Left—were likewise unsuccessful. The Right party "advanced at the double over the intervening ground and soon came under a heavy fire from rifle and machine gun, losing many men; those remaining continued their advance, but when within thirty yards of the wire entanglement were almost annihilated by cross machine-gun fire. Others threw themselves on the ground, as they could not get through the entanglement, which had nowhere been breached and which consisted of trestles and high wire entanglements. Only a very small number succeeded,in reaching the wire, and none got into the enemy's trenches." The Left party were slightly more successful. " This party succeeded in crawling through (the wire), and established themselves in the enemy's front trench by blocking two places and a communication trench, and maintained possession, notwithstanding heavy fire and bomb-throwing, till nearly 2 p.m., by which time only one sergeant and two men were unwounded, and they succeeded in crawling back to our line. . . . There were 2 officers (Captain Grazebrook and Second-Lieut. Ward), 2 sergeants, and 10 men in the party, and both officers were wounded early in the morning. Two supporting parties which were sent to assist the party were practically wiped out by fire—rifle and machine-gun." Second-Lieut. H. H. Slater did good work in saving two machine guns, which had been carried forward as far as the entanglements but could get no farther ; he saved them both.

The gallantry of these three assaulting parties had not availed, and heavy casualties had been suffered. And yet, defeat at times is not without honour. It was so in this attack by the 6th Brigade, for owing to their splendid tenacity, and their persistence in the face of unsurmountable difficulties, the Staffords, King's, and Rifles had actually drawn enemy reinforcements to that part of the line which would obviously have been used farther north at Neuve Chapelle. Thus, although the attack was unsuccessful, it had contributed in no small way to the success which the First Army was at this time obtaining at Neuve Chapelle.

In the afternoon a further attack was made by the South Staffords; but it had to be abandoned, for the wire was not sufficiently cut even after a second bombardment. The artillery were not to blame, for owing to the conformity of the ground good observation was not possible, and the guns had to range over the village.

Both officers and men of the 6th Infantry Brigade were congratulated by the Army, Corps, and Divisional commanders on their very gallant but unsuccessful attempt.

The casualties were : Officers 26, other ranks 582, killed, wounded, and missing.[1]

No further attacks took place on the 2nd Divisional front during March and April. The operations of the First Army from 10th to 12th March had been a distinct success. Two miles of German trenches, including the whole of the village of Neuve Chapelle and some strongly defended works, had been captured, together with nearly 2,000 prisoners ; and casualties estimated at about 16,000 had been inflicted upon the enemy. Strong hostile forces had been held to their positions, preventing the sending of reinforcements to Notre Dame de Lorette—that part of the line where the French had been attacked and were attacking.

Trench Warfare, 14th March to 30th April 1915.

Although for a few weeks a period of comparative quietude set in after the capture of Neuve Chapelle, various items of interest took place in the 2nd Division. The 35th (Heavy) Battery R.G.A., which had been with the Division during the whole campaign in France and Belgium, became " Army Artillery " and was struck off the strength of the Division on 2nd March. The " Heavies " had done good work, and their transfer from the Division was much regretted, though the battery continued to lend support to the Divisional Artillery. The gunners had few opportunities such as fell to the infantry of gaining battle honours, but their casualties were always heavy, and are an eloquent tribute to the part they played in supporting their comrades in the front-line trenches ; the " guns " not infrequently " saved the situation."

The 7th King's (Liverpool) Regiment (Territorial), Lieut.-Colonel Stott commanding, joined the Division on 12th March, and were posted to the 6th Infantry Brigade, which now comprised

[1] See Appendix XI.

six battalions : 2nd South Staffords, 1st King's Royal Rifles, 1st Royal Berks, 1st, 5th, and 7th King's Liverpools.

On 24th March three brigades of the 2nd (London) Division were attached to the 2nd Division for instruction in trench warfare. After a short course they were replaced by three more brigades.

For the first time the March Diaries report that the British trench mortars were repeatedly successful in silencing the enemy's " minenwerfer " and snipers, and that gradually the Germans were losing their ascendancy in this direction.

One item of interest concerning the evolution of trench warfare is contained in the 6th Infantry Brigade Diary for 31st March : " A catapult has now been issued to each section of our line (Guinchy) —it works well, but a suitable bomb has yet to be devised." The vagaries of those catapult bomb-throwers will be remembered by all who used them !

" Whizz-bangs " also first made their appearance in March 1915.

The health of the troops improved as the weather became finer, and to relieve the dull monotony, ceaseless watching, and constant strain entailed during the weary hours in the trenches, games behind the front lines were instituted : football matches, horse shows and races were encouraged ; whilst concerts and theatricals were indulged in, " Divisional Troupes " being formed for the latter purpose.

The Regimental Diary of the 1st Royal Berks of April 1915 contains a description of yet another new engine of warfare, the " Bangalore Torpedo." This instrument was invented and used for wire-cutting purposes, and the following is an account of it in use : " As soon as it was dark, B Company found two men who volunteered to cut the enemy's wire entanglements in front of their trenches. These men were given a ' Bangalore Torpedo ' each. These articles are tubes about six feet long and four inches in diameter, filled with an extremely powerful explosive. The method of employing them is to push the pointed end into the wire, and by means of a safety lighter to explode the torpedo. This was successfully accomplished about 9.30 p.m., but the effect on, or the extent of damage done to, the wire could not be ascertained from our lines the next morning ; the explosion was terrific."

During the Second Battle of Ypres (and on the evening of 22nd April) the enemy first made use of asphyxiating gas, and on the 24th, in the 2nd Division, improvised gas-masks were issued to the troops as protectives should the enemy launch gas against the trenches of the Division.

The Division sustained another loss on 13th April—B Squadron of the 15th Hussars, which had acted as Divisional Mounted Troops at and from Mons, being replaced by three troops of the South Irish Horse, under Captain Watt. The Hussars had gained a great reputation, their scouting and patrol work during the early days of the War being performed with the greatest skill and devotion. They had gained one Victoria Cross, and so long as open warfare lasted and the Division was on the move, acted well their part as "the eyes of the Division." But from the beginning of trench warfare the officers of the squadron had been used for liaison work, and the troopers were mostly employed as mounted orderlies. The Hussars went to the 9th Cavalry Brigade.

A new type of minenwerfer shell was used by the enemy on 16th April ; this was cigar-shaped, and about three feet long. It burst with a roar ; but as it could be seen coming, the troops had an opportunity of taking cover before it burst, thus minimizing its effect.

Mining and counter-mining became very active on both sides. During April many mines were exploded by British and German miners, but it was difficult to say which held the advantage. The 1st East Anglian Field Company R.E. fast became proficient in mining, the 5th Field Company and the 11th Field Company performing wonders in this direction.

THE BATTLE OF FESTUBERT.

May opened warm, with occasional winds, and spells of misty weather which frequently impeded artillery registration.

North, in the Ypres Salient, British, French, and Belgians were continually engaged with the enemy, whose massed artillery was " superior to any concentration of guns which had previously assailed that part of the line." Heavy guns had been lost by the Allies during the first gas attack in April, and for a while the enemy's artillery dominated that of the Allies. But the initial advantage gained by the enemy by his dastardly use of asphyxiating gas had been almost wiped out by vigorous Allied attacks ; the element of surprise had gone and anti-gas apparatus had been issued to all troops, though in the early stages it was necessarily somewhat elementary in construction.

The vigorous offensive from the southern portion of the British line, which took place during May with marked success, was of twofold advantage to the Allies. The British gained considerable stretches of the enemy's trenches, and at the same time afforded the French offensive east of Arras and Lens valuable assistance ; for, owing to the pressure on his position north-west of Fromelles and between Neuve Chapelle and Festubert, the enemy was unable to reinforce that part of his line attacked by General Joffre.

An attack arranged for the 8th May by the Ist Corps, from Richebourg l'Avoué, was to synchronize with that of the French between Arras and Lens.

On 2nd May a gas attack on the Ist Corps was anticipated. Eight objects which might be rods or pipes were seen projecting above breastworks opposite Festubert, suggesting the possibility that the Germans were installing apparatus for projecting poisonous gas. Certain measures were immediately taken. Sentries specially detailed for the purpose were to watch these pipes as soon as they appeared, and the artillery were to register at once on the enemy's trenches, and at the first signs of a greenish-yellow gas, the whole of the artillery available, including the " Heavies," was to open fire on the hostile trenches and on the cloud of gas. Infantry were to don their gas-masks immediately. A few days later, special spraying apparatus and thiosulphate of soda were sent to units for the purpose of dealing with poisonous gas.

At dawn on 8th May the Divisional Artillery began registration. Later during the morning heavy firing was heard, coming from the French area south of the Béthune–La Bassée road. The attack of the Ist and IVth British Corps was to begin in the evening, but at 6.55 p.m. orders were issued that the operation had been postponed until the 9th. " Operation Order No. 39 " issued on the 7th contained the following instructions :

" (1) The First Army is to advance to-morrow with the object of breaking the enemy's line and gaining the La Bassée–Lille road between La Bassée and Fromelles. Its further advance will be directed on the line Bauvin–Don.

" (2) The Ist Corps is to attack from the Rue du Bois and advance on Rue du Marais–Illies, maintaining its right at Givenchy and Cuinchy.

" (3) The Indian Corps is to attack on the left of the Ist Corps and is to capture the Distillery and the Ferme du Biez ; its subsequent advance being directed on Ligny-le-Grand–La Cliqueterie Farm.

" The road Ferme du Biez–Ligny-le-Petit is assigned to the Indian Corps.

" (4) The 1st Division is attacking from its breastworks in front of Rue du Bois. Its first objectives are the hostile trenches P8–P10, the road junction P15, and the road thence to La Tourelle. Its subsequent advance is to be directed on Rue du Marais–Lorgnies, a defensive flank being organized from ' The Orchard,' P14, by La Quinque Rue to Rue du Marais.

" (5) The 2nd Division (less 4th (Guards) Brigade) with No. 1 Motor Machine-Gun Battery attached, will be in Corps Reserve in the area Loisne–Le Touret–Le Hamel in readiness to continue the advance."

The 4th (Guards) Brigade was at this period holding the Givenchy and Cuinchy fronts.

Heavy firing was heard all through the night of the 8th–9th coming from a southerly direction where the French were successfully attacking.

9TH MAY. Just before 5 o'clock on the morning of the 9th, the 5th and 6th Infantry Brigades were assembled in their concentration areas : the former in Loisne, the latter in Le Touret, in readiness to advance. The 2nd Division was to take over the line from the 1st Division, and continue the attack if the assault proved successful.

The first assault, between 5 and 6 a.m., made no progress ; a second, later, shared the same fate ; and a third, launched between 3 and 4 in the afternoon, failed also. Orders were then issued for the 6th Infantry Brigade to take over the 1st Division's trenches from the Crater Trench to the right of the Meerut Division (about V6), and attack at 8.30 p.m.

Two battalions of the 6th Infantry Brigade—1st King's Royal Rifles and the 1st Royal Berks—were moved forward to Richebourg St. Waast early in the afternoon (at 2.50), and shortly afterwards the 1st and 5th King's (Liverpools), followed later by the 2nd South Staffords and 7th King's, joined up with the Rifles and Berks.

The attack was to take place from the breastworks held by the 1st Division, from the Crater Trench to the right of the Indian Corps ; and already when the orders to attack were received (6.30 p.m.) the officers of the Berks and Rifles had gone forward to reconnoitre the ground, which was all quite strange to the brigade. But it was found that all the approaches to the front line were blocked, not only by the constant stream of wounded men walking or being carried back to the clearing station, but also by troops of the 1st Division whose units had not unnaturally become rather mixed up during the day's fighting in the three assaults which had taken place. The communication trenches were narrow, and in consequence it was seen that the front line could not be organized in time for an attack at 8.30 p.m. The Berks and King's Royal Rifles had been detailed for the attack; but fortunately orders cancelling the attack were received, though only just in time. Had the battalions moved forward their casualties must have been very heavy and the results uncertain.

At 7 p.m. the 2nd Division was ordered to relieve the 1st Division.

The 6th Infantry Brigade then moved into the trenches, the Berks (right) and the Rifles (left) holding the front line ; the remainder of the brigade assembled in Richebourg St. Waast.

The 5th Infantry Brigade moved up to Le Touret in place of the 6th Infantry Brigade, but later took over the trenches of the 2nd Infantry Brigade—*i.e.*, from the right of the Indian Corps to the " Cinder Track." The 5th Infantry Brigade was thus in line on the left of the 6th Infantry Brigade. The Oxford and Bucks and the 2nd Highland Light Infantry of the former brigade were in the front line, and the Inniskillings, Worcesters, and Glasgow Highlanders (9th Highland Light Infantry) in support.

Shortly before midnight on the 9th, 1st Corps Headquarters ordered the 2nd Division to attack on the following morning at 11. But the proposed attack did not materialize, for on the morning of the 9th the 8th Division of the IVth Corps, although capturing the enemy's front-line trenches, found the position too strong to admit of further success without a more extensive artillery preparation. And the Indian Division on the left of the 1st Division had been unable to advance. The General Officer Commanding First Army, therefore, proposed, and received permission from Sir John French, to concentrate his efforts on the southern front of attack.

On the morning of the 10th the IVth Corps was back on its 10TH MAY. original line of the 9th. The attack of the 2nd Division projected for the 10th was therefore abandoned, though active reconnaissances were made by officers of the 5th and 6th Infantry Brigades.

The 11th, 12th, 13th, and 14th were reported as " All quiet." On the 12th the 1st Division took over the Cuinchy and Givenchy sections from the 4th (Guards) Brigade, the Guards moving up to the La Casan–Le Touret area in reserve. A very useful reconnaissance by the R.A. 2nd Division was made on this day, for the artillery preparation in the coming attack was to be on a large scale. Deliberate bombardments of the enemy's lines were carried out on the 13th, 14th, and 15th.

At 12.10 p.m. on the 15th, Ist Corps Headquarters ordered the attack to take place on the night 15th–16th.

" 2nd Division Operation Order No. 41 " was issued at 12.30 p.m.:

" The First Army is renewing its offensive to-night with the object of pressing forward to Violaines and Beau Puits, and establishing a defensive flank on the La Bassée–Estaires road on the left, while maintaining the right at Givenchy. The task of the Ist Corps (2nd and 7th Divisions) is to secure the line of the road Festubert– La Tourelle from Points M3 to R13, and to consolidate that line.

" The Indian Corps is to assault the German front system of trenches between the ditches running S.S.E. to N.N.W. through Points V5 and V6, secure the German second-line breastworks and Point V6, and establish a flank at this point, connecting with our present line. This assault is to be delivered to-night simultaneously with that of the 2nd Division.

" The Indian Corps is to push on and secure the road from Port Arthur to La Tourelle as the attack of the 2nd Division progresses.

" The 7th Division is to assault the German position at 3.15 a.m. to-morrow on the front N1–P5, and is to establish there close touch with the 2nd Division.

" The task of the 2nd Division is to assault the German front system of trenches between Point R1 and the right of the Indian Corps, and to secure the line R1–R3–R5–R7–V4 under cover of darkness ; at 3.15 a.m. to-morrow to press its attack simultaneously with that of the 7th Division, to secure the Ferme Cour d'Avoué and the line of the Festubert–La Tourelle road from Points P14 to R13, both inclusive.

" The assault will be carried out to-night at 11.30 by the 6th and 5th Infantry Brigades under arrangements already notified to all concerned. The assault will be delivered simultaneously and in close touch with the assault of the Indian Corps.

" *Frontages.*—6th Infantry Brigade : From R1 to the bend in the German line between R6 and V1 (inclusive). 5th Infantry Brigade : from that point (exclusive) to the north-west corner of the salient between V3 and V6.

" *Objectives.*—6th Infantry Brigade : the first and second line of German parapets between R1 and R7 (exclusive). R1 and Q2 to be blocked. 5th Infantry Brigade : the first and second line of German parapets from R7 inclusive to a point north-west of V5 and to get into touch with the Meerut Division at that point.

" The position when gained will at once be consolidated.

To Neuve Chapelle

Port Arthur

MEERUT DIVISION

Rue du Bois

INDIAN CORPS

APEX OF

ATTACK

ATTACK

INDIAN CORPS

V6

V5

V4

Fe. du Bois

ADVANCE
DRESSING STATION

2ND H.L.I.

LINE FROM WHICH THE
SECOND DIVISION
ATTACKED – MAY 15TH 1915.
First Attack – 11·30. p.m.
Second   ,,   3·15. a.m. 16/

5TH KINGS
(Liverpool)

2ND WORCESTERS

3RD OXFORD

5TH INF BDE.
AREA OF
ATTACK

2ND OXFORD

3RD BLOCK

2ND S. STAFFORDS

2ND
INNIS. FUS.

6TH INF BDE.
AREA OF
ATTACK

1ST K.R. RD

5TH KINGS
(Liverpool)

1ST R. BERKS

KINGS
(Liverpool)

Chocolate Menier
Corner

Rue du Bois

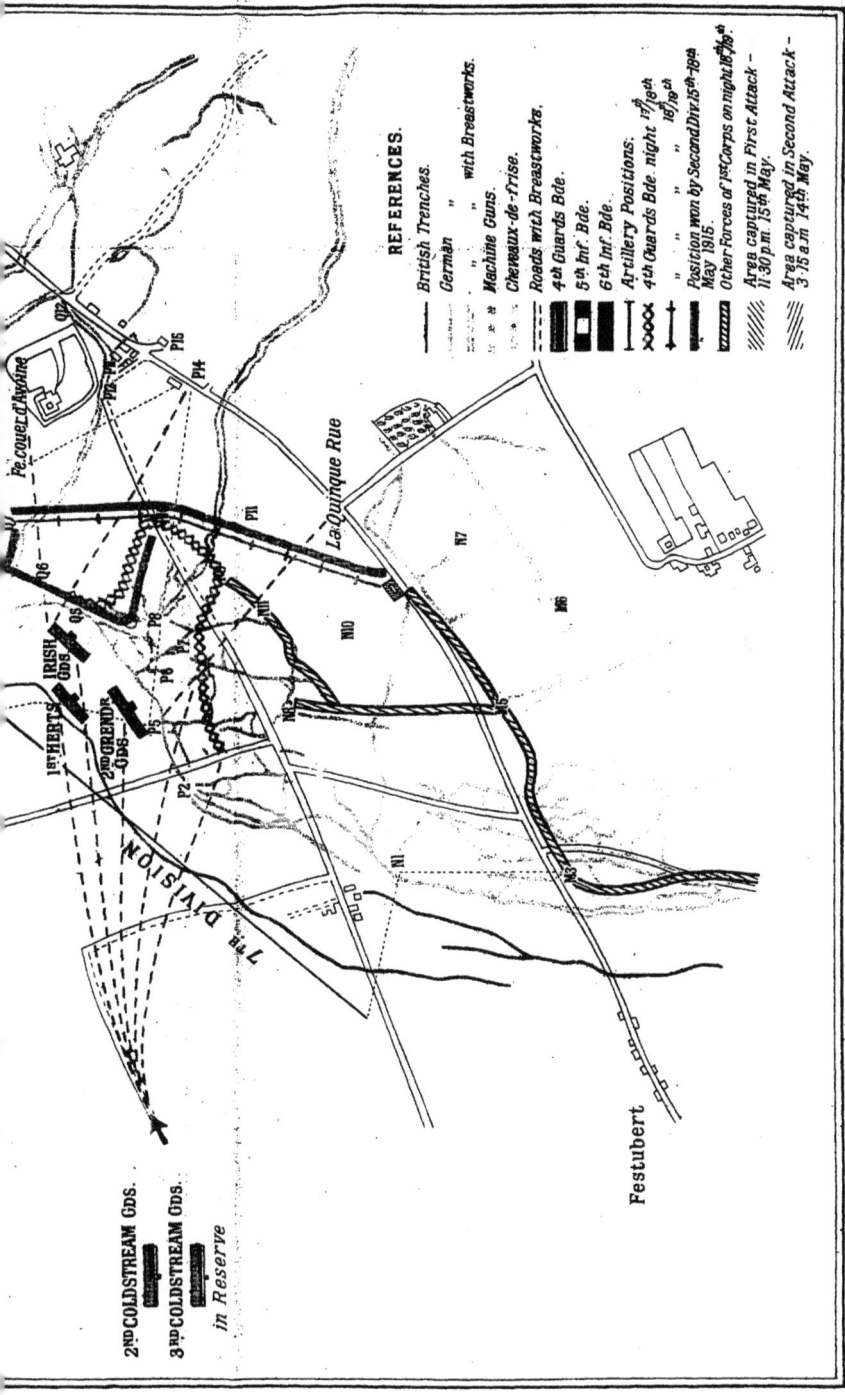

THE BATTLE OF FESTUBERT, 15th–25th May 1915.

Positions of Forces other than 2nd Division are approximate.

REFERENCES.

British Trenches.
German "
" " with Breastworks.
Machine Guns.
Chevaux-de-Frise.
Roads with Breastworks.
4th Guards Bde.
5th Inf. Bde.
6th Inf. Bde.
Artillery Positions:
4th Guards Bde. night 17th/18th
18th/19th
Position won by Second Div. 15th–19th May 1915.
Other Forces of 1st Corps on night 18th/19th
Area captured in First Attack – 11.30 p.m. 15th May.
Area captured in Second Attack – 3.15 a.m. 14th May.

THE MAPPA CO. LTD. LONDON.

(Facing A. 202.)

" At 3.15 a.m. to-morrow the attack will be pushed forward from the line consolidated simultaneously with the attack of the 7th Division.

"*Objectives.*—6th Infantry Brigade: to capture Ferme Cour d'Avoué, to establish itself on the line P14–Q12, both inclusive, and to gain touch with the 7th Division, especially about P14. The German communication trench running south-east to north-west through Q15 will be included in the 6th Infantry Brigade front.

"5th Infantry Brigade: to capture Ferme du Bois, to establish itself on the line Q12 (exclusive)–R13 (inclusive), and to maintain touch with the Indian Corps."

The artillery of the 2nd Division and the 1st Group H.A.R. were ordered to support the night attack of the 15th and the advance on the 16th. The XLIst Brigade R.F.A. was affiliated to the 6th Infantry Brigade and the XXXIXth Brigade R.F.A. (1st Division) to the 5th Infantry Brigade. The 4th (Guards) Brigade was held in Corps Reserve, in readiness to move at short notice from the hour of attack—11.30 p.m. on the 15th.

The bombardment of the enemy's trenches continued throughout the day, and from the official " Return of Ammunition Expended " it is clear that guns of all calibres were brought into action. For just as new methods of warfare had been evolved in the trenches, so behind the lines the artillery had been augmented by guns of all sizes : the disproportion between the artillery of the Allies and that of the enemy was fast disappearing. From the huge 15-inch howitzer (called " Granny," and first used at the Battle of Neuve Chapelle as a signal for the attack) to the small trench mortar, the Divisional Artillery had grown out of all proportions, compared with those early days at Mons where the British army employed only the 13, 18, and 60 pounders and the 4.5-inch howitzer. There are no records of the uses of the 15-inch howitzer at the Battle of Festubert in May 1915, but the records do show that 13, 18, and 60 pounders, 4.5 (Field) and 5 and 6 inch howitzers were all employed ; and that 95 mm. and 1.7 and 4 inch trench mortars were in use, as well as rifle and hand grenades and " Bangalore Torpedoes."

As the hour of attack crept on, the troops who were to form the assaulting parties gradually assembled in and about the front-line trenches. The attack was meant to be a surprise, but the enemy's artillery had been very active all day, and many casualties had, when night fell, been suffered by the 2nd Division.

The assault had been practised some days before the night of attack, and the troops had been very carefully rehearsed in their respective parts. The assaulting parties were to move forward in waves, followed by sandbag and engineer parties, bearing shovels and implements with which to consolidate positions won.

From right to left the troops of the 6th and 5th Infantry Brigades were as follows :

6th Infantry Brigade. Assaulting troops: 1st Royal Berks (centre) with the 7th King's (Liverpools) on their right, supported by the 1st King's (Liverpools) ; 1st King's Royal Rifles on the left of the Berks, supported by the 2nd South Staffords : the 5th King's (Liverpools) were in Brigade Reserve, detailed to supply working parties.

5th Infantry Brigade. Assaulting troops: 2nd Royal Inniskilling Fusiliers (right), supported by the 2nd Oxford and Bucks ; 2nd Worcesters (left), supported by the 9th Highland Light Infantry ; the 2nd Highland Light Infantry were in Brigade Reserve.

" The method employed for getting the men out of the trenches for the night attack was to form them up in successive lines outside our own parapet. Advantage was taken of intervals when the enemy's flares were not being sent up to push men out, and the forming up in this manner was successfully carried out. For the most part the men got over the parapet . . . the exits dug under the parapet not being sufficiently completed." [1]

Just after 11 p.m. the troops who were to form the first line of assault crept over the parapet, and advancing a few yards lay down ; they were followed immediately afterwards by a second line, which also lay down behind the first party ; a third followed the second, until by 11.15 p.m. all the assaulting troops were ready to advance.

Along the front of the 6th Infantry Brigade these movements had not been perceived by the enemy, but opposite the 5th Infantry Brigade rifle and machine-gun fire broke out soon after 11 o'clock, as if the enemy expected an attack, though the night was dark and it was impossible to see farther than a few paces ahead.

Punctually at 11.30 p.m. the first attack moved forward along the front of the Meerut Division (Indian Corps) and 2nd Division. At first the troops advanced in " quick time," but as they neared the enemy's trenches they were ordered to double to the attack. The 7th King's, C Company of the Berks, with D close behind and B and A in the order given, and portions of D and B Companies of the King's Royal Rifles, followed by C and then A Companies, assaulted from the 6th Brigade front.

As the 7th King's, Berks, and the Rifles went forward, the 1st King's (right) and 2nd South Staffords (left) moved up into their places.

The distance between the two lines of trenches was from 300 to 350 yards. The first 150 yards were crossed in silence, save for the machine-gun and rifle fire which had been opened on the 5th Infantry Brigade. But suddenly the Liverpools, Berks, and Rifles also came under violent fire and the remaining 200 yards were rushed. Of the Berks, C Company led the charge on to the enemy's parapets—" Here they bombed, and in many cases actually caught hold of the Germans' rifles and shot the firer. D Company, close on the heels of C, advanced through a perfect hail of rifle and machine-gun bullets, and passing through the front-line trenches, which were now in the possession of C, captured the second line about eighty yards to the rear of the first."

Meanwhile, the Rifles had also won forward with considerable gallantry under a severe cross-fire from the salient opposite the 5th Infantry Brigade (V3). " A burst of rifle fire broke out on our left, and the enemy began to send up lights in all directions. One could then see, silhouetted against the light, our front line, which appeared to be close to the German trenches. The whole space between the lines was dotted with men, some lying on the ground, but the majority still advancing. As our front line reached the German trenches, the lights from that part ceased to go up ; but it was possible to get glimpses of what was going on when the enemy fired lights farther to our right or behind the front line. All this time a very heavy machine-gun fire had been coming across from the salient on our left and sweeping our front, and this fire did not seem to diminish much as time went on."

At about 12 midnight an electric torch flashed from the trenches attacked—the enemy's second line had also been captured !

Thus in the first stride the 1/7th King's, Berks, and Rifles had captured two lines of hostile trenches, and these were being consolidated. The Rifles had called for reinforcements, and D Company of the South Staffords was sent forward and occupied the German front-line trenches ; the 1st King's sent one company forward to support the Berks.

On the 5th Infantry Brigade front the attack was held up. The right-half battalion of the 2nd Inniskilling Fusiliers did indeed succeed in reaching and occupying the German front-line trenches from V1 to the left flank of the Rifles, but the Worcesters were unable to advance at all.   The whole ground was swept by a very heavy rifle and machine-gun fire, the enemy's position bristling with machine guns.   Any attempt by the Worcesters to advance was quickly annihilated.

The Meerut Division (Indian Corps) also failed in its attempt, the line along the front of the Indians being very strongly protected by machine guns.

At 2 a.m. the position of the 2nd Division was—6th Infantry Brigade : 7th Liverpools, 1st Berks, and 1st King's Royal Rifles occupying the line R1, R2, R5, R6 ; 5th Infantry Brigade : half of the 2nd Inniskilling Fusiliers on the left of the 1st King's Royal Rifles between R6 and V1, but the remaining units of the brigade held up in their original trenches.

Preparations were then made for the next attack at 3.15 a.m. (16th) in which the 7th Division was to join.

16TH MAY.   At 2 a.m. the 4th (Guards) Brigade had sent forward two battalions to the existing lines north of the Rue du Bois, the 2nd Grenadiers holding a position behind the 6th Infantry Brigade and the 1st Irish Guards behind the 5th Infantry Brigade.

At 2.45 a.m. the guns again opened on the enemy's trenches at V3, 4, 5, and 6, and the communication trenches at Q15 and Q12.

The Worcesters were to make another attack at 3.15 a.m., to synchronize with that of the 7th Division and a second attempt by the Meerut Division.

For half-an-hour the artillery plastered the enemy's position. At 3.15 the guns lengthened their range, and the infantry once more went forward to the attack.   The Worcesters had reported that they were unable to reorganize in time for the second assault, and the 9th Highland Light Infantry were therefore detailed ; but the latter battalion found on arrival in the Worcester's trenches so much congestion that it was impossible to form up, and finally the attack from this point had for the time being to be abandoned, though preparations for launching an assault when the Scotsmen were in position were continued.

The 2nd Inniskillings, supported by two and a half companies of the Oxford and Bucks, captured the enemy's second-line trenches about R7, and formed a defensive flank to the left of the 6th Infantry Brigade—i.e., the Rifles.

The 6th Infantry Brigade had been ordered to capture the line Q7 to Ferme du Bois (both inclusive), but were unable to advance owing to machine-gun fire in enfilade ; the King's, Berks, and

Rifles therefore held fast to the trenches won, and dug themselves in despite heavy losses.

The attack of the 7th Division was successful, and the first and second lines of the enemy's defences were captured, the position of the Division at 7.30 a.m. on the 16th running from M3 through M5, N8, P2, and P5.

The policy of both the 2nd and 7th Divisions was now to join hands, the 2nd Division forming a defensive flank on its left.

The attacks of the Indian Corps had again unfortunately failed.

The Rue du Bois and the front-line trenches held by the Division were now being very heavily shelled, which considerably hampered operations. The 6th Infantry Brigade, with great gallantry, attempted to extend its right flank towards Q2 and Q3, but at 9.30 a.m. abandoned the attempt, the enemy's fire being too severe.[1] The three main German communication trenches (one north and two south-west of Ferme Cour d'Avoué) were not yet captured, and down these trenches the enemy continued to reinforce his trenches from R5 to P6 under very heavy covering fire. In particular the nest of trenches contained in the quadrilateral P6, Q5, P9, P10 defied all attempts at capture, and held up the attack of the 7th Division ; added to which deep ditches running north-west to south-east, and from north-east to south-west everywhere impeded the advance and made direct frontal attacks most difficult.

Between 11.30 a.m. and 1 p.m. both the 6th Infantry Brigade and the 7th Division attempted further attacks, but they were unsuccessful.

At 2 p.m. the position was : 5th Infantry Brigade were still in their original trenches, though the 2nd Highland Light Infantry had dug a line of trench from the right flank of the brigade straight across to V1, where it joined up with the old German front line, and here the Oxford and Bucks and Inniskillings carried on the line to R7. The 6th Infantry Brigade held the line R6 to R1 and R5 to R3. The 7th Division's line ran from P5–N9–La Quinque Rue–N13–M9, M8–M6–M5 to M3.

At 2.15 p.m. General Fanshawe reported that his brigade (6th) could not undertake another big attack that day, and a little later it was determined that the 5th and 6th Infantry Brigades

---

[1] It was here that Lance-Corporal J. Tombs of the 1st King's (Liverpool) Regiment gained his Victoria Cross, " for most conspicuous bravery on the 16th May 1915 near Rue du Bois. During a very heavy bombardment Lance-Corporal Tombs, on his own initiative, crawled from his trench for 100 yards into the open, and notwithstanding the terrific machine-gun and artillery fire, succeeded in dragging four wounded men under cover."—*London Gazette*, 24th July 1915.

should consolidate the ground won, dig communication trenches, and give the men some rest. The Divisional artillery were, however, ordered to co-operate in another attack by the 7th Division on P6, P7, P8, P9, and P10 at 4.30 p.m.

This attack made no headway !

At nightfall, therefore, the front of the 2nd Division was as already given, the 4th (Guards) Brigade being still held in reserve.

Throughout the 16th a group of French " 75's " and three batteries of heavy artillery had materially assisted the attacks of the Ist Corps.

Casualties in the 2nd Division had been heavy, some units having lost almost 50 per cent. of their effectives, the losses in officers being especially severe. The attack had been pressed with great gallantry, but too much reliance seems to have been placed upon the supposition that the right flank of the 2nd Division and the left of the 7th Division would be able to squeeze the enemy out of the line between R1 and P5. Had the enemy's line between these two places been subjected to a direct frontal attack, the whole line would almost certainly have given way.

17TH MAY. At 2.26 on the morning of the 17th orders were received for the attack to be continued—" The first objective for to-morrow's (17th) operation is to secure the line from the right of the 7th Division about L2–M5–La Quinque Rue–Ferme Cour d'Avoué–Ferme du Bois–V1.—To effect this the junction of the 7th and 2nd Divisions must be attained about P5 and P10.—The artillery of the 7th Division is to carry out a deliberate bombardment of the area P6–P8–P9.—Artillery of the 2nd Division will simultaneously bombard area Q2–Q7–Q5–P10, commencing at 5.30 a.m.—A report of result of bombardment to be rendered to Advanced 2nd Division Headquarters by 6.30 a.m.—Ist Group H.A.R. (Heavy Artillery Reserve) is to bombard the triangle P8–P9–P10 and the Ferme Cour d'Avoué and the group of houses P14–P15–P16.— The artillery of the 7th Division also is to bombard the hostile communication breastworks P8–N15.—The hour of the infantry attack will be fixed by the General Officer Commanding Ist Corps, and will be notified later.—It will not be before 8 a.m.—

" *Objectives*—5th Infantry Brigade to capture Ferme du Bois and to form a defensive flank from V1–Ferme du Bois–Q14, and to maintain touch with the 6th Infantry Brigade.—6th Infantry Brigade to capture Ferme Cour d'Avoué and the line of the La Quinque road, the area Q3–Q7–Q6, and to gain touch with the 7th Division.—Dividing lines between brigades ; the German communication trench through Q11, which will be inclusive to the 5th Infantry Brigade.—Troops are to be provided with masks or respirators for use against asphyxiating gases."

In addition to these orders it was announced that the 3rd Canadian Brigade was in Ist Corps Reserve in Le Touret. The Indian Corps on the left of the 2nd Division, as the latter progressed, was gradually to extend its right and relieve the troops of the 2nd Division as opportunity offered.

The attacks of the 5th and 6th Infantry Brigades on Ferme du Bois and Ferme Cour d'Avoué respectively were fixed for 9 a.m., but were later postponed until 10.30 a.m. Shortly after 8 a.m., however, considerable numbers of the enemy's troops left their trenches, and rushing towards the British line with their hands above their heads, and waving white flags, surrendered. The General Officer Commanding 2nd Division thereupon telephoned to Ist Corps Headquarters, and obtained permission to attack at 9.30 a.m.

At that hour the battalions of the 5th Infantry Brigade were disposed as follows : During the night 16th–17th the Inniskillings and the Oxford and Bucks, who had lost heavily, had been withdrawn from the front line, and were replaced by the 2nd Highland Light Infantry and the Glasgow Highlanders (9th Highland Light Infantry). The 2nd Highland Light Infantry occupied the trench dug from the old breastworks of the 5th Infantry Brigade up to and including Point V1 ; the Glasgows were in support, and the 2nd Worcesters were ordered to take over the trenches occupied by the Glasgows as the latter moved forward to the support of the attacking battalion—the 2nd Highland Light Infantry.

The 1st King's Royal Rifles and the 1st Royal Berks of the 6th Infantry Brigade (both battalions having suffered terribly in the attack of 15th–16th) had also been relieved during the night by the 2nd South Staffords and 1st King's (Liverpools) respectively. The 7th King's still held on to the right of the line about R1, with the 5th King's in support.

The 4th (Guards) Brigade, which had been held in reserve, received orders about 8.30 a.m. to be ready to move at short notice. The 2nd Grenadiers and the 1st Irish Guards were pushed forward behind the left flank of the 7th Division, there to await orders for the attack.

At 9.30 a.m. A and B Companies of the 2nd Highland Light Infantry "went over the top" and rushed forward from the line R7–R5 towards the Ferme du Bois, but immediately came under a very heavy enfilade fire from the east and intense rifle and machine-gun fire. Heavy losses were incurred, and the survivors fell back to their original starting-points.

The South Staffords and the 1st King's (6th Infantry Brigade) simultaneously left their trenches, and by 11.30 the former battalion was reported on a line running north-east. Between the triangle R4–Q15–Q8 the 1st King's at 11.45 had won as far as a line running east between Q2 and Q3, almost to the right flank of the Staffords. In these positions, however, both battalions were held up. Artillery, rifles, and machine guns poured upon them a continuous hail of shells and bullets ; further progress was impossible. The left of the Staffords had been uncovered by the failure of the 2nd Highland Light Infantry to advance, and enfilade fire from the east caused many casualties. Here Lieut.-Colonel P. C. L. Routledge, commanding the 2nd South Staffords, was killed whilst gallantly leading his men. Finally, the Staffords were forced to evacuate their position, which had been won only after hard fighting ; the battalion retired to its original starting-point.

At midday it was again obvious that the operation could not be considered satisfactory until the right of the 2nd Division and the left of the 7th Division joined hands. A juncture with the latter division about Q5 had been reported by the 6th Infantry Brigade, but it is doubtful if at this period (midday) the juncture was permanent. The 1st King's had pushed forward by bombing up the enemy's trenches, and at one period succeeded in reaching Q7 ; but the official accounts of the Battle of Festubert by 6th Infantry Brigade Headquarters and 1st King's (Liverpool) Regiment are missing, and this cannot be confirmed.

At 2 p.m. arrangements were made by 5th and 6th Infantry Brigades to continue the attack at 3 p.m. after half an hour's bombardment. Orders were also sent to the 4th (Guards) Brigade to move up on the right of the 6th Infantry Brigade and gain the line of the La Quinque Rue, relieving *en route* part of the 7th Division and keeping touch with the 6th Infantry Brigade and the 7th Division.

The attacks of the 5th and 6th Infantry Brigades at 3 p.m. failed to make any substantial progress—hostile fire being too heavy. The 6th Infantry Brigade, however, was now able to report definitely that its right (1st King's) was in touch with the 7th Division at Q5. A further attack by the 5th Infantry Brigade at 6 p.m. was projected, but later found impracticable ; the congestion in the trenches, which were crowded with troops moving up to, or back from, the front line and with dead and wounded, made reorganization impossible.

Orders were then issued that the Sirhind Brigade (Indian Corps) would take over the 5th Brigade line at 5.45 p.m., and as much as possible of the 2nd Division line.

At 7 p.m. the two attacking battalions of the 4th (Guards) Brigade —*i.e.*, the 1st Irish Guards (left) and the 2nd Grenadiers (right)— passed the line P5–Q5. The Irish Guards' objective was the Ferme Cour d'Avoué facing north-east, with its left in touch with the 6th Infantry Brigade in the region of Q5, its right on the road between P14 and La Quinque Rue, where it was to join up with the left of the 2nd Grenadiers. The latter were to attack on the right of the Irish Guards, and gain touch on their right flank with the left of the 20th Infantry Brigade (7th Division)—objective, La Quinque Rue.

At 9 p.m. the left of the 4th Brigade was still just east of Q5, but not in touch with the right of the 6th Infantry Brigade. The right of the brigade had, however, joined up with the left of the 7th Division (1st Grenadiers). Excepting for one short burst of rifle fire the Irish Guards and Grenadiers pushed on, and about midnight began to dig themselves in, unmolested by the enemy. At 2.30 on the morning of the 18th touch had been gained with the right of the 6th Infantry Brigade (1st King's). 18TH MAY.

Dawn broke very wet and misty, and the objectives could not be seen clearly. As the preliminary artillery bombardment could not be carried out owing to adverse weather conditions, the attack timed to take place at 9 a.m. was postponed. In the meantime, battalions were warned to take every opportunity of pushing forward and establishing a good line from which to begin the attack when ordered.

At 2.30 p.m. 2nd Division Operation Orders were issued : " Ist and Indian Corps have been ordered to attack again this afternoon. Objective : to capture and consolidate the line M5– P14–Cour d'Avoué–Ferme du Bois—3rd Canadian Brigade under 7th Division is to attack the line of La Quinque Rue from P14 (exclusive) south-eastwards on the right of the 4th (Guards) Brigade ; Meerut Division is attacking Ferme du Bois ; 4th (Guards) Brigade will attack P14 and Ferme Cour d'Avoué, and will maintain touch with 3rd Canadian Brigade ; 6th Infantry Brigade, while ensuring the safety of the line now held by them, will support the left of the 4th (Guards) Brigade, and will maintain connection between the left of that brigade and the right of the Meerut Division. The infantry attacks will be delivered simultaneously at 4.30 p.m. after a bombardment of two hours commencing at 2.30 p.m., in which the first group of Heavy Artillery Reserve is taking part, under instructions which have been issued to artillery commanders concerned."

Punctually at 4.30 p.m. the Irish Guards left their trenches, but were met by a heavy burst of rifle and machine-gun fire, and men began to fall rapidly. Very little progress could be made. A company of the 1st Herts then went forward to reinforce the attacking parties, but they also could make very little progress. Only 300 yards of ground had been won when orders came to dig in on the positions held.

The 2nd Grenadiers were in a similar predicament. The flat terrain over which they were to advance was well planned for defensive purposes, and the enemy swept the ground by a terrific shell, machine-gun and rifle fire. At 7.30 p.m. the Grenadiers were ordered to keep their right at La Quinque Rue (exclusive of road) and dig through P11 and P10. The Irish Guards were definitely ordered to establish their left at Q7 and get touch with the Grenadiers about P10, and the 5th Field Company R.E. and one section of the East Anglian Field Company R.E. were sent forward to help consolidate the new line.

About midnight the Irish Guards were relieved by the 1st Herts, the former battalion withdrawing to trenches 800 yards behind the new line.

During the night all ground gained by the 4th (Guards) Brigade was consolidated, and the Meerut Division (Sirhind Brigade) continued the relief of the 2nd Division line as far as R6. The 3rd Canadian Brigade on the right of the 4th (Guards) Brigade consolidated the line M6–P11 during the night.

The General Officer Commanding 1st Corps (General Monro) decided not to order a definite attack on the 19th, and with that decision, so far as it concerned the 2nd Division, the Battle of Festubert was over.[1]

On the 20th the Division was ordered to be relieved by the 51st (Highland) Division—the relief to be completed by 5 a.m. on the 21st. On the afternoon of that day the Division was once more billeted in and west of Béthune. Only the Divisional artillery remained in action with " Alderson's Force," [2] rejoining the

---

[1] The fighting was continued until 25th May, during which time the 2nd Division was in reserve.

[2] Canadians and 51st Division with artillery of 2nd and 7th Divisions, under the command of Lieut.-General Alderson.

2nd Division later. The 7th Division was also drawn out of the line to rest.

The general results of the Battle of Festubert were as stated in Sir John French's Dispatches : " The enemy was driven from a position which was strongly fortified, and ground won on a front of four miles to an average depth of 600 yards. The enemy is known to have suffered very heavy losses, and in the course of the battle 785 prisoners and 10 machine guns have been captured."

The casualties in the 2nd Division were : officers killed 46, wounded 120, and missing 12 ; whilst in other ranks the Division lost 521 killed, 3,560 wounded, and 1,187 missing—a total of 5,446.[1] Some battalions had lost half their effectives.

But the Division had at least the grim satisfaction of knowing that it had inflicted upon the enemy very severe losses. One diarist described the hostile trenches when captured as a mere shambles, the dead and wounded lying thick upon the ground, and hundreds more lay buried amidst the wreckage created by the intense bombardment to which the enemy's position had been subjected.

Trench Warfare, 21st May to 24th September 1915.

Several changes had taken place in the 2nd Division : Lieut.-Colonel C. Pereira, who had commanded the 2nd Coldstream from Mons onwards, received orders on 17th May to take over command of the 85th Infantry Brigade (28th Division, Vth Corps). On the 30th Major F. F. Ready, D.A.A. and Q.M.G., left the Division to take over the duties of A.A. and Q.M.G. to the 4th Division. Brigadier-General R. Fanshawe (G.O.C. 6th Infantry Brigade) left on the 31st on appointment to the command of the 48th Division, and Brigadier-General A. Daly arrived and assumed command of the 6th Infantry Brigade. Major Ready was replaced by Major C. T. M. Hare.

On the 30th and 31st May the 2nd Division marched south of the La Bassée Canal and took over a portion of the French front, on the right of the 47th (London) Division. The new sections were known as X and W.

Secret instructions issued on 30th May ordered the temporary reorganization of the First Army. The Indian Corps—8th, 49th Meerut and Lahore Divisions, under Sir J. R. Willcocks, K.C.B.,

21ST MAY-24TH SEPT.

[1] See Appendix XII.

was to take over the defensive front of the left[1] of the First Army as far south as La Quinque Rue (exclusive); the IVth Corps, formed of 7th, 51st, and Canadian Divisions, under Sir H. Rawlinson, K.C.B., was to hold the front from La Quinque Rue inclusive as far south as the La Bassée Canal; the Ist Corps, formed of 1st, 2nd, and 47th London Divisions, under Sir C. Monro, K.C.B., was to take over the front from the La Bassée Canal to the left of the French Tenth Army then just west of Loos.

The 2nd Division, therefore, moved down to sections X and W, but a few days later changed over with the 47th London Division and occupied sections Z and Y. By the end of June, however, the Division was once more back in the Givenchy and Cuinchy sections (B and A).

The 1st Battalion Queen's (Royal West Surrey) Regiment was attached to the Division on 30th June, also the 176th Tunnelling Company.

On 23rd June the Howitzer Brigades R.F.A. were broken up, and the batteries allotted to the different corps at the rate of two per corps. This involved the XLIVth Brigade R.F.A. of the 2nd Division, which, to the general regret of the Division, was broken up, the 60th Battery being transferred to the Indian Corps. The 47th and 56th Batteries remained with the 1st Corps. The Divisional artillery consisted (besides the Field Artillery Brigades) of the 7th Mountain Battery R.G.A., IIIrd Heavy Brigade R.G.A., VIth Siege Brigade R.G.A., and No. 3 and No. 6 Trench Mortar Batteries, the former with the 4th and the latter with the 6th Infantry Brigades.

For some weeks after the Battle of Festubert the 2nd Division was not involved in any attack on the enemy's trenches, though elsewhere along the British front (in the Ypres salient) attacks and counter-attacks were made by both British and Germans, with varying results. On 30th July the enemy adopted a new device—the projection of burning liquid into the British trenches—thereby obtaining a small temporary success which was more than balanced in a brilliant attack by the 6th Division on 9th August, which resulted not only in the recapture of the lost trench, but in addition 400 yards of German trenches. Apart from these operations, " until the last week in September there was relative quietude along the whole of the British line, except at those points where the normal conditions of existence comprised occasional shelling or constant mine and bomb warfare."

About Richebourg.

Bombing had now become a regular feature of warfare.

"The hand-grenades themselves have passed from the experimental stages, and we have now two types of hand-grenades, the 'Mills' and the 'T. and P.,'[1] which are simple, effective in action, and as safe to handle as it is reasonably possible to make them. The time has therefore come when the use of the hand-grenade must cease to be considered as a 'special' form of fighting, and when training therein must be extended to all infantry soldiers."[2]

Heavy shelling and bombing by the enemy was an everyday occurrence during the early part of July, but the Divisional trench mortar batteries replied so successfully that after a little while violent hostile bombing ceased and on some days not a grenade was thrown by the enemy.

The following is taken from a Brigade Diary: "After dark the Staffords in B2 bombarded the enemy's trenches opposite Duck's Bill with trench mortars and bombs thrown by the West Bomb Thrower. The enemy retaliated by using vulgar and obscene language!"

Mining and counter-mining went on unceasingly, and the field companies of the Division (5th, 11th, and 1st Anglian), assisted by large working parties of infantry, were most successful in frustrating the enemy's endeavours to blow in the Division's front-line trenches. An instance of these mining operations is given in the Diary of the 4th (Guards) Brigade for 1st August: "Three mines opposite the Rabbit Warren (B section) were exploded simultaneously. The result was to form one large crater. The enemy did not reply at first. This enabled the men told off to occupy the near edge of the crater to do so without loss. A patrol pushed out to discover if any portion of the enemy's line had been damaged by the explosions, found the wire absolutely intact. About 9 p.m. the enemy began to fire shrapnel and machine guns. Later on he also threw hand-grenades and fired trench-mortar bombs and a few heavy shells. A new line was dug during the night round the near lip of the crater. The battalion bombers largely assisted this move by keeping the enemy under a continual shower of hand-grenades—233 'Mills' bombs were used and 180 'Battye' bombs. About 11.30 p.m. the enemy had two machine guns in action. As these were interfering with the digging of the new line the 95 mm. trench mortars and the $1\frac{1}{2}$-inch trench battery came into action. The machine guns ceased firing. From 1.30 a.m. the enemy was quiet."

---

[1] Time and Percussion.   [2] General Staff Diary, 2nd Division.

On 21st July the 2nd Royal Inniskilling Fusiliers became Corps Troops and left the 5th Infantry Brigade and the 2nd Division. They were replaced by the 1st Queen's Royal West Surrey Regiment.

On 29th July Lieut.-Colonel Matheson, commanding the 3rd Coldstream Guards, left to take over command of the 46th Infantry Brigade.

Various Staff changes took place during July. On the 13th Brigadier-General Chichester relinquished the command of the 5th Infantry Brigade and was replaced by Brigadier-General Corkran. Major J. D. Belgrave, D.S.O., arrived on 24th July as G.S.O.2 *vice* Major F. A. Buzzard, who had been transferred to the 9th Division. Lieut.-Colonel S. W. Robinson took over the duties of A.A. and Q.M.G. (15th July) from Lieut.-Colonel G. D. Jebb, D.S.O., who went to the Xth Corps. Captain Viscount Fielding, D.S.O., became D.A.A. and Q.M.G. (21st July) in succession to Major J. E. S. Brind, who also went to the Xth Corps.

On 3rd–4th August the 1/5th and the 1/7th King's (Liverpools) were temporarily detached from the 6th Infantry Brigade and attached to Divisional Headquarters as Pioneers.

On the 20th August, to the general regret of all ranks, the 4th (Guards) Brigade left the 2nd Division to form part of the newly formed Guards Division. On the same day Sir Douglas Haig issued the following letter : " The 4th (Guards) Brigade leaves my command to-day after over a year of active service in the field. During that time the brigade has taken part in military operations of the most diverse kind and under many varied conditions of country and weather, and throughout all ranks have displayed the greatest fortitude, tenacity, and resolution. I desire to place on record my high appreciation of the services rendered by the Brigade, and my grateful thanks for the devoted assistance which one and all have given me during the year of strenuous work." [1]

With the 4th (Guards) Brigade went No. 2 Section 2nd Signal Company R.E., 4th Field Ambulance, and No. 11 Company 2nd Divisional Train. The 1st Herts (Territorials) did not leave with the Guards but were attached to the 6th Infantry Brigade.

The Guards were replaced by the 19th Infantry Brigade (Brigadier-General P. R. Robertson), consisting of 2nd Argyll and Sutherland Highlanders, 2nd Royal Welsh Fusiliers, 1st Cameronians

---

[1] The Guards Division was formed from the 1st and 4th Guards Brigades, two battalions from the 20th Infantry Brigade (7th Division), and some newly raised Guards regiments. It was a coincidence that von Winckler's Guards Division which fought at Ypres was also formed from the 1st and 4th German Guards.

(Scottish Rifles), 1st Middlesex Regiment, 1/5th Cameronians (Scottish Rifles). The 19th Field Ambulance and a Company of the 19th Divisional Train also joined.

Towards the end of August the Commander-in-Chief sent a letter to the General Officer Commanding 2nd Division, in which he commended the mining work and crater fighting of the Division: " The Commander-in-Chief has intimated that he has read with great interest and satisfaction the reports of the mining operations and crater fighting which has taken place in the 2nd Division area during the last two months. He desires that his high appreciation of the good work performed be conveyed to the troops, especially to the 170th and 176th Tunnelling Companies R.E., the 2nd Battalion Grenadier Guards, the 1st Irish Guards, the 1st Battalion King's Royal Rifles, and the 2nd Battalion South Staffords."

This was followed a few days later by another letter to the 2nd Division from the 1st Corps commander (Lieut.-General H. Gough) : " The Corps Commander has read with great pleasure the report of Major-General H. S. Horne, General Officer Commanding 2nd Division, on the mining work of the 170th and 176th Companies R.E. and of the detachments 2nd Oxford and Bucks Light Infantry, 1st Royal Berkshire Regiment, and 2nd Highland Light Infantry, and congratulates the officers and men on their courage and tenacity in their arduous work."

Early in August the enemy brought into use a new projectile —aerial torpedoes—which at first caused much trouble, for in the General Staff Diary of the 2nd Division for that month there is a note on this particular engine of war : " Hostile aerial torpedoes are causing much annoyance and doing us some damage. They appear to fire from about 600 metres away, which is beyond the range of our trench mortars. Sentries are posted in our trenches to watch for them and give warning of their approach ; but they come with greater velocity than the ordinary minenwerfer, are more difficult to judge, and have a terrific explosion with a wide radius. Either two or three firing trenches are in use, or the same trench and alternate positions. Present remedy is to mark down the three or four places from which the torpedoes are usually fired, and as soon as the enemy opens with torpedoes to retaliate at once on these places with 4.5-inch high-explosive. This remedy is generally effective provided retaliation is quick enough."

In fact, the enemy had a wholesome dread of " retaliation," and fear of it often prevented him shelling and bombing the British trenches.

During August (on the 26th) Major O. Ivers, D.A.D.M.S., returned to England, and his duties were taken over by Captain W. B. Purdon, D.S.O.

THE BATTLE OF LOOS.

:5TH SEPT.

MAP.

The summer of 1915 was drawing to a close when the sanguinary struggle called by the Germans " The Battle of Loos and Hulluch " took place. So far as the 2nd Division was concerned, the September operations were mainly confined to the Givenchy and Cuinchy sections, though " Carter's Brigade " (formed of units belonging to the 2nd Division) attacked just south of the Hohenzollern Redoubt.

Preparations for the Battle of Loos were, for that period, vast and methodical. For the first time in the Great War the 2nd Division was to use asphyxiating gas, for after long discussion the Allies had reluctantly decided that the treacherous introduction by the enemy of this barbarous method of making warfare necessitated similar retaliatory measures.

Just as every sin brings its own punishment, so every violation of the principles governing civilized warfare introduced by the enemy—and they were not a few—resulted in swift and adequate retribution. The Allies' counter-measures were eventually always more successful, though at the outset (in the experimental stages) many casualties were suffered as the result of inexperience—the use of gas at the Battle of Loos was an example !

The official dispatches on the subject of the operations which began on September 25, 1915, are very meagre. No reasons are given, and a very few lines sum up discussions between Generals Joffre and Sir John French which must have lasted some days : " It was arranged that we should make a combined attack from certain points of the Allied line during the last week in September."

From their aerial and intelligence reports the Allied commanders were aware that the enemy had transferred, and was actually in the process of transferring, many of his troops from the Western to the Russian front, and that certain points in his line from Verdun to the Belgian coast were but thinly held. With this information at their disposal—information confirmed daily by reports from all sections of the line—Sir John French and General Joffre worked out their plans for two principal offensives, one east and south of Rheims, in the Champagne country, and the other

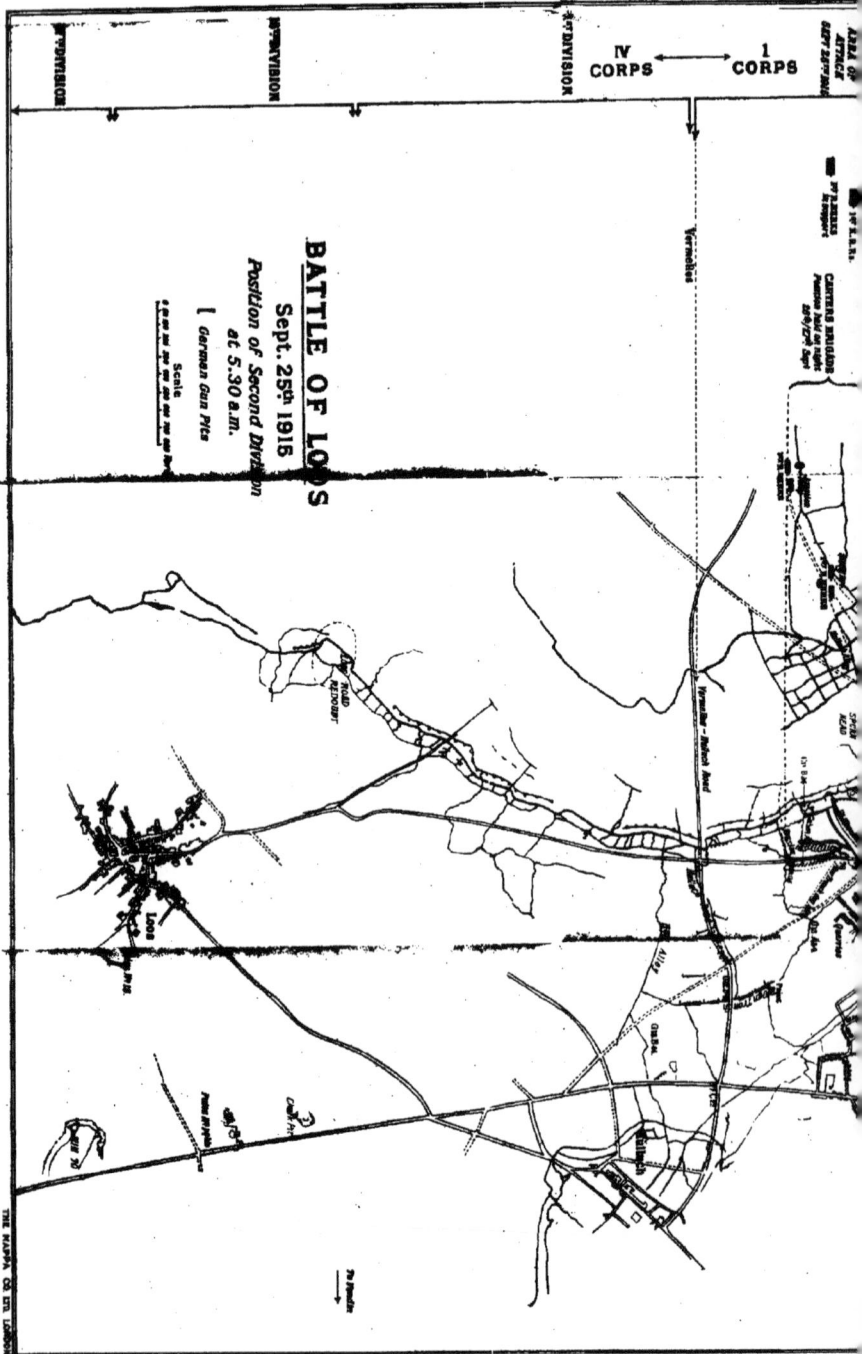

BATTLE OF LOOS

Sept. 25th 1915

Position of Second Division
at 5.30 a.m.

[German Gun Pits

Scale

IV CORPS ← → 1 CORPS

3rd DIVISION

9th DIVISION

7th DIVISION

AREA OF
ATTACK
24/25th SEPT.

Vermelles

Vermelles – Hulloch Road

Loos

Hill 70

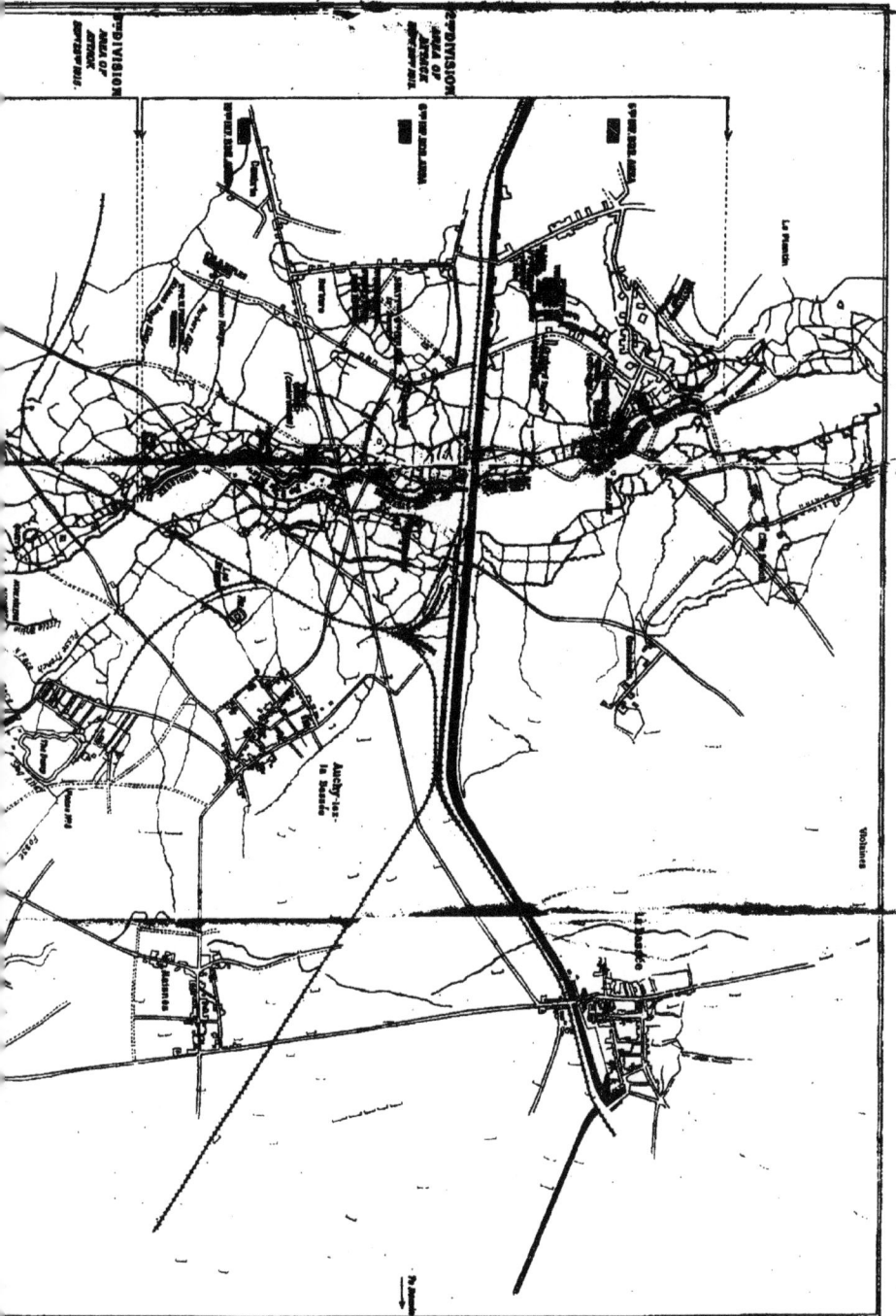

north and south of Arras ; holding attacks were to be made from
other portions of the line. The main object of these attacks was
to break the enemy's front. Having pierced his front the Allies
then hoped to prevent him re-establishing his line, and finally to
defeat his forces, which would be somewhat divided.

For the Rheims attack four French Armies were to be employed
—i.e., the Fourth, Ninth, Third, and Fifth. Two Armies, the First
British and the Tenth French, were to assault the enemy north and
south of Arras.

The positions of the British Armies at this period were as follows :
from north to south, the Second Army, consisting of the VIth,
Vth, Canadian, and IInd Corps (in the order given from north to
south) from Ypres to just south of Armentières, where it joined up
with the First Army, consisting of the IIIrd, Indian, Ist, and IVth
Corps, the right flank of the latter resting just south-west of Loos.
The Third Army, formed of the VIIth and Xth Corps, lay between
Monchy, south-west of Arras and the Somme.

The Tenth French Army intervened between the First and
Third British Armies.

During the summer of 1915 the New Armies had begun to arrive
in France, and Sir John French deemed these reinforcements
sufficient to enable him to undertake the proposed offensive.

On the British front the principal attack, between the La Bassée
Canal and Loos, was to be carried out by the Ist and IVth Corps
of the First Army. In this part of the line Sir John French was
opposed by the Sixth German Army.

Portions of Ist Corps and 2nd Division Operations Orders are
given below :

" *Ist Corps Operation Order No. 106, 21st September* 1915.

" The First Army will assume the offensive on 25th September,
and advance between Lens and La Bassée Canal towards the line
Henin–Lietard–Carvin.

" The Ist and IVth Corps south of the La Bassée Canal will
attack with the object of securing the line Loos–Hulluch and the
ground extending to the La Bassée Canal. Immediately · after
piercing this line units will be pushed forward to gain possession
of the crossings of the Haute-Deûle Canal, between Harnes and
Bauvin.

" North of the La Bassée Canal the enemy will be engaged
vigorously, in order to prevent him withdrawing troops for a counter-
attack. Wherever the enemy gives ground he must be followed up
with the greatest energy.

" The IVth Corps will advance with its left on the Hulluch-Vendin road, and operate so as to secure the passage of the Haute-Deûle Canal at Pont-à-Vendin and the Loos Carvin road south of Annay.

" The 3rd Cavalry Division (less one brigade) will be in Army Reserve in the Bois des Dames in readiness to advance on Carvin as soon as possible.

" The general intention of the General Officer Commanding Ist Corps is to break the enemy's line south of the La Bassée Canal, and to advance to the line of the canal Pont-à-Vendin–Bauvin with his right on the Hulluch–Vendin-le-Vieil road.

" A main attack will be made by the 7th, 9th, and 2nd Divisions against the enemy's front from Vermelles–Hulluch road (inclusive) to the La Bassée Canal, with the view to an immediate advance on Hulluch–St. Elie–Haisnes railway line from Haisnes to La Bassée Canal. A subsidiary attack will also be made by the 2nd Division from Givenchy."

The objectives were then detailed : " 7th Division, the enemy's front trenches from the Vermelles–Hulluch road (inclusive) to Quarry trench. 9th Division, from Hohenzollern Redoubt to Vermelles Triangle Railway (inclusive). 2nd Division, the enemy's front trenches from the left of the 9th Division to the La Bassée Canal. Subsidiary attack : the left brigade of the 2nd Division holding the line north of the canal—the enemy's trenches opposite Givenchy and to push on to the line Chapelle St. Roch–Canteleux."

After detailing the orders given in Corps Operation Orders, 2nd Division Operation Order No. 63 of 21st September adds :

" The main and subsidiary attacks will be prepared by a bombardment commencing 21st September, and by special programme detailed in 2nd Division Instructions 8oG."

This special programme contained instructions for the projection of asphyxiating gas to be used by the Division for the first time. These details, though interesting, are lengthy ; but briefly, the quantity of gas to be expended was : 19th Infantry Brigade from 21 emplacements, each having 12 cylinders ; 6th Infantry Brigade from 37 emplacements, each of 12 cylinders ; 5th Infantry Brigade from 60 emplacements, each having 3 cylinders. The emplacements were dug by the Sappers, but the gas was to be projected by specially trained personnel. Smoke candles for burning simultaneously with the projection of the gas were also to be used to cover the advance of the troops.

" The dividing line between the 9th and 2nd Divisions will

be Tram Alley, Lone Farm, Cemetery Alley, Pekin—all inclusive to the 9th Division."

The 5th Infantry Brigade occupied the Givenchy sector north of the La Bassée Canal. The 6th Infantry Brigade came next in the Cuinchy sector, and the 19th Infantry Brigade was on the right of the 6th Brigade, with its right in touch with the left of the 9th Division. Thus the line from north to south ran : 2nd, 9th, and 7th Divisions. The Corps of the First Army from north to south were IIIrd Corps, Indian Corps, Ist Corps and IVth Corps.

Subsidiary attacks north of the La Bassée Canal (apart from the attack to be made by the 5th Infantry Brigade of the 2nd Division) were :

First Army : Indian Corps to attack Moulin-du-Pietre ; IIIrd Corps, the enemy's trenches at Le Bridoux.

Second Army : Vth Corps to attack Bellewaarde Farm, east of Ypres.

Third Army : Operations along its front between Monchy, south-west of Arras and the Somme.

Just south of Loos the Tenth French Army joined up with the right flank of the IVth Corps.

The attacks of the French and British Corps were to be simultaneous.

During the three weeks which preceded the battle the attack had been rehearsed, and all ranks carefully instructed in their respective *rôles*. The trench mortars had also been reorganized. On 18th September the following allotments were made : 5th Infantry Brigade, two 2-inch mortars, two Stokes mortars ; No. 15 Trench-Mortar Battery, eight 95-mm. mortars. 6th Infantry Brigade, one section No. 6 Trench-Mortar Battery, eight 95-mm. mortars. 19th Infantry Brigade, one section No. 6 Trench-Mortar Battery, eight 95-mm. mortars.

The preliminary bombardment began on the morning of the 21st September, and is excellently recorded by an artillery officer :

" *21st September, Tuesday.*—Bombardment began at dawn all along the front IVth Corps, Ist Corps, Indian Corps, and IIIrd Corps ; also the French on our right and Second Army on our left. Continued all day, and 18-pounders and 4.5 howitzers at night. . . . Enemy's artillery generally quiet, but some firing from Loos, Hulluch, Cité St. Elie. Firing at Vermelles, Noyelles, Grenay. Also opposite Indian Corps, at trenches, Bois Grenier, etc. Effects of our fire generally good. Fires started at Loos, La Bassée ; explosion at Fosse No. 11.

"*22nd September.*—Second day of bombardment; results generally satisfactory, and many gaps cut in wire. Enemy's guns showed little activity, and those that did open fire were soon silenced. Several fires in Loos.

"*23rd September.*—Third day of bombardment; report satisfactory. Enemy showing little activity, and probably has evacuated his front-line trenches. French artillery down south very active.

"*24th September.*—Fourth day of bombardment. Enemy's artillery rather more active, especially opposite IIIrd Corps front. Report satisfactory. Weather reports at 10 p.m. were satisfactory, and the General Officer Commanding decided to carry on with the programme."

The weather reports were very closely watched at this period for changes in the direction of the wind, seeing that on the 25th the initial projection of gas was to be made.

"Zero" hour had been postponed until the last possible moment, but during the night 24th–25th, it was definitely fixed for 5.50 a.m. on 25th September, when the projection of gas was to begin and smoke candles burned.

When dawn broke on the 25th it seemed as if the elements had conspired to make the attack abortive, for heavy rain fell and the wind—what there was of it—shifted almost continually. It was a bad day for the projection of gas!

The 2nd Division was disposed for attack as follows:

5th Infantry Brigade north of La Bassée Canal in the Givenchy section: in front-line trenches from left to right, 2nd Oxford and Bucks (from Deadman's Trench to a few yards north of Berkeley Street); 1st Queen's (from Berkeley Street to Shaftesbury Avenue); 2nd Highland Light Infantry (from Shaftesbury Avenue along the front of the Duck's Bill to Corunna Road); 2 companies of 9th Highland Light Infantry (just north of the La Bassée Canal) to attack in conjunction with the 6th Infantry Brigade south of the canal. In support: 1 company 7th King's, behind Sunken Road; 1 company 9th Highland Light Infantry north of Marie Redoubt; 1 company 9th Highland Light Infantry at Orchard Terrace. In reserve: 1 company 7th King's at New Cut; 1½ companies 7th King's at Newgate Road; the 2nd Worcesters at Sidbury Defences; and a half-company 7th King's at Gunner Siding.

6th Infantry Brigade south of the La Bassée Canal to Gun Street: in the front-line trenches from left to right, 2nd South Staffords (from the Canal Bank to Ridley Walk); 1st King's (from

Ridley Walk to Gun Street). In reserve : 1st Royal Berks, 1st
King's Royal Rifles, and 1st Herts, about Woburn Abbey.

19th Infantry Brigade from Gun Street to due east of Sim's
Keep ; in the front-line trenches from left to right, 2nd Argyll
and Sutherland Highlanders (from Gun Street to road due east of
Point 14) ; 1st Middlesex (from Point 14 to R1). In support : 1st
Cameronians (Scottish Rifles) north-west of Russell's Keep. In
reserve : 2nd Royal Welsh Fusiliers between Burbure Alley and
Maison Rouge Alley ; 5th Scottish Rifles about Maison Rouge.

The attack of the 5th Infantry Brigade was timed for 6 a.m.,
those of the 9th Highland Light Infantry, 6th and 19th Infantry
Brigades, to begin at 6.30 a.m.

Objectives : 5th Infantry Brigade the enemy's first and second-
line trenches in front of the attacking battalions, thence to the line
Chapelle St. Roch–Canteleux ; 6th Infantry Brigade the face and
eastern end of the Triangle and the line of the Vermelles railway to
due east of the right flank of the brigade ; 19th Infantry Brigade
from the right flank of the 6th Infantry Brigade, La Briques
Farm, and the Vermelles railway line due east.

Batteries of 18-pounders firing shrapnel and 4.5-inch howitzers
firing high-explosive were to lay down barrages.

At 5.45 a.m. the guns opened on the enemy's trenches, and
punctually at 5.50, along the whole front of the line of the 2nd
Division, the gas cylinders began to pour out their fumes. But
the wind was so light that the dense clouds of gas hung in the
air and seemed not at all inclined to move towards the enemy's
trenches.

Simultaneously with the discharge of gas the 5th Infantry
Brigade put down two smoke barrages, one just south of the Duck's
Bill and the other just north of the Sunken Road ; they were
intended to screen the flanks of the brigade, but the smoke also
hung in clouds, and with the gas clung to the British trenches
instead of blowing over the enemy's lines. As one Battalion Diary
states : " The air was practically motionless, with the result that
the gas hung back considerably, and in our part of the line did more
harm to our men than to the enemy." This delay was disastrous,
for the enemy had received warning and had already begun to light
small fires along the parapets of his trenches, some of his troops
donning gas masks and using sprays.

Similar difficulties were encountered south of the canal. At
5.52 a.m. 6th Infantry Brigade Headquarters reported that the
wind was unfavourable, but was ordered to proceed with the gas

projection. So the gas was turned on, but here, as north of the canal, the fumes hung about the front-line trenches held by the South Staffords and 1st King's, the wind being almost negligible.

In front of the 19th Infantry Brigade also the gas hung with exasperating stillness, and was inclined to blow back into the faces of the troops waiting for the signal to " go over the top."

At 6 a.m. the Oxford and Bucks, 1st Queen's, and 2nd Highland Light Infantry from just south of the Duck's Bill to opposite the Sunken Road, left their trenches and advanced rapidly across No Man's Land. The Queen's and Scotsmen succeeded without much difficulty in occupying the front line of hostile trenches; the right company of the Oxfords also obtained a footing, but the left company was held up by heavy machine-gun fire and retraced its steps, advancing again south of the southern groups of mine craters which lay out in No Man's Land between the two lines of trenches.

A move was then made towards the enemy's second line, but the attacking battalions had been weakened, first, by the loss of men temporarily out of action suffering from the effects of gas, and secondly, by the enemy's fire from machine guns and snipers, which had gradually increased and was of deadly accuracy. Moreover, the number of bombs issued to the 5th Infantry Brigade—ten to each bomber—had been totally inadequate for the conduct of a bombing attack. And what was even more disastrous, many of these bombs could not be used. They were of the " ball " pattern, and had to be ignited from a kind of match-box striker strapped to the wrist of the bomber. The damp atmosphere and the falling rain made ignition impossible. The enemy used the " stick " grenade, a much better and more formidable weapon, which could be thrown farther.

Thus the advance towards the enemy's second line was begun under the most unfavourable conditions. The result was that although the attack was pressed with great gallantry, the three battalions were bombed back first to the enemy's first-line trenches and later to their own original trenches from which the attack had been launched. As one diarist states : " The whole brigade was back in our original front line by 9.40 a.m."

Of five machine guns and a 4-pounder trench mortar carried forward with the attack, three machine guns and the mortar were knocked out of action and had to be abandoned.

Back in their original trenches, the three battalions of the 5th Infantry Brigade set to work to reorganize and clean up the trenches, which had been much damaged by the hostile artillery bombardment. The brigade had already received orders that if the first attack failed a further attempt was not to be made unless under orders from Divisional Headquarters.

However, in spite of failure to maintain itself in the enemy's trenches, the 5th Infantry Brigade had succeeded in the task allotted to it—*i.e.*, that of containing the enemy on his front and preventing him sending reinforcements elsewhere where the principal attacks were being made.

At 6.30 a.m. the main attack had taken place.

The 9th Highland Light Infantry, although belonging to the 5th Infantry Brigade, had been ordered to attack with the 6th Infantry Brigade along the line of the canal, but about 6.25 a.m. a volume of gas, which had apparently collected just south of the canal, blew northwards over the position of the Glasgows and enveloped their front trenches lined with troops ready to advance. The two leading platoons almost immediately became casualties. "Within five minutes our leading two platoons had only seven and nine men left respectively who were fit to carry on. Two fresh platoons were brought up at the double to take their place, but were not in position till after 6.40 a.m. A reconnoitring party was sent forward towards our objective, but were met with rifle and machine-gun fire and were all killed except one man. . . . Our attack was therefore abandoned for the time being, and our assaulting companies reorganized. Our machine gunners suffered heavily from the gas, and at 6.50 a.m. we had only eight of them left for three guns." [1]

By 6.30 a.m., the time at which the 6th Infantry and 19th Infantry Brigades launched their attacks south of the canal, the element of surprise had been dissipated by the attack of the 5th Infantry Brigade. The enemy's trenches were seen to be full of troops, and he had numbers of machine guns trained upon the ground over which the British troops would advance.

As in the sections north of the canal, the gas attack was almost entirely a failure. The 6th Infantry Brigade reported : " Practically all along our front the gas blew back into our own trenches."

At 6.30 a.m. punctually the South Staffords and the 1st King's climbed the parapets of their trenches and advanced against the enemy.

The terrain along this portion of the front, as it existed in 1915, is worth consideration. Between the La Bassée Canal and the main La Bassée–Cambrin road, the British and German lines ran through a brickfield at an average distance of 200 yards apart. On the right

[1] Diary, 9th Highland Light Infantry.

of the South Staffords' front were several groups of Brickstacks, facing similar groups behind the German front-line trenches, in which machine guns had already been located. These Brickstacks had been the scene of desperate fighting since the beginning of the year (1915). The intervening ground was broken up by a series of mine craters made by the enemy to increase the strength of his position for defensive purposes. Saps had been run out from both front lines towards these craters, and the occupation of the sap-heads had in one place at least brought the opposing forces to within twenty-five yards of one another. The paths between the craters were very narrow, limiting the frontage of any attacking force to small parties of men in single file. Across this network of mine craters A and B Companies of the Staffords were to advance, the former on the right, the latter in the centre; for C Company, which held the trenches next to the canal bank, had been ordered to attack from along the tow-path a fortified position known as "Embankment Redoubt."

Such was the terrain in front of the Staffords when at 6.30 a.m. the order was given for the three companies to scale the parapet and assault the enemy's trenches. What followed after the gas had been projected with disastrous effects is very clearly told in the Battalion Diary: "Many were so badly gassed as to be incapable of advancing, whilst all suffered more or less." Thus the assault was launched under conditions "such as," in the words of the brigadier, "would have demoralized any but the staunchest and most highly disciplined troops." "Immediately the gas was projected the enemy lighted fires at intervals of a few yards all along the first-line parapets."

"To deal with the right attack (A Company) first: As the signal for the assault was given, our men . . . rushed gallantly forward, only to be met by cross-fire from concealed machine guns and heavy rifle fire from the German front-line trench, the enemy evidently being quite unaffected by the gas. A and B Companies were held up on the edge of the crater nearest to their parapet and were unable to advance.

"Meanwhile C Company on the left had advanced with superb gallantry along the tow-path. Most of the men of this company were badly gassed before leaving our front-line trench, and on going forward were met by a murderous fire from both sides of the canal. Many of them actually reached the German wire, which was only a few yards in front of the hostile trenches. A most gallant attempt to support this attack was made by Second-Lieut. D. M. Williams, who pushed forward a machine gun close in rear of the assaulting line. He succeeded in establishing it in position on the railway embankment, where he kept the gun in action until all the team were killed except himself and one other man—he himself being wounded. The 5th Brigade north of the canal had been unable to get forward, and we were thus exposed to concentrated rifle and machine-gun fire at very close range."

It was during this attack on the Embankment Redoubt that Captain A. F. G. Kilby of C Company of the South Staffords won for the 2nd Division the first of the three Victoria Crosses gained by the Division during the Battle of Loos. The company had, by his own request and on account of the gallantry which he had displayed on many occasions, been placed under the command of Captain Kilby.

" The company charged along the narrow tow-path, headed by Captain Kilby, who, though wounded at the outset, continued to lead his men right up to the enemy wire under a devastating machine-gun fire and a shower of bombs. Here he was shot down, but although his foot had been blown off, he continued to cheer on his men and to use a rifle." [1] After the battle Captain Kilby was reported " wounded and missing," and later his death was presumed.

Shortly after 7 a.m. the position of the Staffords was : C Company had been unable to reach the Embankment Redoubt and was suffering heavy losses from rifle and machine-gun fire ; B Company was held up just in front of its own parapet ; A Company had reached the lip of the nearest crater and could not advance farther, being heavily bombed. At 8 a.m., therefore, the battalion was ordered to withdraw from the forward saps and from the front line in order that the artillery might bombard the enemy's trenches. But the bombardment only reached the German second-line defences and did not touch the front line or in any way cut the wire entanglements ; neither had any damage been done to the Brickstacks which formed the enemy's principal strong points. A second assault was therefore not made, the battalion having already suffered very heavy casualties.

The 1st King's advanced to the attack simultaneously with the Staffords, but the gas had affected them also. A company had been placed on each side of the La Bassée–Cambrin road. The company south of the road was almost immediately wiped out by machine-gun fire, and, as the enemy's wire was found to be intact,

[1] *London Gazette*, 30th March 1916.

it was impossible to go on, and the attack was abandoned. North of the road the platoons advanced rapidly and some men reached the hostile wire, but finally this company also, having lost heavily, was withdrawn to its own trenches.

The 19th Infantry Brigade was not as seriously affected by the gas as were the other two brigades of the 2nd Division, but the advance was hampered by the fumes which hung about, there being very little wind to carry them forward.

The 2nd Argyll and Sutherland Highlanders on the right flank of the 1st King's, and the Middlesex on the right of the Highlanders, pressed forward to the attack at 6.30 a.m., but they had scarcely covered a few yards before both battalions were met by an accurate, steady, and deadly fire, delivered from thickly-lined parapets. All along the line it had been noticed that the enemy's front-line trenches were but lightly held until the attack began ; then after opening a very heavy fire from his support trenches, he rushed men up to the front line in time to meet the assaulting parties and decimate them almost on the wire. These tactics were new and saved the enemy many men.

From the first it was evident to the assaulting parties of the Highlanders and Middlesex that the attack could not succeed, for the wire was practically intact ; and where in a few places it had been cut, it was of such thickness and profusion as to form a fresh barrier where it fell without any arranging. One platoon of Highlanders with extraordinary pluck and perseverance had succeeded in getting through the wire : it was never seen again !

For some time the left flank of the 19th Infantry Brigade lay out in front of the brigade's trenches, but was eventually withdrawn. The right flank (Middlesex) had only been able to make slight headway across the open fire-swept ground between the two lines of trenches, and then had to dig itself in as best it could lying on the ground.

The 2nd Royal Welsh Fusiliers, who, as the Middlesex left their trenches, had filed into them, then tried to retrieve the situation ; but almost as soon as the leading platoons were " over the top " the battalion lost 100 men, and the attempt was abandoned.

The situation along the fronts of the 6th and 19th Infantry Brigades at 8 a.m. is summed up in the 2nd Division General Staff Diary thus : " On our right the Middlesex were lying out in front of the German trenches ; the 2nd Argyll and Sutherland Highlanders had been driven back to our trenches—both with heavy losses. The King's were in front of the German trenches on the right of the 6th Infantry Brigade, having suffered heavily; the South Staffords had made a gallant attack on the Embankment Redoubt in spite of the failure of our gas attack, but had been obliged to retire to their own trenches. Both these battalions had suffered heavily."

A second attempt along the front of these two brigades was ordered, and the guns opened fire again at 9 a.m., with orders to continue until 9.30 a.m., when the next assault was timed to take place.

The 1st Cameronians (Scottish Rifles) had replaced the 2nd Argyll and Sutherland Highlanders and the 2nd Royal Welsh Fusiliers the Middlesex, who had gradually worked their way back to their own front line. But finding that reorganization for another attack would take much longer, Divisional Headquarters, after consultation with General Officer Commanding Ist Corps, cancelled the second attack until further orders; the artillery, however, continued firing until 11.30 a.m.

The 1st Herts (T.F.) at 11.30 a.m. moved up one company and a platoon to reinforce the South Staffords, and the 1st Berks one company to reinforce the 1st King's.

During the afternoon the Berks took over the whole of the South Staffords' trenches, and the latter battalion, sorely in need of rest, moved back into the support area.

So far as the 2nd Division was concerned the attack of the 25th September was over.

On the northern flank of the Division—i.e., along the front of the IIIrd and Indian Corps—the attack, like that of the 5th Infantry Brigade, had at first succeeded, and the German trenches were entered near Bridoux and Mauquissait; but later strong counterattacks compelled the assaulting parties to fall back to their original trenches.

South of the Division, however, on the fronts attacked by the 9th and 7th Divisions of the Ist Corps and the 1st, 15th, and 47th (London) Divisions of the IVth Corps, successes had been gained which more than counterbalanced the failure along the front of the 2nd Division.

An admirable summary of the attack south of the 2nd Division is given in an artillery officer's Diary:

" 9th Division, left attack on Madagascar failed twice, but right pushed forward and gained Fosse 8. They then formed a defensive flank from Fosse 8 back to our original trenches on the Vermelles–Auchy railway.

" 7th Division took the Quarries and got as far as trenches in front of Cité St. Elie, but were then held up. An attack later on Cité St. Elie failed.

" The IVth Corps attacked with the left of the 1st Division on Vermelles–Hulluch road, 15th Division on their right, 47th Division opposite Loos with their right on the Double Crassier. The whole of the IVth Corps made good progress, and by nightfall they were on the line Hulluch–Puits 14 Bis–Hill 70 [1] east of Loos. Loos was in our possession, but Hulluch still held by the enemy. On the whole front we have captured 1,800 prisoners and 7 guns. The French on our right report good progress between Angres and Souchez. Also good progress near Perthe, north-east of Rheims."

The 2nd Division's casualties during the fighting on 25th September (the first day of the Battle of Loos) were, in killed, wounded, and missing : officers 91 ; [2] other ranks 2,234. The battalions which suffered most severely in other ranks killed, wounded, and missing were : 1st Middlesex, 439 ; 2nd Argyll and Sutherland Highlanders, 319 ; 2nd South Staffords, 280 ; 1st Queen's (Royal West Surrey), 270 ; 2nd Highland Light Infantry, 252 ; and 1st King's, 202.

Interest in the battle now passes from the front held by the 2nd Division on the night of the 25th September to the " Quarries," situated west of Cité St. Elie, soon to be the scene of attacks by " Carter's Brigade "—a force formed of units from the 2nd Division but attached to the 7th Division. And in order that these operations may be the better understood, it is necessary to give word for word the official " Situation Report " issued by the 1st Corps Headquarters at 5.15 p.m. on 25th September :

" Situation on IVth Corps front as follows : right secured on Double Crassier, thence south of Loos Chalk Pit to Hill 70 inclusive. The line runs thence northwards to include Puits 14 Bis and German trenches immediately south and west of Hulluch, but Hulluch is not in our hands—enemy is reported to be making strenuous efforts to recapture Hill 70.

" Situation on 1st Corps front as follows : right of 7th Division about 1,300 yards south of crossroads H7, C52, along road to same crossroads, thence due west to G12, B44, along Gun Trench to Pt. 39 north of road and the Quarries.—9th Division reported to be holding Pekin Trench from crossroads G6, B52, to A30.

[1] Hill 70 was captured, but only a footing on the western slopes of the hill was held at 1 a.m. on the 26th.
[2] See Appendix XIII.

A74—Fosse 8 back to our old front line on Vermelles–Auchy road.—Beyond this point no appreciable advance has been made on the north of the Ist Corps line.—No change in situation on Indian Corps front."

The formation of " Carter's Brigade " was the outcome of a telephone communication between the General Officer Commanding Ist Corps and 2nd Division, which took place at 10 o'clock on the night of the 25th. The composition was :

General Officer Commanding : Lieut.-Colonel B. C. M. Carter, C.M.G., 1st King's. Brigade-Major : Captain E. C. Davidson, G.S., 2nd Division. Staff Captain : Captain J. L. Dent, South Staffords. Special Brigade Signal Section under Lieut. B. Howarth, R.E. Troops : 1st King's Royal Rifles ; 1st Royal Berks, from 6th Infantry Brigade ; 2nd Worcesters, from 5th Infantry Brigade. Brigade Ammunition Column : 2 G.S. Wagons and 5 S.A.A. carts from XXXIVth D.A.C. ; 2 G.S. Wagons from XXXIVth D.A.C. Medical : 2 Bearer Sub-divisions 19th Field Ambulance, 5 Motor Ambulances 19th Field Ambulance.

The troops were ordered to assemble at 7 a.m. just west of Annequin.

The formation of this new force necessitated the relief of the 1st Royal Berks, who had during the afternoon taken over that section of the front line held by the South Staffords ; the latter battalion therefore had to move back into its old line, and the Berks were withdrawn.

The 1/5th King's were also brought back to the Divisional area and assembled at Le Quesnoy.

About midnight the enemy, by a cleverly executed outflanking movement, recaptured the Quarries, held by the 7th Division ; this loss was reported to 2nd Division Headquarters about 2 a.m.

A counter-attack was organized immediately. In the meantime " Carter's Brigade " was ordered to proceed at once to Vermelles, and the troops marched off independently, reaching that place at 5 a.m. Here they were ordered to prepare for an attack on Cité St. Elie as soon as the Quarries had been recaptured, an attack on which was in progress. But by 10 a.m. on the 26th this attack had failed, and the attack on Cité St. Elie was cancelled.

The brigade was then ordered to attack the Quarries—the attack to take place during the afternoon : " G58, Carter's Force, will at 3.30 p.m. attack the Quarries from approximately the line

26TH SEPT.

G11, B34–G5, D12 ; the 9th Division will assist this advance by a movement from Fosse 8, the details of which will be communicated later.   The attack will be preceded by a bombardment of heavy artillery and field artillery lasting one hour, the last 5 minutes of which will be intensive.—The 20th Brigade (7th Division) will furnish an engineer's party, consisting of one section, to assist in the consolidation of the Quarries when captured.—The heavy artillery will lift off the Quarries at the hour, the field artillery will be detailed to continue firing till two minutes after the assault has been launched, when a barrage will be fired north-east of the Quarries.''

The battalion detailed for the attack was the 2nd Worcesters, with two companies—A and C—of the 1st King's Royal Rifles in support.

The attack, however, was postponed until 4.30 p.m., as the Worcesters, in moving forward up the various communication trenches with five boxes of bombs per company to carry, found it impossible to get into the front-line trenches and the jumping-off point by 4 p.m.   Moreover, in going forward a leaky gas cylinder barred the way, and a few men were affected by the fumes and had to be left behind.   Eventually, however, at 4.15 the battalion arrived in the front line, and at 4.30 the signal was given for the attack to be launched.

The battalion moved forward in two lines—each of two companies (each company on a two-platoon front, followed by the remaining two platoons) ; D Company on the right, C on the left ; in the second line A on the right, B on the left.

The successive lines advanced at the double until the first German trench was reached, which was found to be occupied by some men of the 9th Norfolks.   The latter belonged to the 71st Infantry Brigade (24th Division), which had been lent to the 7th Division. The Worcesters advanced through the Norfolks, who were holding the old German front-line trenches from which the assault on the Quarries earlier in the day had started and failed.

Very few casualties occurred between the British lines and the old German line.   Almost without halting the Worcesters were over the parapets, and advanced magnificently towards the enemy's line, which was strongly held.   Rapid rifle and machine-gun fire now opened on the advancing lines, and casualties were numerous. But still the advance continued until an old German half-dug trench was reached, where the first line took what little cover the parapet afforded and opened fire on the hostile trench about 200 yards in front. Beyond this point it was impossible to advance, and as dusk fell the consolidation of this position was begun, and continued throughout the night, the troops using the small entrenching tool carried as part of the equipment. The second line halted about fifty yards in rear of the first, and also began digging in. A bomb attack was then organized in order to clear St. Elie Avenue, which connected the trench then occupied by the enemy with his old front line. The avenue was cleared, and a double-back made and fire-steps constructed to form a defensive flank.

During the attack the Worcesters had somewhat lost direction by advancing too far to the right. The two companies of Rifles, therefore, acting as supports, were moved up to the left flank, and in this position gave valuable support to the Worcesters as they bombed and fought their way forward towards the Quarries. The latter stronghold was never reached, though in the confusion reports had been sent back that it had been captured.

When darkness fell " Carter's Brigade " was entrenched some 200 yards west of the Quarries, thence through Point 22 to Points 78 and 90. On the left and right flanks of the brigade were the 21st and 22nd Infantry Brigades respectively.

The gallant efforts of the brigade to reach the Quarries, though unsuccessful, drew a congratulatory telegram from General Gough : " Please express my pleasure with Colonel Carter's Brigade for their gallant attack on the Quarries, and convey my appreciations to them, especially the Worcesters, and hope they will continue to maintain all they have won."

After dark the stretcher-bearers began their work of searching for the wounded and dying. And here in the Official Diaries for the first time is mentioned the work of the army chaplains : " Captain the Rev. R. J. Stewart, Chaplain to the Forces, and attached to the battalion (Worcesters), was present during the operation, and rendered valuable assistance in attending the wounded."

The Worcesters lost heavily—13 officers and 275 other ranks killed, wounded, and missing was the cost of the ground the battalion held that night. All the company commanders were killed or wounded, the former including Captain P. S. G. Wainman, Lieut. G. H. J. Daubeney and Second-Lieut. L. H. Oldham. The 1st King's Royal Rifles lost 1 other rank killed, and 1 officer and 10 other ranks wounded.

Captain E. W. Carrington, R.A.M.C., attached 2nd Worcesters, was also killed whilst gallantly attending the wounded.

Casualties in other parts of the 2nd Divisional line : 1 officer

(Captain G. O. Thomas, 2nd Royal Welsh Fusiliers) and 10 other ranks killed, and 2 officers and 61 other ranks wounded and missing.

No incident of importance had taken place during the 26th in the Givenchy and Cuinchy areas north and south of La Bassée Canal.

Elsewhere on the front of the Ist and IVth Corps the Division reported the situation " rather obscure all day, as the fight swayed to and fro ; but at nightfall we were holding the line railway Fosse 8—western edge of Quarry—east edge of Loos—Double Crassier." Other items in the Diaries are interesting. " Casualties yesterday (25th) were very heavy—500 officers and 16,000 men. Our attack, however, drew off the German forces from the French front on our right, and the French attacked at 1 p.m. They took Souchez and advanced through Givenchy-en-Gohelle Wood. The French main attack in Champagne made good progress ; total number of prisoners there is 16,000 and 20 guns. Our captures yesterday were 2,000 prisoners and 20 guns. Latest reports from French state number of prisoners captured as 18,000 and 31 guns."

27TH SEPT.   At 5.30 on the morning of the 27th the situation remained unchanged : " During the night the 6th and 19th Infantry Brigades reorganized and increased their supply of gas ; cylinders were made up to 7 per emplacement." No change had taken place on the front of the 5th Infantry Brigade, though the 7th King's had been withdrawn to Essars, and later relieved the 9th Highland Light Infantry in the trenches just north of the canal.

From 7 a.m. onwards reports were continually received at Divisional Headquarters of the precarious position at Fosse 8, until finally, 2.10 p.m., Ist Corps Headquarters reported its recapture by the enemy. The 2nd Division was therefore ordered to make a gas attack at 5 p.m., followed by an infantry assault on the enemy's trenches from the Vermelles–La Bassée road to the canal. The attack was to be made by the 1st King's and the 1st Herts. The latter had moved into the front-line trenches on the 26th.

In the meantime another attack on the Quarries by " Carter's Brigade " was ordered for 4 p.m., and the battalions concerned were busy organizing for the assault ; but shortly before " zero " hour the attack was postponed until 5.30.

At 5 p.m. gas was projected all along the front of the 19th and 6th Infantry Brigades, and the troops were in readiness to assault the trenches. But again the gas failed to make any impression on the enemy, who immediately lighted fires along the parapets of his trenches ; to make matters worse, the wind changed and rain fell, which dissipated the gas.

Both attacks—*i.e.* from the Vermelles–La Bassée road to the canal and on the Quarries—were then abandoned.

During the time the troops were waiting for the order to advance a large minenwerfer bomb fell into the trenches occupied by the Herts, where the men were ready lined up. No. 1665 Corporal A. A. Burt, 1st Battalion (T.), " who well knew the destructive power of this class of bomb, might easily have got under cover behind a traverse ; but he immediately went forward, put his foot on the fuse, wrenched it out of the bomb and threw it over the parapet, thus rendering the bomb innocuous. His presence of mind and great pluck saved the lives of others in the traverse." [1]

For this gallant act Corporal Burt was awarded the Victoria Cross.

" Carter's Brigade " had been " standing to " all day long. At 10.30 a.m., and again at 3 p.m., orders had been received to attack the Quarries, only to be cancelled subsequently. The " ding-dong " nature of the stubborn and terrible struggle for the possession of Fosse 8 was the cause. Finally, about 11.30 p.m., the Royal Berks were ordered to attack the Slag Heap (Fosse 8) at 2.30 a.m. on the 28th. The half-battalion of the 1st King's Royal Rifles lying in reserve was ordered to support the Berks.

The battalion when these orders were received was at Siding No. 4 and Junction Keep, very much scattered, having been engaged during the day in fatigue duties and in digging trenches. In consequence some time elapsed before the men were assembled for the attack. The position to be assaulted was strange to both officers and men, and a reconnaissance was impossible. 28TH SEPT.

" The battalion formed up in company column, and advanced towards their objective (the Dump or Slag Heap) 800 yards away. During the advance two lines of captured German trenches and two lines of barbed wire had to be crossed ; these were manned by British troops. Owing to the bright moonlight the enemy saw us advancing when we were 400 yards from our objective (Fosse 8) ; they put up Véry lights and kept up a continuous rifle-fire on us from our right front ; this grew heavier as we got nearer."

The battalion advanced steadily, A, B, and half of C Companies going straight for the Fosse. They were unable, owing to the heavy fire from the enemy (who by this time was manning the top of the Fosse) to gain the Slag Heap, being checked about

[1] *London Gazette,* 22nd January 1916.

seventy yards from it. The regimental bombers could also make no headway. D and part of C Companies meanwhile had advanced and manned the front British trench. A communication trench stuffed with Germans, who threw showers of bombs and kept the assaulting parties under heavy fire, was the chief cause of the delay.

A young subaltern (Second-Lieut. A. B. Turner, 3rd Battalion attached 1st Battalion), then stepped forward and volunteered to lead a new bombing attack. " He pressed down the communication trench practically alone, throwing bombs incessantly with such dash and determination that he drove back the Germans about 150 yards without a check. His action enabled the reserve to advance with very little loss, and subsequently covered the flank of his regiment in its retirement, thus probably averting a loss of some hundreds of men." But whilst performing this gallant act Lieut. Turner was mortally wounded, and died later of his wounds. He had, however, gained for the 2nd Division the very highest reward a brave man can receive—the Victoria Cross : [1] the third awarded to the Division in the Battle of Loos.

" By this time it was known that the Commanding Officer (Major L. W. Bird) was wounded, and Captain M. C. Radford, D.S.O., the second-in-command, killed. In consequence the command devolved upon Captain C. W. Frizell, who was in command of the rear company D. Also by this time Colonel Carter, the brigadier, was up in the front trench. Seeing that the first-line companies were checked Colonel Carter gave Captain Frizell the order to charge with the remaining men available. This order was carried out. The leading men, with Captain Frizell in front, got half-way up the Slag Heap when the Germans from the top threw bombs on our heads ; this checked our further advance, and the men retired to the front British trench, a distance of 150 yards. As it was now getting daylight and the men were much exhausted, Colonel Carter decided not to attack again. He ordered Captain Frizell to reorganize in our old trenches."

The Berkshires' casualties in this attack were : 3 officers killed, 4 missing, and 6 wounded (including the Commanding Officer) ; and 265 other ranks killed, wounded, and missing. Besides Captain Radford and Second-Lieut. Turner, Second-Lieut. R. A. Summers was also killed.

Search parties were immediately organized under Captain Large, R.A.M.C. (medical officer 1st Berks), who " worked with

---

[1] *London Gazette*, 18th November 1915.

untiring devotion in evacuating the wounded from his dressing station in the advanced British line."

At 9 a.m. on the 28th Colonel Carter was ordered to assume command of the 85th Infantry Brigade, and the three battalions forming " Carter's Brigade " were handed over temporarily to the General Officer Commanding 22nd Infantry Brigade.

The condition of " Carter's Brigade " in front of the Quarries (the Worcesters and King's Royal Rifles) was now getting serious. The former battalion could only muster a commanding officer, adjutant, 6 lieutenants, and 600 men. Constant hostile bombing attacks and shelling with gas and lachrymatory shells made rest impossible, as the utmost vigilance was necessary.

At 3.30 p.m. the enemy started a strong bombing attack on the left of the King's Royal Rifles near Point 90. Temporary shortage of bombs forced the Rifles to retire some forty yards. A fresh supply of bombs having been obtained the Rifles counter-attacked, and for two hours the fight raged bitterly, ending in a victory for the Rifles, who recovered all the lost ground and re-built their barricade. The Battalion Diary records : " Second-Lieut. L. E. Hall, C.M.S. A. Hopkins and Rifleman Todd threw bombs continuously for two hours, and it was almost entirely owing to them that the German attack failed. Second-Lieut. L. E. Hall was completely exhausted at the finish, having strained his heart. We used a great many German bombs in this attack. The day closed wet and miserable.

" On the evening of this day the situation remained practically unchanged."

During the night of 28th–29th the 5th Infantry Brigade was relieved in Section A (Givenchy) by the Sirhind Brigade and withdrawn temporarily into billets in Béthune, Essars, and Le Préol.

On the morning of the 29th, at 5 o'clock, the King's Royal 29TH SEPT Rifles were again heavily bombed by the enemy. But D Company having during the night relieved A Company, and being completely rested, were able after two hours to resist all endeavours of the enemy to turn them out of their position.

A simultaneous attack made on the right of the King's Royal Rifles against the Worcesters' trenches and the barricades in St. Elie Avenue was, however, immediately successful ; the fuses of the bombs used by the Worcesters were damp and refused to ignite. The enemy took St. Elie Avenue, and a few actually got within twelve yards of the main trench ; but Lieut.-Colonel Lambton, D.S.O., took effective measures and at once ordered some of the

King's Royal Rifles to charge over the parapet. This prompt action saved what might have been a serious situation. The enemy was driven back and out of St. Elie Avenue, and the Worcesters' line was restored, the battalion inflicting heavy losses on the enemy as he retired. Second-Lieut. F. D. E. Cayley of the Rifles was killed during this attack.

At 8 a.m. the situation was once more normal.

During the afternoon word was received that the 22nd Infantry Brigade, and with it " Carter's Brigade," would be relieved at night by the 83rd Infantry Brigade (28th Division) and the three battalions of " Carter's " returned to the 2nd Division. The reliefs were completed in the early hours of the 30th, and the Worcesters marched off to billets in Essars, the King's Royal Rifles to Béthune ; the Berks had preceded the two other battalions of " Carter's Brigade " by some hours, and had reached their billets in Le Quesnoy just before midnight.

" Carter's Brigade " no longer existed !

There were many instances during the Great War of the formation of these small temporary detachments or forces, but none acquitted itself more bravely than " Carter's."

From the 28th to the evening of the 30th the position in front of the 6th Infantry Brigade was described in the Official Diaries as " normal," for although a good deal of shelling took place no further attacks were made either by the brigade or by the enemy. At 6 p.m. on the 30th the brigade was relieved by the 58th Infantry Brigade and moved to billets in Béthune.

On the afternoon of the 29th the Hohenzollern was the scene of another attack in which the 9th Division won a little more ground ; the Division was relieved later.

The 5th Infantry Brigade on the night of the 29th took over the trenches of the 28th Infantry Brigade (9th Division) east of the Vermelles–La Bassée railway, having the 19th Infantry Brigade on the left flank, but spent only a few hours in this position, for during the afternoon of the 30th the 19th Infantry Brigade was ordered to extend its line and take over the portion held by the 5th Infantry Brigade. The latter then returned to billets in Le Préol, Essars, and Beuvry.

On this day also the IXth French Corps extended its left and took over the western portion of Hill 70 and the village of Loos. Farther south the French Tenth Army had gained the crest of the Vimy Ridge. In Champagne a further advance had also been made ; over 20,000 prisoners had already been captured.

Heavy fighting was now gradually dying down along the fronts of the Ist and IVth Corps.

And now, as Sir John French said in his dispatches : " Our troops all along the front were busily engaged in consolidating and strengthening the ground won ; and the efficient and thorough manner in which this work was carried out reflected the greatest credit upon all ranks. Every precaution was made to deal with the counter-attack which was inevitable."

With these counter-attacks (which took place early in October) it is not possible to deal fully, as the 2nd Division as a whole was not involved, the brunt of the fighting on the Divisional front falling on the 5th Infantry Brigade.

On the night of 30th September–1st October the 5th Infantry Brigade took over Gun Trench occupied by the 21st Infantry Brigade (7th Division) north and south of the Vermelles–Hulluch road to Point 57 south of the Quarries ; the 6th Infantry Brigade relieved the 83rd Infantry Brigade (28th Division) and carried on the line from Point 57 to the junction of Big Willie with Quarry Trench—*i.e.*, north of the 5th Infantry Brigade. 1ST OCT.

Gun Trench occupied by the latter brigade was partly held by the enemy, whose communication trench from the east butted into the British line, then turned north and south ; the British and German troops being separated by barricades or " blocks." Between that portion of Gun Trench held by the enemy and the British was a strong line of wire entanglement.

The 2nd Highland Light Infantry and the Oxford and Bucks held front line, with the Worcesters and Glasgow Highlanders in support ; and the 1st King's Royal Rifles and 1st King's the line of the 6th Infantry Brigade from Point 54 to Big Willie, with the 1st Herts and 1/5th King's in support, and the South Staffords and Berkshires in Brigade Reserve.

Gun Trench was held by the Highland Light Infantry, intersected in the middle by about 200 yards held by the enemy. On the evening of 2nd October the General Officer Commanding 5th Infantry Brigade received orders to attack this position and clear the trenches of hostile infantry. The attack, preceded by an artillery bombardment, was timed for 8.30 p.m., when the artillery barrage on the enemy's communication trench would increase.

Both flanks were to launch bombing attacks, and an attempt to reach the trench from the front was to be made as soon as the bombing parties had got to the enemy's position.

At 8.30 the brigade bombers started their attack from both

flanks, but immediately came under a heavy machine-gun fire from the enemy's communication trenches. The attack from the north made no progress ; that from the south succeeded three times in getting into the hostile trench, but on each occasion was beaten back. This attack was very ably led by Second-Lieut. Hutton. The attempt to rush the trench from the front was abortive : " Owing to a failure of the signal and the difficulty of passing orders along the narrow support trench, the frontal attack appears to have started late and by driblets, and to have failed to reach the German trench, with the result that the bombing party were driven out. The troops were tired out, and the communications so bad that it was not possible to organize a further effort that night." The casualties in this attack were Second-Lieut. G. M. Leslie (2nd Highland Light Infantry) and 8 other ranks killed, and 2 officers and 61 other ranks wounded.

The afternoon of the 3rd October witnessed another attack by the enemy west of the Quarries against the King's Royal Rifles. At 2.30 hostile artillery opened fire on the front lines, supports, and communication trenches held by the Rifles. The bombardment lasted two hours, and was accompanied by heavy bombing from minenwerfers and aerial torpedoes. The enemy was then reported massing for an attack, which he launched about 4.30 p.m. His bombers made an attempt to advance from about Point 90, but could make no headway against an accurate machine-gun and rifle fire maintained by the Rifles. The successful manner in which the King's Royal Rifles dealt with this attack was due to the fine efforts of the battalion bombers, who in the course of two and a half hours expended no less than 2,000 bombs, the supply of which had been splendidly organized.

In this affair the Rifles lost two officers (Second-Lieuts. E. H. Bentall and K. J. B. Addy) killed, and 5 other ranks killed and wounded.

On the night of 3rd–4th October the 5th and 6th Infantry Brigades were relieved by the Guards Division and marched into rest-billets and joined the 19th Infantry Brigade in and about Béthune.

From 4th to 9th October inclusive the 2nd Division was out of the line, resting, training, and re-fitting. The strenuous operations which had begun on 25th September had tried even the most hardened troops. Life in the trenches during those anxious days was a horror ; on all sides the dead lay unburied. Men walked with Death, growing callous, careless even if they survived the bloody and terrible struggle which seemed to have no cessation.

ACTIONS OF THE HOHENZOLLERN REDOUBT, 13th–19th October 1915.

(*Facing p. 240.*)

The Mappa Co. Ltd. London

The counter-attacks which Sir John French expected took place on 8th October all along the line from (and including) the French left on Loos to Fosse 8, and only in two places, at the Double Crassier and north-east of the Hohenzollern, had the enemy anything at all to show for the thousands of dead which for days lay out unburied in front of his trenches.

The Guards Division had temporarily been forced out of its position just north of the Hohenzollern, but a counter-attack restored the line; the French lost a small portion of the Double Crassier. " At midnight on the 9th October the line held by the First Army was identically the same as that held before the enemy's attack started."

Actions of the Hohenzollern Redoubt.

The possession of the Hohenzollern Redoubt, Fosse 8, and the Quarries were, however, necessary before any further permanent advance by the First Army could be made. An attack on this formidable group of defences had been planned for 10th October, but the unfavourable direction of the wind and weather conditions necessitated postponement until the 13th, when, at 2 p.m., further attempts to break down the enemy's defences in and about these three powerfully defended positions were made by the First Army. North of the canal the Indian and IIIrd Corps carried out feint attacks, using smoke, and bombarding the enemy's position.

13TH OCT.
MAP.

The XIth Corps (12th, 46th, and 11th Divisions) assaulted the Quarries and Fosse 8. The 1st Division of the IVth Corps was directed on the enemy's position along the Lens–La Bassée road.

Only the 5th Infantry Brigade of the 2nd Division was involved in this attack. The brigade had relieved the 2nd Guards Brigade (Guards Division) and part of the 21st Infantry Brigade (7th Division) on 10th October, and had occupied a line from left Boyeau (opposite the north-west salient of the Hohenzollern) to R (northwest of the Vermelles railway). The relief was completed at 7 p.m., when the General Officer Commanding 2nd Division assumed command of that part of the line occupied by the brigade. The 6th and 19th Infantry Brigades were still in reserve.

On the left flank of the 5th Infantry Brigade the line to the canal was held by the 7th Division ; the right flank of the brigade was held by the 46th Division.

242 THE HISTORY OF THE SECOND DIVISION.

The *rôle* assigned to the 5th Infantry Brigade was : " To form a gas and smoke curtain from its trenches at 1 p.m. ; to form a smoke barrage on Mad Point (the point jutting out from the German trenches just north of Little Willie) with trench mortars ; to open machine-gun fire on the opposing trenches, and finally to carry out a bomb attack at 2 p.m. up New Trench to co-operate with the bombing parties of the 46th Division."

" New Trench " was a trench dug from the British line due east up to the centre of Little Willie.

The 1st Queen's and 9th Highland Light Infantry were in the front-line trenches, the first-named battalion on the right, the Highlanders on the left.

Having bombed up New Trench and captured the junction of the latter with Little Willie, the brigade was then to turn right (southwards) in Little Willie and join hands with the 138th Infantry Brigade (46th Division), coming up northwards from the Hohenzollern ; also to turn left (northwards) up Little Willie to the junction of the latter with Fosse Trench ; then to bomb eastwards along Fosse Trench until touch was gained with a bombing attack made by the 46th Division coming from south-east.

The discharge of smoke and gas took place punctually, but without any effect upon the enemy. Just before 2 p.m. a screen of smoke was put up from an advanced point in New Trench.

At 2 p.m. the brigade bombers, led by Second-Lieut. Ramsey of the Oxford and Bucks, moved forward up New Trench, followed by the right, left, and supporting parties of 1st Queen's. Immediately the first party left the sap-head it came under a cross machine-gun and heavy frontal rifle fire, and was practically wiped out. The enemy had apparently concentrated his fire upon this sap-head.

Of the second party only Lieut. Abercrombie and one man succeeded in getting to the junction of New Trench and Little Willie, and here they waited for reinforcements. As they did not arrive, Lieut. Abercrombie sent his companion back with a message asking for support ; but the man was wounded and the message was never received. Lieut. Abercrombie then advanced up Little Willie alone ; finally, having put an enemy machine gun out of action and expended all his bombs, he retired to the Queen's front lines and reported.

14TH OCT.   A fresh attack, timed for midnight 13th–14th, did not take place until between 4 and 5 a.m., and then failed owing to lack of bombs and proper organization.

As a result of this attempt the 1st Queen's lost Second-Lieut.

A. Tweedie-Smith killed, Second-Lieut. St. L. Perfect (3rd King's Own, attached) died of wounds, and 62 other ranks killed, wounded, and missing. The battalion was relieved by the Oxford and Bucks, and marched back to billets in Annequin.

Elsewhere the attacks which took place on the 13th met with varied results ; the western portion of the Hohenzollern Redoubt, the intersected portion of Gun Trench, and the south-west corner of the Quarries were captured, but Fosse 8 defied all attempts, nor could any advance be made on the enemy's trenches west of Hulluch. These positions were consolidated.

" In the course of the next two days the whole attack died down without attaining the objective aimed at."

Thus ended the operations which began on 25th September.

" The position assaulted and carried with so much brilliancy and dash by the Ist and IVth Corps on 25th September was an extremely strong one. It extended along a distance of some 6,500 yards ; consisted of a double line, which included works of considerable strength ; and was a network of trenches and bomb-proof shelters. Some of the dug-outs and shelters formed veritable caves thirty feet below the ground, with almost impenetrable head cover. The enemy had expended months of labour upon perfecting these defences. The total number of prisoners captured during these operations amounted to 57 officers and 3,000 other ranks. Material which fell into our hands included 26 field guns, 40 machine guns, and 2 minenwerfer."

The losses of the 2nd Division during the Battle of Loos (nineteen days) were approximately as follows. Total number, including those in " Carter's Brigade " : officers killed 43,[1] wounded 73, missing 21 ; other ranks, killed 518, wounded 1,994, missing 748 ; grand total, officers 137, other ranks 3,259.

The losses in " Carter's Brigade " were : officers killed 6,[1] wounded 20, missing 6 ; other ranks, killed 81, wounded 355, missing 219. In addition to the names already given, other officers killed during the battle were : Lieut. F. J. Roberts, 1st King's : Lieut. F. M. Wayte, 1st Cameronians.

On 8th September Brigadier-General W. H. Onslow, the C.R.A. of the 2nd Division, who had been appointed C.R.A. to the XIIth Corps, handed over his duties to Brigadier-General C. H. Saunders.

[1] See Appendix XIII.

Trench Warfare, November 1915 to July 1916.

After the Battle of Loos and the series of small but exhausting operations which concluded on 19th October, it was obvious that before another attack on a large scale could be undertaken, a considerable period must elapse. Not only were the troops much weakened, but winter was approaching. Large numbers of troops of the New Armies were arriving, all of whom had to be trained and given their first instruction in trench warfare; re-organization was therefore necessary. Fresh material (more and more guns of larger calibre, and vast stores of ammunition in order to cope with the enemy's artillery) was essential; the troops required rest and recuperation.

Whatever hopes of an early peace humanity had once indulged in by now were everywhere recognized as futile—the grim struggle would continue to the bitter end. Therefore, however awful the prospect, the British, French, and Belgian armies in France and Flanders prepared for their second winter in the trenches.

For the 2nd Division, November and December of 1915 and the first six months of 1916 passed without any action of a general character taking place. Sir John French spoke of the concluding months of 1915 as being " somewhat barren in incidents of military importance "; while of the first five months of 1916 Sir Douglas Haig reported : " On the British front no action on a large scale such as that at Verdun has been fought . . . nevertheless our troops have been far from idle or inactive." Indeed, extreme vigilance at all times of the day and night was necessary, and although the periodical communiqués announced " There is nothing to report," trench fighting, bombing, raiding, mining and counter-mining, and bombardments were of almost daily occurrence.

" Artillery and snipers are practically never silent, patrols are out in front of the line every night, and heavy bombardments by the artillery of one or both sides take place daily in various parts of the line. Below ground there is continual mining and counter-mining, which, by the ever-present threat of sudden explosion and the uncertainty as to when and where it will take place, causes perhaps a more constant strain than any other form of warfare. In the air there is seldom a day, however bad the weather, when aircraft are not reconnoitring, photographing, and observing fire. All this is taking place constantly at any hour of the day or night, and in any part of the line. . . . A steady and continuous fight has gone on day and night above ground and below it. . . . One form of minor activity claims special mention—viz., the raids or 'cutting-out' parties, which are made at least twice or three times a week against the enemy's line. They consist of a brief attack with some special object on a section of the opposing trenches, usually carried out by a small body of men. The character of these operations, the preparation of a road through our own and the enemy's wire, the crossing of the open ground unseen, the penetration of the enemy's trenches, the hand-to-hand fighting in the darkness, and the uncertainty as to the strength of the opposing forces, give peculiar scope to the gallantry, dash, and quickness of decision of the troops engaged; and much skill and daring are frequently displayed in these operations."

For all these minor attacks constant training and practice were essential; the troops of the New Army especially needed the guidance of those who had become veterans. The old Divisions of the regular British army were fast losing their original character; battalions and even brigades were transferred to the new Divisions in order to stiffen the more recent formations. Officers and senior N.C.O's were taken from regular battalions and posted to freshly-formed units in order to train the latter for their part in the grim struggle.

Thus, on the 25th November, the 19th Infantry Brigade of the 2nd Division was permanently transferred to the 33rd Division. No. 2 Company of the 2nd Divisional Train and the 19th Field Ambulance also went with the brigade. The 99th Infantry Brigade from the 33rd Division, with No. 3 Company 33rd Divisional Train and No. 100 Field Ambulance, replaced the 19th Infantry Brigade. A fortnight earlier (on 10th November) the 1/7th King's (Liverpool) Regiment had been transferred to the 7th Division.

Early in December two more units which had been with the 2nd Division since it left England in August 1914 were transferred to the 33rd Division—i.e., the 11th Field Company R.E. left on the 2nd and the 2nd Worcesters on the 8th of December. On the 9th December the 7th Mountain Battery left the Division.

The 2nd Worcester Regiment and the 1st Queen's (Royal West Surrey) Regiment, also transferred to the 33rd Division, both battalions belonging to the 5th Infantry Brigade, were replaced by the 13th Essex and the 17th Middlesex Regiment.

The 99th Infantry Brigade consisted of the 17th, 22nd, 23rd, and 24th Royal Fusiliers—a New Army Brigade. During December, however, the brigade was split up—two battalions, the 17th and

24th, going to the 5th Infantry Brigade ; they were replaced by the 1st Royal Berks and the 1st King's Royal Rifles from the 6th Infantry Brigade, which thus lost its pre-war formation.

On December 15, 1915, the three infantry brigades of the 2nd Division were organized as follows :

> 5th Infantry Brigade : Brigadier-General C. E. Corkran.
> > 2nd Oxford and Bucks Light Infantry : Lieut.-Colonel A. J. F. Eden.
> > 2nd Highland Light Infantry : Lieut.-Colonel R. E. S. Prentice.
> > 1/9th Highland Light Infantry (Glasgow Highlanders) : Major J. C. Stormonth-Darling, D.S.O.
> > 17th Royal Fusiliers : Major C. G. Higgins (2nd Oxford and Bucks).
> > 24th Royal Fusiliers : Lieut.-Colonel F. J. C. Bonnyman.
> 6th Infantry Brigade : Brigadier-General A. C. Daly.
> > 1st King's (Liverpool) Regiment : Lieut.-Colonel H. C. Potter.
> > 2nd South Staffords : Lieut.-Colonel R. W. Morgan.
> > 1st Herts (T). : Lieut.-Colonel H. P. Croft, C.M.G.
> > 17th Middlesex Regiment : Colonel H. F. Fenwick.
> > 13th Essex Regiment : Lieut.-Colonel P. R. Papillon.
> 99th Infantry Brigade : Brigadier-General R. O. Kellet.
> > 1st King's Royal Rifle Corps : Lieut.-Colonel G. A. Armitage.
> > 1st Royal Berks Regiment : Lieut.-Colonel J. C. May, D.S.O.
> > 1/5th King's (Liverpool) Regiment : Major J. J. Shute.
> > 22nd Royal Fusiliers : Lieut.-Colonel R. Barnett-Barker.
> > 23rd Royal Fusiliers : Colonel Viscount Maitland.

To add to the difficulty—always more or less present where reorganization takes place—the Division in these eight months was constantly moving in and out and up and down the line, from the Cuinchy section to south of Lens. And these changes meant the continual reconnoitring, repairing, rebuilding, and reorganizing of fresh positions and trenches.

*   *   *   *   *   *   *

1/5th King's (Liverpool) Regiment left the 2nd Division to join the Third Army on 7th January, and the 1/9th Highland Light Infantry (Glasgow Highlanders) were withdrawn from the Division to General Headquarters on the 30th of the same

MAJOR-GENERAL W. G. WALKER, V.C., C.B.,
COMMANDED THE 2ND DIVISION FROM 5TH NOVEMBER 1915
UNTIL 27TH DECEMBER 1916.

month. On 24th February the 1st Herts (T.) left the Division for General Headquarters. Thus in March the three infantry brigades of the Division were back to their four-battalion strength. On 10th May the Divisional Mounted Troops (S. Irish Horse and the Divisional Cyclist Company) became Corps Troops. The Cyclists had served the Division splendidly ever since the early days of the war. Their devotion during the Battle of Mons, where with the gallant Hussars they were the first to join action with the enemy, and later during all the stages of the retreat, their fine work in reconnaissance and dispatch riding, had won for them a great reputation.

The 10th Battalion Duke of Cornwall's Light Infantry (Pioneers) joined the Division on 23rd June.

Late in October the 2nd Division held command of the Cuinchy section ; on 30th December the Division was resting and training at Busnes ; January 25, 1916, saw Divisional Headquarters back again in Béthune ; on 28th February the Division relieved the French in the Angres section south of Lens, and two days later Divisional Headquarters opened in Sains-en-Gohelle. Three weeks were spent in the latter section, and then (22nd March) the Division moved back to Bruay for another period of rest and training.

On 19th April the front-line trenches were again occupied, this time in the Aix section until taken over by the 23rd Division. The 2nd Division next went into the line just south of Lens, until finally, on 20th July, after the Somme battles had begun, Divisional Headquarters opened at Rue de Collège, Corbie, with the Division located in the Corbie–Sailly-le-Sac–Morlancourt area. Two days later the Division was in the reserve area, warned to move forward to the battle-front on short notice. The Somme battles had opened with excellent results, and the enemy's line had in places been broken on a front of from three to four miles.

* * * * * * *

Many changes in commands and staff had taken place. Major-General H. S. Horne, C.B., who had commanded the Division from December 1914, was ordered to the War Office on special duty, and on 6th November Major-General H. S. Walker, V.C., C.B., assumed command. On 12th April Lieut.-Colonel L. R. Vaughan, D.S.O., G.S.O.1, was transferred to Headquarters XVth Army Corps, and Lieut.-Colonel C. P. Deedes, D.S.O., was appointed in his place and took over on the 14th. Captain Davidson, G.S.O.3, who had been appointed on June 11, 1915, went to Headquarters Fourth Army, and was replaced by Captain J. D. Boyd, D.S.O., on

January 12, 1916. Brevet-Major Viscount R. Feilding, D.S.O., who had been D.A.Q.M.G., took over the duties of D.A.A. and Q.M.G. from Major C. T. M. Hare on 12th February, the latter officer being invalided to England, and Captain D. P. Dickinson, D.S.O., M.C., became D.A.Q.M.G. The A.D.M.S. of the Division, Colonel M. P. C. Holt, D.S.O., was on October 22, 1915, appointed to the 22nd Division and handed over to Colonel N. L. Gray, A.M.S. The D.A.D.M.S., Captain W. B. Purdon, D.S.O., left the Division on March 25, 1916, to command the 19th Field Ambulance—he was replaced by Captain E. Scott. D.A.D.O.S., Major H. E. Smyth, also had a successor in Captain H. Palmer, who took over from Major Smyth on January 16, 1916, the latter officer going to Headquarters First Army. Captain C. H. H. Joliffe, who had succeeded Major D. Bolton as D.A.D.V.S., left the Division on 1st July to go to the 3rd Cavalry Division ; he was succeeded by Major A. N. N. Swanston. Captain G. W. R. Stacpoole, D.S.O., the D.A.P.M., went on December 15, 1915, as A.P.M. to the Vth Corps, and was replaced a few days later by Captain P. F. Foley. The latter officer, however, was posted as A.P.M. Advanced Base, L. of C., at the end of January 1916, and handed over his duties to Captain J. C. Halstead.

On 15th May Brigadier-General Corkran, commanding the 5th Infantry Brigade, was appointed to command the 3rd (Guards) Brigade, and handed over his brigade to Brigadier-General G. M. Bullen-Smith, D.S.O.

Schools for training officers and men for the next big attack were by now firmly established in the Division. Permanent staffs were appointed to these schools, of which there were several : Divisional Officers School, Divisional Grenade School, Divisional Signal School, and Divisional Gas and Mortar School. These schools were mobile, and instructors, students, and the permanent staff periodically rejoined their units.

* * * * * * *

For some weeks from November 1, 1915, the Divisional Diaries record " Situation unchanged," and yet, as Sir Douglas Haig said in his first dispatch, the troops were " far from idle or inactive." Minor operations were very frequent, and trench raids and bombing, mining and counter-mining always more or less continuous.

Of these minor operations the 2nd Division had its full share.

On 22nd November the Division held the line due east of Cambrin with the 19th Infantry Brigade in the front-line trenches : the 2nd Argyll and Sutherland Highlanders holding Z2, a section

opposite the Etna salient. Just east and slightly north of the
salient in No Man's Land there was a crater (known as "Etna
Crater"), and another south of the salient formed by a mine explosion
in the Battle of Loos on 25th September. About 6.45 on the
morning of the 22nd, as the enemy had been working during the   22ND NOV.
night, the 180th Tunnelling Company R.E. exploded a mine just
south of the salient between the two craters already mentioned. The
new crater was about thirty yards from the Highlanders' fire trench.
After the explosion, and under cover of the smoke, "ten grenadiers,
under Corporal Gibson, with water and rations, five spades, and as
many grenades as they could carry, rushed across and occupied
the crater." [1] Having reached the crater, messages were sent back
for more men, as the crater was found to be double the size it was
reported to be. Twice these messages under rifle and grenade-
fire were carried to and fro by Private Webster. The men in the
crater began to sap backwards to their own front-line trenches,
whilst their comrades holding the latter dug vigorously outwards
to connect up with those holding the crater. Bombs and grenades
were thrown over to Gibson and his party, who with considerable
gallantry kept the enemy at bay. About 11 a.m. the enemy could
be heard digging towards the new crater, but was kept back by
bombs. Soon after 3 p.m. a heavy mist came down, under cover
of which the wounded in the crater—now called "Gibson's Crater"—
were carried back into the front trenches and Gibson and his party
relieved. Two subalterns and a working party then set to work
to consolidate the crater, but the crumbling nature of its sides
made the building of a parados of sand-bags impossible, until support was obtained by building upwards almost from the bottom
of the crater. At 4.30 p.m., however, though an enormous number
of sand-bags had to be used, the work was completed. But half
an hour afterwards a rigorous hostile bombardment of the new
position began. Trench-mortar bombs and rifle grenades began
to fall in numbers in and about the crater. The 47th Field Howitzer
Battery and the 17th Battery R.F.A. lent assistance and bombarded
the enemy's front lines, whilst the 19th Infantry Brigade Trench
Mortars and the 6-inch Trench-Mortar Battery opened fire, and
eventually the hostile attack died down, though many casualties
had occurred amongst the troops holding the crater. The 1/5th
Scottish Rifles sent up a party of fifty grenadiers, and these were
organized into reliefs. Work was continued during the night,
and by daylight the following morning a parados of at least four feet

---

[1] Diary, 2nd Argyll and Sutherland Highlanders.

high had been completed, head cover put up in places, and the lip of the crater sand-bagged all round.

The following note occurs in the Diaries : " During the attack an officer dressed in English uniform was in the sap shouting ' Retire ! ' He ceased on torrents of abuse being hurled at him by Lieut. M——. He was not recognized. Owing to things at the time being rather critical there was no time to take action. A strange officer shortly before the attack reported himself to me as having been sent to take over command of the Tunnelling Company, and was directed to its headquarters."

There is a sequel to the story of the capture of Gibson's Crater.

23RD NOV.

On the day following the explosion of the mine and consolidation of the crater, the 6th Infantry Brigade relieved the 19th Infantry Brigade, the 2nd South Staffords taking over the trenches and Gibson's Crater held by the Argyll and Sutherland Highlanders. About 4.20 on the afternoon of the 24th, the enemy exploded a mine which had been dug immediately beneath Gibson's Crater. The explosion buried the whole of the garrison, consisting of 1 officer and 24 other ranks, with the exception of two men who were blown some distance over the crater. Another officer was also in the crater at the time of the explosion. Some of the unfortunate men were eventually dug out, but of the two officers—Second-Lieuts. J. H. Powell and S. H. Smith—and 13 other ranks, " no trace of them could be found." Bombing and fighting continued during the night, but Gibson's Crater remained in the hands of its gallant defenders.

Rain fell abundantly during November, and towards the end of the month snow came. The trenches were in a very bad condition. The " Tactical Progress Reports " are full of the daily work—of clearing, repairing, of floor boards being put down and the trenches cleared of water and mud. Yet never again were conditions as appalling as in 1914, during that terrible winter in the salient and the first battles of Ypres. For behind the lines there were now amusements, and steps were taken to remove for the time being the terrible mental and physical strain from the minds and bodies of the men whilst they were in reserve.

Systematic bombardments of the enemy's trenches and communications, followed by gas attacks and incursions of patrols into the enemy's trenches, were begun in December. The objects of these operations were to destroy hostile mine-shafts, cause loss to the enemy, obtain identifications and take prisoners, get infor-

mation regarding the enemy's dispositions, and break the enemy's
moral ; to damage his trenches and communications, and keep him
busily employed whilst the British troops were strengthening their
defences, training, and generally organizing their lines for and against
attack. These bombardments drew retaliations from the enemy,
but for every shell he fired he received full measure in return and
in time learned the wisdom of silence ! An illustration of the
manner in which these bombardments were carried out was given
in a report by the C.R.A. 2nd Division to Corps Headquarters: " A
bombardment of the Brickstacks (the Cuinchy Sector) was carried
out on 10th December by the 10th Siege Battery (2–9.2 inch   10TH DEC.
howitzers, 33rd Siege Battery (4–8 inch howitzers) and part of
the artillery of the 2nd Division. The heavy howitzers bombarded
the Brickstacks and mine works in the vicinity ; 350 rounds 4.5
howitzers, bombarded German trenches on either flank and minenwerfer positions. Eighteen-pounders searched approaches to the
bombarded area. Other 18-pounder batteries cut wire at certain
places on the 2nd Division front. The main bombardment lasted
three and a half hours. Much timber, etc., was sent flying, and the
Brickstacks . . . were knocked about sufficiently to disclose signs of
German work inside them. Loopholes and timber were uncovered,
and in D (stack) a large excavation in the top became apparent.
If the faces of these Brickstacks could be dealt with by a hard-
hitting gun such as the 60-pounder more internal arrangements
would probably be disclosed, but I fear it is impossible to do this
because the low trajectory of these guns would not clear our own
Brickstacks."

At night patrols were sent out to observe the damage done by
these bombardments. Reports from two of these patrols stated :
" Officers whom I dispatched to ascertain damage to German wire
by our bombardment have returned after making a successful
reconnaissance ; Lieut. —— reports our bombardment has effected
a breach about twenty-five yards in breadth ; the wire appears to
have been thoroughly cut ; the crater to the right of the La Bassée
road appears to be full of Germans, who were heard laughing,
talking, and singing ; there appears to be extensive repairs
going on in the German trenches on the La Bassée road. Sounds
as if emanating from shovels patting sandbags, and stakes being
driven into the ground, were heard.

" Officer commanding my left company reports as follows :
First patrol found out practically nothing ; second patrol under
Lieut. —— reached thirty yards from German wire ; Germans

re-wiring gap made this morning, also making a mine both sides of it ; the officer is of the opinion that German line is held very much stronger than ours, judging by the noises, flares, lights, and shots from it ; ground between lines very bad ; Germans appear to be making new first and second lines."

The gas attacks, however, often failed to achieve their object—the elements seemed to conspire against the use of this terrible method of rendering an enemy helpless ; though, so far as the Germans were concerned, they could not with any justice complain.

Another bombardment of the enemy's front line took place on 24th–25th December.

*   *   *   *   *   *   *

19TH DEC.   On the 19th December, Field-Marshal Sir J. D. P. French, G.C.B., O.M., G.C.V.O., K.C.M.G., Commander-in-Chief of the British Army in the Field, relinquished his command and returned to England. General Sir Douglas Haig, G.C.B., K.C.I.E., K.C.V.O., who had first commanded the Ist Corps (1st and 2nd Divisions) at Mons and later the First Army, then assumed command of the British Army in France and Flanders.

8TH–9TH   On the night of 8th–9th January 1916, the Division went into
JAN. 1916. General Headquarters Reserve until midnight 15th–16th, when it relieved the 12th Division in Sections B and C (Givenchy and Festubert). The 38th Division took over these sections on 20th February, when the 2nd Division once again passed into Corps Reserve. Eight days later (28th–29th February) the Division was transferred from the Ist to the IVth Corps and took over the
2ND   Angres–Calonne sectors (south of Loos) from the 18th French
MARCH. Division. On the 2nd March the Division extended its line and took over also a portion of the Souchez front.

In this new portion of the line the 2nd Division was opposed by the 17th Reserve Division of the IXth German Reserve Corps. This corps was formed of the 17th and 18th Reserve Divisions, the former consisting of 162nd, 163rd, and 76th Reserve Regiments, and the latter of the 31st, 75th, and 84th Regiments. The 17th Reserve Division was an old opponent of the 2nd British Division.

From the 23rd March to 19th April the Division was again out of the line, resting, training, and furnishing working parties.

A change in the formation of the artillery of the Division took place on 2nd May. The two 6-gun batteries of the XLIVth (Howitzer) Brigade R.F.A. were formed into three 4-gun batteries.

23RD MAY.   A minor operation which took place on the 23rd May is recorded, as it was the first in which the 99th Infantry Brigade, after joining the 2nd Division, took part.

The Division at this period was in the Souchez–Angres area, . having been hurriedly moved forward from reserve in Hersin and Calonne to support the 47th (London) Division, which was being subjected to a particularly heavy bombardment, under cover of which the enemy had captured a small portion of the line southeast of Souchez, on Vimy Ridge.

The 99th Infantry Brigade was sent forward to relieve the 140th Infantry Brigade (47th Division) and arrived at Villers du Bois in the early morning of the 23rd. The 22nd Royal Fusiliers and the 1st Royal Berks were sent forward to relieve the 17th and 7th London Regiments respectively ; the 1st King's Royal Rifles and the 23rd Royal Fusiliers being posted in support at Cabaret Rouge.

An attack had been ordered for the 22nd, but was subsequently postponed until 8.25 on the night of the 23rd.

The Berks at this hour were in the line Boyeau Central to a point about midway up the Talus des Zouaves ; thence the line was continued by the 22nd Royal Fusiliers to Landwehr Avenue. The 25th Division was on the right of the Berks, and the 142nd Infantry Brigade (47th Division) on the left of the 22nd Royal Fusiliers. The 99th Infantry Brigade had (for the attack) been placed under the command of the General Officer Commanding 47th Division.

At noon the enemy opened very heavy shell-fire on the Talus des Zouaves, which he continued without cessation until 7.45 p.m. The general bombardment was then changed to a dense barrage on the Zouave Valley communication trenches and Calonne Rouge, which was maintained until 9.30 p.m. Under the first bombardment the Berks were unable to reach the assembly trenches without incurring very heavy losses. The battalion had already suffered a hundred casualties. Messages were therefore dispatched back to Divisional Headquarters detailing the position, and the Berks were ordered to " stand fast for a short time—directly barrage lifts arrange with 22nd Royal Fusiliers to attack." But this message never reached the battalion. The 22nd Royal Fusiliers had been ordered to direct, but they were held up owing to the inability of the Berks to assemble and advance from the " jumping-off " place. Twice the latter attempted to reach the position of assembly, but on each occasion the leading platoons were practically wiped out.

Only one company (B) of the 22nd Royal Fusiliers, through

failing to get an order cancelling the attack, went forward, and reaching the enemy's trenches maintained itself for an hour and a half, but was finally recalled.

Eventually the attack was stopped by First Army Headquarters at 1 a.m.

In this affair the Royal Berks lost 110 other ranks killed and wounded; the 22nd Royal Fusiliers, 2 officers wounded and 87 other ranks killed and wounded. The 226th Field Company R.E. lost 40 other ranks killed and wounded; 1st King's Royal Rifles, 3 officers and 30 other ranks killed and wounded; and the 99th Machine-Gun Company 2 other ranks wounded.

Throughout the 24th May intermittent shelling took place. On the 25th the 6th Infantry Brigade relieved the 141st and 142nd Infantry Brigades in the Carency section of the line; the General Officer Commanding 2nd Division then assumed command of the line.

29TH MAY.   At 11 p.m. on the 29th the 6th Infantry Brigade, assisted by an artillery barrage, made a small bombing attack, but did not succeed in driving the enemy out of his position. The attack was carried out by the 2nd South Staffords, and though a failure, was a very gallant attempt. The battalion lost Second-Lieut. C. R. Hind killed, Second-Lieut. J. Beech wounded, and Second-Lieut. J. Perry missing, 3 other ranks killed and 4 wounded.

1ST JUNE.   On 1st June, at 8.30 p.m. three mines were blown opposite Souchez, and a bombing raid was made by the 1st King's and 17th Middlesex (6th Infantry Brigade); the 5th and 99th Infantry Brigades did not take part in this operation. The attack was preceded by an intense artillery bombardment, which began at 4.5 p.m. and ended at 8.30 p.m. immediately the three mines had been blown, when the guns lengthened their range and put down a heavy barrage on the enemy's support and second-line trenches. The enemy's artillery was also active, and a very heavy bombardment, with a barrage on Zouave Valley, caused many casualties in the Division, apart from those suffered by the two attacking battalions.

The official narrative of the 1st King's attack reports that " at 8.30 p.m. the mine was blown up, and this was the signal for the attack. There were three attacking parties of 21 men: each party had 20 men in support. The right party was detailed to attack up Ersatz Trench. This party lost heavily. As soon as the enemy realized that the assault had begun (which was after about thirty seconds) he sent up a number of red lights. Our front line was bombarded with heavy shells, which inflicted about 40 casualties on the company which supplied the right party. This party was unable to start owing to confusion caused by the bombardment. The enemy opposite to them was holding his trenches in strength, and opened heavy machine-gun fire and rifle fire and sent up a quantity of flares.

" The centre party made its way up Hartung Trench and succeeded in reaching a German trench. This party made barricades and remained in the German trench for half an hour. When the attack on the right and left had failed the party was ordered to withdraw. It was exposed to heavy machine-gun fire and only avoided casualties by crawling. It would have been very difficult to reinforce them.

" The left party was detailed to assault up Gubron Trench, and they also came under machine-gun fire. They obtained a certain amount of cover until they reached a point twenty-five yards from the German barricade. The Germans then threw bombs continuously and formed a barrage at this point. The party made four separate attempts to assault the enemy's barricade, but the leading men were shot down every time. At the fourth attempt one sergeant reached the barricade and jumped over, but the enemy discharged a volley of bombs at him as he was jumping over. This sergeant (Sergeant Howard) is missing. It is practically certain he has been killed. The officer in charge of the party was severely wounded.

" Total casualties during attack, about 60 killed and wounded."

The 17th Middlesex made a gallant attempt to carry out their orders in the face of fierce opposition. A report by the Officer Commanding (Lieut.-Colonel H. Fenwick) stated : " Our mines being blown the enemy raised a fierce burst of fire which lasted till 9.40 p.m., at which time it began to slacken, and I ordered the arranged-for parties to start in following order :

" (1) Raiding party under Second-Lieut. E. C. Lee.

" (2) Three covering parties under Lieut. Engleburtt.

" (3) Consolidating parties, consisting of 40 men each, of A and B, the rest of these two companies resuming their places in the front line, whence they had been withdrawn shortly before 4 p.m. for the purpose of taking cover from shelling.

" The expectation was that on reaching the (enemy's) line it would be found that great damage had been done to the German front line by the explosion, and also by the five hours' continuous bombardment by our artillery. In fact, it was anticipated that the German front line would be practically non-existent. However, the reverse was the case. Our front line and communication trenches suffered very severely from both the explosion and the German artillery, and the Germans were quite ready to meet our troops on their arrival with machine-gun fire.

" The right party under Second-Lieut. Lee passed through Broadbridge Crater and Mildren Crater, when machine-gun fire opened on them and Lieut. Lee was killed. The remainder of this party, who were expert bombers, fell back and joined in with the covering parties under Lieut. Engleburtt.

" The covering parties were three groups of ten each, whose endeavour it was to seize the far lip of the new craters and hold them, while consolidating parties behind them took up and made tenable the near lip of the craters. It was first of all reported to me that these covering parties had succeeded in occupying the front lip, as was their object; but this I found afterwards had not and could never have been done. What they did was to establish themselves between the craters and on the sides of the craters, and by constant bombing to keep off the enemy. In this they were greatly helped by the two Lewis guns which accompanied them, many of the teams of which were wounded. On learning the situation I sent an order to Lieut. Engleburtt to retire on the consolidating party, and to guard the near lip of the crater while consolidation proceeded. This was done, and Lieut. Engleburtt got his men and guns back to our lines. All the time these parties were out continuous bombing contests kept taking place between small parties. Lieut. Engleburtt, though wounded in head and arm, remained at his post, and did real good work. I consider that these covering parties, though they did not achieve their purpose of occupying the farther lip of the crater, nevertheless enabled the general objective to make progress satisfactorily, which was to occupy the near lip. As regards consolidation of the line of near lip of crater this may be divided into two parts as follows : First, the left, led by B Company under Captain Salter. Here a crater of considerable size was formed on the left of Broadbridge. Explosions have only damaged our line in two places. The crater itself was of a favourable nature to consolidate. Much work was done here, and by daylight on the 2nd inst. was pretty safe. Second, as regards the crater on the right. This was a matter of much magnitude and difficulty, which difficulty was enhanced by the fact that two platoon leaders, Second-Lieuts. L. A. Bradstreet and J. B. Skerry, were killed within five minutes of entering trenches by machine-gun fire. It took some time to send up two officers to replace them, and consequently work proceeded much slower. Also Captain Rollason, who commanded this part of the line, did not have the advantage of any expert advice, the Engineer officer who accompanied the consolidating parties confining his attentions strictly to crater on left. Of two sappers who accompanied this party one was instantly killed by shell-fire before reaching the trench. Captain Rollason found himself without any technical advice and assistance, and had to do the best he could, which consisted in clearing and digging trench and sap to the crater to gain as much cover as possible. The front trench here was completely obliterated, and a dangerous position thus created."[1]

The above report of the gallant attempt by the 17th Middlesex to gain and consolidate the crater is given in full, as this was the first occasion the battalion since its arrival in France, six months previously, had been engaged in an important operation. As the General Officer Commanding 2nd Division stated in his report to IVth Corps Headquarters: "This is the first occasion on which the 17th Middlesex have been engaged in serious fighting, but I consider they carried out the operation with steadiness and gallantry under very trying circumstances."

Besides the 3 officers killed and 1 officer wounded (whose names have already been given) the Middlesex lost 7 other ranks killed and 51 wounded; the 1st King's Royal Rifles (5th Infantry Brigade) had one officer (Lieut. A. J. Austen Cartmell) and three other ranks killed, and 1 officer and 30 men wounded; the 23rd Royal Fusiliers lost 3 other ranks killed and 33 wounded; the 13th Essex, 1 officer wounded, 4 other ranks killed and 36 wounded; the 2nd South Staffords lost 1 officer and 4 other ranks killed and 1 officer and 14 other ranks wounded.

A gallant action is mentioned in the Diary of the 1st King's (Liverpool) Regiment on the 3rd June, and is here given as it is written:

"*Vimy Ridge, June 3rd.*—Camouflet blown by Germans near Kennedy Crater. Lieut. Wilson (Second-Lieut. F. Wilson, 3rd Battalion, attached 1st Battalion), killed by gas in endeavouring to effect the rescue of two miners caught in fallen gallery. Several N.C.O's and men also went down suffering from gas poisoning."

The three days' fighting—1st to 3rd June—had cost the 2nd Division 6 officers killed and 11 wounded, and 45 other ranks killed and 294 wounded.

On the night of the 26th-27th June the 1st Royal Berks made

[1] Diary, 17th Middlesex Regiment.

an unsuccessful attack on the southern end of Momber Crater, with the object of investigating and if possible damaging the enemy's mine shaft. For the latter purpose a party of the 176th Tunnelling Company R.E. was attached to the assaulting party of the Berks, which numbered 100 men, under Captain West. Valuable information was obtained, but no prisoners were taken, nor were the enemy's mine shafts damaged. Some 40 casualties were suffered by the Berks in this attempt.

1ST–2ND JULY.

Another raid on the enemy's trenches was fixed for the night 1st–2nd July, and artillery preparation and " shoots " were carried out with the object of cutting the enemy's wire and generally preparing the way for the assaulting parties, which were to be found by the 13th Essex Regiment. For some days before the attack the Essex had rehearsed the raid in the rear of the front line, using dummy trenches.

The story of the raid is taken from the Diary of the 13th Essex Regiment :

" *Southern Sub-section, Berthonval, July 1st–2nd.*—A raid was carried out on the enemy's strong point at the junction of Vincent Street with the German front line. The raiding party consisted of Captain A. C. Hayward, Lieut. W. W. Busby, Lieut. Keeble and 199 N.C.O.'s and men, including A/R.S.M. G. E. Cattermole.

" The whole party crawled out in the dead ground between the two lines to within sixty and seventy yards of the objective, and they were in position there by 12.30 a.m. At 'zero' hour, 12.39 a.m., an intense fire of the artillery, trench mortars, and Stokes guns was opened, the artillery and trench mortars forming a box barrage round the objective, also firing on suspected emplacements, minenwerfer positions, and communication trenches in rear. These continued to fire on the same points throughout the raid. The Stokes guns opened rapid fire on the objective for one minute, and the instant the minute was up a dash was made for the enemy's trenches and the whole party succeeded in getting in, suffering only one casualty. The strong point was found to be full of Germans, some ten or a dozen of whom had already been killed by the fire from the Stokes guns. A fierce fight ensued ! A party on the left told off to deal with the sap in Vincent Street found it unoccupied, nor were they any more successful with the supposed machine-gun emplacement to the south of it, which was found to be a mine shaft. A few Germans, however, were seen by the party, and five of them were killed. The left-centre party also found a few Germans, of whom one was killed, and five of them who took refuge in a dug-out were also killed. The right-centre party found more Germans in their part of the trench. They killed five of them and ran seven to ground in a shallow dug-out, six of whom were killed and one made prisoner. The bulk of the garrison attempted to withdraw down a communication trench leading eastwards. These were heavily bombed by the right party, and twenty more killed and a number wounded.

"The raiding party withdrew after being about a quarter of an hour in the enemy's trenches, and came under rather heavy shrapnel fire on the way back. About a dozen prisoners were taken.

"The casualties amongst the raiding party were: Captain A. C. Hayward and Lieut. F. R. Keeble wounded, 6 other ranks killed, 40 wounded, and 3 missing."

Most of the casualties occurred during the retirement from the enemy's trenches; many as the men were actually getting over the top into their own trenches.

The South Staffords were in the line on the left of the Essex, and during the raid a shell fell in their trenches, killing Second-Lieut. W. R. C. Benson.

The raid reflected considerable credit on the 13th Essex Regiment (Colonel Papillon), as the battalion was a New Army formation and had not very long arrived in France.

It was during the tour of the Division in this sector of the line that the enemy first used lachrymatory shells, which fell in Carency on 2nd July. He had also recently made use of box kites for observation purposes.

Heavy artillery bombardments, and considerable trench mortar shelling, was on the increase; the enemy appeared very "jumpy," as if he expected to be heavily attacked.

The 2nd Division was relieved by the 47th Division in the middle of July, and on the 18th was "resting and training." A strenuous time was in front of it, for farther south, desperate fighting was taking place—the battles of the Somme had begun.

III.

THE ALLIED OFFENSIVE, 1916.

THE BATTLES OF THE SOMME, 1916.

THE BATTLE OF DELVILLE WOOD.
THE BATTLE OF GUILLEMONT.
Trench Warfare, 19th August to 31st October.
THE BATTLE OF THE ANCRE:
Capture of Beaumont Hamel.

THE BATTLES OF THE SOMME, 1916.

In his Dispatch dated 23rd December 1916 Sir Douglas Haig outlined the situation on the Western front which led up to the Somme battles of that year :

"The principle of our offensive campaign during the summer of 1916 had," he said, "already been decided on by all the Allies. The various possible alternatives on the Western front had been studied and discussed by General Joffre and myself, and we were in complete agreement as to the front to be attacked by the combined French and British armies. Preparations for our offensive had made considerable progress ; but as the date on which the attack should begin was dependent on many doubtful factors, a final decision on that point was deferred until the general situation should become clearer."

The "final decision," however, could not be postponed very long, for "the Germans were continuing to press their attacks on Verdun ; and both there and on the Italian front, where the Austrian offensive was gaining ground, it was evident that the strain might become too great to be borne unless timely action was taken to relieve it. . . . By the end of May the pressure of the enemy on the Italian front had assumed such serious proportions that the Russian campaign was opened early in June, and the brilliant successes gained by our Allies against the Austrians at once caused a movement of German troops from the Western to the Eastern front. This, however, did not lessen the pressure on Verdun," and "in view therefore of the situation in the various theatres of war, it was eventually agreed between General Joffre and myself that the combined French and British offensive should not be postponed beyond the end of June. The object of that offensive was threefold — (1) to relieve the pressure on Verdun ; (2) to assist our Allies in the other theatres of the war by stopping any further transference of German troops from the Western front ; (3) to wear down the strength of the forces opposed to us."

The preparations for the Somme battles were elaborate :

" Vast stocks of ammunition and stores of all kinds had to be accumulated beforehand within a convenient distance of our front. To deal with these many miles of new railways, both standard and narrow gauge, and trench tramways were laid. All available roads were repaired, many others were made, and long causeways were built over marshy valleys. Many additional dug-outs had to be provided as shelter for the troops, for use as dressing-stations for the wounded, and as magazines for storing ammunition, food, water, and engineering material. Scores of miles of deep communication trenches had to be dug, as well as trenches for telephone wires, assembly and assault trenches, and numerous gun emplacements and observation posts. Important mining operations were undertaken, and charges were laid at various points beneath the enemy's lines.

" Except in the river valleys the existing supplies of water were hopelessly insufficient to meet the requirements of the numbers of men and horses to be concentrated in this area as the preparations for the offensive proceeded. To meet this difficulty many wells and borings were sunk, and over 120 miles of water mains were laid, and everything was got ready to ensure an adequate water supply as our troops advanced.

" Much of this preparatory work had to be done under trying conditions, and was liable to constant interruption from the enemy's fire. The weather, on the whole, was bad, and the local accommodation totally insufficient for housing the troops employed, who consequently had to content themselves with such rough shelter as could be provided in the circumstances. *All this labour, too, had to be carried out in addition to fighting,* and to the everyday work of maintaining existing defences. It thus threw a very heavy strain upon the troops, which was borne by them with a cheerfulness beyond all praise."

The dispatches then describe the enemy's position to be attacked, which was of a very formidable character, " situated on a high, undulating tract of ground, which rises to more than 500 feet above sea-level, and forms the watershed between the Somme on the one side and the rivers of south-western Belgium on the other. On the southern face of this watershed, the general trend of which is from E.S.E. to W.N.W., the ground falls in a series of long irregular spurs and deep depressions to the valley of the Somme. Well down the forward slopes of this face the enemy's first system of defences, starting from the Somme near Curlu, ran at first northwards for 3,000 yards, then westwards for 7,000 yards to near

Fricourt, where it turned nearly due north, forming a great salient angle in the enemy's line.

"Some 10,000 yards north of Fricourt the trenches crossed the river Ancre, a tributary of the Somme, and still running northwards passed over the summit of the watershed, about Hébuterne and Gommecourt, and then down its northern spur to Arras.

"On the 20,000 yards front between the Somme and the Ancre the enemy had a strong second system of defences, sited generally on or near the southern crest of the highest part of the watershed, at an average distance of from 3,000 to 5,000 yards behind his first system of trenches.

"During nearly two years' preparation he had spared no pains to render these defences impregnable. The first and second systems each consisted of several lines of deep trenches, well provided with bomb-proof shelters and with numerous communication trenches connecting them. The front of the trenches in each system was protected by wire entanglements, many of them in two belts forty yards broad, built of iron stakes interlaced with barbed wire often as thick as a man's finger."

The defences behind these formidable belts of wire were then described: "The numerous woods and villages in and between these systems of defence had been turned into veritable fortresses. The deep cellars usually to be found in the villages, and the numerous pits and quarries common to a chalk country, were used to provide cover for machine guns and trench mortars. The existing cellars were supplemented by elaborate dug-outs, sometimes in two stories, and these were connected up by passages as much as thirty feet below the surface of the ground. The salients in the enemy's line from which he could bring enfilade fire across his front were made into self-contained forts, and often protected by mine-fields ; while strong redoubts and concrete machine-gun emplacements had been constructed in positions from which he could sweep his own trenches should these be taken. The ground lent itself to good artillery observation on the enemy's part, and he had skilfully arranged for cross-fire by his guns. These various systems of defence, with the fortified localities and other supporting points between them, were cunningly sited to afford each other mutual assistance and to admit of the utmost possible development of enfilade and flanking fire by machine guns and artillery. They formed, in short, not merely a series of successive lines, but one composite system of enormous depth and strength."

Between the Somme and the Ancre the British front-line trenches ran parallel with, and close to, those of the enemy, but below them.

The terrain of the Somme battlefield is given in full, in order that the operations of the 2nd Division in relation with those other divisions of the Fourth and Third British Armies may be more easily understood.

During Sir Douglas Haig's final preparations for the offensive the enemy twice attempted to interfere with his arrangements. On 21st May he attacked the Vimy Ridge, but gained only a very small portion of trench of no importance. On 2nd June he launched another attack near Hooge Cemetery, capturing several hundred yards of trench, which, however, were recaptured on the 13th.

Neither of these attacks interrupted the preparations for the Somme offensive, which had been definitely ordered for 1st July.

The subsequent operations which began on that date divided themselves into phases—but with the first phase, from 1st to 13th July, the 2nd Division was not actively concerned.

1ST JULY.

The offensive[1] was launched on the 1st July at 7.30 a.m. after an intense bombardment.[2] Mines were exploded under the enemy's trenches and smoke was discharged at many places along the front, under cover of which a great infantry attack by five Army Corps was launched. Between the Ancre and the Somme the attack was successful, but north of the former river no progress was made.

14TH JULY.

The second phase of the battle began on the evening of 14th July and lasted for three days, at the end of which the enemy's second main system of defence had been captured on a front of over three miles : he had been forced back more than a mile, and the Fourth Army (Sir H. Rawlinson) held possession of the southern

17TH JULY.

crest of the main ridge on a front of 6,000 yards. On 17th July the line of the Fourth Army ran from Maltz Horn Farm (where

[1] The British forces engaged were : Fourth Army (Sir H. Rawlinson), XIIIth Corps (30th and 18th Divisions), XVth Corps (7th and 21st Divisions), IIIrd Corps (34th and 8th Divisions), Xth Corps (32nd and 36th Divisions), VIIIth Corps (29th and 4th Divisions). Third Army (General Sir E. H. H. Allenby), VIIth Corps (56th and 46th Divisions).

[2] In the preliminary bombardment (from 24th June until the morning of 1st July) 1,178,772 rounds were fired. The 18-pounders fired 591,939 rounds : " Mother " (the 9.2-inch) 24,011, and " Granny " (the 15-inch) 776. The objectives were : wire-cutting, destruction of trench systems and fortified localities, neutralization and destruction of hostile guns, and bombardment of communications, billets, and back areas. On the opening day of the battle (1st July) 376,256 rounds were fired (18-pounders 182,681, " Mother " 9,661, and " Granny " 70 rounds). Fifteen divisions attacked, and in the Fourth Army the casualties totalled 42,000. The bombardment had obviously not accomplished all that was required of it.

the right of the Fourth Army joined up with the left of the French Army) northwards along the eastern edge of Trônes Wood to Longueval; thence westwards past Bazentin-le-Grand to the northern corner of Bazentin-le-Petit and Bazentin-le-Petit Wood ; thence westwards again past the southern face of Pozières to the north of Ovillers.

Since 1st July the total captures were 8 heavy howitzers, 4 heavy guns, 42 light and field guns and field howitzers, 30 trench mortars, and 52 machine guns. The enemy had also suffered enormous casualties, and had lost over 10,000 prisoners.

The next phase of the battle opened on 18th July : " There was strong evidence that the enemy forces engaged on the battle front had been severely shaken by the repeated successes gained by ourselves and our Allies ; but the great strength and depth of his defences had secured him sufficient time to bring up fresh troops, and he had still many powerful fortifications, both trenches, villages, and woods, to which he could cling on our front and our flanks."

This was indeed so, for by 18th July the enemy had more than doubled his forces. He had just over 60 battalions in this part of the line on the 1st July—but when the second phase of the struggle opened he had between 130 and 140 battalions. The German Second Army had been reinforced from the First German Army, and it was obvious that with these new forces a strong counter-attack would be made.

" During the afternoon of 18th July the enemy developed his expected counter-attack against Delville Wood, after heavy pre-liminary shelling. By sheer weight of numbers and at very heavy cost he forced his way through the northern and south-eastern portions of the wood and into the northern half of Longueval, which our troops (3rd Division) had cleared only that morning. In the south-east corner of the wood he was held up by a gallant defence (9th and 18th Divisions), and farther south three attacks on our position in Wartelot Farm, held by the 35th Division, failed." [1] It is not possible to follow in detail the gradual widening of the front of the Fourth Army, nor the attacks of the gallant Divisions who slowly but surely pressed the enemy back. But the Official Dispatches provide an excellent survey of the operations from the time of the enemy's counter-attack on 18th July to 27th July, on which date the 2nd Division attacked and fought the Battle of Delville Wood which ended in the capture of that place : " The enemy's attack on Delville Wood marked the commencement of

[1] Official Dispatches.

18TH JULY.

the long closely contested struggle which was not finally decided in our favour till the fall of Guillemont on 23rd September, a decision which was confirmed by the capture of Guinchy six days later. Considerable gains were indeed made during this period, but progress was slow and bought only by hard fighting. A footing was established in High Wood by the 33rd Division on 20th July, and our line linked up there with Longueval by the 7th and 5th Divisions. A subsequent advance by the Fourth Army on 23rd July on a wide front from Guillemont to Pozières found the enemy in great strength[1] all along the line, with machine guns and forward troops in shell-holes and newly constructed trenches, well in front of his main defences. Although ground was won, the strength of the resistance experienced showed that the hostile troops had recovered from their previous confusion sufficiently to necessitate long and careful preparation before further successes on any great scale could be secured."[2]

" An assault delivered simultaneously on this date by General Gough's army (1st Australian and 48th Divisions) against Pozières gained considerable results, and by the morning of 25th July, the whole of that village was carried, including the cemetery, and important progress was made along the enemy's trenches to the north-east. That evening (24th July), after heavy artillery preparation, the enemy launched two more powerful counter-attacks —the one directed against our new position in and around High Wood (51st Division) and the other delivered from the north-west of Delville Wood. Both attacks were completely broken up with very heavy losses to the enemy.

" On 27th July the remainder of Delville Wood was recovered by the 2nd Division (Major-General W. G. Walker, V.C.)."

THE BATTLE OF DELVILLE WOOD.[3]

When the enemy's counter-attack of 18th July was made the 2nd Division was still " resting and training " in the Dieval (5th and 99th Infantry Brigades)–Gouy Servins–Estrée–Cauchie–Maisnil-Bouche–L'Abbée (6th Infantry Brigade) areas. Divisional Headquarters were in a château just east of Dieval.

About midday on the 18th, Divisional Headquarters received orders from IInd Corps Headquarters instructing the Division to

---

1 The whole of the Second German Army had been brought up.
2 Official Dispatches.
3 The official date of the Battle of Delville Wood is 15th July–3rd Sept. 1916.

entrain and proceed to join the IXth Corps (Fourth Army) at Talnas. On the 20th the Division entrained, and three days later was located in the reserve area of the Fourth Army—Happy Valley (5th Infantry Brigade), Sand Pit Valley (99th Infantry Brigade), and Bois des Tailles (6th Infantry Brigade), having reported its arrival to the XIIIth Corps (Lieut.-General W. N. Congreve, V.C.).

At 11 on the night of 24th July, 2nd Divisional Order No. 116 was issued : " 99th Infantry Brigade and Bearer Division 5th Field Ambulance will relieve units of the 3rd Division in the left sub-section of 3rd Divisional area on the night 24th–25th July. 99th Infantry Brigade and Bearer Division 5th Field Ambulance will move from its present area *via* Caftet Wood and Montauban. On arrival at Montauban, 99th Infantry Brigade and 5th Field Ambulance will come under the orders of the General Officer Commanding 3rd Division. 5th Infantry Brigade will relieve units of the 3rd Division in the right sub-section of the 3rd Divisional area on the night 25th–26th July. 6th Infantry Brigade will move to-morrow, the 25th inst., into the Reserve Brigade area of the 3rd Division and will come under orders of the General Officer Commanding 3rd Division. Montauban Village will be held by a permanent garrison of two companies under command of Major C. C. Harman, 22nd Royal Fusiliers, who will remain in command during the tour of the Division in the line. The two companies may be changed at the discretion of the General Officers Commanding Infantry Brigades in order to provide necessary reliefs, but continuity of work must be ensured. The garrison is on no account to be used for counter-attacks. The 2nd Division Artillery will relieve 9th Division Artillery in the line on nights 26th–27th and 27th–28th. Medium trench mortars will be moved into the line as soon as possible."

The Field Companies R.E. and Field Ambulances of the 2nd Division were ordered to relieve similar units of the 3rd Division, and the 10th D.C.L.I. (Pioneers), the Pioneers of the 3rd Division.

On completion of these reliefs the General Officer Commanding 2nd Division would assume command of the left section XIIIth Corps area.

The contents of this order were communicated verbally some hours previously to the General Officer Commanding 99th Infantry Brigade, he being ordered to move immediately ; and by 6.30 p.m. the brigade had marched off to relieve the left sub-section of the 3rd Divisional line—the Delville Wood sector.

The 1st King's Royal Rifles relieved the 4th Royal Fusiliers, taking over the northern trenches in Delville Wood, with one company in reserve in Montauban Alley. The 1st Royal Berks relieved the 1st Royal Scots Fusiliers in Longueval Village and the western portion of Delville Wood ; the 22nd and the 23rd Royal Fusiliers were in Bernafay Wood and Montauban Alley.

25TH JULY. The reliefs were completed early on the morning of 25th July. Brigade orders were then issued, which stated that " the immediate digging of very deep and narrow trenches is of the utmost importance." In this work the brigade was assisted by the Divisional Engineers. No casualties were incurred during the relief.

The 5th Infantry Brigade on the night 24th–25th July was still in the Happy Valley, and the 6th Infantry Brigade at Bois des Tailles.

During the 25th, the 99th Infantry Brigade was heavily shelled. Two companies of the 22nd Royal Fusiliers which had been moved up to relieve the 18th Highland Light Infantry in some trenches north of the Quarry, had 19 other ranks killed and wounded. The 1st King's Royal Rifles also suffered casualties.

At 7.50 p.m. 2nd Division Advanced Headquarters opened in a small copse known as " Copse B " just west of Mericourt, and the General Officer Commanding assumed command of the left section of the XIIIth Corps line.

The 5th Infantry Brigade by 9 p.m. had relieved 8th Infantry Brigade (5th Division) in Wartelot Farm section : " The battalions relieved were the 2nd Royal Scots D.C.L.I. and East Yorkshire. They were all very depleted." The 2nd Highland Light Infantry and the 24th Royal Fusiliers were in the front line ; the 17th Royal Fusiliers in Trônes Wood (one company) and Longueval Alley (three companies) ; the 2nd Oxford and Bucks were in Brigade Reserve south of Montauban.

At 10.30 p.m. XIIIth Corps Operation Order No. 33 was received at 2nd Division Headquarters : " The XVth Corps has been ordered to secure the eastern corner of High Wood as early as possible. The capture of the strong point in the orchard north of Longueval and the village of Longueval and Delville Wood will form one combined operation to be carried out by the XIIIth and XVth Corps on the morning of 27th July. The whole of the northern end of Longueval Village will be the objective of the XVth Corps : Delville Wood will be the objective of the XIIIth Corps. The 2nd Division (XIIIth Corps) will attack Delville Wood on the morning of the 27th inst. in conjunction with the 5th Division (XVth Corps)

XV CORPS ARTILLERY

XIII C... ARTIL...

FINAL BARRAGE

Final Barrage 8.40 a.m.

Second Lift at 8.10 a.m. to this line.

First Lift at 7.10 a.m. to this line.

Barrage began 6.10 a.m. on this line.

Delville W...

Longueval

Windmill

Clarge...

Sloane...

5TH DIVISION AREA OF ATTACK

XV CORPS

Dover St.

Down St.

Cheapside

Ch...

Pall Mall

Longueval Alley

Trones Wood

6TH INF. BDE. in Carnoy

... Britis...
o Stron...
---- Tren...
■■■■ 99th...
☐ 6th In...
■■■■ 5th In...

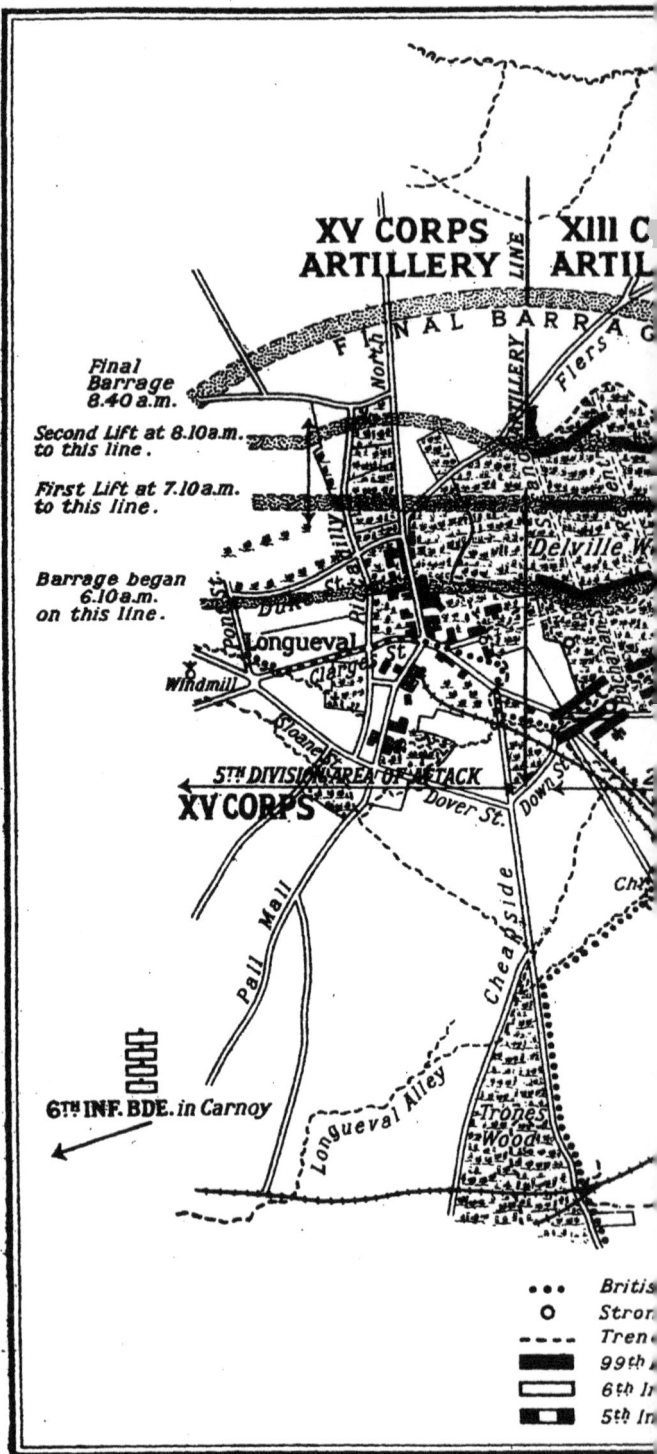

THE BATTLE
Attack on 27th

8.40 a.m.

Final Line reached by
Second Wave - 8.50 a.m.

Line reached by Second Wave
(Fusiliers - 8.30 a.m., Rifles - 8.8 a.m.)

Line reached by First Wave
(Fusiliers - 7.19 a.m., Rifles - 7.15 a.m.)

First Wave: B. D. Coys. 23rd R.Fus., D. B. Coys. 1st K.R.R.
Second Wave: A. C. Coys. 23rd R.Fus., C. A. Coys. 1st K.R.R.
1st R.Berks: A. B. C. D. Coys. in support
with sections - 99th M.G.C. & 99th T.M.B.
& 1st E.A. Field Coy. R.E.

7.10 a.m.
Princes St
6.10 a.m.

Rotten
Row

Haymarket

85 Men
1st K.R.R. with
L.Gs. & M.Guns

uth Street
Platoons Rifles
2nd H.L.I. (5th Bde.) with
ЄА OF ATTACK   L.Gs. & M.Guns

Ginchy

Ginchy
Farm

RPS

ot Farm

Holborn

STATION

Quarry

mont

on Morning (6.a.m.) July 27th 1916.

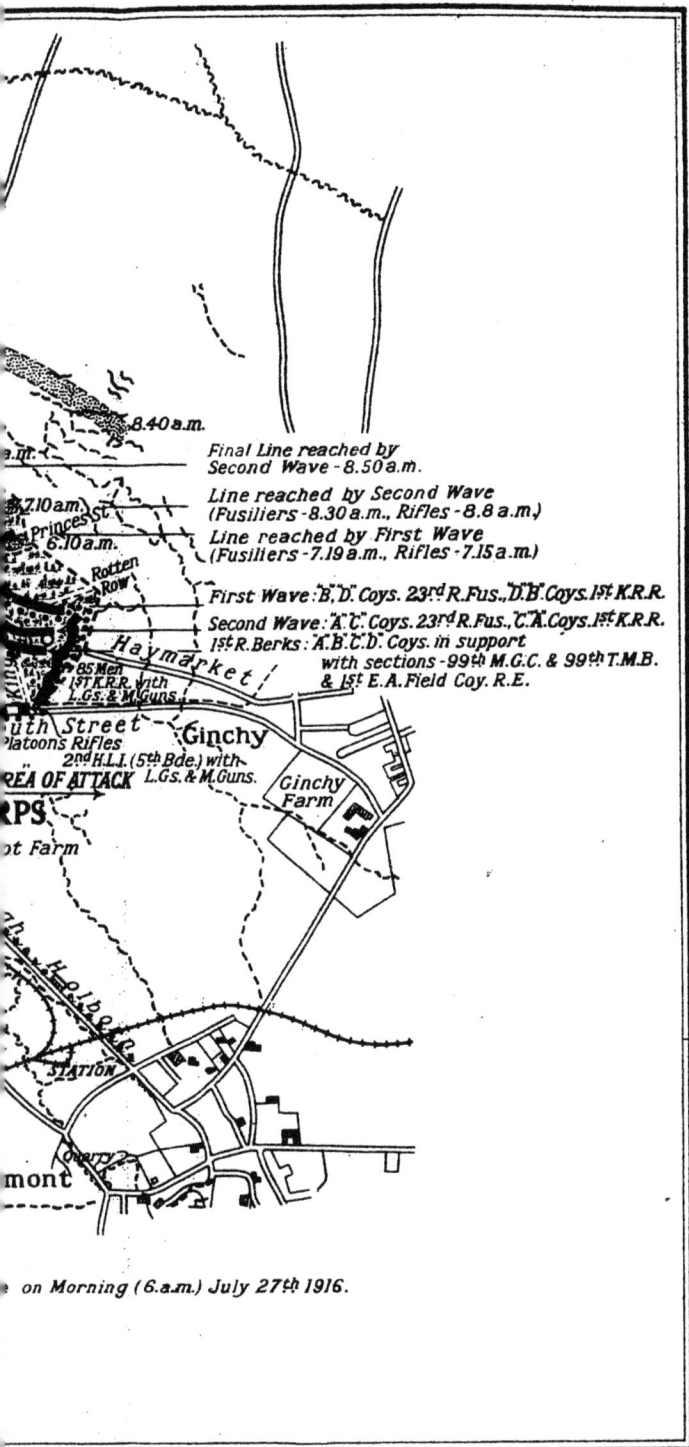

THE MAPPA CO., LTD., LONDON.

LVILLE WOOD.
by 2nd Division.

(Facing p. 272.)

which is attacking Longueval and the orchards north of it, including that north of the Flers road "—*i.e.*, opposite the north-west corner of Delville Wood.

The objectives of the 2nd Division were : To secure the whole of the wood as far north as a line drawn approximately from the eastern end of Princes Street to the south-east corner of the Flers road orchard, in touch with the 5th Division which had been ordered to secure the orchard : to consolidate the ground gained, and to construct an intermediate line between the line held before the attack and the objective.

A heavy artillery bombardment was to precede the attack : " The whole of the available artillery of the XIIIth and XVth Corps will be employed for this operation."[1]

The guns were to carry out a one-hour's bombardment of the enemy's line on the morning of the 26th, and later instructions to the 2nd Division ordered the 99th Infantry Brigade, then holding the trenches in Delville Wood, to push forward patrols immediately the bombardment lifted at 7.10 a.m. on the 26th, " to explore the wood and capture prisoners, and endeavour to ascertain the position of any machine guns and strong points or trenches in the wood which may be manned by the enemy."

At 2 o'clock on the morning of the 26th, the enemy opened weak rifle fire upon the King's Royal Rifles and threw a few bombs, but otherwise the situation was normal. The guns opened at 6.10 a.m., and until 7.10 poured a stream of shell upon the enemy's position. At the latter hour (the guns having ceased fire) the Rifles sent out six patrol parties to explore the wood and observe the enemy's trenches, each party consisting of 1 N.C.O. and 10 Riflemen. Good information was obtained by these patrols, but many casualties were incurred. The enemy fired large numbers of " tear shells " and heavy " high-explosive " almost continuously the whole day. The casualties of the 99th Infantry Brigade were 3 officers wounded, 8 other ranks killed and 53 wounded.

The assaulting waves, supports, consolidating parties, etc., of the 99th Infantry Brigade who were to attack Delville Wood got into position during the night of 26th–27th, and in the early hours of the 27th,[2] when dawn broke, were assembled as follows : The 1st King's Royal Rifles (right) held the front-line trenches

26TH JULY.

27TH JULY.
MAP.

[1] This involved the use of 18-pounders, 4.5-inch, 6-inch, 8-inch, and 9.2-inch howitzers and the big 12-inch and 15-inch howitzers.
[2] The 2nd Divisional Artillery arrived during the 26th in the Divisional area and began the relief of the artillery of the 9th Division.

(2,242) 18

from Campbell Street (inclusive), King Street, nearly to Rotten Row, and along South Street in an easterly direction ; the 23rd Royal Fusiliers (left) held the front-line trenches from Campbell Street (exclusive) across Buchanan Street to the south-west corner of the wood, and along South Street westwards. The south-east end of the wood (*i.e.*, from Angle Trench eastwards along South Street) was held by a permanent garrison of 2nd Highland Light Infantry ; two half-companies of the 1st King's Royal Rifles, with two machine guns and Lewis guns, held the south-east face of the wood from South Street nearly to Rotten Row, thence in three islands for about 150 yards westwards.

The 1st Royal Berks, with all four companies extended from west to east, were in support, behind the second wave. The battalion was detailed to do " mopping-up " work, clearing out hidden machine guns passed over by assault, clearing out trenches, bombing and clearing dug-outs, etc., and was to be responsible for the consolidation of the eastern exits of Delville Wood from Rotten Row to Princes Street ; also for consolidating on a line approximately conforming to the line of the first barrage and clearing communications through the wood. No. 1 Section of the 99th M.G.C., supported by B and C Companies, No. 2 Section D and No. 3 Section A Companies of the Berkshires ; No. 4 Section was in reserve.

One section of the 1st East Anglian Field Company R.E. was allotted to each flank company of the Berks for consolidation purposes, and one section remained at Brigade Headquarters.

The attack was to be delivered in two waves :

First wave (from west to east) : B and D Companies 23rd Royal Fusiliers, C and A Companies 1st King's Royal Rifles.

Second wave (from west to east) : A and C Companies 23rd Royal Fusiliers, B and D Companies 1st King's Royal Rifles.

In support (from west to east) : A, B, C, and D Companies 1st Royal Berks—*i.e.*, one company to each company of the second wave.

With D Company of the 1st Royal Berks—1 Section 1st East Anglian R.E., No. 2 Section 99th M.G.C.

With A Company of the 1st Royal Berks—1 Section 1st East Anglian R.E., No. 3 Section 99th M.G.C., and 1 Section T.M.B.

With B and C Companies of the 1st Royal Berks—No. 1 Section 99th M.G.C.

The 99th Infantry Brigade Reserve was formed of two companies of 22nd Royal Fusiliers in Bernafay Wood, the remaining two companies having been detailed as carrying parties. One section (4 guns) of the 99th T.M.B. was also held in reserve.

The assaulting waves, supports, and consolidating parties were in position when the first bombardment opened at 6.10 a.m. For an hour the "Heavies" poured shell on to the enemy's trenches, almost obliterating the roads through the wood. Punctually at 7.10 a.m. the barrage lifted to the second line, and the first wave of the assaulting troops, who had been lying out in front of their trenches, rose to their feet and rushed towards the enemy's trenches in Princes Street.[1] Barely fifty yards were covered before the enemy appeared, many without arms or accoutrements, and these surrendered ; they were utterly cowed by the bombardment. Others resisted, and were either shot down or bayoneted. Without pausing the wave passed on, and Princes Street was taken with but small loss to the attackers. The fearful havoc created by the first barrage [2] was everywhere evident. The trenches were blown to crumbled masses of earth, and dead and wounded Germans were lying in all directions. Three machine guns had been smashed, and much hostile equipment was scattered about. More prisoners were taken as the assaulting troops jumped into the enemy's trenches. Consolidation began immediately the line was taken, the troops working with feverish haste, for the enemy's shells were already beginning to fall thick and fast.

As the first wave rushed forward the second wave (which had been formed up behind the first), moved into the trenches vacated, and there awaited the second lifting of the barrage.

At 8.10 a.m. the barrage lifted to the third line, and the second wave dashed forward through the first wave, and reached the second line of the objective with but little opposition. Consolidation here was also begun immediately, the enemy offering but slight resistance, though a machine gun firing on the left from the northern exits of Longueval Village enfiladed the waves and caused many casualties. These guns were, however, soon silenced.

Two companies of the 1st Royal Berks had advanced behind the second wave. On reaching the line occupied by the first wave, one company began the consolidation of the eastern exits of the wood from the strong point south of Rotten Row up to Princes Street ; the other company assisted in the further consolidation of Princes Street. But the line dug being some 150 yards from the edge was

---

[1] In this attack the 99th Infantry Brigade was opposed north, north-east, east, and south-east by the 8th, 12th, and 52nd Jägers of the 5th Infantry Division of von Stein's Army Group.

[2] The total number of guns concentrated for these barrages was 369, exclusive of guns engaged in counter-battery work.

too far into the wood, which later gave the enemy an opportunity of effecting a temporary lodgment.

Hostile rifle fire on the second wave being very slight, the "wave" went forward at 8.30 a.m., when the barrage lifted to the final line.

Thus the whole of Delville Wood was captured.

Meanwhile the 23rd Royal Fusiliers had experienced considerable opposition from the direction of Longueval Village and the orchards north of it.

At 8.10 a.m. the second wave passed through the first wave, then consolidating on the left flank of the Rifles along the western end of Princes Street. But progress was hampered by enfilade fire from Longueval Village and from a redoubt in front of the Fusiliers. An attempt to envelop this redoubt was made, but was at first without success. Captain Hayward's company then charged the redoubt, but were unable to obtain a footing in it, their gallant leader being killed at the head of his men. The company was then reinforced by another company with Lewis guns. The guns and bombers worked round the flanks of the redoubt, and under cover of gunfire and a shower of bombs rushed the post and finally captured it. In it were three machine guns, one of which was destroyed, another carried off, and one was turned on to the enemy garrison as it fled from the redoubt. Many of the garrison had been killed and wounded, including two officers. Two officers and about 50 men were captured, and were passed to the rear by the Norfolks, through Longueval Village.

The redoubt was then consolidated, and after re-forming, the Fusiliers continued their advance and finally swept the enemy out of the northern end of the wood. Unfortunately, after describing the advance of the first and second waves to the final objective, the Diary of the 23rd Royal Fusiliers does not relate what happened during the day whilst the Rifles were being heavily attacked. It is probable, however, that sandwiched between the right of the 5th Division and the left of the Rifles, the Fusiliers were attacked only in front (from the north), and were able to repulse the enemy without great difficulty. The battalion suffered heavy casualties, most of these being due to the intense bombardment to which the enemy subjected Delville Wood after he had been ejected from it.

The Fusiliers were given valuable assistance by the left flank company of the 1st Royal Berks (under Captain Weston), who constructed a series of strong points facing west, with the result that when the Fusiliers reached their objective their left flank was well protected.

At 10.30 a.m. two companies of the 23rd Fusiliers held the northern exits of Delville Wood, two more companies were behind them on a line between the front line and Princes Street, with one company of Berkshires guarding the left flank in strong points, and another company of Berks improving the defences along Princes Street facing north and west.

Away on the left of the 99th Infantry Brigade the 15th Infantry Brigade (5th Division) had at first made good progress, but was held up in the northern half of Longueval about the crossroads in Duke Street ; the eastern flank of the attack (Norfolk Regiment) was, however, in touch with the left of the 2nd Division.

From 9 a.m. onwards, the wood was swept by heavy shell-fire, which, coming from the east and north-east, caught the troops of the 99th Infantry Brigade in enfilade. Half an hour later the enemy was seen in large numbers massing north of the wood, evidently for a counter-attack. Parties of his troops began to creep up towards the eastern edge of the wood, and at 10 a.m. a heavy bombing attack was made which for a while gave the enemy a lodgment about seventy yards south of Princes Street.

The King's Royal Rifles were hard pressed. " The Germans gained seventy yards but were driven back forty yards, chiefly owing to the gallantry of Sergeant Woodward, who at the head of his bombers drove the enemy back with very heavy loss. The enemy's bomb attack decimated B Company, and D Company also suffered heavily. Captain Howell was wounded about 9 a.m. but continued to carry on his duties, acting with great gallantry, and it was largely owing to this officer's efforts that the Germans were driven off. A and C Companies were also heavily attacked from north and north-east. Fierce fighting took place at fifteen yards' range with bombs and rifle-fire, and though the enemy lost heavily, both company commanders of the Rifles were wounded. At 11.20 a.m. Colonel Denison of the Rifles reported : " Fighting went on incessantly, chiefly sniping from shell-holes, the Germans trying all the time to creep in on my flank between the various lines." Shortly after 1 o'clock " more bombs arrived, and some bombers from the 23rd Royal Fusiliers, Lance-Corporal Bell of the 23rd Royal Fusiliers behaving with great gallantry, and greatly assisting by his fine throwing in driving back the Germans. The German method of bomb attacks was to bomb up the new trench with snipers on each flank."

It must have been during this attack (though no time is given) that No. 2815, Sergeant Albert Gill, of the 1st King's Royal Rifles, won his Victoria Cross.   " The enemy made a very strong counter-attack on the right flank of the battalion, and rushed the bombing post after killing all the company bombers.   Sergeant Gill at once rallied the remnants of his platoons, none of whom were skilled bombers, and reorganized his defences, a most difficult and danger-ous task, the trench being very shallow and much damaged.   Soon afterwards the enemy nearly surrounded his men by creeping up through the thick undergrowth, and commenced sniping at about twenty yards' range.   Although it was almost certain death, Ser-geant Gill stood boldly up in order to direct the fire of his men. He was killed almost at once, but not before he had shown his men where the enemy were, and thus enabled them to hold up their advance.   By his supreme devotion to duty and self-sacrifice he saved a very dangerous situation." [1]

The 1st Royal Berkshires also sent up a party of twelve bombers to assist the Rifles, and these, with the party from the 23rd Royal Fusiliers, were eventually successful in helping the sorely pressed Rifles to defeat the enemy's determined efforts.

During this attack a pigeon message was sent off to Brigade Headquarters, the bird carrying a request to " Send up bombs : very urgently needed."

From 2.45 p.m. until darkness fell the enemy very heavily bombarded the old British front line—*i.e.*, South Street, Longueval Village and Alley, traversing the road between Angle and South Street with machine-gun fire from the direction of his trenches north-east of Wartelot Farm.   The dressing station in Longueval was included in this bombardment, which made it temporarily impossible for reinforcements to get into the wood to support the hard-pressed troops of the 99th Infantry Brigade.

During the afternoon two companies of the 22nd Royal Fusiliers arrived and reported to the Officer Commanding 1st King's Royal Rifles, who used some of them to assist in carrying bombs and am-munition, whilst others were put in to defend the right flank of the Rifles along the eastern face of the wood.

About 5.15 p.m. two companies (A and B) of the 17th Royal Fusiliers (5th Infantry Brigade) and two of the 17th Middlesex (6th Infantry Brigade) arrived.   They had suffered heavily on the way up.   Two platoons of 17th Royal Fusiliers, with two Lewis guns, were sent up to reinforce the posts, and another company relieved C Company of the Rifles.

[1] *London Gazette*, 26th October 1916.

The 23rd Fusiliers were relieved at 7 p.m. by the 2nd South Staffords, and moved back to the position occupied before the attack.

The 99th Infantry Brigade M.G.C. had fought gallantly. No. 1 Section went into action with the King's Royal Rifles. One gun did not come into action, but the three remaining guns, close together, were in the centre of the line held by the Rifles. These guns fired approximately 17,500 rounds of S.A.A. No. 3 Section was with the 23rd Royal Fusiliers: " All guns were under very heavy enfilading and frontal shell-fire. Communication was impossible to maintain owing to the nature of the shell-fire."[1] The M.G.C. suffered heavy casualties, losing its Commanding Officer, Captain C. B. Grant, and Second-Lieut. D. Crawford, killed, and 6 officers wounded, besides 82 other ranks out of 138. Six guns were put out of action.

From 9.20 p.m. onwards the relief of the three right companies of the 1st King's Royal Rifles by three companies of the 17th Middlesex began, and at 10.30 p.m. two platoons of the latter reinforced the left company of the Rifles, which was finally relieved by the 17th Middlesex at 6.30 a.m. on the morning of the 28th.

The situation at 11 p.m. on the night of the 27th was as follows :

The 2nd South Staffords had relieved the 23rd Royal Fusiliers on the left flank, and were disposed: A Company in the front line near the northern edge of the wood ; B Company in support, C Company forming a defensive flank facing west, and D Company in Battalion Reserve.

One company, 1st King's Royal Rifles, and three and a half companies 17th Middlesex held the line from Regent Street eastwards to south of Princes Street.

One company 1st Royal Berks, thence to Rotten Row.

Three companies 1st King's Royal Rifles, thence to South Street, supported by one company 22nd Royal Fusiliers and one company 17th Royal Fusiliers (5th Infantry Brigade).

Two companies 1st Royal Berks, on Princes Street line.

One company 1st Royal Berks, guarding left flank.

Remainder of force in reserve in the " Old British " line and South Street.

The successful operations by the 2nd Division on 27th July drew congratulations from the Army and Corps commanders. The Division had, however, suffered very heavy casualties, many

[1] Diary, 99th Brigade M.G.C.

of which were caused by the enemy's bombardment after the troops had reached their objective.

The artillery barrage was very effective.

The 1st East Anglian Field Company R.E. did valuable work during the day in the construction of machine-gun emplacements, the deepening and consolidation of the line, and in erecting strong points.   But the work was interrupted, as it was necessary at critical moments (of which there were many throughout the day) to man the front-line trenches.   Indeed, No. 1 Section held a portion of the line during the night 27th–28th.

The 5th Infantry Brigade was shelled heavily throughout the whole day, 5 other ranks were killed, and 5 officers and 51 other ranks were wounded.   The brigade rendered timely help to the 99th Infantry Brigade by the loan of two companies of 17th Royal Fusiliers.

The total casualties suffered by the 2nd Division in the Battle of Delville Wood were 59 officers and 1,339 other ranks killed, wounded, and missing, of which 45 officers and 1,119 other ranks belonged to the 99th Infantry Brigade.[1]

Three officers and 161 other ranks were captured from the enemy.

So terrible had been the bombardment (British and German) of Delville Wood that an air report at 5.30 p.m. on the 27th stated that the wood appeared to be almost entirely destroyed.

The effectiveness of the concentrated fire of 369 guns on the wood was well described in a report by the General Officer Commanding 99th Infantry Brigade (Brigadier-General R. O. Kellett) : "Our artillery was most effective. Hundreds of freshly killed Boches were met with in the line of our advance, and at least three Boche machine guns were destroyed, thus saving hundreds of our lives. Our shells got right into the Boche as they streamed north up the hill after we had cleared them out of the wood, and also during their subsequent massing for and delivering of counter-attacks, doing great execution.   Their shooting inspired our men with complete confidence, and though we apparently suffered a good many casualties from short shells (principally Heavies), the shooting of our guns was admirable and provided a curtain of fire close behind which our men moved with little loss, encountering men (the Boche) out of whom the fight had been knocked by our shell-fire.   So great was the feeling of security by reason of our curtain fire, that our men were clamouring to move before the hour appointed, so that they might get right into the rear fringe of our artillery before it

[1] See Appendix XIV.

lifted and so meet the enemy while still paralyzed by its intensity."

An excellent story concerning the effectiveness of the artillery barrage is told in a private diary kept by an artillery officer belonging to the 2nd Divisional Artillery: "Two Tommies (were) bringing home a Boche prisoner when they ran into a Boche barrage. Both the Tommies jumped at once into a trench, while the Boche sat on the top of the parapet smoking his cigar and smiling. One of the Tommies shouted out to him, 'Come down, you fool; you'll only get killed.' 'Why?' he asked. 'Well, can't you see your friends are putting up a barrage?' they said. 'Barrage?' said the Boche. 'Barrage! do you call this a barrage? If you want to know what a barrage is like, go over to the other side'; and he pointed to his lines."

The 22nd Royal Fusiliers were in support in Longueval Alley, and the 13th Essex were in reserve. During the evening two companies of the Essex relieved the 22nd Royal Fusiliers in the support area—one company to be at the disposal of the 2nd South Staffords, the other at the disposal of the 17th Middlesex.

Early on the morning of the 28th the 1st King's Royal Rifles *28TH JULY.* were withdrawn to Montauban Alley, their line having been taken over by the 17th Middlesex. The 23rd Fusiliers were relieved at 6 a.m. by the South Staffords and withdrew to Bernafay Wood. Delville Wood was now held only by the Staffords and Middlesex.

The 6th Infantry Brigade as a whole relieved the 99th Infantry Brigade, the latter marching back to the reserve trenches along the Montauban–Carnoy road.

Delville Wood, Montauban, and Bernafay Wood were all very heavily shelled throughout the 28th. The 5th Infantry Brigade alone had 8 officers wounded, 43 other ranks killed and 210 wounded and missing.

The 2nd Divisional Artillery south of Montauban also came in for a gruelling: "The Boche started an 8-inch and 5.9-inch barrage just over the battery. . . . They went on a hell of a long time with their shooting and got thirty into the 71st position, knocking out two of their guns, and setting fire to a lot of ammunition. Altogether most unpleasant, especially when two men and two horses of D/36 Battery were literally blown into small pieces and another driver wounded, whereupon my little R.A.M.C. orderly dashed out and helped very gallantly under a heavy fire. . . . They stopped at lunch, and only put a few shrapnel over during the afternoon. It's a merciful thing the Boche does not realize that a shrapnel barrage is twice as bad as any H.E. barrage for killing results ; the H.E. is much more terrifying." [1]

On the night of the 28th a fierce counter-attack, accompanied by a very heavy barrage on the support trenches and southern exits of Delville Wood, was made by the enemy—principally against the South Staffords.[2] The battalion had been disposed as follows : A Company in the front line near the north edge of the wood, B Company in support; C Company had formed a defensive flank facing west, and D Company was in battalion reserve.

At 9 p.m. the bombardment started, and soon portions of the trenches held by B Company were practically obliterated, all the officers were killed, and most of the men buried beneath the debris. In spite of this, however, the survivors stuck to their position. Hostile bombing parties approached the front line, but were easily beaten back. Part of the line held by C Company was also heavily shelled. Most of the fire came from an enemy Heavy battery in the direction of Ginchy. An " S.O.S." was sent up, and soon after the Divisional Artillery opened fire the enemy's barrage died away. Under great difficulties the South Staffords had held on to their line, and their magnificent tenacity was later recognized by congratulations from the Army, Corps, and Divisional Commanders, and from the General Officer Commanding (Brigadier-General Daly) the brigade.

In this affair the South Staffords lost 6 officers killed (Captain W. E. Wansbrough, Captain W. Lake, Lieut. I. L. Malpass, Second-Lieut. S. B. Thornton, Second-Lieut. E. L. Holdcroft, and Captain C. Dutton (died of wounds) ; 42 other ranks killed, 196 wounded, 21 of whom were suffering from shell-shock, and 46 missing—total, 6 officers, 305 other ranks.

The 17th Middlesex were also attacked, but held the line intact and beat the enemy off without difficulty.

The capture of Delville Wood and the defeat of the inevitable counter-attacks during the 27th and 28th was no small achievement ; for the wood formed a most advanced salient in the British line, and while Sir Douglas Haig, General Foch, and General Fayelle [3] were planning a further advance eastwards, had to be held at all costs. This the 2nd Division did. The wood was exposed to

[1] Diary of the late Major Victor Walrond, R.F.A.

[2] The South Staffords were again holding the most easterly point in the battlefield, just as at Ypres in 1914 the battalion held the point in the salient farthest east against the Boche.

[3] Commanding the group of French armies in the north, and the Sixth French Army on the right flank of the British Army, respectively.

hostile shell-fire from three directions, and yet the gallant men who held it did not give way, or lose an inch of ground won on the first day of the battle.

From 1st July to and including 28th July, just one month of warfare, the British army on the Somme had suffered casualties to the extent of 4,185 officers and 110,025 other ranks.

And the Battle of the Somme lasted until 18th November !

. THE BATTLE OF GUILLEMONT.

On 27th July Sir Douglas Haig had interviewed Generals Foch and Fayelle, and had discussed with them the situation north and south of the Somme. Sir Douglas Haig urged that the immediate possession of Guillemont was essential, as he could not advance his line until he had taken that place from the enemy. General Foch was anxious to attack south of the Somme from Lihons to Barleux, but could not do so without a three days' preliminary bombardment.

The bombardment would begin as soon as the weather cleared.

It was then suggested that the British should attack Guillemont, and not await the French offensive on Maurepas. Finally, a plan of action was adopted whereby the XIIIth British Corps (Fourth Army) was to attack Guillemont and Falfemont Farm on the 30th, to synchronize with an attack by the XXth French Corps on and from Maurepas to the Somme. Offensive operations along the whole front of the Fourth Army, where possible, were also to be undertaken.

At noon on the 29th, " 2nd Division Operation Order No ·119 " was issued :

" The XIIIth Corps has been ordered to capture the enemy's defences between Falfemont Farm and Guillemont (both inclusive) in conjunction with attacks by the French to the south.

" The attack by the XIIIth Corps will be carried out by the 30th Division and by the 5th Infantry Brigade of the 2nd Division."

Objectives : 30th Division—the enemy's defences about Guillemont (inclusive) and the establishment of touch with the 2nd Division on the left. 5th Infantry Brigade—the capture of the enemy's defences between Wartelot Farm and Guillemont.

Right attack—30th Division. Left attack—2nd Division.

The hour of attack was notified later—4.45 a.m.

The 2nd Oxford and Bucks and the 24th Royal Fusiliers were detailed for the attack by the 5th Infantry Brigade, and at 4.20

on the morning of the 30th were lying out in front of their trenches, whilst the artillery pounded the enemy's defences. The artillery barrages were heavy, but the morning was misty and observation almost impossible.

At 4.45 a.m. A and B Companies from the direction of Wartelot Farm rushed forward towards the station at Guillemont, but were held up almost immediately by hostile machine-gun fire and bombs from bombing posts just south-east of the farm. The Stokes mortars which had been detailed to deal with these posts had apparently failed, and the ground was swept by machine-gun fire. A few men reached the hostile positions, but were bombed out of them and were forced to return to their own starting-points. The two remaining companies which had attacked towards Ginchy were also unable to make headway.

The 24th Royal Fusiliers on the left of the Oxford and Bucks, who had been ordered to attack the enemy's trenches some 600 yards east of Wartelot Farm, were likewise unsuccessful. Of C Company, which went forward to the attack, only 1 officer (wounded) and 11 other ranks returned to their original trenches, the remainder —three officers and 114 other ranks—being either killed, wounded, or missing. The heavy mist impeded the advance, and owing to the ground being " pock-marked " by huge shell-holes, direction was lost. None of the Fusiliers reached the hostile trenches, and only a few men under Captain C. S. Meares reached the enemy's wire; Captain Meares was killed on the wire whilst leading his men.

Of the 30th Division, the right brigade, attacking south of a line drawn east and west through Arrow Head Copse, failed to reach its objective and got mixed up with the left of the French attack ; one battalion of the left brigade (north of Arrow Head Copse), the 2nd Royal Scots Fusiliers, succeeded in reaching Guillemont and penetrated to the eastern exits of the village ; but it was entirely in the air, owing to the failure on both its flanks, and although the battalion gallantly held on for some time under very heavy fire, it was finally forced to retire, a portion of it eventually being surrounded just west of Guillemont.

As a result of the XIIIth Corps attack, 3 officers and 233 other ranks were taken from the enemy, and the line was advanced in front of Maltz Horn Farm to Arrow Head Copse.

The French were reported to have reached their left objective, but were held up outside Maurepas.

The first attack on Guillemont had failed.

The losses of the 2nd Oxford and Bucks were : Captain J. D.

Hardcastle and Second-Lieut. W. L. Chown killed, and 12 officers wounded ; the number of casualties amongst the rank and file was not recorded.

At 4 a.m. on the 31st the 2nd Highland Light Infantry relieved the Oxford and Bucks and Fusiliers, who were withdrawn to the reserve trenches south-west of Montauban. During the relief, Captain G. J. Edwards, 24th Royal Fusiliers, was killed.

In the meantime the position of the 6th Infantry Brigade in Delville Wood was still desperate. Intense hostile artillery fire was concentrated on the wood and in the vicinity night and day. Snipers and enemy bombers were very active, and minenwerfer and machine-gun fire was kept up almost unceasingly. The garrison of the wood had been thinned out to one battalion, and in conjunction with Lewis guns and machine guns managed to hold the wood. On the afternoon of the 30th a party of hostile snipers gained a footing in the wood, but 40 men of the Essex Regiment drove them out. Lieut.-Colonel P. R. Papillon (commanding officer) and 4 other officers were wounded, and a number of other ranks killed and wounded. A Company of the 1st King's, which had been ordered up to assist the Essex Regiment in clearing the wood, had a few casualties : Second-Lieut. G. G. Lauder being killed, besides 30 other ranks killed, wounded, and missing.

The 2nd Division had been in the line five days only (from the 26th to the 31st), and had already lost 108 officers and 2,957 other ranks. No part of the line, either the front-line trenches or the reserve areas, was free from the terrific shell fire and barrages put down by the enemy. From the first to the last day of July the losses of the Fourth Army were 4,428 officers and 116,270 other ranks—no wonder that the Somme battles of 1916 were veritable infernos ! Some idea of the terrible strain upon the troops may be gathered from a report on the fighting strength of the 2nd Division sent to Corps Headquarters on 1st August. The report stated that only one battalion of the Division was fit for " offensive operations " !

The enemy's casualties cannot have been less. Since the offensive began he had lost 11,041 men in prisoners alone, besides much material, and he was slowly but surely being pressed back.

On the evening of 1st August the 2nd Division was disposed as follows : Divisional Headquarters were at the Citadel, with Advanced Headquarters at Minden Post ; 5th Infantry Brigade in the front line holding the Wartelot Farm section ; 6th Infantry 1ST AUG.

Brigade holding Delville Wood ; 99th Infantry Brigade in reserve in the Montauban area.

The artillery of the Division held the following positions : Headquarters R.A.—Minden Post ; XXXIVth Brigade R.F.A.—Carnoy ; XXXVIth and XLIst Brigades R.F.A.—Montauban Area. The Divisional Ammunition Column was at Maulte.

Of the Divisional Troops : the 10th Duke of Cornwall's Light Infantry (Pioneers) had their Headquarters at Bois de Caftet, but the four companies were employed on the improvement of trenches in Bernafay, Delville and Trônes Woods, and in Carnoy.

The Divisional Train was at Grove Town and the Field Ambulances with their respective brigades.

During the night 1st to 2nd August the 99th Infantry Brigade relieved the 6th Infantry Brigade in Delville Wood ; the 22nd Royal Fusiliers relieved the 1st King's, who had three companies in the wood and the fourth just outside the southern face of the wood ; the 23rd Royal Fusiliers relieved the South Staffords, who had one company in Longueval Alley and three companies in the east end of Montauban Alley ; the 1st King's Royal Rifles relieved the 17th Middlesex, also in Montauban Alley in support ; the 13th Essex (6th Infantry Brigade) and the 1st Royal Berks (99th Infantry Brigade) remained in their trenches—Back Trench and Bund Support Trench south of Montauban—the latter battalion being in reserve to the 99th Infantry Brigade.

It will be seen that Delville Wood was at this time held only by three companies, but the defences included twelve Lewis guns and eight Vickers guns with their teams.

Lieut.-Colonel Barnet Barker, of the 22nd Royal Fusiliers, commanded the Delville Wood garrison, which included the 23rd Fusiliers.

The relief was completed in the early hours of the 2nd.

A second attack on Guillemont had already been decided upon, and when, at 2.30 p.m. on 2nd August, XIIIth Corps Headquarters issued " Operation Orders " for an attack to take place on a date and at an hour to be announced later, preparations had already been begun for renewing the struggle for the village. These preparations consisted principally in digging a trench towards Guillemont, and pushing forward the front lines wherever possible to form convenient " jumping-off " positions. Behind the lines fresh stores of ammunition were being brought up. And through all, the relentless shelling went on day and night. Artillery barrages and counter-battery work continued, though no offensive operations were undertaken. The records of 1st August show that over 63,000 rounds of artillery ammunition were expended, 34,000 odd rounds being fired by 18-pounders alone. And this amount was the least expended on any one day since the beginning of the Somme battles !

The German artillery was not less active, for his guns belched death and destruction day and night. Delville Wood drew the enemy's fire at all hours. On the 2nd the 22nd Royal Fusiliers had one officer wounded and 23 other ranks killed and wounded. Montauban Alley and the Carnoy areas were also subjected to a heavy shelling. Wartelot Farm, held by the 5th Infantry Brigade, was again pounded by the enemy's guns, with the result that 4 officers were wounded and 33 other ranks killed, wounded, and missing, including Major L. M. Owen, 2nd Oxford and Bucks, who was wounded and died later of his wounds. In comparison the artillery suffered heavily. One brigade (XXXIVth Brigade R.F.A.) states in its Diary : " Early this morning an 8-inch buried four men of the 70th Battery—two were dead when extricated. Major W. H. F. Jones was wounded. The XLIst Brigade (having on the 1st had Major Lee Warner and Major Goschen wounded) on the 2nd lost its commanding officer, Lieut.-Colonel Dooner, who was wounded ; Major Goschen was again wounded. The 48th Battery of the XXXVIth Brigade had two of its guns knocked out. And yet it was a quiet day." At 3 p.m. on the 3rd a small party of the enemy attempted to raid the south-east corner of Delville Wood. The attack was unsuccessful : several of the enemy were killed, two more wounded, and one taken prisoner.

At 4.15 a.m. on the 4th the 1st Royal Berks relieved the 22nd Royal Fusiliers in Delville Wood. The Berks at this period were terribly weak, numbering only 280 men ; they were formed into two companies—A and D=A, B and C=B—and these included 20 men drawn from the transport and 20 from the " Drums."

On the night of the 4th–5th, the 51st Infantry Brigade (17th Division) took over Delville Wood from the 2nd Division, whose left flank was ordered to rest on Wartelot Farm. The XVth and XIIIth Corps areas had been readjusted—the northern boundaries of the XIIIth Corps running from the middle of Angle Trench (just south of Delville Wood) to Bernafay Wood. 　　4TH–5TH AUG.

Thus the wood which had cost the 2nd Division so many valuable lives passed from its possession.

The second attack on Guillemont, primarily ordered for the 4th, was postponed until the 7th, and finally fixed for 8th August.

It is not possible to give the full text of the general principles governing the attack which General Headquarters circulated to all General Officers Commanding concerned, but the following excellent outline of the situation on the Somme shows to some extent the enemy's position and with what the Allies had to contend : "The present situation is that the enemy has brought up considerable reinforcements of men and guns, and can continue for some time still to replace tired troops. He has also strengthened and continues to strengthen his positions; and he has recovered to a great extent from the disorganization caused by the success of the Allied attack last month. In consequence, although most of his troops in our front have been severely handled and must be somewhat tired, they are still too formidable to be rushed without careful and methodical preparation ; and they may prove capable of developing strong and well-organized counter-attacks, prepared and supported by the heaviest artillery fire that the enemy can develop."

Apparently General Headquarters were under no delusions as to the length of the operations : the crisis " probably will not be sooner than the last·half of September." The General Officers Commanding the Fourth, Second, and Third British Armies were to hold the enemy to his positions on their fronts, and with all the means at their disposal cause him loss.

Detailed orders for the attack on the 8th were issued at 7 a.m. on the 7th.

The XIIIth Corps was ordered to capture Guillemont : the attack was to be carried out by the 2nd and 55th Divisions. The French XXth Corps would advance its left flank up to the Hardecourt–Guillemont road.

The objectives were : the 55th Division to capture Guillemont and to establish itself on the northern portion of the road to Hardecourt north-east, east, and south-east of Arrow Head Copse ; to join up with the left of the French XXth Corps ; to gain touch with the 2nd Division on the left. The 2nd Division was to capture the enemy's defences between Wartelot Farm and Guillemont (exclusive), including the trench which ran parallel to the Longueval–Guillemont road almost to Wartelot Farm, thence due north to south-east of Angle Trench, to establish touch with the 55th Division, and to maintain touch with the front line in Angle Trench and Delville Wood.

The boundary between the two Divisions : "the road from Wartelot Farm chimney to Guillemont as far as the level railway

crossing (road inclusive to 2nd Division), and just south, thence
east to the crossroads east of the station."
    " The attack will be preceded by a bombardment of heavy artil-
lery lasting seventeen hours ; this bombardment will start at 9 a.m.
on 7th August, but there will be a pause for getting the assaulting
troops into their assembly trenches, between 9 p.m. and 12 midnight 7th–8th.   It will then recommence and continue until zero."
    " Zero " hour had been fixed for 4.20 a.m.
    The 6th Infantry Brigade was detailed for the attack : " The
6th Infantry Brigade, two sections of the 5th Field Company R.E.,
and two companies 10th D.C.L.I. (Pioneers) will carry out the task
assigned to the 2nd Division.   The whole will be under the orders
of the General Officer Commanding 6th Infantry Brigade."
    The attack on the northern portion of the trenches along the
Longueval–Guillemont road was to move forward from the north-
west, and that on the remainder of the objective from the west, the
latter keeping close touch with the 55th Division on its right.
    The 1st King's (Liverpool) Regiment and the 17th Middlesex
were to make the attack, with the 2nd South Staffords in close
support and the 13th Essex in Brigade Reserve in Mine Alley.
No. 2 Section of the 5th Field Company R.E. had been allotted to
the 17th Middlesex and No. 3 Section to the 1st King's.   One company of the Pioneers was attached to each attacking battalion.
    At 9 a.m. on the 7th the XIIIth Corps Artillery opened fire on
the German defences east of Wartelot Farm (known as " Z–Z "
Trench) and in front of Guillemont, and continued until 9 p.m.
Forty 18-pounders, and twelve 4.5-inch howitzers of the 2nd
Division Artillery were in action all day, the former firing three
and the latter two rounds per minute.   " Chinese attacks " were
also made, for the Germans had to be kept in a state of uncertainty
as to when the infantry attack would be launched.   The " Ammunition Expenditure " reports for the 7th August afford ample evidence
of the huge number of rounds fired from guns of all calibres—
howitzers : 4.5-inch, 6-inch, 9.2-inch, 12-inch, and 15-inch ; guns :
18-pounders, 4.7-inch, 60-pounders, 9.2-inch, and 12-inch.
    At 9 p.m. the bombardment lifted, and between that hour and
12 midnight the assaulting troops assembled in their trenches.
    The 1st King's were ordered to attack the German front-line
system from south of Wartelot Farm to Guillemont ; the 17th
Middlesex, " Z–Z " Trench east of the Longueval–Guillemont road.
    Immediately the bombardment lifted at 9 p.m. the Middlesex
sent out patrols to ascertain whether the German trenches east of

290   THE HISTORY OF THE SECOND DIVISION.

Wartelot Farm were held in force, and if the bombardment had been effective. The patrols reported the trenches strongly held, and practically undamaged by the bombardment.

The assaulting troops then took up their positions.

The 1st King's disposed three companies in the front line—B, C, and D—in the New Trench, A Company just east and Battalion Headquarters in the north end of Trônes Wood. The 17th Middlesex occupied Wartelot Farm and the trench along High Holborn, thence to New Trench; also the southern end of Angle Trench.[1]

The 2nd South Staffords in support occupied trenches in Trônes Wood and Bernafay Wood—A Company being placed at the disposal of the 1st King's, and B Company under order of the 17th Middlesex. Instructions were given to the General Officer Commanding to keep the closest possible touch with the situation, reinforcing the attacking battalions on his own initiative. Nos. 2 and 3 Sections of the 5th Field Company R.E. were also in Bernafay Wood, whilst A and B Companies of the Pioneers (under Major G. B. Stratton) were entrenched just west of the wood, awaiting orders to move forward and consolidate the enemy's trenches when won.

8TH AUG.   At midnight the bombardment recommenced. In conjunction
MAP.   with bombardments arranged by the IIIrd and IVth Corps designed to attract the enemy's attention to other parts of the line, the XIIIth Corps Artillery again opened fire at midnight, the intention being to lift the artillery suddenly at 4.20 a.m. without any period of extra intense fire which might give warning to the enemy of the moment of attack. The artillery of the French XXth Corps also assisted by bombarding Leuze Wood and by counter-battery work.

Punctually at 4.20 a.m. the bombardment lifted to the first barrage line; the Stokes mortars then opened rapid fire for from thirty seconds to one minute on the strong points Machine-gun House and " Z–Z " Trench.

As the mortars ceased fire the attacking troops of both the XIIIth and XVth Corps, who had been lying out in front of their trenches, jumped to their feet and advanced across No Man's Land. The morning was very misty, and the Battalion Diary of the 1st King's stated that it was " very hard to see more than ten yards."

---

[1] The exact disposition (by companies) of the 17th Middlesex was unobtainable from the Official Diaries. Very little information also is to be found in the battalion records of the battle which followed.

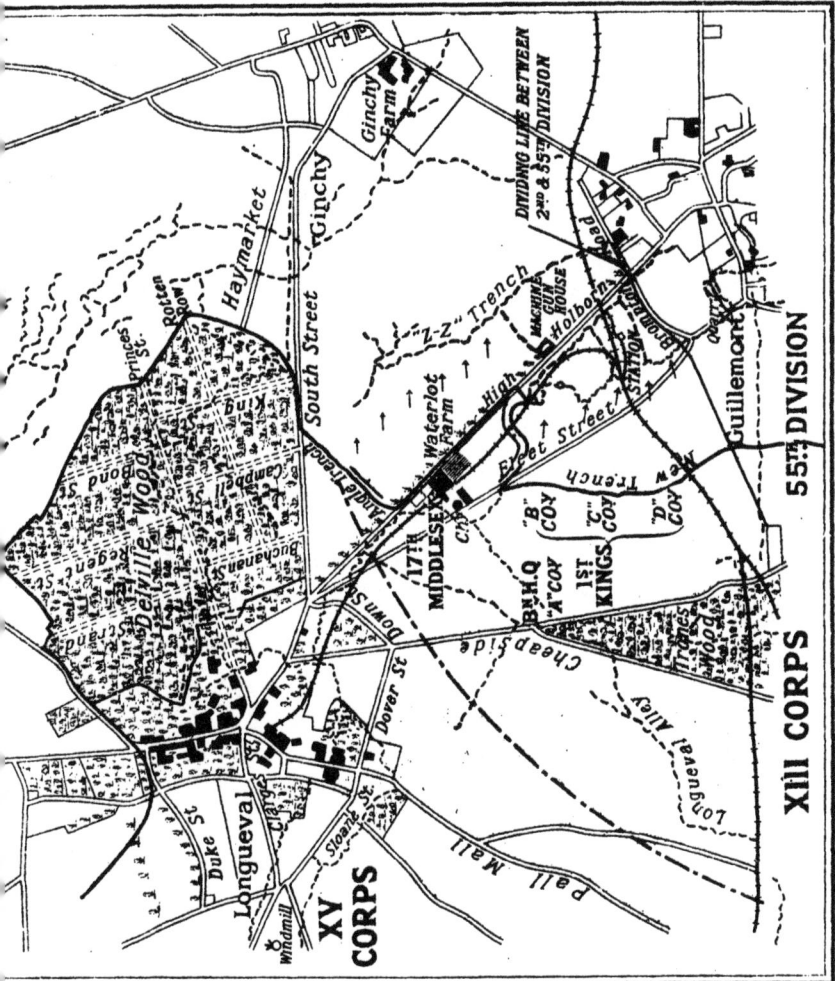

THE BATTLE OF GUILLEMONT.
Attack by 2nd Division, 8th August 1916.

THE MAPPA CO., LTD., LONDON.

Owing to the impossibility of seeing their objectives, the 1st King's seem to have lost direction and had advanced more to the south than they ought to have done. The result was that the enemy's strong points were missed—an unfortunate but apparently unavoidable mistake.

The 1st King's objectives were: first, German front line from strong points to Brighton Road; second, Guillemont railway station; third, High Holborn—trenches north of station.

As B, C, and D Companies of the King's went forward, A Company moved up into New Trench—the latter company having been detailed to carry out " mopping-up " duties. These duties consisted of following in the rear of the attacking troops and thoroughly searching dug-outs and shelters for the lurking enemy. For it had been found that, on the approach of assaulting troops, the Germans betook themselves to their dug-outs, and when the attack had passed over the front line, came out, and, turning their machine guns on to the backs of the advancing troops, caught them in rear. Many a hard-won position had been lost again owing to neglect in rounding up the enemy out of his dug-outs and shelters.

At 5.20 a.m. two flares went up—pre-arranged signals to denote capture of the enemy's front-line trenches; the 1st King's and the 17th Middlesex had reached their first objectives.

A little later a carrier pigeon arrived at 6th Infantry Brigade Headquarters with the following message from Lieut.-Colonel Goff, commanding the 1st King's: " First—we have taken front line and station and I think High Holborn. Everything is rather mixed. Machine guns are firing at us from Guillemont and from our left. I am at present in German front line and am going forward to clear up situation."

" First " was the code word, denoting capture of the enemy first-line trench.

A Company of the King's moved forward towards the old German front line with the intention of " mopping up," but was met by a severe machine-gun fire and a shower of bombs from the strong points.

Meanwhile the three Companies B, C, and D, *had* captured High Holborn and a little later Guillemont station. But from this point there are no records of what happened to the three gallant companies. For a little later, while A Company was still engaged with the enemy at Strong Point, a large number of Germans came streaming down the original German front trench from Guillemont. The left attacking battalion of the 55th Division and a party of Norfolks of the 15th Infantry Brigade (5th Division) had failed in its attempt to capture Guillemont, and thus the enemy was enabled to pass men quickly from the village down his front-line trench and sever communication between the 1st King's and their supports.

Something of what happened was gathered from a wounded officer (Captain Last of the 1st King's), who, shot through the knee, had crawled back towards New Trench, which still sheltered A Company. This officer stated that about 150 men of the 1st King's were consolidating their newly gained position at High Holborn (third objective), and that 70 more were at Guillemont station (second objective). Second-Lieut. Hutson, in command of A Company, thereupon dispatched orderlies to B, C, and D Companies, informing them of the presence of large numbers of the enemy in his old front line. These orderlies never reached the beleaguered companies, for they were killed *en route*. Lieut. Hutson also called for reinforcements. Two half-platoons of the 2nd South Staffords were hurried up to New Trench, and with these and stragglers from the three lost companies the consolidation of New Trench was begun.

Meanwhile, the 17th Middlesex attacking simultaneously on the left of the 1st King's had captured " Z–Z " Trench, but immediately came under enfilade machine-gun fire, and were bombed unceasingly. At 9.45 a.m. the brigadier (General Daly) telephoned to Divisional Headquarters that " All Middlesex in ' Z–Z ' Trench were killed or captured." The Middlesex were then ordered to endeavour to isolate Machine-gun House and bomb southwards towards Guillemont station with the object of joining up with the 1st King's. This apparently was attempted, and although the battalion did not get as far as the station or isolate Machine-gun House, the enemy's front line from a few hundred yards north-west of the railway junction (west of the station) to a point about half-way between Machine-gun House and Wartelot Farm was captured and consolidated.

But of the three companies of the gallant 1st King's Regiment nothing was seen or heard !

A fate similar to that which had overtaken the left battalion of the 164th Infantry Brigade (55th Division) which, attacking Guillemont, got into the northern portion of the village without much difficulty, but was eventually cut off, may have happened to Colonel Goff and his officers and men. An Official Diary thus described what happened to the 164th Infantry Brigade : " As soon as they had got into the village, it appears that the enemy came up out of the ground behind them, and cut them off entirely by means of machine guns. This is practically what happened at the previous attack on Guillemont of the 30th July, and it is possible that the village is an underground warren of passages in which the garrison is immune from shell fire, and from which they can emerge with their machine guns after the attacking infantry has passed over." The need then for strong "mopping-up" parties is admirably brought out in the above quotation.

At 3 p.m. 6th Infantry Brigade Headquarters received orders to continue the attack any time after dark in an endeavour to take all the objectives of the morning.

The afternoon passed quietly, but without any signs of the missing companies of the 1st King's. After dark the remnants of the battalion—A Company and a few stragglers—about 180 all told, were withdrawn to trenches near Brigade Headquarters on the Carnoy–Montauban road.

The night attack was to be carried out by the 13th Essex Regiment. Two companies of the South Staffords were placed at the disposal of the Officer Commanding 17th Middlesex, to assist in the operations. The 2nd Oxford and Bucks were ordered forward between Bernafay and Trônes Woods, at the disposal of the General Officer Commanding 6th Infantry Brigade. At 3.30 a.m. the 13th Essex got into position in the forming-up trenches used by the King's.

Following a preliminary bombardment the attack began at 2.20 a.m. on the 9th. Two bombing attacks by the South Staffords failed to make headway, though they were admirably led by Captain Fluke (17th Middlesex). At 4.10 a.m. the 13th Essex advanced, but were unsuccessful in their attack west of Guillemont station, the enemy's position being too strongly held. The attack of the 55th Division on the right of the Essex Regiment also failed.

9TH AUG.

Instructions were then received from 2nd Divisional Headquarters to break off the attack. At 6.45 p.m. on the 9th, XIIIth Corps Headquarters issued orders that the 2nd Division would be relieved by the 24th Division during the night 9th–10th ; on relief the Division would go into Corps Reserve.

The two attacks on Guillemont had cost the Division 24 officers and 688 other ranks killed, wounded, and missing, the majority of these being of the 6th Infantry Brigade.

The relief of the Division took place as ordered—only the Divisional artillery remaining in the XIIIth Corps area. At 2 a.m.

on the 11th, the Division received orders to march to the Ancre area during the 11th and 12th. On the 14th the Division (less the Divisional artillery) was complete in the area Belloy–Picquigny–Vaux-en-Amiénois.

It is impossible to give an adequate word-picture of the Somme battles of 1916. The wholesale slaughter of men, the almost continuous roar of the guns, left their mark upon the faces of those who carried on in the battle area. If the Germans' casualties were heavy (and there is conclusive evidence they were heavier than the Allies'), those sustained by the Fourth and Reserve Armies were at that period of the war unparalleled. From the first day of the offensive until 9th August, the date on which the 2nd Division went out of the line, the British casualties were : officers, 5,574 ; other ranks, 133,883. Of that total the 2nd Division lost (from 23rd July to 11th August), officers 196, other ranks 4,712, killed, wounded, and missing.[1]

Three distinct attacks had been made by the Division, the first, which resulted in the capture of Delville Wood, and the two abortive attacks on Guillemont. The latter was ultimately captured by the 20th Division and the 47th Infantry Brigade 16th Division between 3rd and 6th September ; Ginchy was taken on 9th September.

The enemy's heavy and continual artillery fire and barrages were responsible for a large percentage of the casualties. And yet, compared with at least one other action, that of the Battle of Festubert in 1915, in which the 2nd Division suffered over 5,000 casualties, the losses of the Division had not been excessive. The casualties in officers *were* very high ; indeed, at this period it was a common saying that a subaltern's life was worth only about a week's purchase.

Trench Warfare, 19th August to 31st October.

The portion of the Somme battlefield, to which the 2nd Division was transferred about the middle of August 1916, was in the northern area, just south of Hébuterne. The VIIIth Corps, which on 1st July, at the opening of the battle, had attacked from this line, penetrated as far as Serre, the Beaucourt–Serre road, and just west

---

[1] The casualties amongst the whole of the British artillery on the Somme from 1st July to 24th August 1916 were 562 officers, of which 124 were battery commanders, and over 6,000 rank and file.

of Beaucourt-sur-Ancre, but eventually had to withdraw to its original trenches. Since that date this portion of the line had defied all attempt at capture ; likewise every attempt of the enemy to advance had been frustrated. As the offensive farther south progressed, it became essential to reduce the salient in the northern part of the battle-front, which was gradually growing more pronounced.

About the same time that the 2nd Division left the Fourth Army area, the Vth Corps was transferred from Ypres to the Somme west and north of the river Ancre, and on 19th August the Division came under orders of this corps. The Vth Corps, with the IInd and VIIth Corps, formed the Fifth (Reserve) Army.

On 19th August the 2nd Division began the relief of the Guards 19TH AUG. Division, the 5th Infantry Brigade taking over the trenches held by the 2nd (Guards) Brigade. On the 20th the 6th Infantry Brigade relieved the 1st (Guards) Brigade, and on the 21st the 99th Infantry Brigade relieved the 2nd (Guards) Brigade. The General Officer Commanding 2nd Division assumed command of the line on 21st August. The three sections of the line (left, centre, and right) south of Hébuterne were then held by the 99th Infantry Brigade, 6th Infantry Brigade, and 5th Infantry Brigade respectively. Each brigade had two battalions in the front line, one in support and one in reserve. From north to south the battalions in line were 22nd and 23rd Royal Fusiliers (99th Infantry Brigade), 2nd South Staffords and 13th Essex (6th Infantry Brigade), 17th Royal Fusiliers and 2nd Highland Light Infantry (5th Infantry Brigade). Divisional Headquarters were in Couin.

The 2nd Divisional artillery were still in action in the Fourth Army area. The gunners were having a strenuous time indeed, and their casualties were gradually mounting up.

The position held by the 2nd Division on 21st August was 21ST AUG. a wide stretch of trenches about 4,000 yards in length from Watling Street (south) to 16 Poplars (north). Hostile trench-mortar activity greeted the Division in its new sector, but the enemy's ardour was cowed by effective retaliation. " This part of the line seemed very quiet after the Somme trenches," said one brigade Diary. There was, however, sufficient excitement to keep the troops busy.

On the night of the 21st the 2nd Highland Light Infantry sent out a patrol, consisting of 2 officers and 4 other ranks, to visit two bombing posts held by the battalion about sixty yards from the front-line trenches. In the darkness the patrol bumped into a German patrol, and a fight ensued. Rifles, bombs, and revolvers were used, till all the ammunition was expended ; the patrols then returned to their respective trenches. No casualties were suffered by the Highland Light Infantry.

About 1 a.m. on the 24th the enemy blew in the gallery of Russian Sap at John's Copse, a portion of the 6th Brigade line held by the South Staffords. Twenty men were seriously injured, 6 of whom were buried and much shaken.

Intermittent shelling took place until the end of the month, which closed quietly ; the situation being described officially in Diaries as " normal."

The 2nd Divisional Artillery arrived in the new area on 27th–28th and 28th–29th August, and at once set to work to register and cut wire. Large working parties of infantry were furnished to assist the " Special Brigade," and were employed on " carrying duties." The Special Brigade was the Gas Section, and the troops were carrying up gas cylinders.

On the 28th a conference was held at Divisional Headquarters of Army, Corps, and Divisional commanders. The Commander-in-Chief also visited the Division and held a discussion with the General Officer Commanding ; active operations were soon to begin again.

Since the Division moved into the Hébuterne section much work had been done in revetting and repairing the trenches, and in wiring the front line ; in deepening the trenches, reclaiming damaged fire bays, and in building new ones. Deep dug-outs had been made, while for the first time the Division is recorded to be in possession of a trench " tramway," which ran from Euston and Vauxhall to La Signy Farm. One hundred yards of tramway had also been constructed in the left section occupied by the 99th Infantry Brigade.

With the close of August came wet weather, and the trenches were in consequence soon muddy and in places deep in water. The rain, moreover, postponed a gas attack which had been ordered to take place from the trenches of the 99th Infantry Brigade on the last day of the month.

South of the Ancre the struggle still went on with great intensity. At Maurepas, Pozières, Guillemont, Thiepval, Martinpuich, and south of the Somme at Arras the Allied attacks had progressed. The French had taken ground on a front of eleven miles from Cléry, through Maurepas to Guillemont. Constant pressure on the enemy south of the Ancre had prevented him making any attack north of the river, though the time was fast approaching when General Gough's Army (Fifth) would be called upon to take the offensive.

The enemy in this northern sector of the line was evidently getting nervous. The 1st September opened with the blowing of mines, during which the Tunnel at John Copse (6th Infantry Brigade front) was seriously damaged, and two sappers were injured. On the 3rd he blew in Mark Runnel, and at 6 p.m. opened a particularly violent bombardment, which continued for two hours. The front line of the 6th Infantry Brigade was completely obliterated, though the brigade suffered only a very few casualties. South, in the neighbourhood of Beaumont Hamel, an attack was made by the 39th and 48th Divisions, but without success ; this attack evidently caused the bombardment of the centre section of the 2nd Division's line. The Divisional and Corps Artillery retaliated with marked effect, the enemy's guns ceasing fire very soon afterwards.

On 12th September the British position on the Somme from Combles to Hébuterne ran as follows : the British right rested about the centre of Bois Douage, a long straggling belt of trees between Maurepas and Combles ; thence the line ran almost north, skirting east and north-east of Ginchy, north-west again of Delville Wood, suddenly dropping back south-west to the forked roads north-west of Longueval ; then north-west again through High Wood, thence in an undulating line west by north-west to Mouquet Farm, south-west for 1,500 yards, west again to a point 1,000 yards east of the Ancre and 1,200 yards south of Thiepval ; the line thence ran directly north, skirting west of Thiepval, and crossed the Ancre south-west of St. Pierre Divion ; north-west to west of Beaumont Hamel ; the 2nd Division continued the line north to 16 Poplars, east of Hébuterne.

Patrol work, mining, counter-mining, and night raids on the enemy's trenches, with periods of mortar and artillery bombardments, continued throughout September, for the weather precluded anything in the nature of offensive operations on a large scale. Whenever the German artillery shelled the Division, retaliatory measures were adopted — his trenches were very heavily bombarded, which invariably had the desired effect. His " minnies " (minenwerfer), however, caused much trouble and many casualties.

Trench raids were frequent, and in these considerable daring and gallantry were displayed by the raiding parties.

The first of these raids took place on the night of 14th–15th September, when all three infantry brigades sent out parties. The object of this raid was to attract attention from the main operations, which were to take place farther south on the 15th. The IInd Corps, on the right of the Vth Corps, had been ordered to co-operate by attacking the Wund Werk (just south of Thiepval) and the trenches on either flank, with the intention of assisting assaults on High Wood and Martinpuich by the IIIrd Corps. Apart from the co-operative value of these trench raids, they were undertaken in order to capture prisoners, secure identifications, and do as much damage as possible.

The proposed raids along the front of the 2nd Division included a discharge of gas, artillery bombardments by field and heavy artillery, and the blowing of mines and one-minute intense bombardment by Stokes mortars; after which the raiding parties were to be pushed into the enemy's trenches. Two distinct series of raids were to be made—one north at midnight, by 50 all ranks of the 99th Infantry Brigade, and the other south by the 5th and 6th Infantry Brigades, following the blowing of a mine at Cat Street.

The raid by the 99th Infantry Brigade was to be preceded by a discharge of gas at 8.30 p.m. and a bombardment of field and heavy artillery, beginning at 10 p.m. and lasting for two hours. The position to be assaulted was the front-line German trench in the vicinity of K.17 central, and opposite Bugeaud, leading to Fore Street.

About midnight a mine was to be blown opposite Cat Street as a' signal for the second assault to begin. This was to take the form of three raids—one opposite the Cat by about 30 all ranks of the 5th Infantry Brigade, a second on the north-west corner of the Quadrilateral by about 25 all ranks, also of the 5th Infantry Brigade; and a third on the German post in a sap about K.35, A7.7, by about 25 all ranks of the 6th Infantry Brigade. The 22nd Royal Fusiliers (99th Infantry Brigade), 17th Royal Fusiliers and 2nd Highland Light Infantry (5th Infantry Brigade), and 1st King's (6th Infantry Brigade) were detailed to carry out the raids.

An intense bombardment by Stokes mortars, lasting one minute, was to precede these raids.

The discharge of gas by the 99th Infantry Brigade was postponed owing to the direction of the wind being unfavourable. The 22nd Royal Fusiliers then received orders to " patrol instead of raid."

At " zero " hour—midnight—the artillery lifted to the German trenches and the flanks of the positions to be assaulted. The Stokes mortars opened fire, and put down a heavy barrage on the enemy's front line. The raiding parties had already left their trenches and had crawled forward as near as possible to the German lines, awaiting the signal to rush the enemy.

At a minute after midnight the Stokes mortars ceased firing, and the raids began.

Owing to the fact that the enemy's wire was found intact, the patrol of the 99th Infantry Brigade, carried out by the 22nd Royal Fusiliers, came to naught, and the party returned to its own trench. The 1st King's of the 8th Infantry Brigade were successful in reaching the enemy's trench in the vicinity of K.35, A7.7, but ten of the raiding party were wounded and a prisoner could not be captured ; two Germans were killed. " It was very bad luck that the whole of our party with the exception of two should be wounded, and thus prevent our fellows from bringing in the Boche," said a Diary. The whole party, however, returned to its trench. The men were justly disappointed, for they had spent great trouble over the raid, even blackening their faces in order that the enemy might not distinguish them ; whilst each man carried a bludgeon with which to dispatch the enemy without the necessity of discharging rifles or revolvers.

The mine in front of Cat Street went up at midnight, and both parties of the 5th Infantry Brigade—i.e., the 2nd Highland Light Infantry and 17th Royal Fusiliers—rushed forward to their objectives. The mine, however, had not exploded under the enemy's wire, which prevented the Highland Light Infantry reaching their objective, as the entanglements were found to be intact. Falling debris knocked out 1 officer and 2 other ranks ; no other casualties were suffered.

The 17th Royal Fusiliers succeeded in getting into the enemy's trench at two points ; but unfortunately it was empty, and the party then returned to its own lines.

The next raid took place on the night of the 15th, and was carried out by the 22nd Royal Fusiliers. It was completely successful, and for some time afterwards was looked upon as an example of how a raid should be conducted. 15TH SEPT.

The object of the raid was the same—i.e., to secure identifications and to harass the enemy. The point to be assaulted was the same as on the previous evening—the Boche line in the vicinity of K.17. " Zero " hour was at 10.45 p.m.

Ten minutes before " zero " the raiding party, consisting of Second-Lieut. Martin and 25 other ranks, including bomb-carriers, identification snatchers, and an orderly, left Fore Street and began to crawl forward to the German trenches. The artillery barrage was then on the enemy's front line. At 10.45 p.m. the artillery lifted from the point of attack—K.17, D.o.8, but continued to fire north and south of and behind the objective. The Stokes mortars next opened an intense and well-directed fire for one minute, behind which the raiding party, split up into three sections, gradually approached the enemy's front line. As the mortars ceased firing the raiding party (then roughly forty yards from its objective) jumped up and rushed forward. A bombing party jumped into the sap at K.17, D.o.8, and clubbed or bayoneted the garrison. The right and left bombing parties then blocked the German main trench, keeping the enemy under a constant shower of bombs. The remainder of the party, headed by Lieut. Martin, sprang into the main German trench. That officer shot one German officer in the face at a yard's range, killing him instantly. Eleven Germans were killed, 10 unwounded prisoners were taken, and not a single man left living in the trench. The raiding party fought splendidly, and the records with grim satisfaction stated that " every raider had blood on his club or bayonet."

At 10.55 p.m. the raiding party left the enemy's trench and returned to its own front line, having suffered not a single casualty. The success of the raid was largely assisted by the splendid artillery co-operation and the effective dispositions and handling of the machine guns, the latter entirely preventing the enemy putting his head up until the raiding party was actually on the parapet of his trench.

The Commanding Officer of the 22nd Royal Fusiliers stated in his report: " I account for the success of the raid as due to the fact that the officer and men meant business, and were determined not to return without some spoil."

The night 15th–16th witnessed also another raid by the 1st King's on the enemy's front line just opposite Flag Avenue. The King's, smarting under the disappointment of the previous evening, determined to make another attempt. Accordingly, at 6 a.m. on the 15th, a raiding party of 1 officer and 25 other ranks marched off to Courcelles-au-Bois, where a dummy trench was marked out, and the whole party rehearsed in the raid, first as a drill and afterwards independently. When darkness fell the raid was again twice practised, after which the party marched back from Courcelles direct to the front-line trench at Flag Avenue, the " jumping-off " place for the raid. The party arrived in its old position at midnight, and at 12.10 a.m., led by Second-Lieut. G. H. H. Scott, went over the parapet. The whole party entered the Boche sap, but found no Germans there. Lieut. Scott and 1 man were wounded. The raiding party again returned empty-handed.

On the 17th the trenches of the South Staffords at Bleneau were again obliterated by shell-fire and bombs. The bombardment lasted about an hour, and the casualties numbered 52 of all ranks. " Owing to the restrictions placed on expenditure of artillery ammunition our guns were unable to retaliate." For weeks the daily expenditure of artillery ammunition on the Somme had been prodigious, and a scarcity now began to be felt !

The enemy blew a mine at Grey Tunnel on the 18th, and the 17th Middlesex lost heavily. Owing to hostile trench-mortar activity a number of men and some officers of the battalion had taken shelter in the Tunnel. The casualties were Second-Lieut. J. D. Stagg (27th Battalion, attached) and 1 other rank killed, and 2 officers and 59 other ranks wounded.

On the 19th the 2nd Division was relieved by the 39th Division, and marched back into the rest area in Corps Reserve, where until the 30th the Division was " resting and training." During this period, however, the 1st King's Royal Rifles of the 99th Infantry Brigade carried out a raid on the enemy's line between K.23, D.8.4, and K.23, D.9.6½. This raid was to have taken place on the night of 18th–19th September before the battalion went out of the line, but owing to bad weather it had to be postponed. A raid was then ordered for the 25th, and as the battalions in the line could not spare the men to make it, the Rifles were detailed to carry out their original plan. _{19TH SEPT.}

During the afternoon of the 25th the raiding party, consisting of 6 N.C.O's and 44 other ranks under Second-Lieut. A. A. Kidd, marched to the front-line trenches. The raid is thus described in the Battalion War Diary : " The object of the raid was to enter the German trenches between K.23, D.8.4 and K.23, D.9.6½, in front of the Hébuterne southern sector, to kill and capture as many Boche as possible, and to bring back identifications, etc. The night was favourable for the enterprise, and at ' zero ' (10.15 p.m.) the party reached the German front line, through the gap in the wire which had been prepared some time ago and was still open. There they suddenly met with an impassable obstacle in the shape of a new type of German ' knife rest.' This knife rest is laid on the ground, and to all intents and purposes is a lot of loose wire, such as might well be left after wire-cutting by artillery. It can be manipulated like an umbrella, and when pulled open, which it can be apparently quite easily, forms a considerable obstacle. In the words of Sergeant Loomes, who was with the party, it seems suddenly to spring from the ground. Simultaneously with the sudden appearance of these knife rests, a bell was heard to ring in the German lines, bombs were thrown by the Germans from the parapet, and machine-gun fire opened immediately in front of the raiders from the enemy's support lines. The party saw about 20 Germans. . . . Second-Lieut. A. A. Kidd decided that it was no use attempting to pursue the enterprise, and after his party had thrown about fifty bombs, ordered them to withdraw into shell-holes and work their way back to our lines. This they did. The Boche bombs had done very little damage, though some burst a yard in front of the men. At 10.27 p.m. the first Boche red light went up, and their artillery opened at 10.35 p.m. Thirty or forty ' pipsqueaks ' were fired, and a few trench-mortar ·bombs. The party reached camp at 2.45 a.m. on the 26th."

The ten days' " resting and training " were spent by the Division in musketry training, bomb-throwing, the use of the Lewis gun, and in wiring practice, whilst the junior officers were instructed in regimental exercises by the Divisional Staff.

During September the Trench-Mortar Batteries of the 2nd Division were augmented, and at this period numbered four—V/2, X/2, Y/2, Z/2.

1st Oct.

On 1st October the Division moved up from Corps Reserve again into the front line, the 6th Infantry Brigade occupying the Hébuterne sector, the 99th Infantry Brigade the Serre-Redan ridge sector, and the 5th Infantry Brigade in Divisional Reserve still engaged in training. Three days later (on the 4th) the Division handed the Hébuterne sector over to the 51st Division, the 152nd Infantry Brigade relieving the 6th Infantry Brigade, which then marched to Mailly Maillet and Bertrancourt. The 5th Infantry Brigade went into the line on the 6th, relieving the 99th Infantry Brigade, the latter moving back to Mailly Maillet Wood and Village.

The Division was again relieved on the 8th, and went out of the line after handing over to the 3rd and 63rd Divisions.

The morning of the 9th October found the Division situated in the following areas : 5th Infantry Brigade, Lealvillers ; 6th Infantry Brigade, Puchevillers ; 99th Infantry Brigade, Raincheval and Arquèves. ·The Artillery was still in the line.

Second Division Headquarters had opened in Hédauville.

A short strenuous period of training was before the Division, for it had been drawn out of the line in order to practise the attack, soon to be launched against the enemy's line north of Thiepval. Thiepval itself, now a shapeless mass of ruins, once a town, had fallen to the British on 27th September, and the Schwaben Redoubt had for the most part been occupied ; the salient north of it was daily growing more pronounced. Bad weather had hitherto made offensive operations from the line Beaumont Hamel–Hébuterne impossible. But still training went forward, for the attack north of the river Ancre could not be postponed much longer.

The two first days in reserve—9th and 10th October—were spent by the troops in company and brigade training and in exercises over the taped practice trenches. On the 11th, however, the Division as a whole rehearsed the attack, when an assault was carried out on dummy trenches. This rehearsal was repeated on the 15th and 16th, whilst between times battalion and brigade training in attacks on dummy trenches, bombing raids, blocking trenches, and blowing up traverses took place each day.

A party of officers from the 2nd Division was also sent to inspect some " Tanks," which for the first time were to attack with the 2nd Division when " zero " hour arrived. The Tanks caused great astonishment amongst the troops when they beheld them, and their somewhat ungainly antics when moving over the ground gave Mr. Atkins innumerable opportunities to exercise his ready wit.

The short period of training passed quickly, and on the 17th the Division made a move back to the line, though only one brigade —the 99th—went into the trenches. The 5th and 6th Infantry Brigades continued training, but were also largely employed in furnishing working parties for duty with the sappers and gunners, digging dug-outs, gun-pits, and in generally preparing for the coming offensive. _{17TH OCT.}

Throughout the whole of this period the indefatigable gunners never ceased their regular and careful bombardment of the enemy's front-line and communication trenches. " Wire-cutting " formed part of the daily programme from early in the month, and big gaps had been made in the thick wire entanglements which the enemy had put down in front of his trenches. Whenever attempts were made to mend the wire or replace it, the machine guns, trench mortars, and artillery opened a brisk fire. In consequence, towards the end of the month the Boche was becoming very anxious about his front line. Under intense bombardments by trench mortars and heavy guns he occasionally succeeded in repairing some of the damage done to his defences, but the methodical pounding of his front line was gradually reducing the strength of his position and making it more vulnerable to infantry attacks.

In conjunction with these artillery bombardments the infantry sent out frequent night patrols to observe the condition of the enemy's wire and trenches. On the 25th, the enemy made another determined attempt to mend his wire, but the Lewis gunners of the Division drove him back to his trenches. Towards dusk on the following day a large flight of enemy aeroplanes attacked the guns of the Division which were then engaged in wire-cutting. A regular air combat ensued between British and German aircraft. Five were brought down, but only two were German. The hostile machines then flew back over their own lines. A raid by the 2nd Oxford and Bucks (6th Infantry Brigade) on the night of the 26th was abortive. The raiding party missed direction and could not find a gap in the enemy's wire.

The weather at this period was wet, dull, cold, and misty, and the roads, trenches, and communications were in an appalling state. Day after day the attack was postponed "forty-eight hours," until at the end of the month it seemed as if the elements would prevent the projected offensive. Heavy rains caused many dug-outs to fall in, whilst the parapets of the trenches were continually tumbling down. Working parties were everywhere engaged in digging and revetting. To add to these difficulties, heavy hostile bombardments frequently blew in the parapets and smashed up communication trenches. Behind the front-line trenches many gun-pits in the artillery lines were deep in water.

In this way October passed.

Farther south the advance was well maintained, and the Fourth Army progressed almost daily towards its final objective.

*   *   *   *   *   *   *

Several Staff changes had taken place in the Division. On 11th September Major P. M. A. Evans joined the Division as G.S.O.3, vice Major C. K. Steward, who went to the 143rd Infantry Brigade. Major J. D. Belgrave, D.S.O., G.S.O.2, left the Division for the IInd Corps on 12th September, having handed over his duties to Major C. A. S. Maitland, D.S.O. Second-Lieut. F. S. Arbuthnot joined the 2nd Division on 12th Oct. as A.D.C. to the General Officer Commanding. On 27th October Major Evans went to the 9th Cavalry Brigade as Brigade-Major, and was succeeded by Captain G. M. Gathorne Hardy, M.C. Lieut.-Colonel J. P. Villiers Steuart, D.S.O., assumed the duties of A.A. and Q.M.G. on 28th October, vice Lieut.-Colonel S. W. Robinson, who was posted to the XIIIth Corps. Captain E. Scott, the D.A.D.M.S., was evacuated sick to England on 29th October, and was replaced by Captain K. W. Mackenzie, D.S.O., M.C.

THE BATTLE OF THE ANCRE, 1916.

Capture of Beaumont Hamel.

The bad weather of October, which had repeatedly delayed operations north of the river Ancre, took a turn for the better during the first few days of November. The 9th was fine, and seemed to offer prospects of a period favourable to an offensive, but the condition of the trenches was truly appalling. In the 6th Infantry Brigade front line the water in places was waist-deep, the average depth knee-deep. The ground about the trenches was pockmarked with shell-holes full of water and inches deep in mud ; the constant traffic up and down the communication trenches had turned the latter into quagmires. Reliefs took hours to accomplish and sometimes had to be completed in daylight, progress to and fro from the front lines being painfully slow. 9TH Nov.

The weather had already compelled curtailment of the plans laid down by Generals Foch and Sir Douglas Haig : " The scheme of the Allied operations, if events went well, included an advance to the general line Le Transloy–south of Bapaume–Bois Loupart. The British forces would then have developed their success in a northerly and south-easterly direction, turning the enemy's defences south of the Scarpe and threatening his troops in that area with capture or destruction. The unfavourable weather, and consequent delay in the Allied advance against Sailly-Saillisel and Le Transloy, made it necessary to abandon this plan at the moment when our September successes seemed to have brought it almost within our grasp. As the season advanced and the bad weather continued, the scope of our plan had constantly to be reduced, until finally it was only possible to undertake the much more limited operation of the 13th November against Beaumont Hamel."

The original Operation Orders issued by VIth Corps Headquarters for the attack bear the date " 22nd October," and the Serre position, Puisieux Trench and Beauregard Dovecote, are given as the final objectives of the Corps. But, as Sir Douglas Haig said in his dispatches, these objectives had to be curtailed, and on the 10th November, when the final orders for the attack were issued, the objective given was the Yellow Line—*i.e.*, the Frankfort and Munich Trenches immediately west of the Beaucourt–Serre road, with an advance on " Z plus 2 days " if the assault was successful and weather permitted. 10TH Nov.

" The enemy's defences in this area (the Ancre) were already extremely formidable when they resisted our assault on the 1st of July ; and the succeeding period of four months had been spent in repairing and adding to them in the light of the experience he had gained in the course of our attack farther south. The hamlet of St. Pierre Divion and the villages of Beaucourt-sur-Ancre and Beaumont Hamel, like the rest of the villages forming part of the enemy's original front in this district, were evidently intended by him to form a permanent line of fortifications while he developed his offensive elsewhere. Realizing that his position in them had become a dangerous one, the enemy had multiplied the number of his guns covering this part of the line, and at the end of October introduced an additional Division on his front between Grandcourt and Hébuterne."

The portion of the enemy's position to be attacked by the Vth Corps lay between a point due west of St. Pierre Divion and northwards to opposite John Copse. North of John Copse the XIIIth Corps held the line ; south of St. Pierre Divion the IInd Corps line ran east and south-east of Hamel, thence due east through Schwaben Redoubt to Stuff Redoubt.

The Vth Corps had in line from north to south in the order given the 3rd, 2nd, 51st, and 63rd (Naval) Divisions.

The 3rd Division's line extended from John Copse to Board Street (inclusive) ; the 2nd Division lay between Board Street and Hunter Street (inclusive) ; the 51st Division from Hunter Street to approximately Q.11, C.1.9, where its right flank joined up with the left of the 63rd (Naval) Division.

The attack of the Vth Corps was to be supported by the artillery of eight Divisions and by the fire of about forty heavy howitzers, in addition to the co-operation of the heavy artillery of the flanking Corps.

The front of attack allotted to the 2nd Division was from Q.4, B.7.0 (about the centre of Hunter Street, due east of the White City) to K.35, A.4.9 (Board Street).

Objectives : Violet and Green Lines—1st Phase ; the Yellow Line—2nd Phase.

The dispositions at " zero " hour were given in " 2nd Division Operation Order, No. 157 " :

" The front of attack allotted to brigades is :

" Right Brigade : from Q.4, B.7.0 (inclusive) to Dog Street (inclusive).

" Left Brigade : from the above point (Dog Street exclusive) to about K.35, A.4.5 (Board Street).

"The 5th Infantry Brigade will be on the right; the 6th Infantry Brigade will be on the left; the 99th Infantry Brigade will be in Divisional Reserve.

"The 51st and 63rd (Naval) Divisions will be attacking on the right of the 2nd Division; the 3rd Division will be attacking on our left. The 37th Division will be in reserve."

Headquarters: 5th Infantry Brigade—White City; 6th Infantry Brigade—Vallade Trench (just south of Cheeroh Avenue); 99th Infantry Brigade—Ellis Square (just north of Roman road).

The artillery arrangements included an intense bombardment to begin at 5 a.m. two days before the attack, to be kept up until the assault took place. At 5 a.m. the siege batteries were to open a gradually increasing fire until 6 a.m. when it would become intense, a proportion of the field batteries joining in at the hour. At 6.15 a.m. the fire of both siege and field batteries was to cease for one hour and resume according to the usual daily programme. The twofold object of these bombardments was to deceive the Boche, and to cut wire and generally damage the enemy's defences.

The following is the Barrage Time Table:

"0.0. Barrage begins, 75 per cent. of 18-pounders and all 4.5-inch howitzers on front trench; 25 per cent. of 18-pounders fifty yards short (to catch snipers in shell-holes).

"0.1. All 4.5-inch howitzers and 25 per cent. of the 18-pounders to lift 100 yards: 4 rounds per gun per minute while troops are moving.

"0.6. All lift 100 yards and continue to lift 100 yards every five minutes until the whole barrage is on a line 150 yards beyond the Violet Line: 2 rounds per gun per minute while stationary.

"0.31. Continue to lift at the same rate until the whole is on a line 150 yards beyond the Green Line.

"0.56. Consolidating barrage, 150 yards beyond the Green Line; ½ round per gun per minute.

"1.51–1.56. Pause.

"1.56. Re-open intense fire 150 yards beyond the Green Line; 4 rounds per gun per minute.

"1.58. Lift 100 yards every five minutes until the whole is on a line 150 yards beyond the Yellow Line.

"2.46. Consolidating barrage 150 yards beyond the Yellow Line; ½ round per gun per minute.'

308 THE HISTORY OF THE SECOND DIVISION.

The 11th November was foggy, and in consequence the artillery could not complete registration. Throughout the Division there were fears that the attack definitely fixed for the 13th would again be postponed. The gunners opened fire as usual, and the short period of intense fire put the enemy on the alert—as it was intended to do. His artillery replied vigorously, and his trench mortars were active, but as no attack developed his anxiety evaporated and his guns ceased fire. On the 12th, similar tactics by the Divisional artillery again drew the Germans, who vigorously shelled the front line and communication trenches of the Division, with light and heavy guns. The light was better and artillery registration was possible. " The enemy was rather unpleasantly active, as he got the usual morning ' strafe ' at 5.45 a.m. to 6 a.m. rather heavier, and a good heavy ' strafe ' from 8–10 a.m. We did very careful registration on to points on the Violet, Green, and Yellow Lines, which the ' show ' has been cut down to, the Blue and Brown lines having been abandoned. Then later it came to registering the front line, which was no easy matter, especially as all the telephone wires were broken. Meanwhile a heavy bombardment was going on, and Serre was practically in flames, 12-inch, 15-inch, 9.2-inch, and 8-inch shells falling in torrents on to it. All the rear communications, O.P's, etc., were being shelled to blazes by the big stuff, and in retaliation the Boche put up two quite good barrages on to the White City and the Redan ridge." [1]

At nightfall on the 12th all units were notified that " zero " hour had been fixed for 5.45 on the following morning, the 13th —news which gave the troops the greatest satisfaction. From the middle of September, when the Division was withdrawn from the Guillemont–Delville Wood sector, the Division had not taken part in any general attack, and all ranks were looking forward to a successful operation. The coming of the Tanks farther south had raised extraordinary enthusiasm amongst the British troops on the Somme, and that enthusiasm had spread north to the left flank of the army. So keen indeed were the troops that, after the Battle of the Ancre had been fought, one battalion Diary stated : " All ranks were extremely cheerful, and success seemed inevitable. Two of the Companies—B and D—went over (the top) playing mouth organs."

During the night of the 12th–13th the troops were moved into their forming-up places ; this operation had to be completed by 4 a.m. The advance was to be made in four waves, following close

[1] Diary of the late Major Victor Walrond, R.F.A.

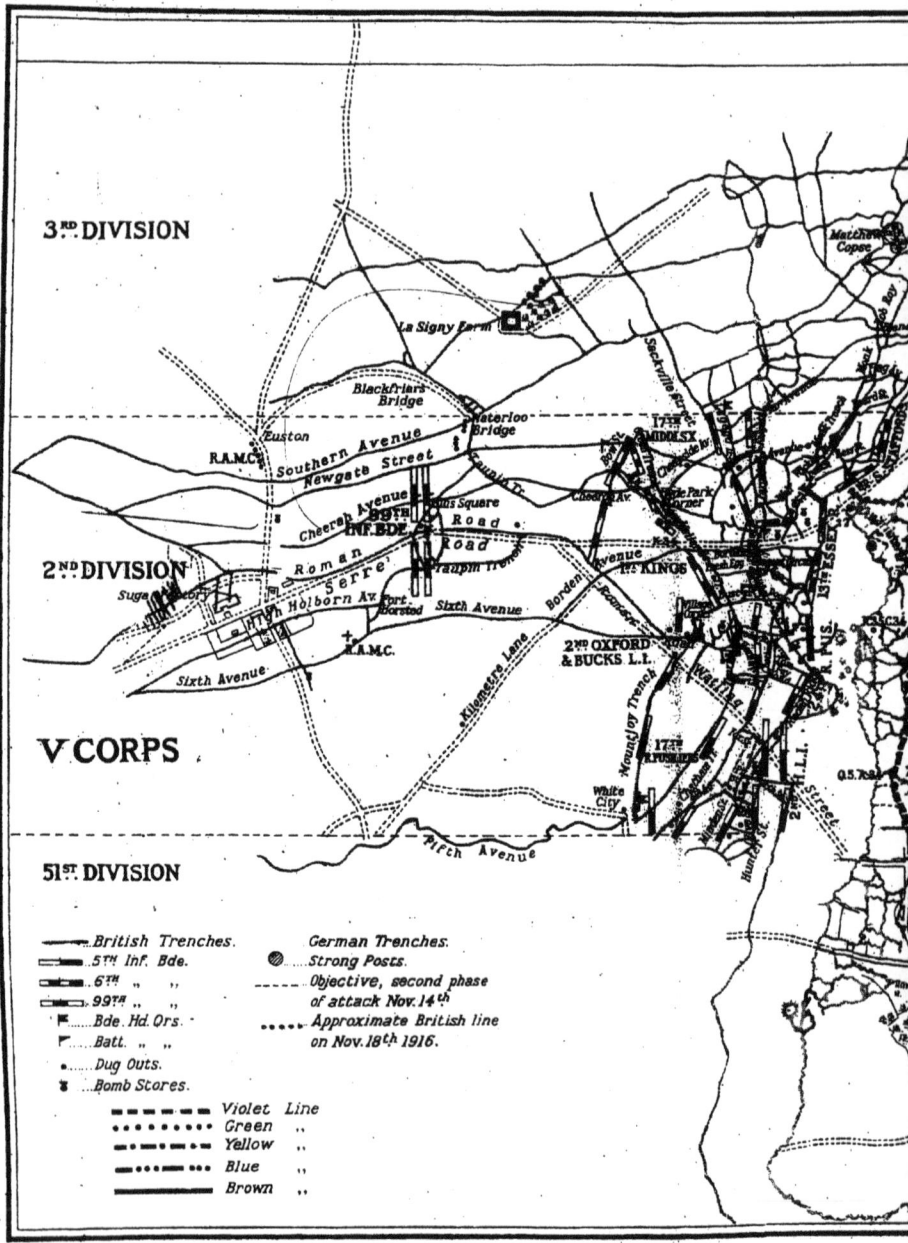

3RD. DIVISION

La Signy Farm

Blackfriars
Bridge

Euston
R.A.M.C.
Southern Avenue
Newgate Street

Waterloo
Bridge

17TH
MIDDLESX

Cheerah Avenue
Road

Hyde Park
Corner

99TH
INF. BDE.

Gun Square
Road

Cheapside Av.

2ND. DIVISION

Roman
Sugar Factory
17TH Holborn Av.
Fort
Borsted

Serre
Traupm Trench

Avenue

1ST KINGS

Sixth Avenue
R.A.M.C.

Sixth Avenue

Kilometre Lane

Borden

2ND OXFORD
& BUCKS L.I.

V CORPS

White
City

Mountjoy Trench

17TH
YORKSHIRE

Hunter St.

Q.S.R.

51ST. DIVISION

Fifth Avenue

Matthew
Copse

Sackville

British Trenches.
5TH Inf. Bde.
6TH „ „
99TH „ „
Bde. Hd. Ors.
Batt. „ „
Dug Outs.
Bomb Stores.

German Trenches.
Strong Posts.
Objective, second phase
of attack Nov. 14th
Approximate British line
on Nov. 18th 1916.

Violet Line
Green „
Yellow „
Blue „
Brown „

THE BATTLE OF THE

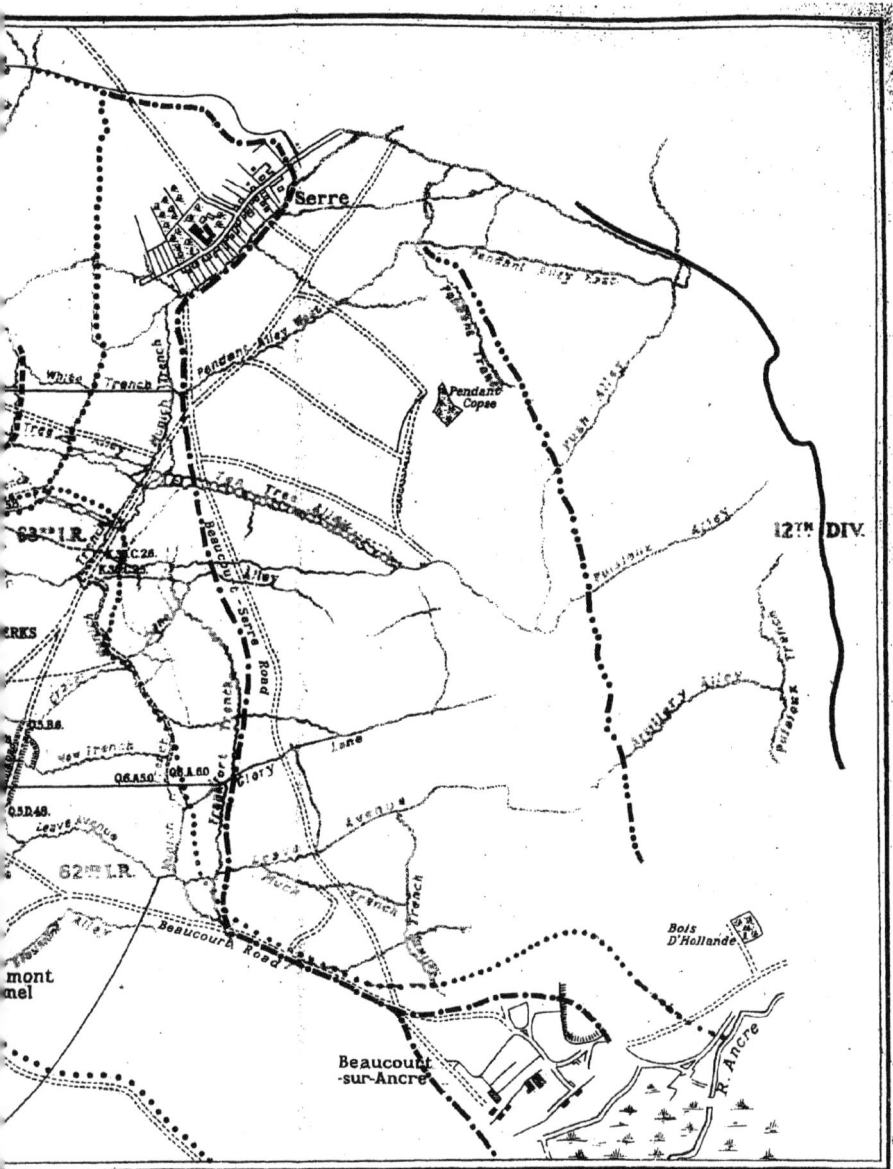

Serre

Pendant Copse

12TH DIV.

White Trench

63RD I.R.

62ND I.R.

Bois D'Hollande

Beaucourt Road

Beaucourt -sur-Ancre

R. Ancre

THE MAPPA CO., LTD., LONDON.

13th–18th November 1916.

(Facing p. 308.)

behind the barrage. On the 2nd Divisional front two battalions of the 5th Infantry Brigade and two battalions of the 6th Infantry Brigade were to take part in the first phase of the attack, the capture of the Green Line ; each battalion going forward in four waves, in column of half-companies in single rank ; the men extended to at least three paces ; a distance of about 100 yards between each wave. The battalions detailed for the first phase were—2nd Highland Light Infantry (right-front battalion) and 24th Royal Fusiliers (left-front battalion) of the 5th Infantry Brigade ; 13th Essex Regiment (right-front battalion) and 2nd South Staffords (left-front battalion) of the 6th Infantry Brigade.

Had the enemy been able to observe what was going on in the Divisional area he would have been considerably surprised, but care had been taken not to disturb his comparative equanimity by any untoward artillery or trench activity ; the increase in the morning strafes of the 11th and 12th had at first aroused him, but as they had not been followed by infantry attacks, he had apparently settled down again to fancied security.

As the night wore on the troops were gradually assembled in their allotted positions. At midnight hot coffee and cocoa and " something to eat " were issued to the men, though not even the discomfort of standing in wet trenches or moving about in seas of mud could damp their enthusiasm. Something in the nature of disappointment had been felt during the evening of the 12th, when it was announced that the Tanks would not take part in the attack.

At 4 a.m., from all parts of the Divisional front, the code word " Smith " began to arrive at Divisional Headquarters : it was the pre-arranged signal that all troops were in position. 13TH Nov. MAP.

The preparations for the Battle of the Ancre had given the Staff many anxious hours of study and hard work. The original orders for the battle (first issued on 22nd October) are contained on twenty closely printed sheets of foolscap paper, and included much which had been acquired in bitter fighting during the early years of the war. These closely printed pages show an extraordinary amount of care and forethought. And when on that November morning the Division stood ready to attack, it seemed as if all that was humanly possible to circumvent the chances of war had been thought out and ordered.

The general dispositions of the Fifth (Reserve) Army—*i.e.*, the XIIIth, Vth, and IInd Corps—have already been given. At " zero " hour on the 13th the battle positions of the 2nd Division were as follows :

6th Infantry Brigade : 2nd South Staffords and 13th Essex Regiment in the front line forming the four waves, each battalion having two half-companies in the first wave, followed by three successive waves of two platoons each from the remaining two companies. Immediately behind the first wave, ready to follow as closely as possible, stood the three " cleaning-up " parties. Each company was accompanied by two Lewis guns to go forward with the " cleaning-up " parties. Other platoons of each battalion were detailed for such work as sapping, police, and pioneer duties, and working parties under the R.E. for the construction of strong points : one platoon from each front-line half-company carrying a Lewis gun detailed to form defensive flanks when the enemy's trenches had been gained. The 17th Middlesex Regiment was behind the South Staffords, and the 1st King's supported the 13th Essex. Of the 6th Brigade Machine-Gun Company four guns were ready to go forward with the 2nd South Staffords and four with the 13th Essex ; the remaining guns were in support and reserve.

5th Infantry Brigade : right-front battalion—2nd Highland Light Infantry ; left-front battalion, 24th Royal Fusiliers ; right support battalion—17th Royal Fusiliers ; left support battalion—2nd Oxford and Bucks Light Infantry. The battalions of the 5th Infantry Brigade were formed up in waves similar to those of the 6th Infantry Brigade.

99th Infantry Brigade : in reserve.

Pioneers : 10th D.C.L.I., some platoons of which occupied positions in Taupin and Mountjoy trenches ; others were attached to the 226th and 1st East Anglian Field Companies R.E.

Engineers : 5th Field Company, assembly trenches opposite Redan ; 226th Field Company, assembly trenches about Fifth Avenue ; 1st East Anglian Field Company, two sections in Green Street and two at Divisional Headquarters.

Each man of the attacking parties carried 150 rounds of small-arms ammunition, 2 Mills bombs, and 2 sandbags ; one iron ration, one day's rations, besides the unexpended portion of his daily ration. His haversack, covered by a piece of red material to facilitate aeroplane observation, was carried on his back. Troops of the 3rd Division used yellow material, and those of the 51st Division a tin disc. About twenty men of each company carried picks and shovels for consolidation purposes.

Between St. Pierre Divion and Serre, the enemy disposed the 95th Infantry Regiment (38th Division), 23rd, 62nd, and 63rd Infantry

Regiments (12th Division), and 169th Infantry Regiment (52nd Division) : each regiment consisted of three battalions.

Patrol reports up to the evening of the 11th had reported No Man's Land in a frightful condition—the mud was inches thick, and made reconnaissance difficult ; the constant shelling to which the enemy's front line had been subjected had ploughed up the ground in and about his trenches, and gaping shell holes and mine craters full of water were everywhere, making the crossing hazardous.

At 5 on the morning of the 13th, in order to deceive the enemy that he was merely about to receive his morning strafe, the siege batteries opened fire as usual. During this bombardment dawn broke gradually. A thick fog hung over the whole battle-field ; No Man's Land and the enemy's trenches were obscured from view ; it was impossible to see more than thirty yards ahead. This condition had, however, been anticipated, and all officers given orders that if, during the assault, the objectives were invisible owing to mist or fog, the advance was to be by compass. " But," as one of the brigadiers afterwards said, " marching by compass bearing as a peace manœuvre is a very different thing to doing so under heavy fire."

Hostile artillery retaliation, in reply to the fire of the siege batteries, was slight. The infantry who were to deliver the first assault were by this time lying out in front of their trenches, having used ladders in " going over."

At 5.45 a.m. all 18-pounders and 4.5-inch howitzers joined in, and put down a heavy barrage on the enemy's front line.

The 5th Infantry Brigade opposite Cat Street blew a mine.

As the first barrage began, the assaulting troops all along the line from the Ancre to just north of Serre moved forward across No Man's Land. The right and centre of the attack was everywhere successful, but on the left of the line, held by the 2nd and 3rd Divisions, the assault met with varying results. The 5th Infantry Brigade took its initial objective almost in the first stride ; the 6th Infantry Brigade was only partially successful ; the 3rd Division failed in its attack. It had been abundantly proved in previous battles, and in particular during the Battle of Delville Wood, that the best results were always obtained when the infantry followed close on the heels of the artillery barrage. Whenever the barrage moved too fast, or the attacking troops were impeded in their advance by adverse ground conditions or uncut wire entanglements, the enemy had time to fix his machine guns, man his trenches, and bring the attack either to a standstill or annul success by the infliction of very heavy casualties.

The attacks of the 5th and 6th Infantry Brigades are more conveniently related separately; for, although the two brigades fought side by side, the conditions prevailing along the front of the 5th Brigade were different from those which practically annulled the gallant efforts of the 6th Brigade.

The artillery barrage, it will be remembered, had been ordered to lift at the rate of 100 yards every five minutes and to halt 150 yards, first beyond the Green and later behind the Yellow Lines. The first shell of the barrage at " zero " hour had scarcely fallen on the enemy's front lines when the assaulting troops of the Division pressed forward to the attack. The South Staffords of the 6th Infantry Brigade, guided by officers marching on compass bearings, went straight towards their objective—though the latter was invisible, the fog being very thick. The going was extremely heavy. In consequence, progress was slow; but the front German line was occupied with very few casualties, most of which were sustained by the left half-company of the Staffords, which in its eagerness to get into the enemy's position, had followed too close upon the heels of the barrage. The front line was reported taken about 6.15 a.m., but twenty minutes later, however, a report reached Battalion Headquarters that " there had been a mix-up with units from our left, of whom a large number had come across our front and then retired."

In the fog they had lost direction, and had marched into the Staffords as the battalion was crossing, and later into the 17th Middlesex (about Fargate), who as the Staffords moved across No Man's Land, had advanced in order to occupy the front-line trenches in the British line. Hopeless confusion now reigned. In the meantime the barrage had gone on ahead with an ever-widening gap between it and the troops of the 6th Infantry Brigade. The wire in front of the German second (the Violet) Line was found practically impassable ; moreover, the ground in front of it had been ploughed up into fine soil, forming a deep sticky mass into which the men sank, in places up to their waists. In vain were gallant efforts made by both officers and men to find a gap in the wire through which they could advance.

Finally a galling machine-gun fire was opened by the enemy, who, when the barrage had passed over his position, came up out of his dug-outs, quickly manned his trenches, and from the direction of Serre poured a storm of bullets on to the wire, which he knew to be uncut and holding up the advance of his adversaries. He also placed a heavy artillery barrage on the British front line, causing many casualties. A gallant subaltern of the Staffords had indeed succeeded in creeping through the wire and bombing down Ten Tree Alley, but had been stopped by further obstacles, and being wounded was obliged to return. The two bombs issued to each man had been expended ; mud clogged the rifles, and made them useless except for bayonet fighting. There was nothing for it but to retire, and the Staffords fell back to the old British front line.

Meanwhile the 13th Essex, whose objective was the Quadrilateral and the German trenches beyond it, had fared very little better. Followed by the 1st King's, the battalion lay out in No Man's Land until the barrage began ; the troops then jumped to their feet and moved across towards the enemy's trenches, close on the barrage. For two hours nothing was heard at Battalion Headquarters of the results of this attack, and Colonel Carter sent out a party of two officers and two men to get what information they could. They reported that the right could be seen nowhere, but that on the left " the men were about the German front line, and that a party of about fifty were lined up behind a small bank a hundred yards in front of our wire and were under very heavy machine-gun and rifle fire, and it was impossible for them to advance." Orders were then given for this party to consolidate the position held.

The right had, however, penetrated the enemy's position. A platoon of C Company, forming the right half of the fourth wave of the 13th Essex, had pressed forward with very little opposition, a few bombs being thrown by the enemy's troops on the left of the platoon. " We pushed forward," said the subaltern in charge of the platoon, " over the second and third German lines, and arrived at the Green Line a few minutes after our own artillery barrage had lifted. I found myself with two Lewis gun teams and sixty men, and the signalling officer ; also one Lewis gun team and a few men of the 1st King's (Liverpool) Regiment, with an officer of the 2nd South Staffords Regiment. On looking round my position I found that the left flank was exposed, owing to the remainder of the waves not reaching their objective. I immediately placed two Lewis guns on this flank, and commenced consolidating the position. A small party of the enemy attempted to bomb us, but were dispersed by Lewis gunfire. I next visited the third line, and found that the junction of Lager Alley (*i.e.*, with the Green Line) was a weak point, so I placed my third Lewis gun and a post at this point."

Thus at midday (apart from the capture of nearly 200 prisoners) the attack of the 6th Infantry Brigade had resulted only in a small lodgment in the Green Line, by the extreme right flank of the brigade, and this flank was in the air! As this position was vulnerable, a trench was immediately begun from the junction of the Green Line with Lager Alley, back to the old British front line, in order to form a defensive flank for the protection of the troops of the 5th Infantry Brigade who had won through to their objective.

During the morning the 6th Infantry Brigade was re-formed into two composite battalions—the 1st King's and the 13th Essex on the right (less those who had successfully advanced to the Green Line), under Lieut.-Colonel Norris, 1st King's and the 2nd South Staffords and 17th Middlesex on the left, under Colonel Fenwick. The right composite battalion numbered about 250 men, and the left, approximately, 300.

The failure of the 6th Infantry Brigade was due to causes outside Staff control. The fog had played havoc with arrangements which must have been successful had the objectives been clearly visible. And although the going was far more heavy on the left than on the right, but for the thickness of the atmosphere, and the consequent mix-up of the 6th and 8th Infantry Brigades, there is but little doubt the Staffords and Essex would have won through to the Green Line.

The 6th Brigade Machine-Gun Company did well in this attack. On the right two guns under Lieut. Birch went forward with the first wave. This officer got separated from his men, as he was slightly wounded. He then went through to the Green Line as an ordinary infantry officer, and with his orderly bombed three dug-outs, which yielded ninety German prisoners. Meanwhile his guns had won through into the first line of the enemy's position, and covered the infantry, who had been ordered to advance. Two more guns on the left succeeded in reaching the enemy's front line, but were then held up. They, however, opened fire on the enemy and considerably reduced his activity.

But during the time that misfortune had fallen upon the 6th Infantry Brigade, the 5th Infantry Brigade had gained all its objectives and had captured large numbers of prisoners. The 24th Royal Fusiliers (left) and the 2nd Highland Light Infantry (right), with the 2nd Oxford and Bucks as left and the 17th Royal Fusiliers as right supports, formed up in No Man's Land about 4 a.m. At "zero" hour, as the barrage became intense, the Fusiliers and Highland Light Infantry moved forward to the attack. Almost immediately the guns lifted to the Violet Line the German front-line trenches were captured, many of the enemy's troops being taken as they came up out of their dug-outs. The "cleaning-up" parties then got to work, bombing and rounding up the Boche in a most efficient manner. The front-line hostile trenches were entered six minutes from "zero" hour. The Battalion Diary of the 24th Royal Fusiliers stated: "The leading troops were within twenty yards of the barrage all along the front allotted to the battalion. A few casualties were caused by our own barrage, but the advantages gained of getting into the enemy's trench immediately the barrage lifted, far outweigh the loss occasioned. On the barrage lifting the line advanced at a walk into the enemy's front-line trench, where the Germans were found to be emerging from their dug-outs. These men all surrendered. The enemy's wire was found completely demolished, and proved no obstacle. The advance proceeded in accordance with orders, until the Green Line was taken."

The Battalion Diary of the 2nd Highland Light Infantry is even more brief: "The battalion assaulted and captured the enemy's front system of trenches just north of Beaumont Hamel. All objectives were reached and consolidated; 207 unwounded prisoners were captured and sent down. . . . Five machine guns, two trench mortars (one 15-inch) and much war material captured."

As the 24th Royal Fusiliers went forward, their front-line trench was occupied by the 2nd Oxford and Bucks; whilst the 17th Royal Fusiliers moved forward into the trenches vacated by the 2nd Highland Light Infantry. Both support battalions then advanced with the object of going through the Green Line to the final objective, the Yellow Line.

From the meagre reports contained in the Divisional Brigade and Battalion Diaries all that can be gathered is that at 6.15 a.m. A and B Companies of the 24th Royal Fusiliers, with a considerable number of men of the 2nd Oxford and Bucks, held the line from Crater Lane to a point about seventy yards south of Lager Alley; there was then a gap between Lager Alley and the strong point at K.35, C.95, held by men of the Essex Regiment (6th Infantry Brigade) with a Lewis gun. On the right of the 24th Royal Fusiliers, the Green Line appears to have been held also jointly by the 2nd Highland Light Infantry and men of the 17th Royal Fusiliers. The first four lines of hostile trenches were already being "cleaned up," and the 24th Royal Fusiliers had established a strong point at the junction of Serre Trench and Crater Lane; a block in the old Ger-

man front line just south of point K.35, C.24, was also placed by
the Fusiliers in order to protect the left flank of the 5th Infantry
Brigade, which, owing to the failure of the 6th Brigade, was open
to attack from the north. For a number of the enemy still held
out in a strong post in the Quadrilateral, opposite the Cat, and they
were not forced out of this position for forty-eight hours after the
attack began. Bombing attacks were made by the Fusiliers
against these gallant Germans, but without success.

The Divisional Pioneers—the 10th D.C.L.I.—and the 226th
Field Company R.E., worked hard at constructing strong points,
and to their devotion was due in no small measure the safety of
the left flank of the 5th Infantry Brigade.

At 7.15 a.m. the Highland Light Infantry reported : " All
appears to be going well."

At 7.40 a.m. a platoon of the 10th D.C.L.I. went over the top
to begin work on the Cat Tunnel, with the object of connecting it
with the old German front line ; but the work was much hampered by machine-gun fire from the Quadrilateral and did not
progress well.

The fog still interfered with the operations. The Oxford and
Bucks, with men of the 17th Royal Fusiliers, had advanced towards
the Yellow Line. But on leaving the Green Line " the leading
waves appear to have lost direction and to have wheeled northwards in the mist, into a communication trench known as Lager
Alley, running east to west between the Green and Yellow Lines,
and so parallel to the real and correct line of advance. This
mistake was discovered, and the Yellow Line was penetrated by
elements of all companies who had by now become thoroughly
mixed up." [1] Some men of the 17th Royal Fusiliers (on the right
of the Oxford and Bucks) had also penetrated as far as the Yellow
Line, but failing to get touch on either flank, had withdrawn.
Considerable fighting, however, took place in Munich Trench and
Lager Alley, and some forward parties of the Oxford and Bucks
were at one time all but surrounded by the enemy, but with the
aid of Lewis guns and bombs effected a safe retirement to Wagon
Road and the Green Line.

The bombers did fine work. One man was seen to throw
twenty-one bombs in succession down the steps of a German
" regimental command post " in Munich Trench.

By 9.30 a.m. the 5th Infantry Brigade had passed 420 prisoners
back to the cages.

[1] Diary, 2nd Oxford and Bucks Light Infantry.

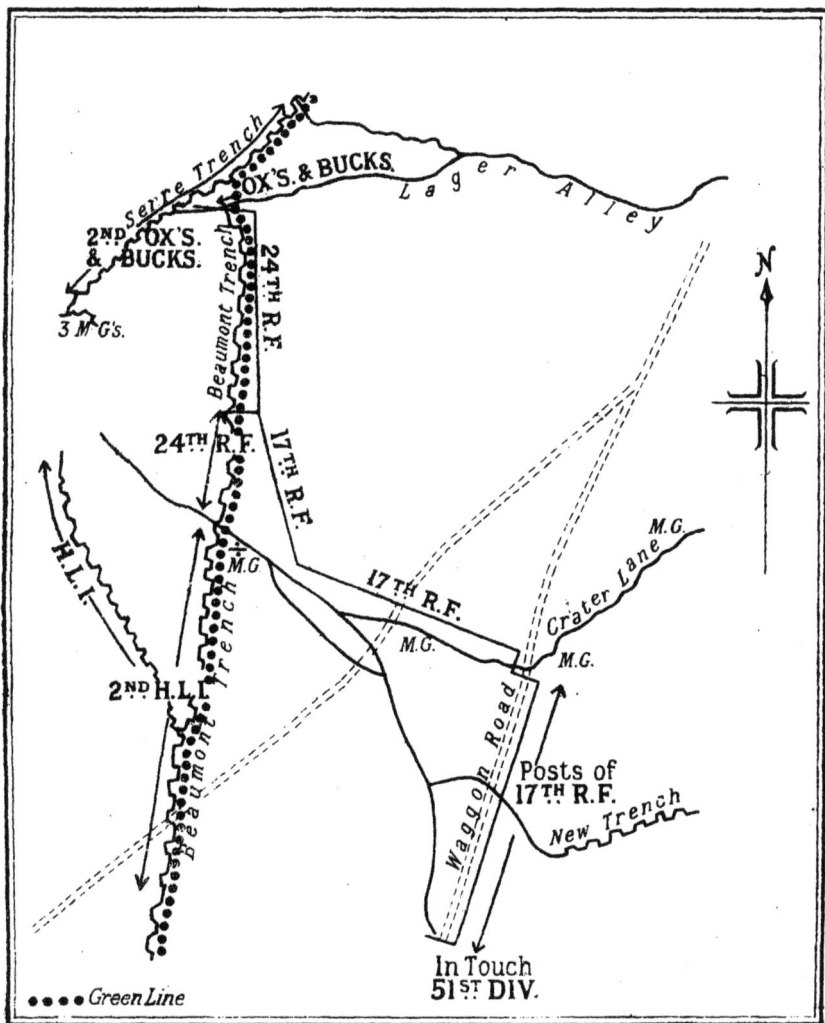

THE BATTLE OF THE ANCRE.

Position of 5th Infantry Brigade, 10.25 a.m., 13th November.

(*Facing p. 316.*)

At 10.25 a.m. all four companies of the 17th Royal Fusiliers were situated between Q.5, B.26, and Q.5, B.50.

During the advance casualties had been light, for the enemy was unprepared for the attack. As the attack progressed, however, artillery fire became intense, and with machine-gun fire, snipers, and bombing parties, the enemy was able to inflict heavy losses on the devoted troops of the 5th Infantry Brigade. At 11 a.m. the Highland Light Infantry asked for 12 officers and 4 company sergeant-majors, the casualties of the battalion then being 50 per cent. of other ranks and 15 officers out of 20.

Despite heavy losses, the troops everywhere held their positions with splendid tenacity. Just after noon an orderly who brought information to Brigade Headquarters giving the position of the 24th Royal Fusiliers and Highland Light Infantry, brought also this message : " A cheerful spirit prevails in the Green Line." And there was good reason for it. For south of the 2nd Division, the 51st and 63rd Divisions and the IInd Corps had made splendid progress. The 51st Division had won through to the Green Line and had captured Beaumont Hamel, taking over 500 prisoners ; the 63rd (Naval) Division was well on the way to Beaucourt-sur-Ancre, having taken large numbers of Germans ; the IInd Corps had captured St. Pierre Divion and had established touch with the Vth Corps (63rd Division) at the mill on the Ancre. But north of the 2nd Division the XIIIth Corps, which, after gallant fighting, had won ground almost to the enemy's third line, had, owing to the failure of the 3rd Division and the left of the 2nd Division, to abandon it.

During the first phase of the attack by the 5th and 6th Infantry Brigades the 99th Infantry Brigade was held in reserve. The brigade left Bertrancourt just after midnight the 12th–13th and marched to Ellis Square. A little later, the 22nd Royal Fusiliers moved up into Sixth Avenue, the 1st Royal Berks to Borden Avenue, the 1st King's Royal Rifles to Cheeroh Avenue, and the 23rd Fusiliers to Fort Hoystead and View Trench, two companies remaining in Ellis Square. One section of the 99th Machine-Gun Company was attached to each battalion.

The General Officer Commanding 99th Infantry Brigade during the morning received an order to place two companies at the disposal of the 5th Infantry Brigade to reinforce the Green Line. A and C Companies of the 23rd Royal Fusiliers were detailed. A little later the two remaining companies of the Fusiliers were also placed under the orders of the General Officer Commanding 5th

Infantry Brigade; these latter companies were held in reserve in the "Old British" line.

A further attack by the 3rd Division proved abortive.

Early in the afternoon the General Officer Commanding 99th Infantry Brigade was ordered to move one battalion to form a defensive flank facing north with its right on Serre Trench, gaining touch at the strong point held by the Essex Regiment, and its left on the Quadrilateral; the 22nd Royal Fusiliers were detailed, and one section of the 99th Machine-Gun Company. Finally, the brigade received orders to continue the attack on the Yellow Line:

" To attack and capture Munich Trench from south of 2nd Divisional area to Lager Alley (inclusive) at 6 a.m. on the 14th, with my two remaining battalions supported by the 23rd Royal Fusiliers, who would be returned to my command in time to take part in the attack. At the time of receipt of the latter order the two battalions remaining under my command were the 1st Royal Berks, situated in the Vallade Line, with their right on Buster Trench, 1st King's Royal Rifles in Taupin and Ellis Square (north of Roman Road). 23rd Royal Fusiliers (less two companies) were in View Trench and Ellis Square (south of Roman Road), but were ordered to Clive and Merindin Trench by the General Officer Commanding 5th Infantry Brigade, and were detailed by him for carrying duty from the Brigade Dump to front line, during the night 13th–14th November."

14TH NOV. At 4.30 a.m. C, B, and D Companies of the 22nd Royal Fusiliers, under Major Phythian-Adams (C Company leading), moved across No Man's Land to form the defensive flank which was to cover the still somewhat exposed left of the 5th Infantry Brigade. On arrival in the old German front line, Second-Lieut. Gell, commanding C Company, was shot in the knee, and the command devolved upon Second-Lieut. Kelly, who moved his troops up to the left flank of the strong point held by the Essex Regiment, and from there sent out a patrol and finally established his right close up to the Essex Regiment with his left towards the Quadrilateral. B Company was sent up to continue the line, but owing to the mist and difficult nature of the ground, which was extremely boggy, lost its way, and finally returned and reported to Major Adams. D Company, followed now by A Company, then set out, and in the early hours of the 14th eventually succeeded in prolonging the line of defence through the southern portion of the Quadrilateral to the "Old British" line. A strong post was then formed in the southern portion of the Quadrilateral. The whole

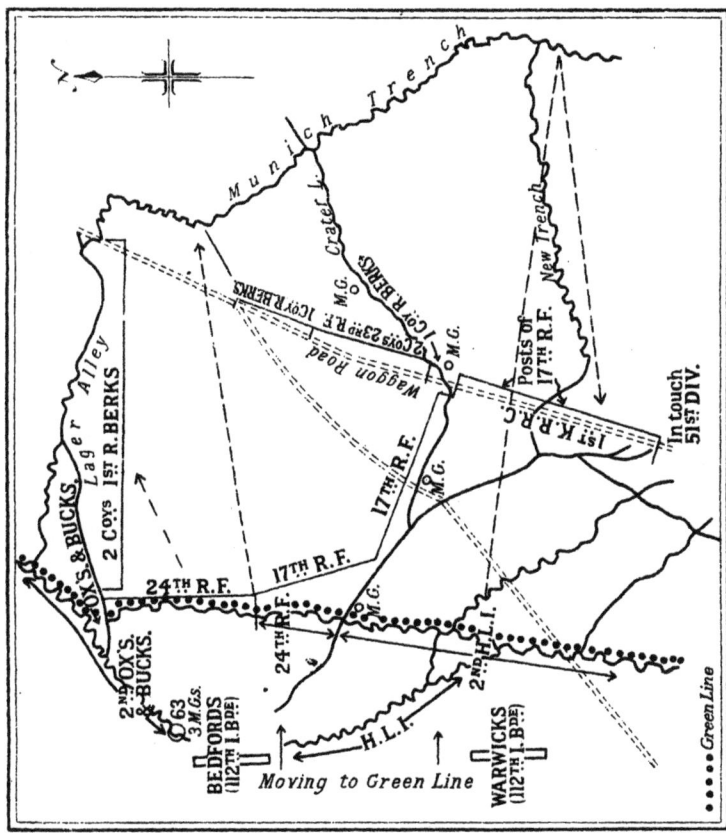

THE BATTLE OF THE ANCRE.

Position at 5 a.m., 14th November.

(Facing p. 318.)

defensive flank (with B Company in support) was finally established by 9 a.m. on the 14th. Throughout the day this position was held under exceptionally heavy shell-fire.

The latter part of the operation—*i.e.*, the formation of the defensive flank—had taken place simultaneously with the attack of the 99th Infantry Brigade on the Yellow Line.

The dispositions for this attack were as follows :

The 1st King's Royal Rifles on the right from Rump Trench to Crater Lane (inclusive) ; 1st Royal Berks on the left from Crater Lane (exclusive) to Lager Alley (inclusive). The 23rd Fusiliers disposed two companies in the rear of the outer flanks of each of the leading battalions.

The attack by the leading battalions was to be made in four waves—the troops forming up in Beaumont Trench (Green Line) at 5 a.m.—one hour before " zero." The 99th Machine-Gun Company had two guns with each of the leading battalions and two with each half-battalion of the 23rd Royal Fusiliers.

As on the 13th, the early hours of the 14th were shrouded in a dense fog, which enveloped the ground and added to the intense difficulties already experienced by the troops in reaching the " forming-up positions " in the Green Line. Deep mud, shell-holes mostly full of water, tangled wire, blown-in German trenches waist-deep in holding mud, all tended to loss of direction and touch. The result was something near chaos. The 1st King's Royal Rifles and the 1st Royal Berks, moving off from their positions in the "Old British " lines five hours and four and a half hours respectively before " zero," were soon in difficulties. Portions of both battalions completely lost their way, and of the Rifles only one company arrived at the Green Line four minutes before " zero " hour : it was then too late to point out on the ground the actual line of advance. As distant objects on the line of advance could not be distinguished compasses were of little value. The diaries also report that the compasses were affected by the steel helmets, rifles, etc., and made unreliable.

During these difficulties the Rifles moved off, first in a south-easterly direction and then north-east. At about 6.30 a.m. two simultaneous attacks were made, one on Leave Avenue and the other on New Trench.

Leave Avenue was attacked from the south by 4 officers and 80 N.C.O's and men, who captured it and began to consolidate the position under the impression that it was Munich Trench. Bombing points were established on the eastern and western flanks, the former about eighty yards short of the junction of Leave Avenue with Munich Trench. It was then discovered (how is not stated) that a mistake had been made. A bombing attack was then organized on Munich Trench, which failed owing to the Divisional Artillery barrage being still on the trench, and especially severe at the junction of Leave Avenue with Munich Trench ; the party was also heavily sniped from the latter trench. Under these conditions, and owing to the impossibility of obtaining touch with troops north or south, the Rifles withdrew to Wagon Road, reaching the latter at 1.30 p.m. The attack had not been quite unsuccessful, for 2 officers and 60 prisoners were brought back.

The attack on New Trench was made apparently by two independent parties. One party got within thirty yards of the junction of New Trench with Munich Trench. The other party having discovered also that it was not Munich Trench, organized an attack on the latter, and 40 men were lined out in shell-holes south of New Trench at about 150 yards from, and facing, Munich Trench. But upon this point also the Divisional Artillery barrage still continued to fall, and finally the attack was abandoned and preparations made to dig in. Soon after the mist lifted, and it was then found that the party were in an impossible position, being in direct enfilade fire from the enemy's trenches and out of touch with troops on either flank. A withdrawal down New Trench was then made between 9 and 9.30 a.m. Simultaneously the other party in New Trench was withdrawn, both parties eventually reaching a position west of Wagon Road, where, after consultation with the Officer Commanding 17th Royal Fusiliers, a position was taken up in Wagon Road. To this position the first party which had retired from Leave Avenue was also joined about 1.30 p.m.

The battalion then proceeded to consolidate the position which ran from Q.5, D.48 to Q.5, B.65.

During the attack by the Rifles the Hon. F. S. Trench was badly wounded in the chest and arm by a shell, and died of wounds a day or two later. Second-Lieuts. T. U. Royden and R. F. Lowndes were hit whilst gallantly standing up to direct the fire of their men. Lieut. J. H. T. Liddell was also badly wounded in the arms and legs. The Rifles lost 2 officers killed, 3 wounded, and 17 other ranks killed, 109 wounded, and 13 missing.

In the meantime the 1st Royal Berks, who owing to the front to be covered had formed up in two waves instead of in four, had moved off at " zero " close (too close) on the barrage. The two right companies reported the barrage falling short, of which there does not seem to be much doubt, the two companies losing 116 men out of 159. The survivors then closed in towards the right to keep touch with their directing flank. In this movement, however, their numbers were still further depleted owing to some 10 or 15 men on the left flank bearing off towards the left in touch with the two left companies of the battalion, who were gradually working north forming strong points as they progressed.

On arriving in front of Munich Trench, therefore, the leading wave of the two right companies numbered only from 10 to 15 men, but these, nothing daunted, forced their way through the enemy's wire, which in parts was still uncut, and, led by Second-Lieuts. E. D. D'O. Astley and G. C. Stoneham, jumped into the trench. The latter officer and some of his men were shot dead almost immediately, but Lieut. Astley and his few gallant comrades pressing on, captured a number of Germans who were standing on the steps of their dug-outs. These men as they saw the British troops threw up their hands and surrendered. Leaving two men to guard the prisoners, Lieut. Astley then proceeded south along the trench in search of his comrades, but finding none returned to his own troops. By this time, however, the Divisional barrage had lifted off the trench, and the enemy's troops rushing up out of their dug-outs began to bomb and snipe Lieut. Astley and his men, who on retiring formed up some twenty or thirty yards in the rear of the trench with the idea of again going forward. At this period two more German officers and about 50 other ranks came out of Munich Trench, and crying out " Kamarade," and holding their hands above their heads, surrendered to the Berkshires. The enemy then lined his trenches in considerable numbers, and under cover of a heavy frontal and flanking fire began moving down Crater Lane. The survivors of the two right companies of Berks then worked their way back, and getting into Crater Lane east of its junction with Wagon Road formed a block. The right company had lost all its officers killed, and the right-centre company lost three out of four wounded.

The two left companies moved forward with their left flank on Lager Alley, which they found practically obliterated and untenable ; they then pushed forward and ultimately established themselves in Serre Trench from K.35, C.95 to K.35, D.39. This trench was much battered by shell fire, but had still some good dug-outs, in one of which 1 officer and 11 other ranks of the 1st King's, all wounded, were recaptured. They had been well treated by the enemy, of whom 1 medical officer and 35 other ranks were also captured. A trench mortar and a machine gun were also taken.

The capture of this small section of trench was very valuable, for it ran over the crest of a ridge and thus safeguarded the line farther south, besides giving a view down Ten Tree Alley.

The total loss of the battalion in this attack was 211 men out of 435. Two Lewis guns were also smashed by shell-fire and one damaged. Throughout the attack the 1st King's Royal Rifles and the 1st Royal Berks were well supported by the 23rd Royal Fusiliers.

The 99th Machine-Gun Company was specially mentioned as lending valuable assistance, not only to the Berkshires and Rifles, but to the 22nd Royal Fusiliers, who during the attack on Munich Trench were engaged in forming the defensive flank northwards from K.35, D.58, westwards through the southern portion of the Quadrilateral to the " Old British " line. In spite of heavy losses—one section alone lost 14 men out of 26—the company is mentioned for its " bravery, cheerfulness, and energy," and " the *moral* of the machine gunners was excellent."

South of the 2nd Division, the 51st and 63rd Divisions and the IInd Corps had made further progress, and more prisoners and much war material had been captured ; on the front of the XIIIth Corps, north of the 2nd Division, there was no change.

During the afternoon the 6th Bedfords and the 11th Warwicks of the 112th Infantry Brigade, which had been placed at the disposal of the General Officer Commanding 2nd Division early on the 14th, made an attack through the 99th Infantry Brigade (between the southern Divisional area and Lager Alley) on Frankfort Trench. The attack of the two battalions was unsuccessful. These troops had little time to reconnoitre the ground, and though the attack was carried out very gallantly against Munich and Frankfort trenches, it failed. The two remaining battalions of the 112th Infantry Brigade moved up from Mailly during the night 14th–15th, into the 2nd Divisional area.

The 2nd Division on the night of the 14th November was disposed as follows :

> Right Section: three battalions of the 99th Infantry Brigade and two battalions 112th Infantry Brigade, from south Divisional boundary to Serre Trench, all under the command of the General Officer Commanding 99th Infantry Brigade.

> Left Section: one battalion 9th Infantry Brigade (3rd Division), one battalion 99th Infantry Brigade, with four battalions 6th Infantry Brigade in " Old British " lines, all under

the command of General Officer Commanding 6th Infantry
Brigade.

In support : the 5th Infantry Brigade, in and in the rear of
the Green Line.

All through the night the R.A.M.C. made strenuous efforts
to cope with the large number of wounded. In this they were
assisted by carrying parties of infantry. In one Aid Post at Q.5,
A.34, over 100 cases were awaiting evacuation. The terrible condition of the trenches made the carrying of wounded extremely
difficult. A hundred trench boards were laid through the old
German front line to the " Old British " line in order to facilitate
evacuation. Detachments from the T.M.B's and 40 gunners were
drafted into the lines, and before dawn had carried over 200 badly
wounded men back to the clearing station.

The medical officers of the 1st King's and 22nd Royal Fusiliers
(Lieut. J. B. Stevenson, R.A.M.C., and Captain W. A. Miller, D.S.O.,
M.C., respectively) were both wounded, and 24 other ranks of the
R.A.M.C. were killed and wounded.

At 3.15 on the morning of the 15th the Cat Tunnel was re- 15TH Nov
ported cut through, and forty more prisoners were captured. But
north, in the Quadrilateral, a pocket of the enemy still held out
and defied capture. An attack on this last stronghold in the old
German front line was ordered, and took place early in the morning.
For the first time Tanks were brought up to assist in the capture
of the Quadrilateral—two being sent up to the Division for this
purpose. But unfortunately they were soon bogged in the deep
mud and never reached their objective. The attack was then
carried out by the 22nd Royal Fusiliers, with bombing parties
from A, B, and D Companies. " The party drawn from B
Company, which worked up the German front line in the Quadrilateral, met with little resistance and made good progress, supported
by mixed elements of the 6th Infantry Brigade. The other two
parties, drawn from A and D Companies, whose objective was
to form strong points on the far side north of the Quadrilateral,
succeeded, after great trouble from deep mud, in establishing a
strong point on the crest of the ridge which commanded the remainder of the Quadrilateral ; so that by 12 noon a good half of the position was actually in our hands and our position commanded all
the remaining ground, which was covered by Vickers and Lewis
guns. These positions were then consolidated under extremely
heavy hostile shelling, which was sustained for many hours, only
abating about 8 p.m. ; and although in one instance the whole

of a post of C Company was obliterated by shell fire, the remaining men never lost their steadiness for one minute under the most trying conditions."

The enemy evacuated the Quadrilateral soon after the establishment of the strong points, as the position (from his point of view) was no longer tenable.

Although the Germans fought well, there are no records in the Official Diaries of enemy counter-attacks on the 2nd Divisional front during the Battle of the Ancre. Only one or two half-hearted attempts were made to recover his lost trenches; but these did not materialize, owing to the dispersal of his troops by the Divisional Artillery, which all through the battle lent splendid support to the infantry. The fine work of the gunners was acknowledged in a letter issued by the C.R.A., 2nd Division, on 16th November, at the close of the battle : " I would like to thank all ranks 2nd Divisional Artillery for their work under the very trying conditions of the past month. The batteries have been at it continually night and day, and by their hard work have accomplished the very difficult task of cutting the wire . . . all ranks of wagon lines and D.A.C. have played up splendidly. They have been living in extreme discomfort and working very long hours, generally at night and in the rain, and the work had been done with a cheerfulness and energy beyond praise. The trench-mortar batteries, under great difficulties and suffering heavy casualties, pegged away unflinchingly at their task, and when the advance gave them a well-earned rest, they all volunteered as stretcher-bearers and have done good work carrying the wounded."

At 11.15 a.m. on 15th November, 2nd Division Order No. 168 was issued—the Division (less artillery) was to be relieved by the 32nd Division.

The relief took place during 16th and 17th November, and the 2nd Division went out of the line for rest and training.

The Division's losses from 13th to 16th November (inclusive) were, in killed, wounded, and missing—officers 129,[1] other ranks 2,767. The Division captured 11 officers and approximately 1,000 other ranks, during the five days' fighting.

On 19th, 21st, 23rd, 24th, 25th, and 27th November the 2nd Division was located successively in the Doullens, Bernaville, Yvrench, Braille, Le Titre, and Brailly areas; in the latter the Division settled down to training, refitting, and resting. On the 30th the 10th D.C.L.I. and the three Field Companies R.E. marched

[1] See Appendix XVII.

to join the 11th Division for temporary duty in the line. On this date also the 2nd Divisional Artillery was still in line with the 32nd Division.

The sanguinary struggle which raged from 1st July to the middle of November 1916 was but the prelude to further and bloodier contests, in which the number of troops and guns employed on both sides increased beyond the wildest dreams of pre-war strategists—heedless of the terrible cost in lives of men and material. In his dispatches, dated 23rd December 1916, Sir Douglas Haig gives the results of the Somme battles of 1916 (" The Opening of the Wearing-out Battle ") : " The three main objects of our offensive in July," he said, "had already been achieved at the date when this account closes ; in spite of the fact that the heavy autumn rains had prevented full advantage being taken of the favourable situation created by our advance, at a time when we had good grounds for hoping to achieve yet more important successes.   Verdun had been relieved ; the main German forces had been held on the Western front ; and the enemy's strength had already been very considerably worn down.   Any one of these results is in itself sufficient to justify the Somme battles."   How very greatly the Allies' cause was assisted by the gallant French at Verdun has passed into history, for had Verdun fallen anything might have happened in the Western theatre of the war.

The number of prisoners captured on the Somme from 1st July to 18th November was 38,000, including over 800 officers.   Twenty-nine heavy guns, 96 field guns and field howitzers, 136 trench mortars, and 514 machine guns were amongst the material also taken from the enemy.   Casualties on both sides were enormous, for the courage of the enemy, before his *moral* in the later stages of the battle had been almost broken, equalled that of the British soldier.   The Germans had, however, been outfought !

" Among all the roll of victories borne on the colours of our regiments there has never been a higher test of the endurance and resolution of our infantry.   They have shown themselves worthy of the highest traditions of our race and of the proud records of former wars." [1]

During the months of strenuous warfare on the Somme, the British army in other parts of the field had been occupied in operations of a secondary nature, though the latter were neither light nor unimportant.   Raids on the enemy for the purpose of keeping him constantly on the alert were made up and down the line from

[1] Official Dispatches.

north of the Somme to Ypres, over 360 of these attacks being made on the enemy's line during these four and a half months.

On 1st December the 2nd Division Artillery came out of the line and marched to Maizicourt, where from the 4th to the 31st the gunners found relaxation in resting, training, Staff rides, and divisional sports.

* * * * * * *

Another Howitzer Battery (the 521st, commanded by Captain Reicke, R.F.A.) joined the 2nd Division on 14th November ; the battery was posted to the XXXIVth Brigade R.F.A. and renamed D/34th Howitzer Battery.

The 2nd Divisional Artillery was formed as follows :

> XXXIVth Brigade R.F.A. : 50th and 70th Field Batteries ; 56th and D/34th Howitzer Batteries.
>
> XXXVIth Brigade R.F.A. : 15th, 48th, and 71st Field Batteries and D/36th Howitzer Battery.
>
> XLIst Brigade R.F.A. : 9th, 16th, and 17th Field Batteries and 47th Howitzer Battery.
>
> V/2, X/2, Y/2, and Z/2 : Trench-Mortar Batteries.

Throughout the month of December 1916 the Divisional Diaries have little to record excepting the training and general routine work, relieved by sports and entertainments whenever possible. The Divisional, Lewis Gun, Bombing, and Gas Schools were busily engaged in the training of officers and men for the next offensive. Captain W. J. Jervois assumed the duties of G.S.O.3 on 26th December, *vice* Captain G. M. Gathorne Hardy, M.C.

On 27th December Major-General C. E. Pereira, C.B., C.M.G., assumed command of the 2nd Division, *vice* Major-General W. G. Walker, V.C., C.B.

APPENDICES.

Appendix I.

ORDER OF BATTLE OF THE SECOND DIVISION AT THE BATTLE OF MONS, 1914.

General Officer Commanding: Major-General C. C. Monro, C.B.

A.D.C. : Captain Viscount Gort, M.V.O.
„ Captain W. E. Rothwell.
G.S.O. : 1. Colonel Hon. F. Gordon, D.S.O.
„ 2. Major (Temp. Lieut.-Colonel) A. J. B. Percival, D.S.O.
„ 3. Captain L. A. E. Price-Davies, V.C., D.S.O.
A.A. and Q.M.G. : Lieut.-Colonel G. Conway-Gordon, D.S.O., A.S.C.
D.A.A. and Q.M.G. : Lieut.-Colonel W. A. White.
D.A.Q.M.G. : Major J. E. S. Brind.
C.R.A. : Brigadier-General E. M. Perceval, D.S.O., R.A.
C.R.E. : Lieut.-Colonel R. H. H. Boys, D.S.O., R.E.
A.D.M.S. : Colonel H. Thompson, R.A.M.C.
D.A.D.M.S. : Major F. S. Irvine, R.A.M.C.
A.D.V.S. : Major F. C. Stratton.
D.A.D.O.S. : Major J. Baker.
A.P.M. : Captain G. A. Sullivan.

4th (Guards) Infantry Brigade.

Brigade Commander : Brigadier-General R. Scott-Kerr, M.V.O., D.S.O.
Brigade Major : Major Hon. W. M. Hore-Ruthven, D.S.O.
2nd Batt. Grenadier Guards : Lieut.-Colonel N. A. L. Corry, D.S.O.
2nd Batt. Coldstream Guards : Lieut.-Colonel C. E. Pereira.
3rd Batt. Coldstream Guards : Lieut.-Colonel G. Feilding, D.S.O.
1st Batt. Irish Guards : Lieut.-Colonel Hon. G. H. Morris.

5th Infantry Brigade.

Brigade Commander : Brigadier-General R. C. B. Haking, C.B.
Brigade Major : Captain D. S. Gilkison.
2nd Worcester Regiment : Lieut.-Colonel C. B. Westmacott.
2nd Oxford and Bucks Light Infantry : Lieut.-Colonel H. R. Davies.
2nd Highland Light Infantry : Lieut.-Colonel A. A. Wolfe-Murray.
2nd Connaught Rangers : Lieut.-Colonel A. W. Abercrombie.

6th Infantry Brigade.

Brigade Commander : Brigadier-General R. H. Davies, C.B.
Brigade-Major : Captain W. J. Maxwell Scott, S.R.
1st King's (Liverpool) Regiment : Lieut.-Colonel W. S. Bannatyne.
2nd South Staffords : Lieut.-Colonel C. S. Davidson.
1st Royal Berks : Lieut.-Colonel M. D. Graham.
1st King's Royal Rifles : Lieut.-Colonel E. Northey.

Divisional Mounted Troops.

B Squadron, 15th Hussars : Captain Hon. W. Nugent.
Divisional Cyclists : 2nd Cyclist Company : Captain Hall.

Royal Artillery.

C.R.A. : Brigadier-General E. M. Perceval, D.S.O.
Brigade Major : Captain F. M. Chenevix-Trench.
G.S.O. : Captain J. L. Mowbray.
A.D.C. : Lieutenant H. M. M. Robertson.
XXXIVth Brigade Royal Field Artillery : Lieut.-Colonel H. G Sandilands.
    22nd Battery R.F.A. : Major H. T. Wynter.
    50th Battery R.F.A. : Major T. O. Seagram.
    70th Battery R.F.A. : Major H. C. Stanley Clarke.
    XXXIVth Brigade Ammunition Column : Captain D. Stewart.
XXXVIth Brigade R.F.A. : Lieut.-Colonel E. F. Hall.
    15th Battery R.F.A. : Major C. C. Barnes.
    48th Battery R.F.A. : Major (Lieut.-Colonel) C. S. Stewart, D.S.O.
    71st Battery R.F.A. : Major C. W. Scott.
    XXXVIth Brigade Ammunition Column : Captain R. H. Haining.
XLIst Brigade R.F.A. : Lieut.-Colonel S. Lushington, C.M.G.
    9th Battery R.F.A. : Major R. D. Wylde.
    16th Battery R.F.A. : Major H. F. E. Lewin.
    17th Battery R.F.A. : Major H. H. Bond.
    XLIst Brigade Ammunition Column : Captain G. St. L. Thornton.
XLIVth (Howitzer) Brigade R.F.A. : Lieut.-Colonel D. Arbuthnot.
    47th Battery R.F.A. : Major H. W. Newcome.
    56th Battery R.F.A. : Major F. E. L. Barker.
    60th Battery R.F.A. : Major H. J. A. Mackey, M.V.O.
    XLIVth Brigade Ammunition Column : Captain G. R. Miller.
35th (Heavy) Battery R.G.A. : Major A. C. Wilkinson.
2nd Division Ammunition Column : Lieut.-Colonel T. F. Ravenhill, R.F.A.
No. 1 Section : Major A. S. Cotton.
No. 2 Section : Captain J. C. E. Jameson.
No. 3 Section : Captain H. B. Dresser.
No. 4 (Howitzer) Section : Captain E. W. Cushen.
No. 4 (Heavy) Section : Second-Lieut. C. H. N. Young.
2nd Division Ammunition Park : Captain A. Corbett Smith, R.F.A., S.R.

Royal Engineers.

C.R.E. : Lieut.-Colonel R. H. H. Boys, D.S.O., R.E.
Adjutant : Captain A. J. Darlington.
5th Field Company : Major Garwood.
11th Field Company : Captain Skipwith.

Signal Service.

2nd Signal Company : Captain R. W. Powell, R.G.A.

Army Service Corps.

2nd Division Train : Lieut.-Colonel E. F. Taylor, A.S.C.

Medical Units.

4th Field Ambulance : Major P. H. Collingwood, R.A.M.C.
5th Field Ambulance : Lieut.-Colonel R. J. Copeland, R.A.M.C.
6th Field Ambulance : Major T. J. Potter, R.A.M.C.
2nd Division Veterinary Section : Major F. C. Stratton.

Appendix II.

Casualties from 23rd to 29th August 1914.

Divisional Headquarters : Colonel H. Thompson, A.D.M.S. ; Major F. S. Irvine, D.A.D.M.S. (missing).

Royal Artillery.—XXXIVth Brigade : other ranks, 3 killed, 19 wounded. XLIst Brigade : 1 officer (Lieut. B. D. Rose) killed ; other ranks, 2 killed, 10 wounded. XLIVth (Howitzer) Brigade : other ranks, 1 killed, 1 wounded, 1 missing.

Divisional Mounted Troops : 1 officer (Lieut. J. N. Taylor) killed ; other ranks, 1 killed, 1 wounded, 7 missing.

Divisional Cyclist Company : 2 officers wounded ; other ranks, 1 killed, 7 wounded, 3 missing.

R.E. 11th Field Company : other ranks, 4 wounded, 1 missing.

2nd Signal Company : other ranks, 1 missing.

5th Infantry Brigade.—2nd Connaught Rangers : 1 officer (Captain F. W. M. Leader) killed, 5 officers (including Lieut.-Colonel A. W. Abercrombie [died prisoner of war, November 5, 1915]) missing ; other ranks, 284 missing.

6th Infantry Brigade.—1st King's (Liverpool) : other ranks, 4 wounded, 56 missing, 2 died. 2nd South Staffords : other ranks, 17 missing. 1st Royal Berks : 1 officer (Captain H. H. Short) killed, 2 officers wounded, 1 officer (Major A. Scott Turner) missing ; other ranks, 2 killed, 35 wounded, 24 missing.

4th (Guards) Brigade.—2nd Grenadiers : 1 officer (Second-Lieut. R. H. M. Vereker) killed, 1 officer wounded ; other ranks, 4 wounded. 3rd Coldstream : 1 officer (Second-Lieut. Hon. Windsor Clive) killed, 3 officers wounded, 1 officer (Lieut. Hon. Viscount Hawarden) died of wounds, August 26, 1914 ; other ranks, 15 killed, 82 wounded, 22 missing. 6th Field Ambulance : 2 officers missing ; other ranks, 12 A.S.C. drivers missing.

APPENDICES.

Appendix III.

Casualties at Villers-Cotterets, 1st September 1914.

The Irish Guards : 2 officers (Lieut.-Colonel Hon. G. Morris, commanding ; Captain C. A. Tisdall) killed, 5 officers wounded ; other ranks, 4 killed, 36 wounded, and 64 missing.
The 2nd Grenadiers : 2 officers (Lieut. and Adjutant I. MacDougall, and Lieut. Hon. J. H. Manners) killed, 2 officers missing ; other ranks, 2 wounded, 147 missing.
The 3rd Coldstream : 1 officer (Lieut. G. Lambton) killed, 2 officers wounded ; other ranks, 7 killed, 16 wounded, and 14 missing.
The 6th Brigade.—2nd South Staffords: other ranks, 1 killed, 26 wounded, and 34 missing. 1st King's Royal Rifles : 1 officer wounded ; other ranks, 15 wounded, 21 missing. 1st Berks : other ranks, 1 killed, 9 wounded, 16 missing. 1st King's (Liverpool) : 3 officers wounded ; other ranks, 1 killed, 57 wounded.
Captain M. Sinclair and Lieut. H. J. S. Shields, both of the R.A.M.C., were reported missing.

Appendix IV.

Casualties at the Passage of the Petit-Morin, 8th September 1914.

4th (Guards) Brigade.—2nd Grenadiers : 1 officer wounded ; other ranks, 18 wounded. 2nd Coldstream : 2 officers wounded ; other ranks, 11 killed and wounded. 3rd Coldstream : 4 officers wounded ; other ranks, 54 killed, wounded, and missing. 1st Irish Guards : other ranks, 48 killed, wounded, and missing.
5th Infantry Brigade.—2nd Oxford and Bucks : other ranks, 1 killed. 2nd Worcesters : other ranks, 29 wounded and missing. 2nd Highland Light Infantry : other ranks, 2 wounded. 2nd Connaughts : 1 officer wounded ; other ranks, 2 wounded.
XLIst Brigade R.F.A. : other ranks, 3 killed and wounded.

Appendix V.

The 2nd Connaught Rangers at the Battle of the Aisne, 14th September 1914.

" At about 1 a.m. on the 14th September operation orders by the G.O.C. 5th Infantry Brigade were received by the battalion at Soupir, in which the information was given that the 4th (Guards) Brigade and the XXXVIth Brigade R.F.A. had been ordered to cross the river at 6 a.m. and to march *via* Soupir to Point 197 (Croix-sans-Tête).
" The Connaught Rangers were ordered to close on Moussy as soon as the Guards Brigade and the XXXVIth Brigade had passed through them.
" On receipt of these orders the O.C. Connaught Rangers, considering that in his position at Soupir he would be of no assistance to this force in their advance, decided to march to La Cour Soupir Farm, which stands in a good position at the head of the valley through which lay the line of advance of the force.

" The battalion arrived at La Cour Soupir Farm at 5.30 a.m. and halted there, sending forward pickets to Croix-sans-Tête and to other points, and the front and flanks. No signs of the enemy had been observed up to that hour, and the inhabitants stated that they believed there were no Germans in the vicinity.

" At about 9.30 a.m. a small party of the Guards Brigade under an officer, forming the point of the advanced guard, arrived at the farm, but no more of the brigade arrived until about 11.30 a.m.

" At about 10 a.m. a message, dispatched at 9.25 a.m. by motor cyclist, was received from Headquarters 5th Brigade, to whom the movements of the battalion had been reported, stating that it would be some time before the Guards Brigade could arrive, and instructing the O.C. Connaught Rangers not to leave his position until they were up and had securely occupied the high ground about Point 197. The battalion was then ordered to close on Moussy as soon as that position was secure.

" At about 10.30 a.m. warning was given by the advanced posts of the near approach of a very large body of the enemy's infantry. The battalion was immediately deployed east and west of the farm, and was barely in position before the enemy attacked. The attack was supported by artillery fire, and was pushed forward with great vigour. The enemy endeavoured to turn our right flank by moving through the woods, and against our centre and left he advanced across the open ground in very large numbers. By 10.30 a.m., in spite of his losses, which were very heavy, he had almost succeeded in turning our right flank, and most of our men who were holding the position close to the farm on the west having been killed or wounded, the enemy had succeeded in pushing forward to within a hundred yards of the farm buildings at this point.

" Two companies of the Coldstream Guards then arrived, and were sent forward to reinforce the battalion—one company on either side of the farm. This relieved the situation, and although the attacks continued to be hotly pressed throughout the day, and desperate efforts were made by the enemy to take the position by turning our left flank, the arrival of the remainder of the Guards Brigade in the afternoon rendered our position secure.

" At about 3.30 p.m. all the enemy remaining in his front line surrendered in two parties, the number of prisoners thus taken being about 250. But fresh troops from the enemy's side were soon pushed forward, and the attack was renewed and continued until dusk.

" Late in the evening the battalion was ordered to march to the village of Soupir, with the object of joining the brigade the following day. The casualties in the battalion on this day were very heavy. The following officers were killed and wounded :—Killed : Lieut. R. I. Thomas, Lieut. R. L. Spreckley, Lieut. J. Fraser, Second-Lieut. V. A. Lentaigne. Wounded : Major H. M. Hutchinson, Captain C. T. O'Sullivan, Second-Lieut. V. N. Aveling, Second-Lieut. Swift." [1]

[1] Battalion Diary of the 2nd Connaught Rangers (5th Infantry Brigade), September 1914.

Appendix VI.

Casualties in the Battle of the 'Aisne, 12th to 15th September 1914.

4th (Guards) Brigade.—2nd Grenadiers : 2 officers killed (Lieut. F. des Vaux and Second-Lieut. Pickersgill-Cunliffe), 5 officers wounded; other ranks, 17 killed, 67 wounded, 77 missing. 3rd Coldstream : 2 officers killed (Lieut. D. C. Bingham and Lieut. P. L. Wyndham), 5 officers wounded; other ranks, 21 killed, 85 wounded, 61 missing. 1st Irish Guards : 3 officers killed (Captain Lord Arthur Hay, Captain Lord H. A. F. Guernsey, Captain H. H. Berners), 2 officers wounded; other ranks, 3 killed, 21 wounded, 147 missing. 2nd Coldstream : 1 officer killed (Second-Lieut. R. W. M. Lockwood), 2 officers wounded; other ranks, 1 killed, 30 wounded.

5th Infantry Brigade.—2nd Worcesters : 2 officers wounded; other ranks, 8 killed, 60 wounded. 2nd Oxford and Bucks : 1 officer wounded ; other ranks, 4 killed, 38 wounded, 33 missing. 2nd Highland Light Infantry : 2 officers killed (Captain Sir A. C. Gibson Craig, Bart., Second-Lieut. R. F. Powell) ; other ranks, 1 killed, 10 wounded. 2nd Connaughts : 4 officers killed (Lieut. R. I. Thomas, Lieut. R. L. Spreckley, Lieut. J. Fraser, Second-Lieut. V. A. Lentaigne), 4 officers wounded ; other ranks, 18 killed, 102 wounded, and 97 missing.

6th Infantry Brigade.—1st King's : 2 officers wounded ; other ranks, 4 killed, 76 wounded. 1st King's Royal Rifles : 3 officers wounded ; other ranks, 9 killed, 38 wounded, 16 missing. 1st Berks : 1 officer killed (Lieut. G. Perkins), 2 officers wounded ; other ranks, 3 killed, 37 wounded.

Divisional Mounted Troops (B Squadron 15th Hussars) : other ranks, 3 wounded.

Divisional Cyclists : other ranks, 4 wounded.

Royal Artillery.—71st Battery : other ranks, 1 killed, 1 wounded, 1 missing. 48th Battery : 1 officer wounded (Lieut. Campbell); other ranks, 4 killed, 7 wounded. XXXIVth Brigade R.F.A. : 3 officers killed (Major H. T. Wynter, Lieut. J. R. Wissman, Lieut. J. E. L. Clarke) ; other ranks, 4 killed, 24 wounded. XLIVth Brigade R.F.A. : 1 officer killed (Captain G. W. Blathwayt), 2 officers wounded ; other ranks, 6 killed, 14 wounded, 2 missing.

Royal Engineers.—Headquarters : other ranks, 2 killed, 1 wounded. 5th Field Company : 1 officer wounded ; other ranks, 8 wounded, 3 missing. 11th Field Company : 1 officer killed (Lieut. G. L. Miller) ; other ranks, 1 killed, 10 wounded. 2nd Signal Company : 1 officer wounded : other ranks, 1 killed, 3 wounded.

Total : 16 officers killed, 41 officers wounded ; other ranks, 89 killed, 316 wounded, 515 missing.

Appendix VII.

Casualties on the Aisne from 16th September to 14th October 1914.

16th September.

4th (Guards) Brigade.—2nd Grenadiers : 2 officers killed (Lieut. Hon. W. A. Cecil, Lieut. R. W. G. Welby). 3rd Coldstream : 1 officer killed

(Lieut. Huggan, R.A.M.C.); other ranks, 6 killed, 39 wounded, 12 missing. Irish Guards : other ranks, 1 killed, 1 wounded.

5th Infantry Brigade.—2nd Worcesters : other ranks, 6 wounded. 2nd Highland Light Infantry : other ranks, 8 killed, 3 wounded, 21 missing.

6th Infantry Brigade.—2nd South Staffords : other ranks, 2 killed, 7 wounded. 1st Royal Berks : other ranks, 3 killed, 2 wounded, 4 missing. 1st King's Royal Rifles : other ranks, 12 killed, 55 wounded, 6 missing.

17th September.

2nd Signal Company, R.E. : other ranks, 1 wounded.

4th (Guards) Brigade.—3rd Coldstream : other ranks, 12 wounded.

5th Infantry Brigade.—Headquarters : 1 officer wounded ; other ranks, 1 wounded. 2nd Worcesters : other ranks, 1 killed, 7 wounded. 2nd Connaughts : other ranks, 1 killed, 1 wounded. Oxford and Bucks : 3 officers killed (Lieut. R. C. Worthington, Lieut. H. Mockley-Ferryman, Second-Lieut. P. C. Giradot), 3 officers wounded ; other ranks, 7 wounded, 3 missing.

6th Infantry Brigade.—1st King's : other ranks, 5 wounded. 2nd South Staffords : other ranks, 3 wounded. 1st King's Royal Rifles : other ranks, 2 killed, 2 wounded, 4 missing.

18th September.

XLIVth Brigade R.F.A. : other ranks, 1 killed, 1 wounded.

4th (Guards) Brigade.—2nd Coldstream : other ranks, 1 killed, 1 missing. Irish Guards : other ranks, 1 wounded.

5th Infantry Brigade.—2nd Worcesters : 2 officers killed (Captain M. R. Carr, Second-Lieut. F. F. Smythe) ; other ranks, 1 killed, 5 wounded. 2nd Highland Light Infantry : other ranks, 1 wounded. 2nd Connaughts : other ranks, 1 killed, 6 wounded.

6th Infantry Brigade.—2nd South Staffords : other ranks, 3 wounded. 1st Berks : other ranks, 1 killed, 8 wounded.

R.A.M.C. : 1 officer missing (Lieut. G. R. Walker) ; other ranks, 1 missing.

19th September.

XXXVIth Brigade R.F.A. : other ranks, 1 wounded.
XLIVth Brigade R.F.A. : other ranks, 2 wounded.

4th (Guards) Brigade.—2nd Grenadiers : other ranks, 2 killed, 5 wounded. 2nd Coldstream : other ranks, 2 killed, 5 wounded. 3rd Coldstream, 1 officer wounded ; other ranks, 4 wounded.

5th Infantry Brigade.—1st King's Royal Rifles : 1 officer wounded ; other ranks, 2 killed, 18 wounded. Oxford and Bucks : 1 officer killed (Captain R. C. Evelegh), 2 officers wounded ; other ranks, 26 wounded. 2nd Highland Light Infantry : other ranks, 2 wounded.

6th Infantry Brigade.—1st King's : other ranks, 8 killed, 5 wounded. 2nd South Staffords : other ranks, 1 wounded. 1st Berks : other ranks, 4 killed, 18 wounded. 2nd Signal Company R.E. : other ranks, 1 killed, 3 wounded.

20th September.

XXXVIth Brigade R.F.A. : other ranks, 1 wounded.
XLIVth Brigade R.F.A. : other ranks, 1 wounded.

10

4th (Guards) Brigade.—2nd Grenadiers : other ranks, 4 wounded. 2nd Coldstream : other ranks, 1 killed, 5 wounded.

5th Infantry Brigade.—Headquarters : 1 officer killed (Captain D. S. Gilkison). 2nd Connaughts : 4 officers killed (Lieut. R. H. H. Henderson, Lieut. G. R. Fenton, Second-Lieut. R. B. Benison, Second-Lieut. R. A. de Stacpoole) ; other ranks, 4 killed, 15 wounded. 2nd Worcesters : 4 officers wounded, 1 officer died of wounds (Lieut. A. W. Hudson) ; other ranks, 3 killed, 53 wounded, 16 missing. 2nd Highland Light Infantry : 4 officers killed (Second-Lieut. C. G. Mackenzie, Second-Lieut. E. R. M'Donald, Second-Lieut. J. A. H. Ferguson, Lieut. O'Connell, R.A.M.C.), 2 officers wounded ; other ranks, 20 killed, 60 wounded, 40 missing. 2nd Oxford and Bucks : other ranks, 1 wounded.

228

6th Infantry Brigade.—1st King's : 1 officer killed (Lieut. M. R. Sweet Escott), 3 officers wounded, 1 officer missing (Lieut. L. E. H. Horton) ; other ranks, 20 killed, 37 wounded, 1 missing. 2nd South Staffords : other ranks, 1 killed, 8 wounded. 1st Royal Berks : other ranks, 4 killed, 22 wounded.

98
336

21st September.

3

XLIVth Brigade R.F.A. : other ranks, 1 killed, 2 wounded.

3

XXXVIth Brigade R.F.A. : other ranks, 2 wounded. 2nd Signal Company R.E. : other ranks, 1 wounded.

14

5th Infantry Brigade.—2nd Worcesters : other ranks, 2 killed, 4 wounded. 2nd Highland Light Infantry : other ranks, 2 wounded. 2nd Oxford and Bucks : other ranks, 3 wounded, 3 missing.

2

4th (Guards) Brigade.—2nd Coldstream : other ranks, 1 wounded. 3rd Coldstream : other ranks, 1 wounded.

62
84

6th Infantry Brigade.—1st King's : other ranks, 1 wounded. 2nd South Staffords : other ranks, 2 wounded. 1st Royal Berks : 1 officer wounded ; other ranks, 3 killed, 24 wounded. 1st King's Royal Rifles : 1 officer wounded ; other ranks, 27 wounded, 3 missing.

22nd September.

11

4th (Guards) Brigade.—2nd Coldstream : other ranks, 1 killed, 4 missing. 3rd Coldstream : 1 killed. 1st Irish Guards : other ranks, 1 killed, 4 wounded.

55
66

6th Infantry Brigade.—1st King's : other ranks, 4 missing. 2nd South Staffords : 1 officer wounded ; other ranks, 4 wounded. 1st Royal Berks : other ranks, 3 killed, 3 wounded, 40 missing.

23rd September.

1

XLIVth Brigade R.F.A. : other ranks, 1 killed.

5
~

4th (Guards) Brigade.—2nd Grenadiers : other ranks, 1 killed. 2nd Coldstream : other ranks, 1 wounded. 1st Irish Guards : other ranks, 4 wounded.

24th September.

2

35th (Heavy) Battery R.G.A. : other ranks, 2 wounded.

14
16

4th (Guards) Brigade.—2nd Grenadiers : other ranks, 2 killed, 2 wounded. 2nd Coldstream : other ranks, 4 wounded. 3rd Coldstream : other ranks, 1 wounded, 4 missing. 5th Field Company R.E. : other ranks, 1 wounded.

APPENDICES. 337

25th September.

XLIVth Brigade R.F.A. : other ranks, 1 wounded.
4th (Guards) Brigade : Headquarters, 1 officer wounded. 2nd Grenadiers : other ranks, 1 wounded. 2nd Coldstream : other ranks, 1 killed, 6 wounded. 1st Irish Guards : other ranks, 1 wounded.

26th September.

XLIVth Brigade R.F.A. : other ranks, 1 killed, 5 wounded.
XXXVIth Brigade R.F.A. : other ranks, 1 wounded.
4th (Guards) Brigade.—2nd Grenadiers : 1 officer wounded.
6th Infantry Brigade.—2nd South Staffords : 1 officer killed (Lieut. D. O. W. Ball, R.A.M.C.) ; other ranks, 1 killed, 4 wounded, 3 missing.
Headquarter Staff 2nd Division : 1 officer wounded.

27th September.

XLIVth Brigade R.F.A. : other ranks, 1 wounded. 5th Field Company R.E. : other ranks, 1 wounded.
4th (Guards) Brigade.—1st Irish Guards : other ranks, 1 wounded.
6th Infantry Brigade.—1st Royal Berks : other ranks, 1 wounded. 1st King's Royal Rifles : 1 officer wounded ; other ranks, 2 wounded. 1st King's : other ranks, 1 killed, 1 wounded.

28th September.

XLIVth Brigade R.F.A. : other ranks, 1 wounded.
XLIst Brigade R.F.A. : other ranks, 1 wounded.
4th (Guards) Brigade.—2nd Coldstream : other ranks, 1 killed, 1 wounded. 1st Irish Guards : other ranks, 1 wounded.
6th Infantry Brigade.—2nd South Staffords : other ranks, 2 wounded. 1st Royal Berks : other ranks, 1 killed. 1st King's Royal Rifles : 1 officer wounded ; other ranks, 2 wounded.
5th Infantry Brigade.—2nd Worcesters : other ranks, 1 killed, 4 wounded. 2nd Highland Light Infantry : other ranks, 2 wounded. 2nd Connaught Rangers : other ranks, 2 wounded.

30th September.

XXXVIth Brigade R.F.A. : other ranks, 4 wounded.
4th (Guards) Brigade.—2nd Grenadiers : other ranks, 1 wounded.
6th Infantry Brigade.—1st King's : other ranks, 1 wounded. 1st King's Royal Rifles : other ranks, 1 killed, 15 wounded.

1st October.

XLIst Brigade R.F.A. : other ranks, 1 missing. 1st Siege Battery R.G.A. : 1 officer wounded ; other ranks, 3 wounded.
6th Infantry Brigade.—2nd South Staffords : other ranks, 4 wounded. 1st Royal Berks : other ranks, 1 killed.

2nd October.

4th (Guards) Brigade.—2nd Grenadiers : other ranks, 1 wounded. 2nd Coldstream : other ranks, 1 wounded.
5th Infantry Brigade.—2nd Worcesters : other ranks, 1 killed, 5 wounded. 2nd Oxford and Bucks : other ranks, 1 killed.
6th Infantry Brigade.—2nd South Staffords : other ranks, 3 wounded.
XLIVth Brigade R.F.A. : other ranks, 3 wounded.
(2,242) 22

3rd October.

XXXVIth Brigade R.F.A. : 1 officer wounded.

5th Field Company R.E. : other ranks, 1 wounded.

4th (Guards) Brigade.—2nd Grenadiers : other ranks, 1 killed, 1 wounded. 2nd Coldstream : other ranks, 1 wounded.

5th Infantry Brigade.—2nd Oxford and Bucks : other ranks, 1 killed, 18 wounded. 2nd Highland Light Infantry : other ranks, 1 killed, 1 wounded.

6th Infantry Brigade.—1st King's : other ranks, 1 killed, 1 wounded.

4th October.

XLIst Brigade R.F.A. : other ranks, 1 killed, 3 wounded.

5th Infantry Brigade.—2nd Oxford and Bucks : other ranks, 1 killed, 8 wounded.

6th Infantry Brigade.—1st King's : other ranks, 3 wounded. 1st Royal Berks : other ranks, 1 wounded.

5th October.

4th (Guards) Brigade.—2nd Grenadiers : other ranks, 1 killed. 2nd Coldstream : other ranks, 1 killed, 4 wounded. 1st Irish Guards : 1 officer wounded ; other ranks, 1 killed.

5th Infantry Brigade.—2nd Oxford and Bucks : other ranks, 5 wounded. 2nd Highland Light Infantry : other ranks, 1 wounded.

6th Infantry Brigade.—1st King's : other ranks, 1 wounded. 2nd South Staffords : other ranks, 2 wounded. 1st Royal Berks : other ranks, 1 killed. 1st King's Royal Rifles : other ranks, 1 killed, 4 wounded.

XXXVIth Brigade R.F.A. : 1 officer wounded ; other ranks, 1 wounded.

6th October.

4th (Guards) Brigade.—2nd Grenadiers : other ranks, 1 wounded.

5th Infantry Brigade.—2nd Worcesters : other ranks, 1 wounded. 2nd Highland Light Infantry : other ranks, 1 wounded.

7th October.

XLIVth Brigade R.F.A. : other ranks, 2 wounded.

6th Infantry Brigade.—1st King's : other ranks, 1 wounded.

8th October.

Headquarters 2nd Division : other ranks, 1 wounded.

5th Infantry Brigade.—2nd Oxford and Bucks : other ranks, 1 wounded.

5th Field Company R.E. : other ranks, 1 wounded.

6th Infantry Brigade.—1st Royal Berks : other ranks, 1 wounded. 1st King's Royal Rifles : 1 officer wounded ; other ranks, 2 wounded.

XLIst Brigade R.F.A. : other ranks, 1 wounded.

9th October.

5th Field Company R.E. : other ranks, 1 killed.

5th Infantry Brigade.—Headquarters : other ranks, 1 wounded. 2nd Worcesters : other ranks, 1 wounded.

6th Infantry Brigade.—1st Royal Berks : other ranks, 1 killed. 1st King's Royal Rifles : other ranks, 5 wounded.

APPENDICES. 339

11th October.

4th (Guards) Brigade.—2nd Coldstream : other ranks, 1 wounded.
5th Infantry Brigade.—2nd Worcesters : other ranks, 1 wounded.

12th October.

5th Infantry Brigade.—2nd Highland Light Infantry : other ranks, 5 wounded.
6th Infantry Brigade.—1st King's Royal Rifles : other ranks, 1 killed.

13th October.

5th Infantry Brigade.—2nd Highland Light Infantry : other ranks, 1 wounded.
6th Infantry Brigade.—2nd South Staffords : 1 officer wounded.
1st Royal Berks : other ranks, 1 wounded.   1st King's Royal Rifles : other ranks, 1 wounded.
4th (Guards) Brigade : other ranks, 1 wounded.

14th October.

6th Infantry Brigade.—1st King's Royal Rifles : 1 officer wounded ; other ranks, 1 killed, 1 wounded.

Appendix VIII.

Casualties at the Battle of Langemarck, 21st to 24th October 1914.

4th (Guards) Brigade.—3rd Coldstream : 3 officers killed (Captain Hon. C. H. S. Monck, Lieut. H. D. Wallis, Lieut. D. W. Rintoul, R.A.M.C.) and 3 wounded, including the C.O., Lieut.-Colonel G. Feilding ; other ranks, 80 killed, wounded, and missing. 2nd Coldstream : other ranks, 35 killed, wounded, and missing. Irish Guards : other ranks, 8 killed and wounded. 2nd Grenadiers : other ranks, 8 killed and wounded.
5th Infantry Brigade.—2nd Oxford and Bucks : 5 officers killed (already given), 6 officers wounded, including Major Eden ; other ranks, 202 killed, wounded, and missing. 2nd Connaught Rangers : other ranks, 34 killed and wounded. 2nd Worcesters : 2 officers killed (Captain R. H. Nolan, R.A.M.C., Lieut. F. F. Curtler) ; other ranks, 84 killed, wounded, and missing. 2nd Highland Light Infantry : 2 officers wounded ; other ranks, 117 killed, wounded, and missing.
Of the Artillery the XXXVIth Brigade R.F.A. had 2 officers wounded, including Lieut.-Colonel C. G. Stewart, and 7 other ranks killed and wounded ; the XLIst Brigade R.F.A. 2 officers wounded and 10 other ranks killed and wounded ; the 5th Field Company R.E. 3 other ranks killed and wounded.

Appendix IX.

Casualties during January and February 1915.

The casualties in the 2nd Division during January were : 10 officers killed, 11 wounded ; other ranks, 88 killed, 235 wounded, 3 missing.

The officers killed were : Captain L. H. Birt, D.S.O., 1st Royal Berks ; Captain F. C. Norbury, 6th King's Royal Rifles, attached 1st King's Royal Rifles ; Second-Lieut. A. D. Tylden-Pattenson, 2nd Oxford and Bucks ; Lieut. H. J. Snowden, 1st Herts ; Second-Lieut. D. Henderson, 6th King's Royal Rifles, attached 1st King's Royal Rifles ; Lieut. H. S. Keating, 1st Irish Guards ; Second-Lieut. W. W. W. Godman, 1st King's Royal Rifles ; Lieut. D. J. F. Galbraith, 9th Highland Light Infantry ; Second-Lieut. V. J. Austin, XXXIVth Brigade R.F.A. ; Second-Lieut. E. J. Munby, 1st East Anglian Field Company R.E. ; Second-Lieut. C. Whitehouse, XXXVIth Brigade R.F.A. (died of wounds).

During February the casualties were : 8 officers killed, 32 wounded ; other ranks, 159 killed, 613 wounded, 3 missing.

The officers killed (not previously mentioned) were : Captain A. B. R. Gosselin, D.S.O., 2nd Grenadier Guards ; Lieut. L. B. Hardy, 2nd Worcesters ; Lieut. T. Allen, 1st Irish Guards. Wounded : Second-Lieut. B. H. Francis, 3rd Royal Scots, attached 2nd Highland Light Infantry (died later) ; Lieut. F. C. Tyrrell, 3rd Coldstream Guards (died of wounds, 15th Feb. 1915) ; Captain J. H. Stokes, 3rd Royal West Kent, attached 1st Royal Berks (died of wounds, 22nd March 1915).

Appendix X.

Casualties at Cuinchy, 1st February 1915.

The casualties were as follows : 2nd Coldstream : 1 officer killed (Lieut. J. A. Carter-Wood) ; other ranks, 21 killed, 51 wounded. 1st Irish Guards : 2 officers killed (Lieut. R. St. J. Blacker-Douglas, Lieut. F. H. N. Lee), 3 officers wounded ; other ranks, 10 killed, 24 wounded, 2 missing.

Appendix XI.

Casualties in Attack from Givenchy, 10th March 1915.

2nd South Staffords : 5 officers killed (Lieut. C. E. A. Parker, Second-Lieut. H. C. Stonor, Second-Lieut. A. D. Sprunt, Lieut. L. F. Yeo, Second-Lieut. G. M. F. Hewat), 2 officers wounded ; other ranks, 24 killed, 74 wounded, 23 missing. 1st King's : 6 officers killed (Captain F. E. Feneran, Lieut. P. M. Young, Lieut. H. M. J. Webb, Second-Lieut. H. Hayes-Newington, Second-Lieut. T. H. Madden, Second-Lieut. H. P. O'Donoghue), 3 officers wounded ; other ranks, 14 killed, 93 wounded, 77 missing. 1st King's Royal Rifles : 7 officers killed (Captain F. P. Shakerley, Captain C. A. Grazebrook, Second-Lieut. F. P. Crawhall, Lieut. P. J. Bevan, Second-Lieut. A. R. Herron, Second-Lieut. R. Fellowes, Second-Lieut. K. H. W. Ward), 1 wounded ; other ranks, 34 killed, 94 wounded, 119 missing. 1st East Anglian Field Company R.E. : 1 officer wounded ; other ranks, 4 killed, 19 wounded. 5th Field Company R.E. : 1 officer killed (Second-Lieut. D. M. Parsons) ; other ranks, 5 wounded, 2 missing.

Appendix XII.

Casualties at the Battle of Festubert, 15th to 25th.May 1915.

The Irish Guards lost 17 officers ; the 2nd Royal Inniskilling Fusiliers, 19 ; the 2nd Oxford and Bucks, 20 ; the 1st King's (Liverpool) Regiment, 14 ; the 2nd South Staffords, 1st King's Royal Rifles, and the 1/5th King's (Liverpool) Regiment, 13 each; whilst other units lost from 4 upwards. The 2nd Grenadiers, 2nd South Staffords, and 1st King's Royal Rifles lost their commanding officers (Lieut.-Colonel W. R. A. Smith, C.M.G. ; Lieut.-Colonel P. C. L. Routledge ; and Lieut.-Colonel C. G. Shakerly, D.S.O., respectively—killed). The names of the officers killed (not already mentioned) were given as :— Royal Artillery : Second-Lieut. C. Q. Roberts, R.F.A. ; Royal Engineers : Lieut. A. Trewby, 11th Field Company ; 2nd Grenadier Guards : Major B. H. Barrington-Kennett ; 1st Irish Guards : Captain J. N. Guthrie, Second-Lieut. V. W. D. Fox ; 2nd Royal Inniskilling Fusiliers : Lieut. R. W. S. Hinds, Second-Lieuts. L. St. G. Mordaunt-Smith, J. J. L. Morgan, W. J. Whittington ; 2nd Worcesters : Lieuts. A. W. H. Scott, F. C. F. Biscow, Second-Lieut. J. S. McCormick ; 2nd Oxford and Bucks : Capt. F. H. Beaufort, Lieuts. D. H. W. Humfrey, R. E. B. Bull, Second-Lieut. L. A. Dashwood ; 2nd Highland Light Infantry : Captains A. W. D. Gaussen, H. E. Johnston-Stewart, Lieut. H. B. O. Hughes, Second-Lieuts. B. Crossley, W. H. Oldfield ; 9th Highland Light Infantry : Captain A. J. Martin, Lieut. W. Spens ; 1st King's Regiment : Second-Lieuts. J. D. W. Kenyon, J. S. Rich, G. Martin ; 2nd Staffords : Captain K. J. Maples ; 1st Royal Berks : Captain S. Belcher, Lieuts. W. J. Cox, C. R. Taffs ; 1st King's Royal Rifles : Captain Hon. J. M. Bigge, Lieut. W. H. Grenville-Grey, Second-Lieut. J. S. H. Jones ; 1/5th King's : Lieuts. G. H. Cohen, A. H. Plummer ; 1/7th King's : Major A. Hughes, Captain M. Tweedale, Lieuts. L. K. Adams, W. S. Allan, Second-Lieuts. W. G. Alexander, N. L. Hannon, T. McClelland, R. G. Gamble.

Appendix XIII.

Casualties at the Battle of Loos, 25th September 1915.

Officers killed :—1st Middlesex Regiment : Captain N. Y. L. Welman, D.S.O., Captain F. V. A. Dyer, Captain L. G. Coward, Captain B. J. Deighton, Second-Lieuts. C. A. J. Mackinnon, C. Pery, B. U. Hare, A. L. Hill, R. C. Mellish, J. H. Linsell, Lieut. A. W. R. Carless (died of wounds). 2nd Argyll and Sutherland Highlanders : Captain J. C. Aitken, Lieut. I. M. Miller, Lieut. J. L. Bullough, Lieut. G. E. Smith, Second-Lieuts. H. Kerr, W. G. Fallowfield, I. C. Fraser, W. A. Kennedy, J. D. Fordyce, H. D. Gillespie. 2nd Royal Welsh Fusiliers : Captain A. L. Samson, Captain J. A. Childe-Freeman. 1st King's (Liverpool) Regiment : Captain J. H. A. Ryan, Second-Lieuts. W. Harvey, G. W. Baillon, N. C. Marsh. 2nd South Stafford Regiment : Captain A. D. Johnson, Captain A. F. C. Kilby, Lieut. B. Hall, Lieut. R. W. Fawcett (died of wounds), Second-Lieut. C. W. King. 1st Royal Berks Regiment : Captain C. P. Wheeler. 2nd Oxford and Bucks

342 APPENDICES.

Light Infantry : Lieut. P. F. Newton-King, Second-Lieuts. C. Hurst-Brown, V. V. Jacob, E. R. C. Hughes, L. A. Vidal. 2nd Highland Light Infantry : Captain C. W. Hooper, Lieut. H. W. Whitson, Captain H. B. Coghill, Second-Lieuts. C. H. Shipton, D. A. Medley. 1st Queen's Royal West Surrey Regiment : Lieut. C. D. M. Fowler, Second-Lieuts. A. W. A. Bradshaw, M. I. B. Howell, F. G. Plant.

Appendix XIV.

Casualties in the Battle of Delville Wood, 27th July 1916.

99th Infantry Brigade.—1st King's Royal Rifles : 7 officers killed (Captain and Adjutant A. H. Brocklehurst (died of wounds), Captain R. H. Slater, Captain E. L. Howell, Lieut. C. Collins (died of wounds), Second-Lieut. C. R. S. Turner (3rd Dorsets attached), Second-Lieut. A. Y. Bailey, Second-Lieut. J. W. E. Paul), 8 officers wounded, 2 officers missing; other ranks, 308 killed, wounded, and missing. 23rd Royal Fusiliers : 5 officers killed (Captain C. B. Hayward, Captain D. C. Ranken, Second-Lieut. R. H. C. Bushell (7th Batt. attached), Second-Lieut. E. F. H. Taylor (30th Batt. attached), Second-Lieut. E. A. Oliver (15th Batt. attached), 7 officers wounded ; other ranks, 276 killed and wounded. 1st Royal Berks : 3 officers killed (Second-Lieut. R. J. Childs (3rd Batt. attached), Lieut. J. R. Reid, Second-Lieut. H. J. Stidwell), 5 officers wounded ; other ranks, 244 killed, wounded, and missing. 99th Infantry Brigade M.G. Company : 2 officers killed (Captain C. Grant, Second-Lieut. D. Crawford), 6 officers wounded ; other ranks, 82 killed and wounded.

6th Infantry Brigade.—1st King's (Liverpool) Regiment : 1 officer wounded, 1 gassed; other ranks, 40 wounded. 6th Infantry Brigade M.G. Company : other ranks, 6 killed, wounded, and missing.

5th Infantry Brigade.—2nd Highland Light Infantry : 1 officer killed ; other ranks, 22 killed and wounded. 17th Royal Fusiliers : 2 officers killed—Lieut. R. H. Fletcher (14th Batt. attached), Second-Lieut. S. Penny (died of wounds ; 14th Batt. attached), 3 wounded ; other ranks, 113 killed, wounded, and missing. 24th Royal Fusiliers : 3 officers wounded ; other ranks, 14 killed, wounded, and missing.

Divisional Troops.—10th D.C.L.I. (Pioneers) : 3 officers wounded ; other ranks, 29 killed, wounded, and missing. Royal Engineers—5th Field Company R.E. : other ranks, 1 wounded. 1st East Anglian Field Company R.E. : other ranks, 1 wounded.

Appendix XV.

Casualties at the Battle of Guillemont, 8th to 9th August.

1st King's (Liverpool) Regiment : 5 officers killed (Lieut.-Colonel C. E. Goff, M.C. (commanding), Major McErvel (second-in-command), Second-Lieut. D. O. Evans, Second-Lieut. J. T. St. Clair Tisdall, Second-Lieut. J. R. Swallow), 6 officers wounded, 4 captured by the enemy. 17th Middlesex : 3 officers killed (Captain W. Salter, Second-Lieut. E. L. Cocks, and Second-Lieut. W. F. Henderson), 2 wounded ; other ranks, 19 killed, 143 wounded, 43 missing. 2nd South Staffords :

I officer killed (Lieut. S. T. Spicer, died of wounds) ; other ranks, 30 killed, wounded, and missing. 13th Essex Regiment : 2 officers killed (Lieut. B. R. Page, Second-Lieut. G. H. T. Ross), 1 wounded ; other ranks, 82 killed, wounded, and missing.

Appendix XVI.

Officers killed on the Somme from 23rd July to 11th August 1916.

The 2nd Oxford and Bucks Light Infantry : Major R. M. Owen, Captain J. B. Hardcastle, Lieut. N. S. Harrison, Second-Lieut. W. L. Chown (3rd Batt.), Second-Lieut. B. C. C. Warde (3rd Batt.), Second-Lieut. R. S. L. Maul, Second-Lieut. W. R. Goffe. 2nd Highland Light Infantry : Second-Lieut. T. F. Phillips (3rd Batt.), Second-Lieut. W. A. H. Lindsay (4th Batt.), Second-Lieut. A. Allen, Second-Lieut. J. F. O'Halloran. 17th Royal Fusiliers : Lieut. R. H. Fletcher (14th Batt.), Second-Lieut. R. Ramsbottom (29th Batt.), Second-Lieut. E. P. Underwood (29th Batt.), Second-Lieut. A. F. H. Lelievre (died of wounds). 24th Royal Fusiliers : Captain C. S. Meares, Captain G. T. Edwards, Second-Lieut. F. J. Fathorne. 1st King's : Second-Lieut. G. G. Lauder. 2nd South Stafford Regiment : Captain W. E. Wansbrough, Captain C. Dutton, Captain W. Lake, Lieut. J. L. Malpas, Second-Lieut. S. B. Thornton, Second-Lieut. W. L. Holdcroft. 13th Essex Regiment : Second-Lieut. G. H. T. Ross, Second-Lieut. B. R. Price. 17th Middlesex Regiment : Second-Lieut. W. Hendry, Second-Lieut. J. A. Guest. 6th Infantry Brigade M. G. Company : Second-Lieut. C. B. Campbell. 1st Royal Berks : Lieut. J. R. Reid, Second-Lieut. R. J. Childs, Second-Lieut. H. J. Stidwell. 22nd Royal Fusiliers : Captain A. Macdougall. 99th M. G. Company : Second-Lieut. T. L. Kendall, Second-Lieut. F. E. Gallichan. 10th D.C.L.I. : Second-Lieut. H. G. Miles. Royal Artillery : Major J. L. Mowbray, D.S.O., Major P. S. Fraser-Tytler.

Appendix XVII.

Officers killed in the Hébuterne Section from 19th September to 12th November 1916.

Second-Lieut. J. R. Stagg, 27th Batt. Middlesex Regiment, attached 17th. Second-Lieut. S. W. Hunt, 12th Essex Regiment, attached 13th.

Officers killed in the Battle of the Ancre, 13th to 16th November (inclusive).

24th Royal Fusiliers : Second-Lieut. A. W. Burnham (15th Batt.), Second-Lieut. S. H. Gregory (15th Batt.), Second-Lieut. F. S. Bracey, Second-Lieut. W. H. G. Parry (died of wounds, 29th). 2nd Oxford and Bucks Light Infantry : Captain H. W. H. Rawson (3rd Batt.), Lieut. V. E. Fanning, Second-Lieut. A. O. W. Webster-Jones (3rd Batt.), Second-Lieut. J. P. C. Holland, Second-Lieut. H. Davies (6th Batt.), Second-Lieut. R. H. Cresswell. 22nd Royal Fusiliers : Second-Lieut. N. Fitton. 23rd Royal Fusiliers : Second-Lieut. L. A. Green (6th

344   APPENDICES.

Batt.). 1st King's : Second-Lieut. D. A. Green (3rd Batt.), Second-
Lieut. A. Cross. 10th D.C.L.I. : Lieut. H. G. F. Hall. 2nd South
Stafford Regiment: Second-Lieut. F. J. Brooks (4th Batt.), Second-
Lieut. R. P. Phipps (6th Batt.), Captain G. D. Perrin (3rd Batt.), Second-
Lieut. E. S. Wilmot (4th Batt.), Second-Lieut. N. L. Winstanley (4th
Batt.), Second-Lieut. C. W. Goodall. 13th Essex Regiment : Captain
E. M. Charrington, Captain C. G. Carson (died of wounds, 28th), Second-
Lieut. C. L. B. Lyne (11th Batt.), Captain J. M. Round (3rd Batt.),
Lieut. W. L. Busby, Lieut. L. H. B. Wilcock (3rd Batt.), Second-Lieut.
G. H. Gemmell, Second-Lieut. B. W. Finn (13th Batt.), Second-Lieut.
F. G. English (3rd Batt.), Second-Lieut. J. G. Fulkes (3rd Batt.).
1st Royal Berks Regiment : Second-Lieut. H. W. Dobbie (3rd Batt.),
Second-Lieut. J. A. V. Wood (9th Batt.), Second-Lieut. C. A. S. Ham-
ilton (3rd Batt. ; died of wounds, 24th), Second-Lieut. G. C. S. Stone-
ham. 17th Middlesex Regiment : Captain J. O. C. Kessack (25th
Batt.), Second-Lieut. W. H. Austen (27th Batt.), Lieut. P. J. Fall
(15th Batt. ; died of wounds, 15th), Second-Lieut. L. F. Christmas,
Second-Lieut. S. E. O. Rothe (15th Batt.), Second-Lieut. E. B. D.
Brunton (27th Batt.). 1st King's Royal Rifle Corps : Second-Lieut.
R. F. Lowndes (5th Batt.), Second-Lieut. T. U. Royden (19th Batt.),
Lieut. J. H. T. Liddell (6th Batt. ; died of wounds, 17th), Lieut. Hon.
F. S. Trench (died of wounds, 16th). 2nd Highland Light Infantry :
Captain G. H. Austen-Cartmell, Lieut. J. B. C. Starkey (3rd Batt.),
Lieut. F. B. Muir (3rd Batt.), Second-Lieut. J. Y. F. Dick (13th Batt.).
99th Infantry Brigade M. G. Company : Second-Lieut. R. Gordon
(died of wounds December 4, 1916), Lieut. G. Howard. XXXIVth
Brigade R.F.A. : Second-Lieut. E. W. Flinn.

END OF VOL. I.

PRINTED & BOUND BY ANTONY ROWE LTD, EASTBOURNE

Lightning Source UK Ltd.
Milton Keynes UK
UKHW021007060121
376511UK00006B/38

9 781843 423331